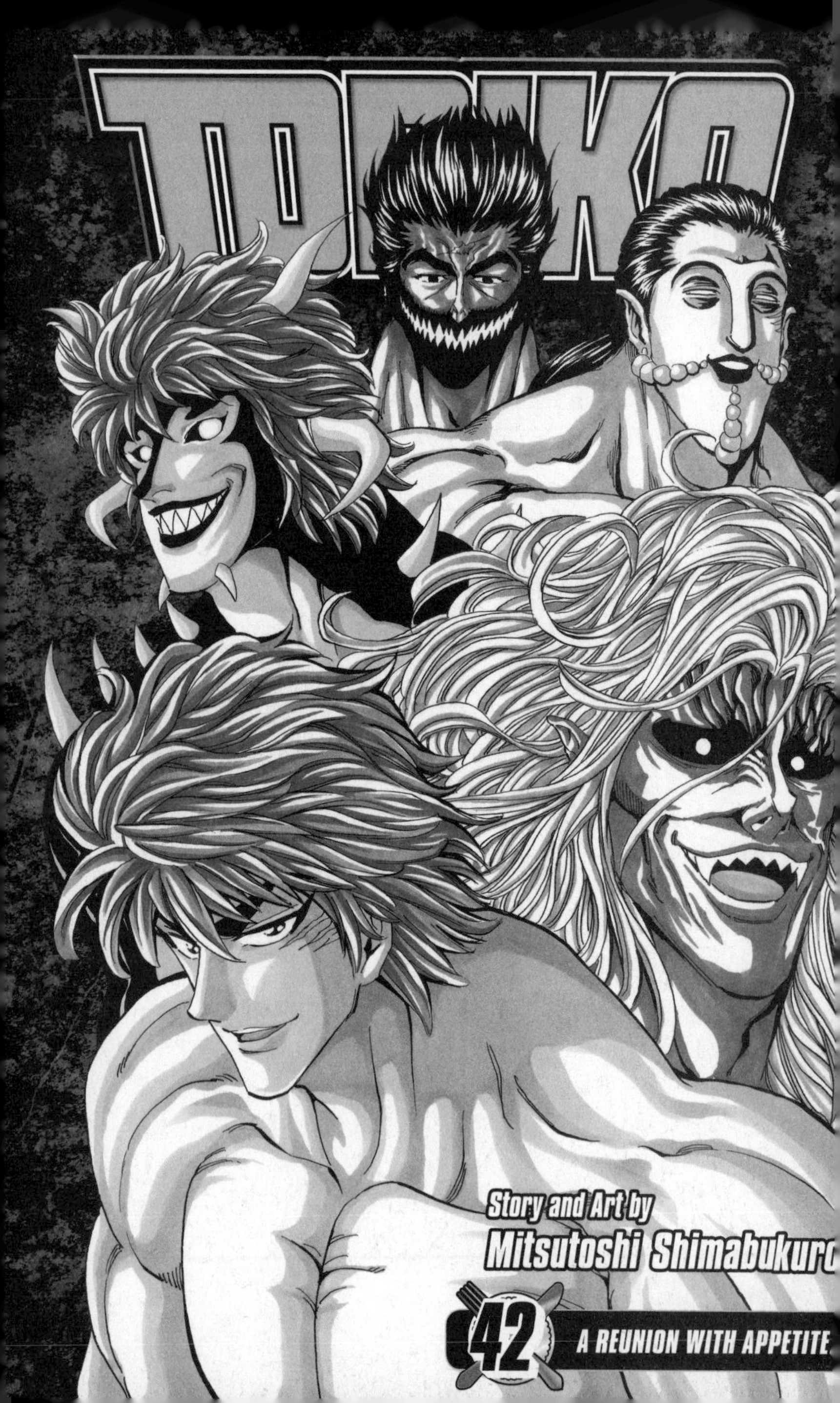
TORIKO
Story and Art by
Mitsutoshi Shimabukuro
42
A REUNION WITH APPETITE

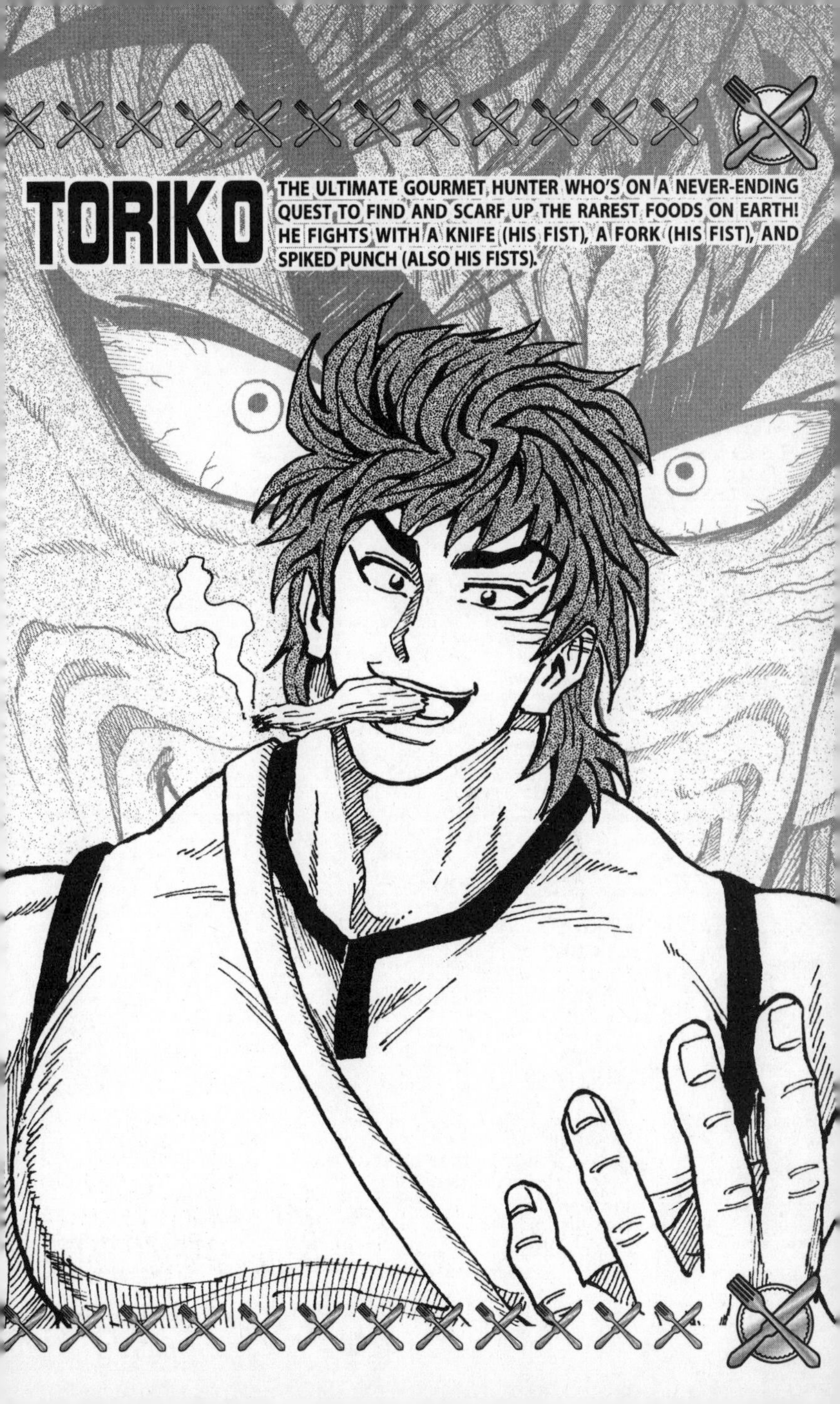
TORIKO
THE ULTIMATE GOURMET HUNTER WHO'S ON A NEVER-ENDING QUEST TO FIND AND SCARF UP THE RAREST FOODS ON EARTH! HE FIGHTS WITH A KNIFE (HIS FIST), A FORK (HIS FIST), AND SPIKED PUNCH (ALSO HIS FISTS).

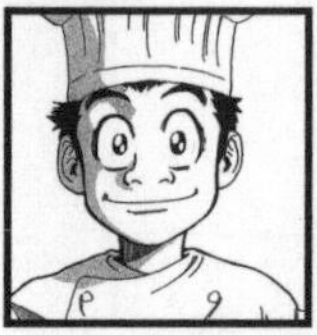

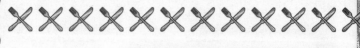

● KOMATSU
TALENTED IGO HOTEL CHEF AND TORIKO'S #1 FAN. HE POSSESSES FOOD LUCK.

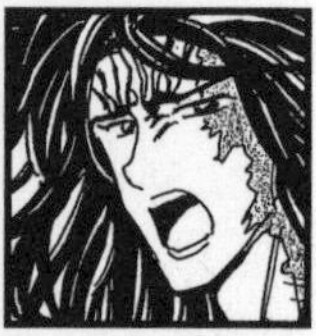

● STARJUN
A VICE CHEF FROM GOURMET CORP. MIDORA ORDERED HIM TO HELP TORIKO AND THE GANG DESPITE BEING A FORMER ENEMY.

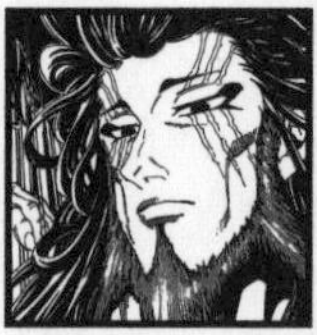

● MIDORA
GOURMET CORP. BOSS AND ACACIA'S YOUNGEST PUPIL. HE'S WORKING WITH TORIKO TO REVIVE GOD.

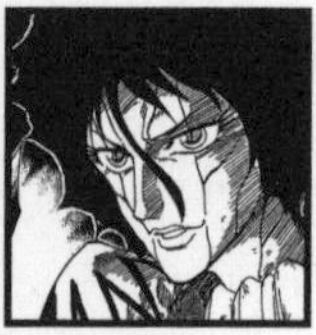

● JOIE
A SHADY CHEF WHO DEFECTED FROM GOURMET CORP. TO JOIN NEO. POSSESSES FROESE'S REVIVED BODY.

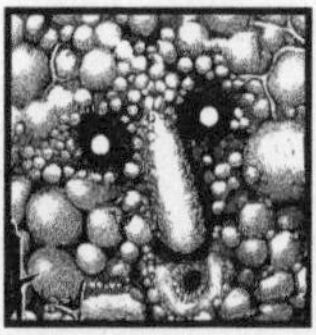

● NEO
A GOURMET CELL DEMON THAT'S BEEN REINCARNATED MANY TIMES OVER THE PAST TEN BILLION YEARS. HE DWELLS INSIDE ACACIA.

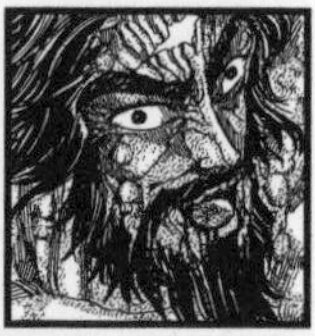

● ACACIA
A LEGENDARY GOURMET HUNTER KNOWN BY MANY AS THE GOURMET GOD. HE PLANS TO REVIVE HIS GOURMET CELL DEMON, NEO.

WHAT'S FOR DINNER

THE WORLD IS IN THE AGE OF GOURMET! THE GOURMET HUNTER TORIKO, AND HIS CHEF WHO POSSESSES THE UNIQUE ASSET OF "FOOD LUCK," KOMATSU, HAVE A FATEFUL MEETING AND EMBARK ON NUMEROUS ADVENTURES TOGETHER. MEANWHILE, THE IGO AND THE EVIL ORGANIZATION GOURMET CORP., START AN ALL-OUR WAR. THE WAR DESTROYS MOST OF THE INGREDIENTS ON EARTH AND THE HUMAN WORLD ENTERS A FOOD SHORTAGE CRISIS! GOURMET CORP. TAKES THE BRUNT OF THE DAMAGE THANKS TO A NEW EVIL POWER KNOWN AS NEO, LED BY THE INFAMOUS CHEF JOIE!

IN ORDER TO SAVE HUMANITY, TORIKO AND KOMATSU, ALONG WITH THE OTHER FOUR KINGS, COCO, SUNNY AND ZEBRA, EMBARK ON AN ADVENTURE TO THE GOURMET WORLD TO GO AFTER ACACIA'S FULL-COURSE MEAL!

MEANWHILE, THE GOURMET ARISTOCRATS, THE BLUE NITRO, HAVE BEEN SPENDING THOUSANDS OF YEARS WORKING TO PREPARE ACACIA'S FULL-COURSE MEAL ON THEIR OWN. THEIR GOAL IS TO FULLY RESURRECT ACACIA'S GOURMET CELL DEMON, NEO, AND SEAL HIM AWAY.

TO PREVENT NEO FROM DESTROYING THE WORLD AND STOP HIS RESURRECTION, TORIKO AND THE GANG SPLIT UP TO CAPTURE THE REMAINING INGREDIENTS IN THE FULL COURSE. AFTER GATHERING THE COURSES, TORIKO AND HIS FRIENDS CONSUME THEM TO REVEAL THEIR GOURMET CELL DEMONS AND POWER UP BEFORE THE FINAL BATTLE.

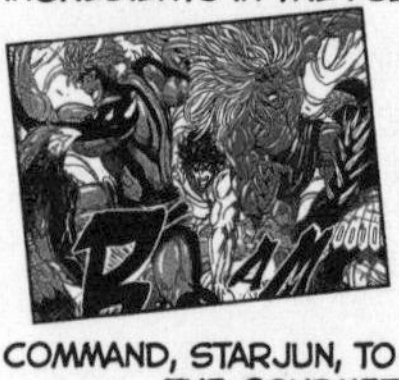

MEANWHILE, JOIE SEALS AWAY MIDORA, THE BOSS OF GOURMET CORP, AND CHALLENGES HIS SECOND-IN-COMMAND, STARJUN, TO A BATTLE TO THE DEATH!

THE GOURMET ECLIPSE CLOSES IN, AND GOD SUDDENLY APPEARS AND INSTANTLY EATS KOMATSU, LEAVING ITS PREPARATION UP TO OTAKE AND NAKUME.

THE BLUE NITRO CONTINUE THEIR MISSION TO SEAL AWAY NEO WHILE ACACIA ATTEMPTS TO REVIVE HIM TO HIS MOST POWERFUL STATE, AND TO MAKE MATTERS EVEN MORE COMPLICATED, THE EIGHT KINGS SUDDENLY APPEAR TO ASSIST TORIKO AND HIS FRIENDS IN CORNERING NEO! ANOTHER ALLY SOON RUSHES IN TO HELP THEM AS THE RED NITRO, CHICHI, ALSO JOINS THE BATTLE, TRANSFORMING HIMSELF INTO A MONSTROUS BEING AND RUSHING INTO THE HEAT OF BATTLE. WILL IT BE ENOUGH TO SLOW ACACIA DOWN AND STOP NEO'S FULL REVIVAL?!

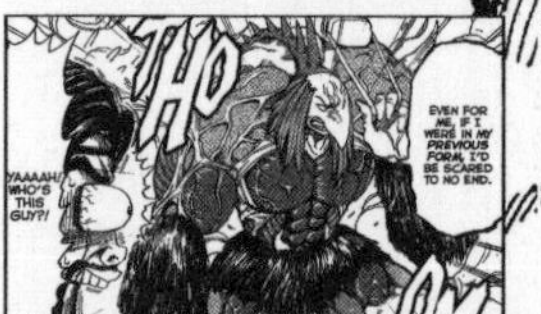
EVEN FOR ME, IF I WERE IN MY PREVIOUS FORM, I'D BE SCARED TO NO END.
YAAAAH! WHO'S THIS GUY?!
THO
OM

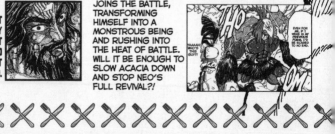

Contents

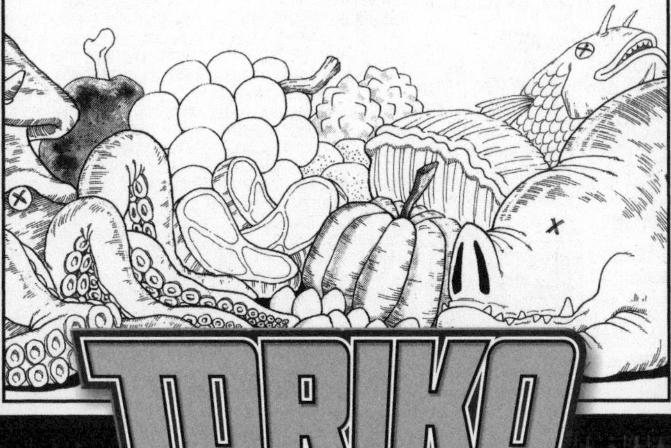

TORIKO

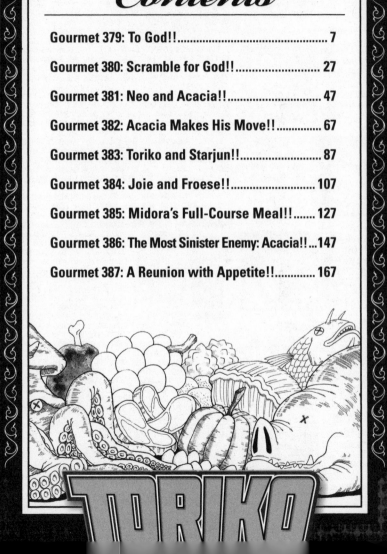

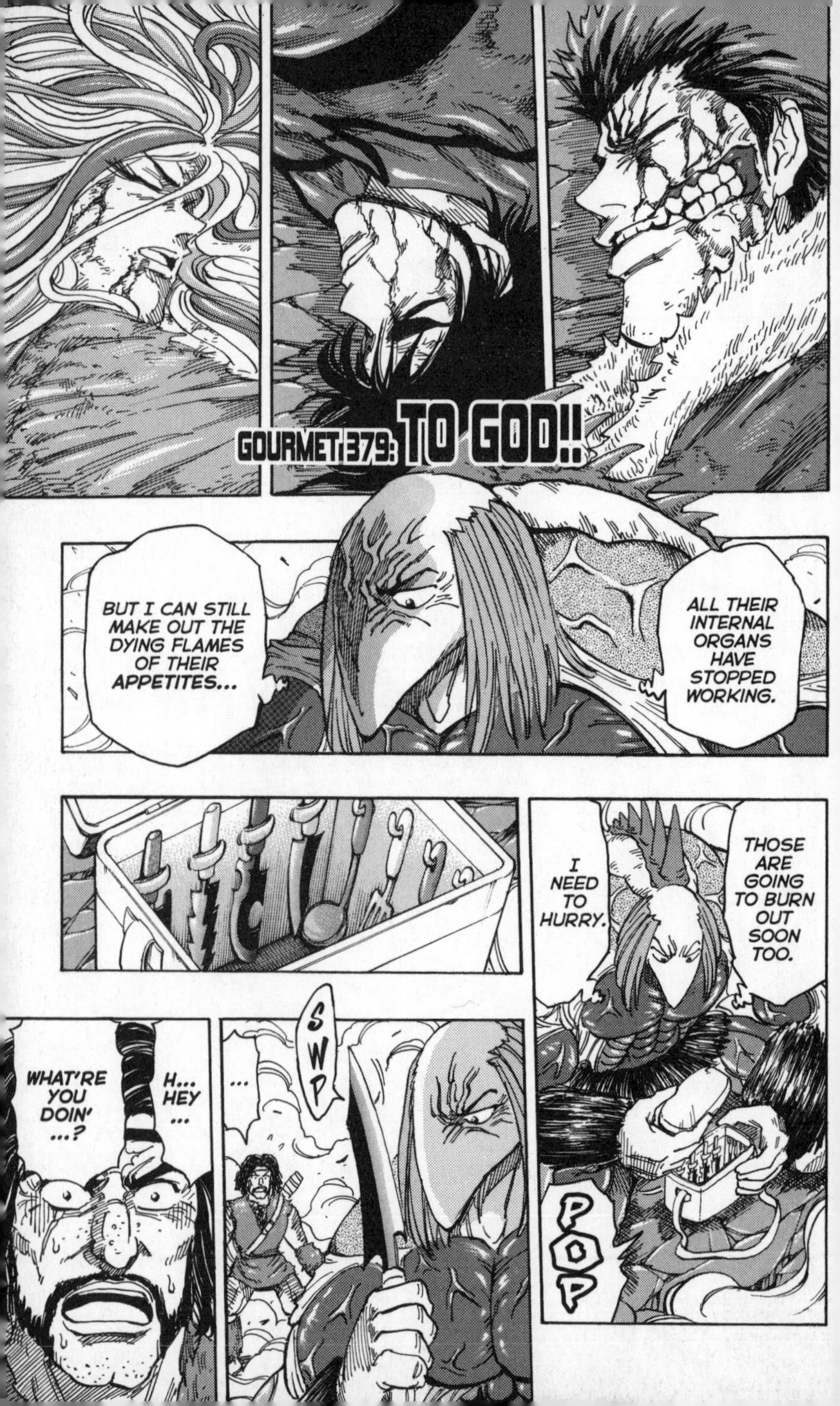
GOURMET 379: TO GOD!!
ALL THEIR INTERNAL ORGANS HAVE STOPPED WORKING.
BUT I CAN STILL MAKE OUT THE DYING FLAMES OF THEIR APPETITES...
THOSE ARE GOING TO BURN OUT SOON TOO.
I NEED TO HURRY.
POP
SWP
...
H... HEY ...
WHAT'RE YOU DOIN' ...?

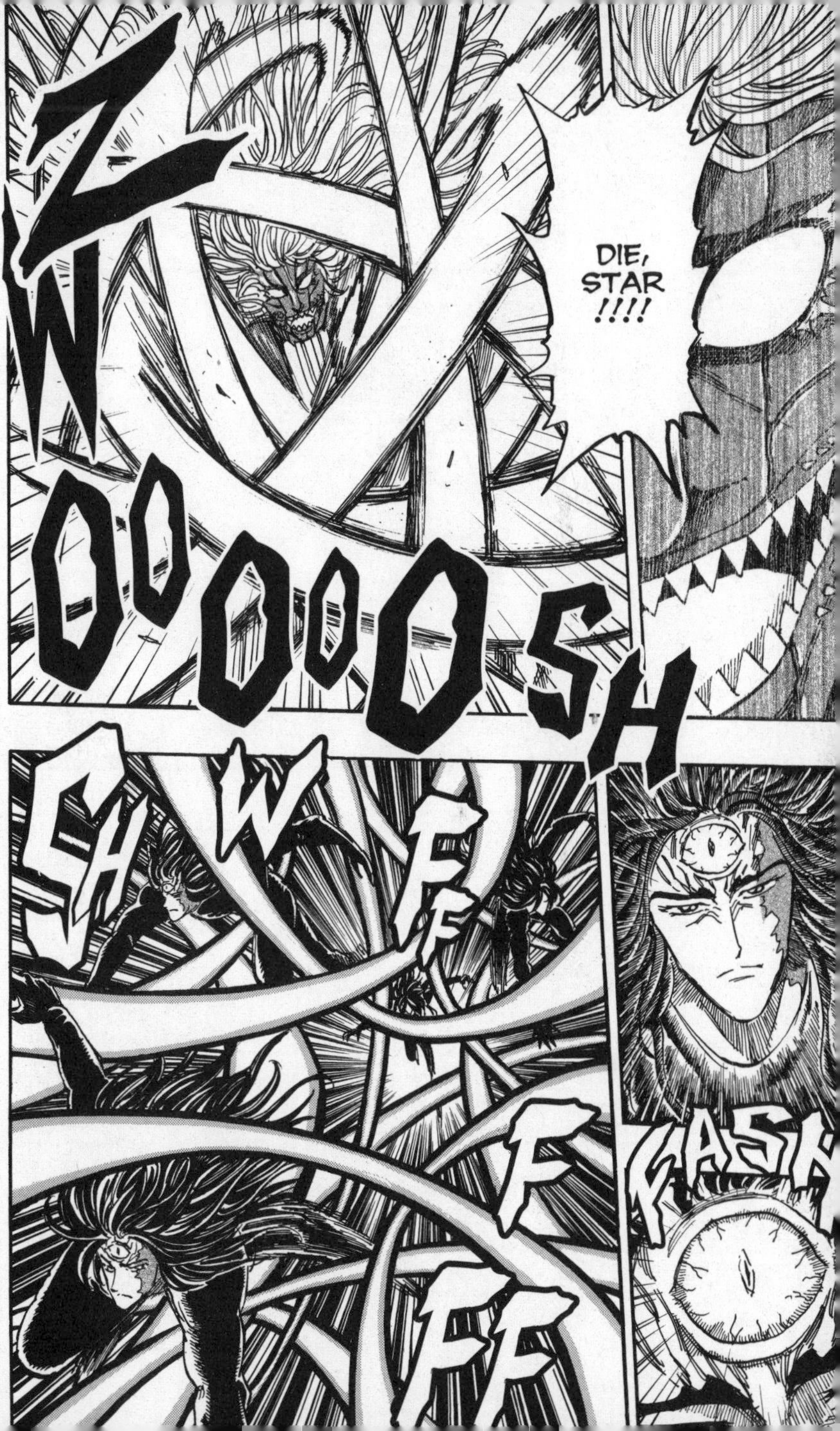
DIE, STAR!!!!
ZWOOOOOSH
FLASH
CHWFF
FFF

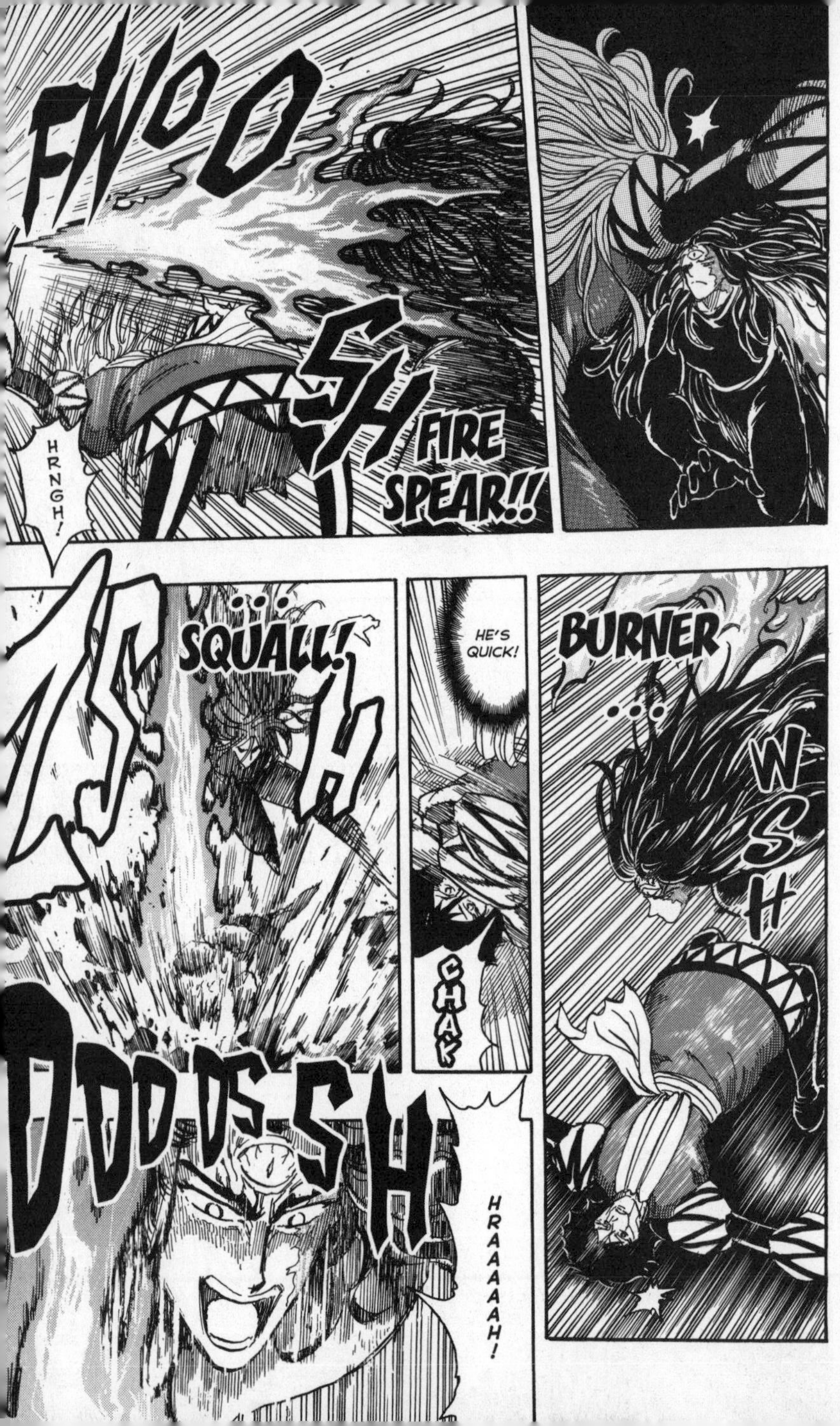
FWOO
SH
FIRE SPEAR!!
HRNGH!
BURNER
...
WSH
HE'S QUICK!
CHAK
ZSH
...
SQUALL!
D-DD-DS-SH
HRAAAAAAH!

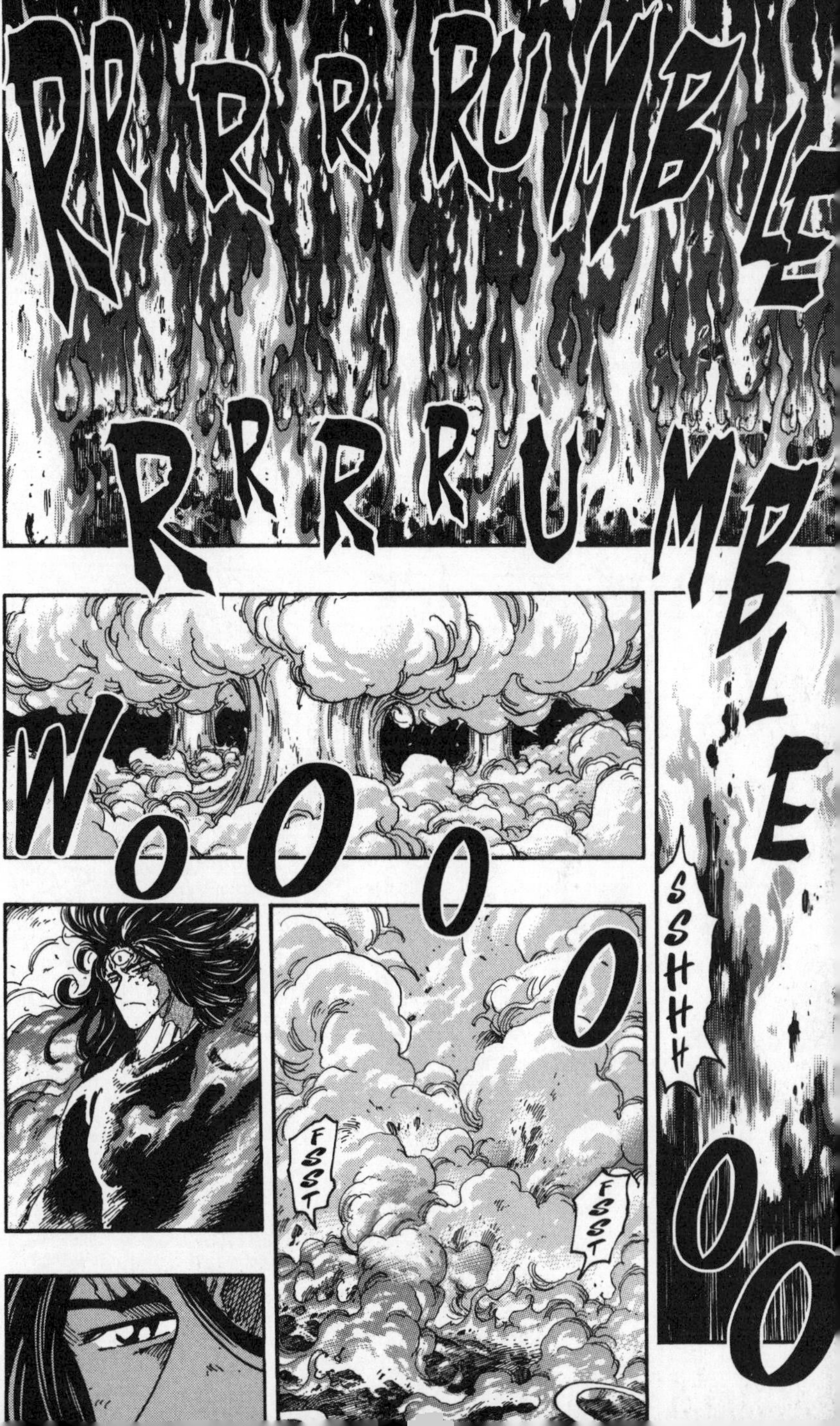
RRRR RUMBLE
RRRRRUMBLE
SSHHH
WOOOOOOO
FSSST
FSSST

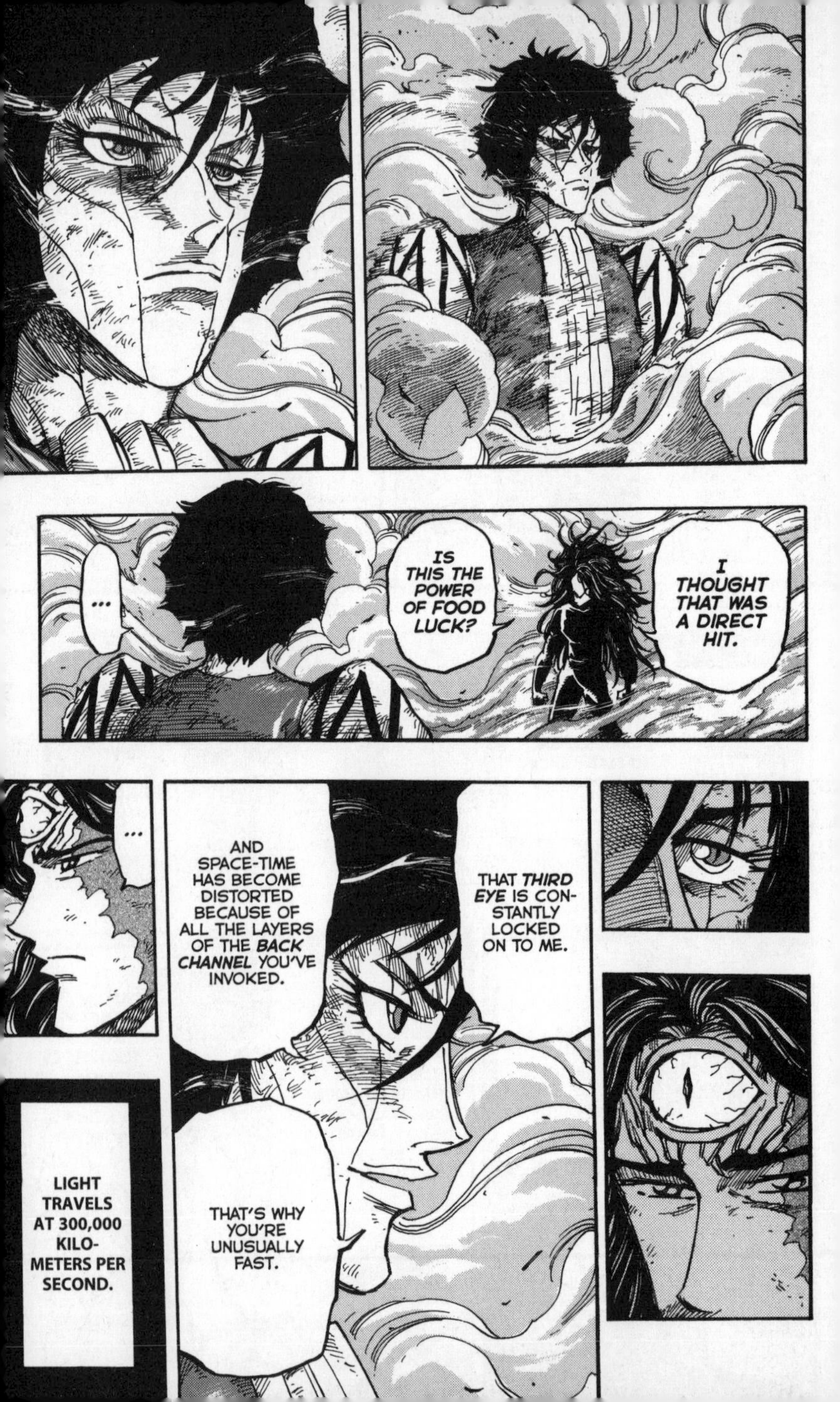

I THOUGHT THAT WAS A DIRECT HIT.
IS THIS THE POWER OF FOOD LUCK?
...
THAT *THIRD EYE* IS CONSTANTLY LOCKED ON TO ME.
AND SPACE-TIME HAS BECOME DISTORTED BECAUSE OF ALL THE LAYERS OF THE *BACK CHANNEL* YOU'VE INVOKED.
THAT'S WHY YOU'RE UNUSUALLY FAST.
...
LIGHT TRAVELS AT 300,000 KILOMETERS PER SECOND.

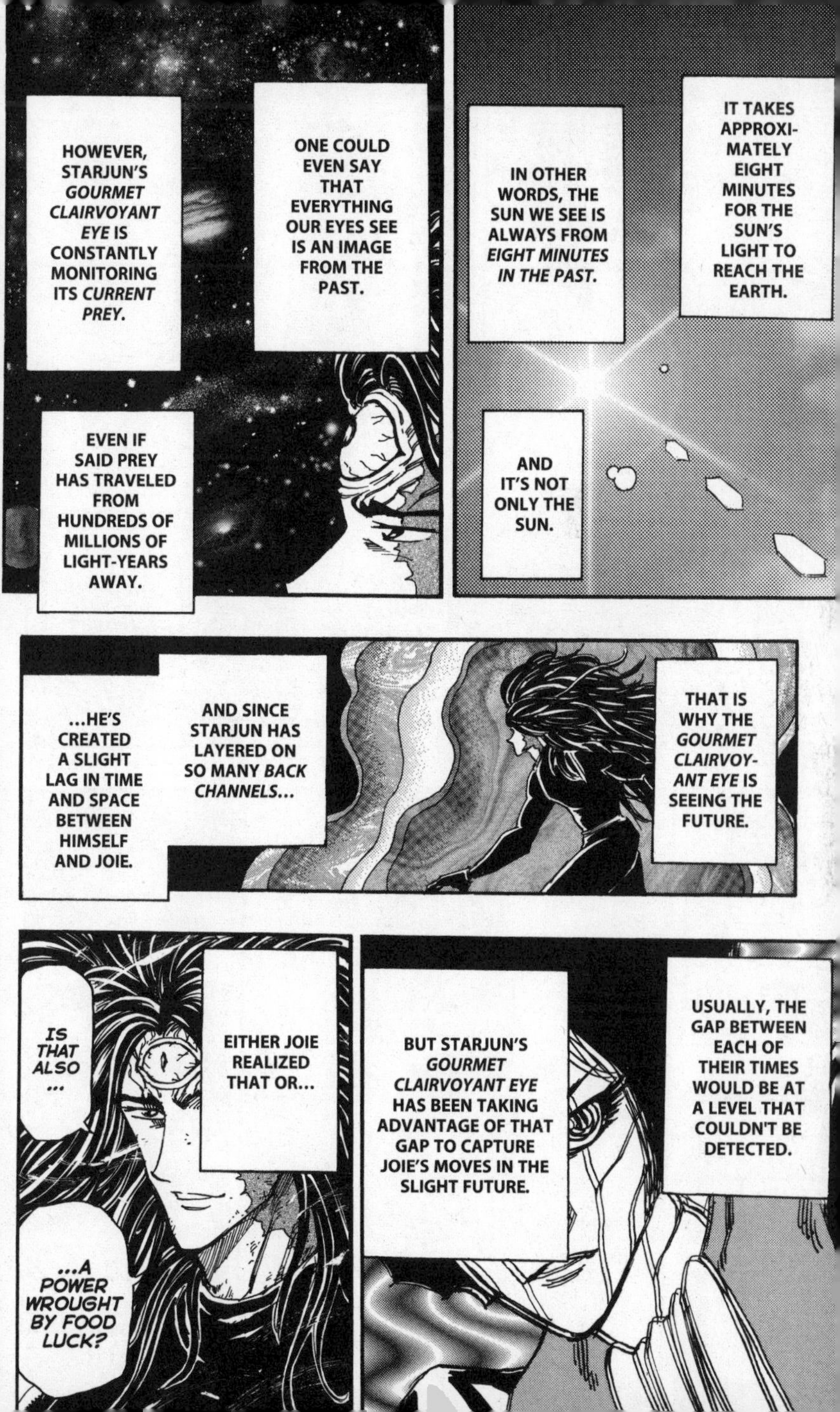
IT TAKES APPROXIMATELY EIGHT MINUTES FOR THE SUN'S LIGHT TO REACH THE EARTH.
IN OTHER WORDS, THE SUN WE SEE IS ALWAYS FROM *EIGHT MINUTES IN THE PAST.*
AND IT'S NOT ONLY THE SUN.
ONE COULD EVEN SAY THAT EVERYTHING OUR EYES SEE IS AN IMAGE FROM THE PAST.
HOWEVER, STARJUN'S *GOURMET CLAIRVOYANT EYE* IS CONSTANTLY MONITORING ITS *CURRENT PREY.*
EVEN IF SAID PREY HAS TRAVELED FROM HUNDREDS OF MILLIONS OF LIGHT-YEARS AWAY.
THAT IS WHY THE *GOURMET CLAIRVOYANT EYE* IS SEEING THE FUTURE.
AND SINCE STARJUN HAS LAYERED ON SO MANY *BACK CHANNELS...*
...HE'S CREATED A SLIGHT LAG IN TIME AND SPACE BETWEEN HIMSELF AND JOIE.
USUALLY, THE GAP BETWEEN EACH OF THEIR TIMES WOULD BE AT A LEVEL THAT COULDN'T BE DETECTED.
BUT STARJUN'S *GOURMET CLAIRVOYANT EYE* HAS BEEN TAKING ADVANTAGE OF THAT GAP TO CAPTURE JOIE'S MOVES IN THE SLIGHT FUTURE.
EITHER JOIE REALIZED THAT OR...
IS THAT ALSO ...
...A POWER WROUGHT BY FOOD LUCK?

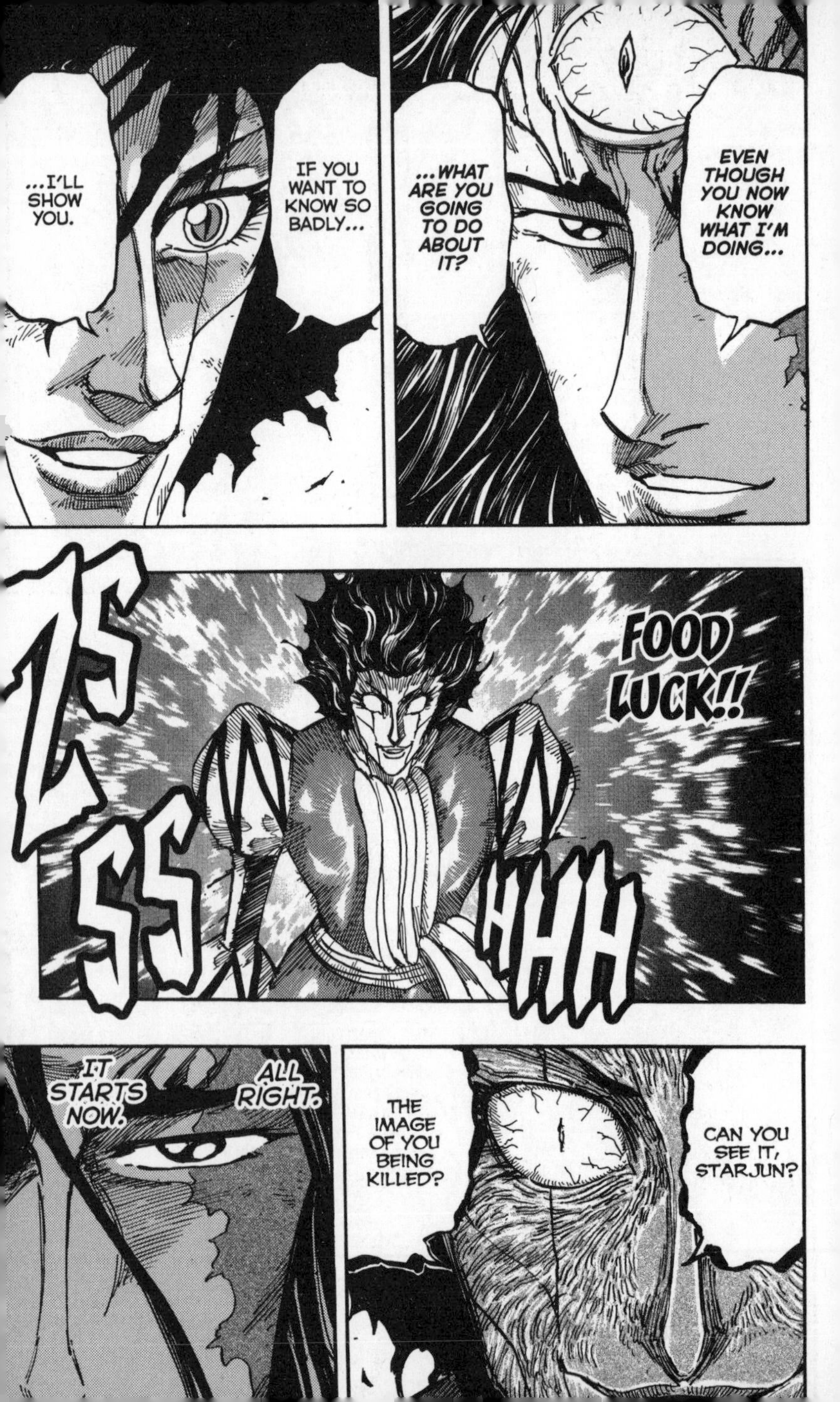
EVEN THOUGH YOU NOW KNOW WHAT I'M DOING...
...WHAT ARE YOU GOING TO DO ABOUT IT?
IF YOU WANT TO KNOW SO BADLY...
...I'LL SHOW YOU.
FOOD LUCK!!
ZSSSHHH
CAN YOU SEE IT, STARJUN?
THE IMAGE OF YOU BEING KILLED?
ALL RIGHT.
IT STARTS NOW.

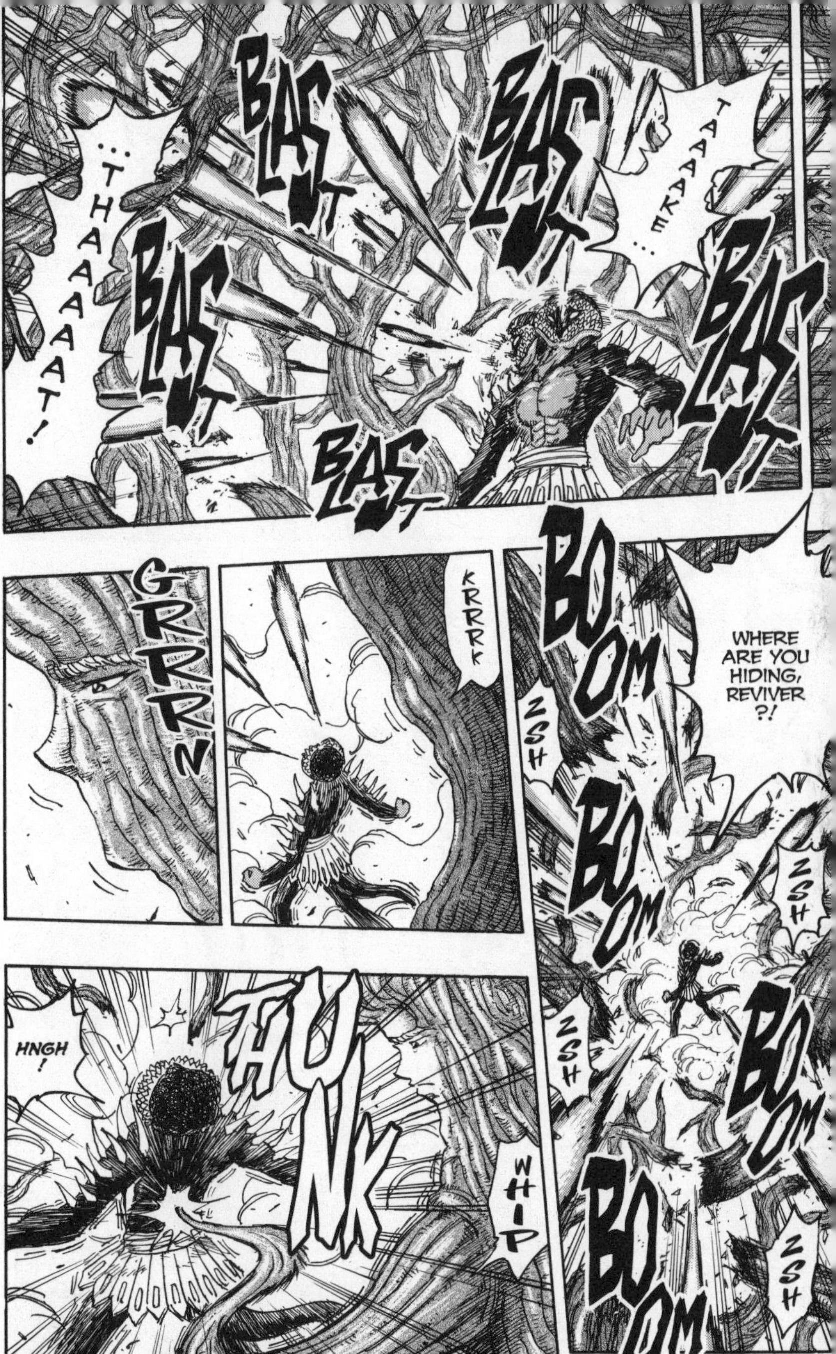
TAAAAKE...
BLAST
BLAST
BLAST
BLAST
BLAST
...THAAAAAAT!
WHERE ARE YOU HIDING, REVIVER?!
BOOM
ZSH
BOOM
ZSH
ZSH
BOOM
BOOM
ZSH
KRRRK
GRRRRN
THUNK
WHIP
HNGH!

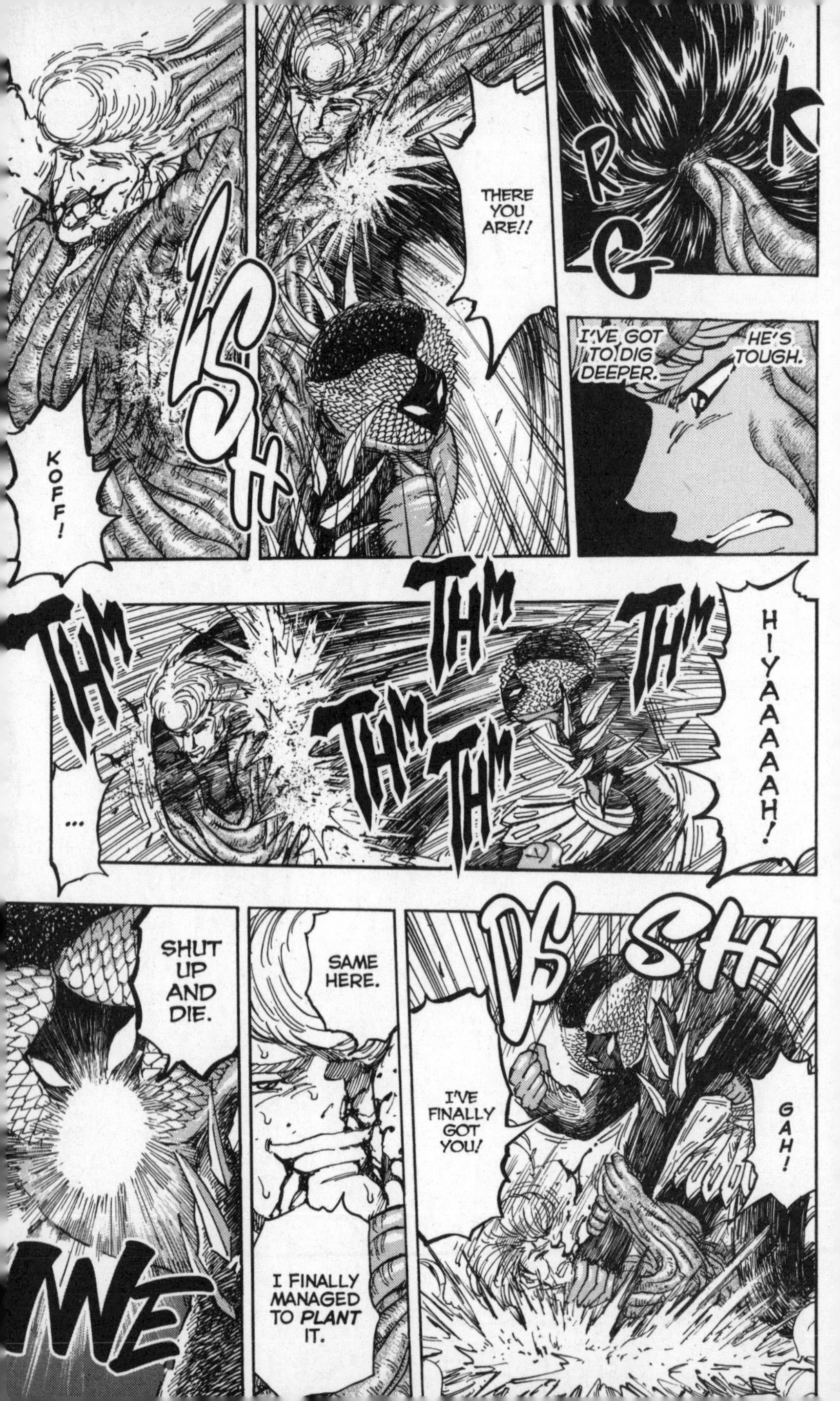

RGK
HE'S TOUGH.
I'VE GOT TO DIG DEEPER.
THERE YOU ARE!!
SH
KOFF!
HIYAAAAAH!
THM
THM
THM
THM
THM
...
DSSH
GAH!
I'VE FINALLY GOT YOU!
SAME HERE.
I FINALLY MANAGED TO *PLANT* IT.
SHUT UP AND DIE.
WE

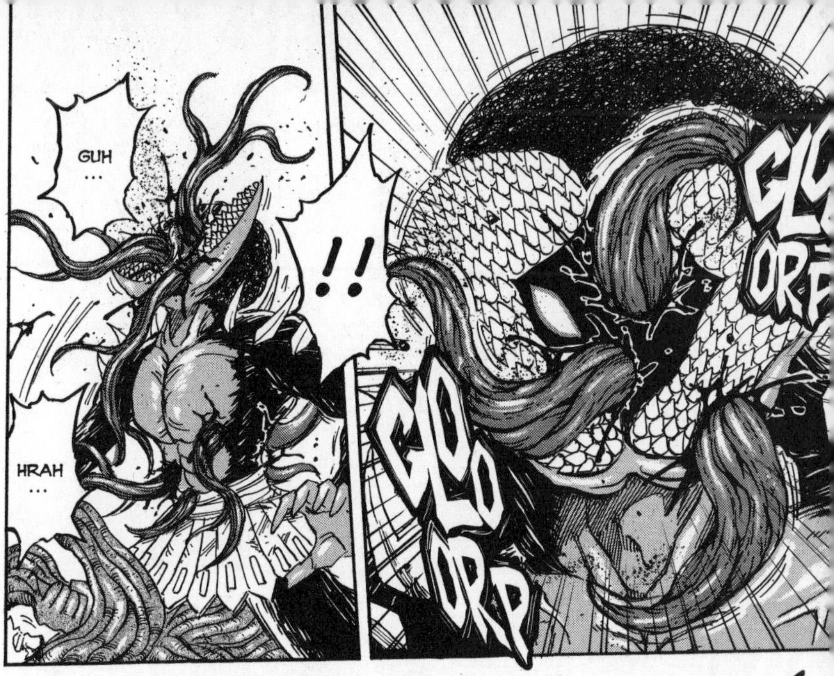
!!
GLOORP
GLOORP
GUH...
HRAH...

*SUBMITTED BY IZURU INUBUSE FROM OSAKA!

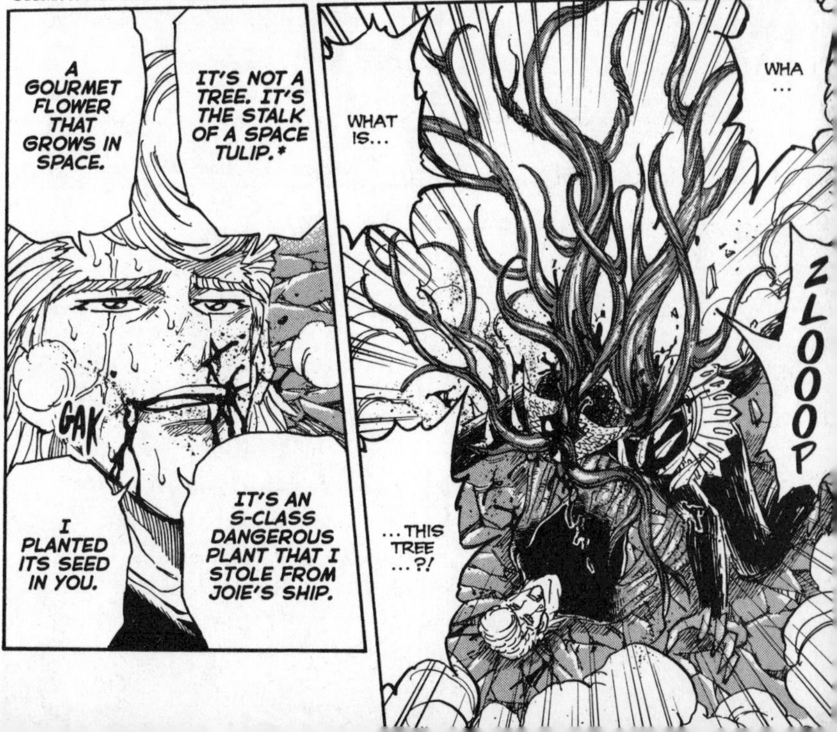
WHA...
WHAT IS...
ZLOOOOP
...THIS TREE ...?!
IT'S NOT A TREE. IT'S THE STALK OF A SPACE TULIP.*
A GOURMET FLOWER THAT GROWS IN SPACE.
GAK
IT'S AN S-CLASS DANGEROUS PLANT THAT I STOLE FROM JOIE'S SHIP.
I PLANTED ITS SEED IN YOU.

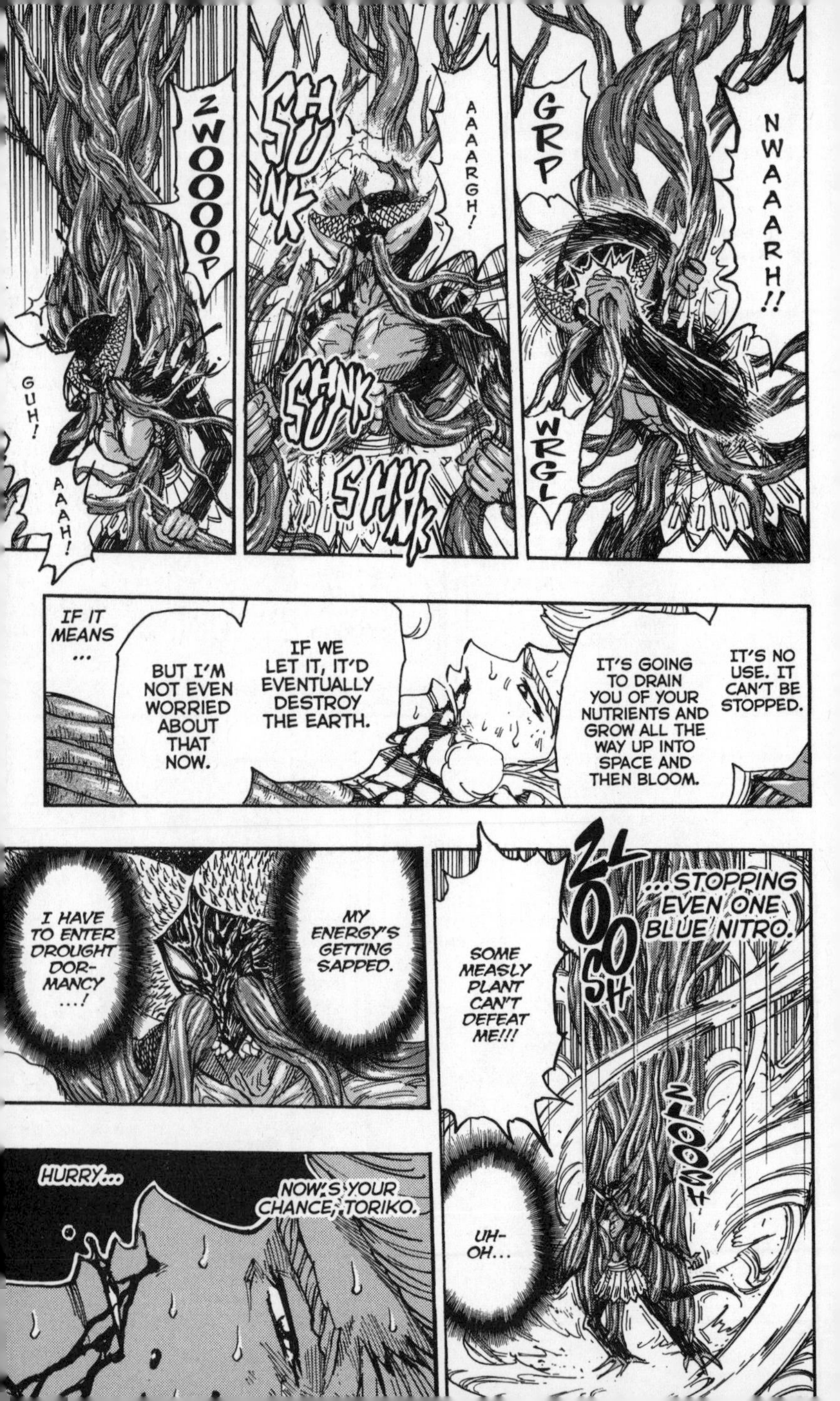
NWAAAARH!!
GRP
WRGL
AAAAARGH!
SHUNK
SHUNK
SHUNK
ZWOOOOOP
GUH!
AAAH!
IT'S NO USE. IT CAN'T BE STOPPED.
IT'S GOING TO DRAIN YOU OF YOUR NUTRIENTS AND GROW ALL THE WAY UP INTO SPACE AND THEN BLOOM.
IF WE LET IT, IT'D EVENTUALLY DESTROY THE EARTH.
BUT I'M NOT EVEN WORRIED ABOUT THAT NOW.
IF IT MEANS ...
...STOPPING EVEN ONE BLUE NITRO.
ZLOOOSH
SOME MEASLY PLANT CAN'T DEFEAT ME!!!
ZLOOOSH
UH-OH...
MY ENERGY'S GETTING SAPPED.
I HAVE TO ENTER DROUGHT DORMANCY ...!
NOW'S YOUR CHANCE, TORIKO.
HURRY...

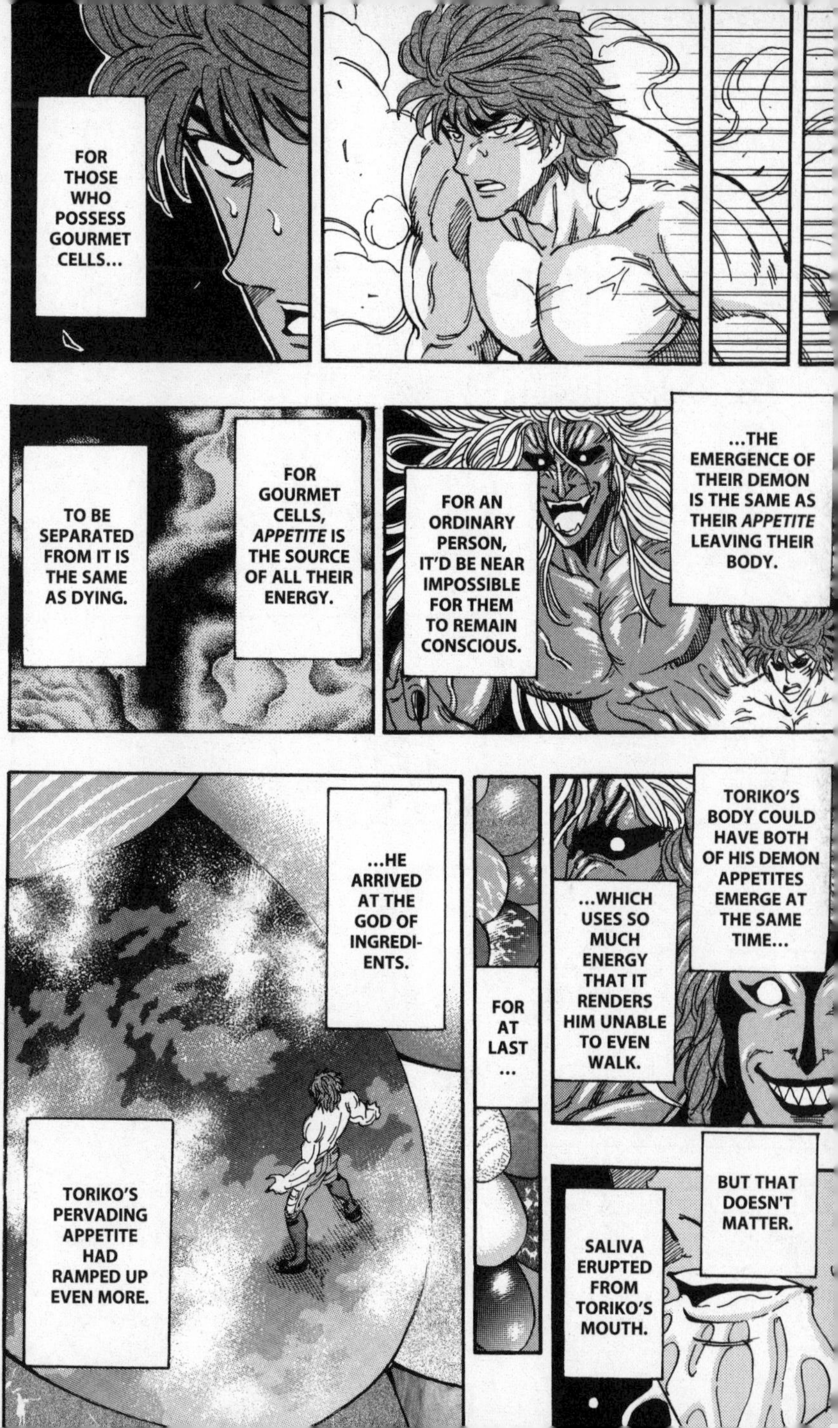
FOR THOSE WHO POSSESS GOURMET CELLS...
...THE EMERGENCE OF THEIR DEMON IS THE SAME AS THEIR *APPETITE* LEAVING THEIR BODY.
FOR AN ORDINARY PERSON, IT'D BE NEAR IMPOSSIBLE FOR THEM TO REMAIN CONSCIOUS.
FOR GOURMET CELLS, *APPETITE* IS THE SOURCE OF ALL THEIR ENERGY.
TO BE SEPARATED FROM IT IS THE SAME AS DYING.
TORIKO'S BODY COULD HAVE BOTH OF HIS DEMON APPETITES EMERGE AT THE SAME TIME...
...WHICH USES SO MUCH ENERGY THAT IT RENDERS HIM UNABLE TO EVEN WALK.
BUT THAT DOESN'T MATTER.
SALIVA ERUPTED FROM TORIKO'S MOUTH.
FOR AT LAST ...
...HE ARRIVED AT THE GOD OF INGREDI- ENTS.
TORIKO'S PERVADING APPETITE HAD RAMPED UP EVEN MORE.

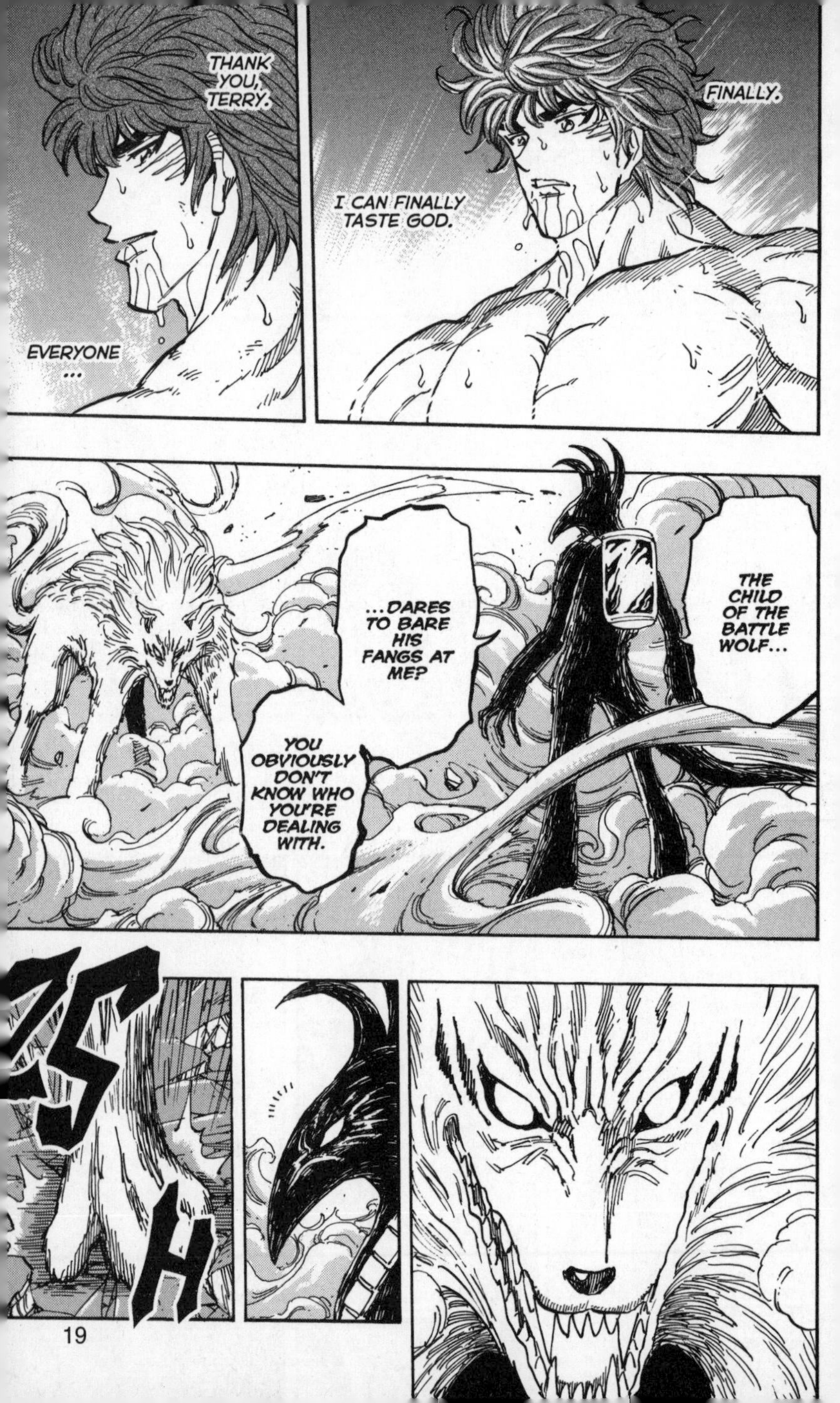

FINALLY.
I CAN FINALLY TASTE GOD.
THANK YOU, TERRY.
EVERYONE ...
THE CHILD OF THE BATTLE WOLF...
...DARES TO BARE HIS FANGS AT ME?
YOU OBVIOUSLY DON'T KNOW WHO YOU'RE DEALING WITH.

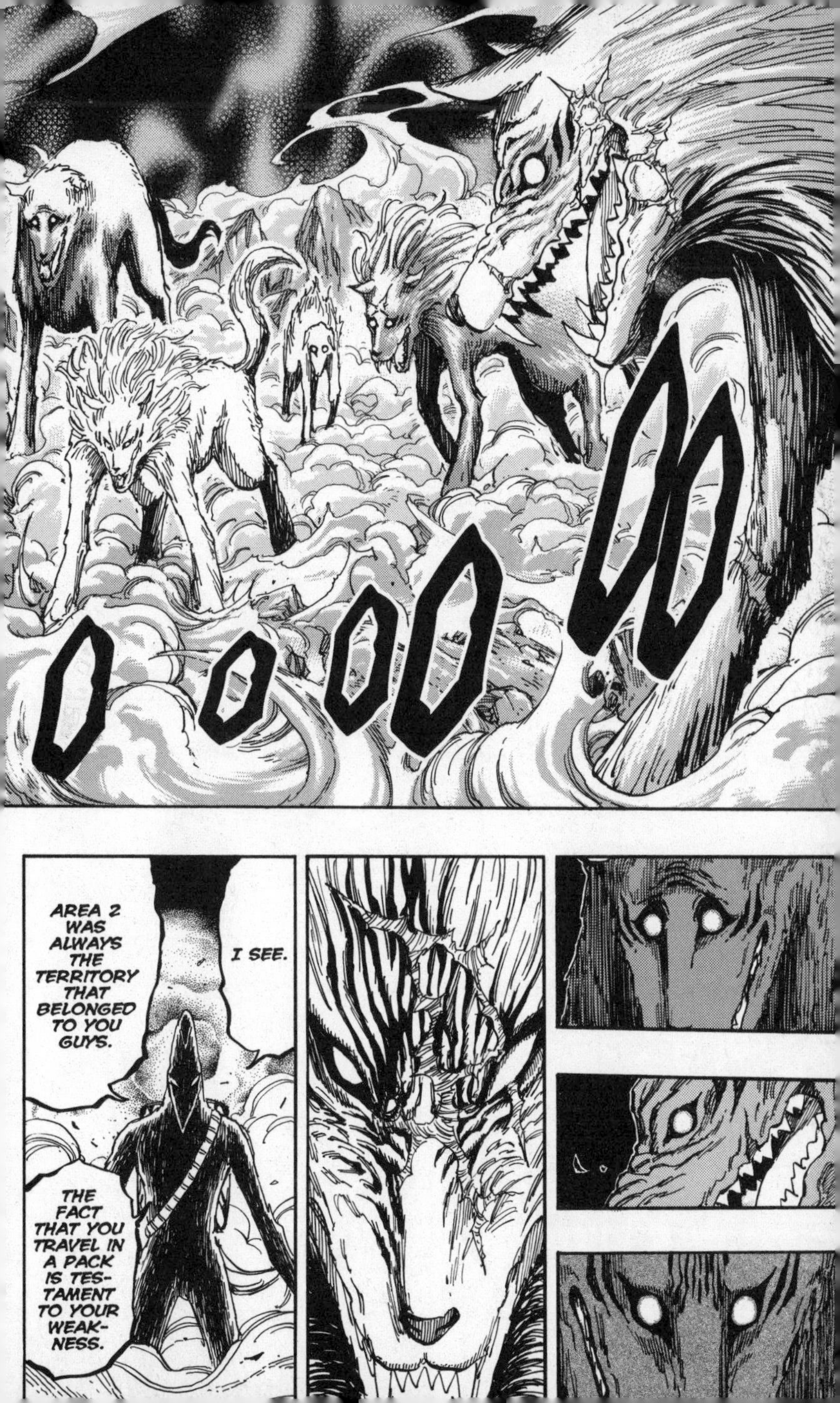

OOOOM
I SEE.
AREA 2 WAS ALWAYS THE TERRITORY THAT BELONGED TO YOU GUYS.
THE FACT THAT YOU TRAVEL IN A PACK IS TES-TAMENT TO YOUR WEAK-NESS.

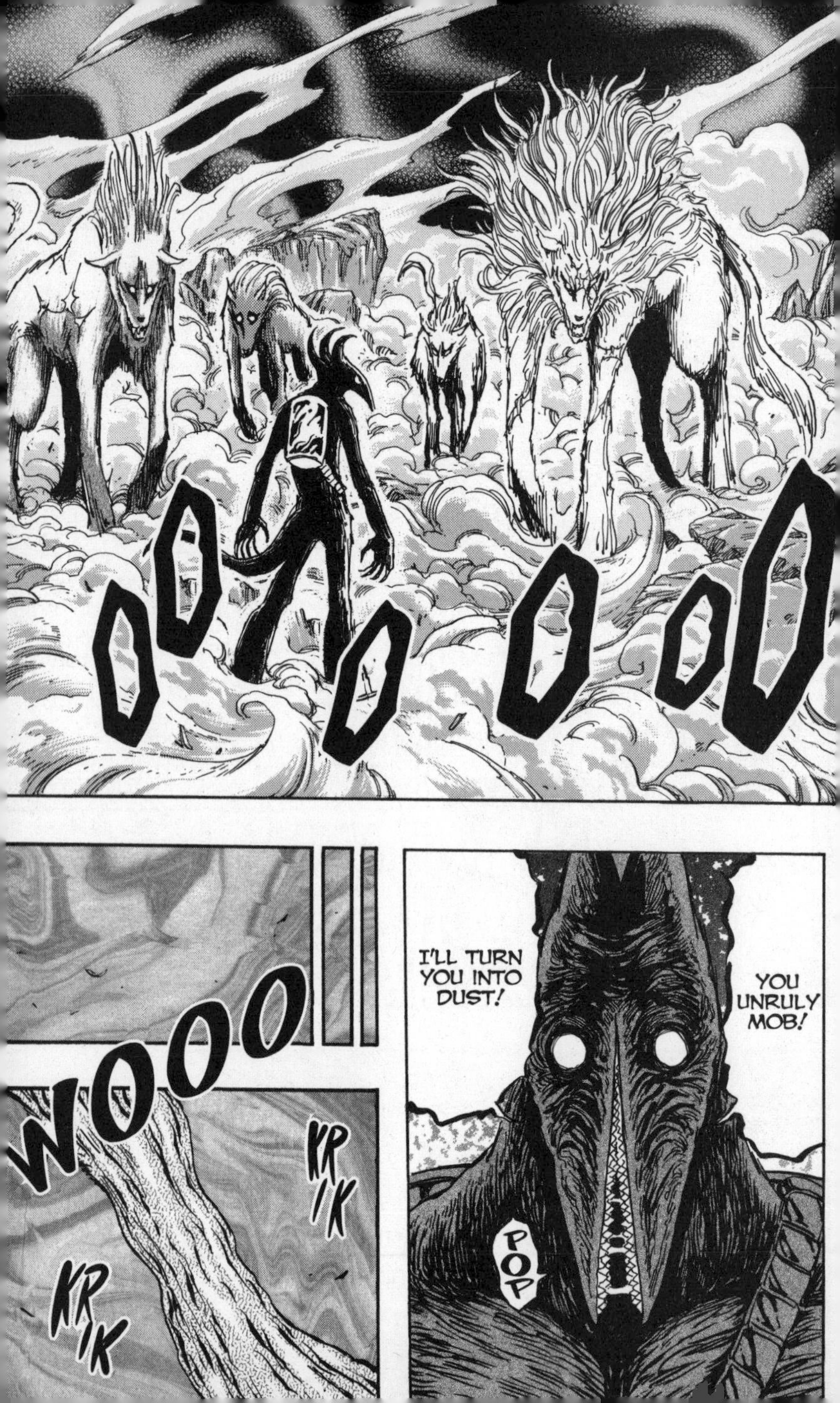
OOOOOO
YOU UNRULY MOB!
I'LL TURN YOU INTO DUST!
POP
WOOOO
KRIK
KRIK

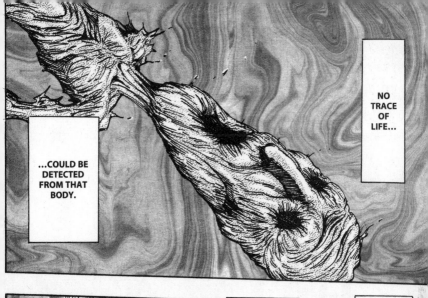

NO TRACE OF LIFE...
...COULD BE DETECTED FROM THAT BODY.
THERE ARE MANY DEFINITIONS OF DEATH, BUT...
...WHEN CELLS ARE DYING AND BREAKING DOWN...
...THEY'RE THE FIRST TO GO BEFORE THE BODY THAT WILL EVENTUALLY FADE AWAY.
NOT ONE OF THE CREATURES ...
...DOUBTED ACACIA'S *DEATH.*
BUT THE DEER KING DIDN'T REMOVE THE *BACK CHANNEL.*
IN FACT, IT CONTINUED TO SPEED UP TIME...
...UNTIL THE SMOLDERING EMBER OF APPETITE...
...LURKING WITHIN HIS CELLS...

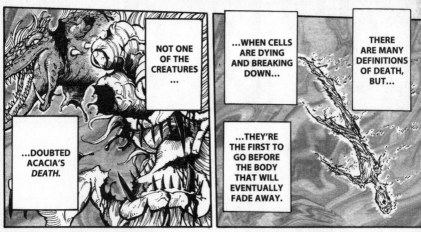

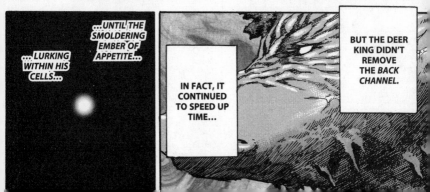

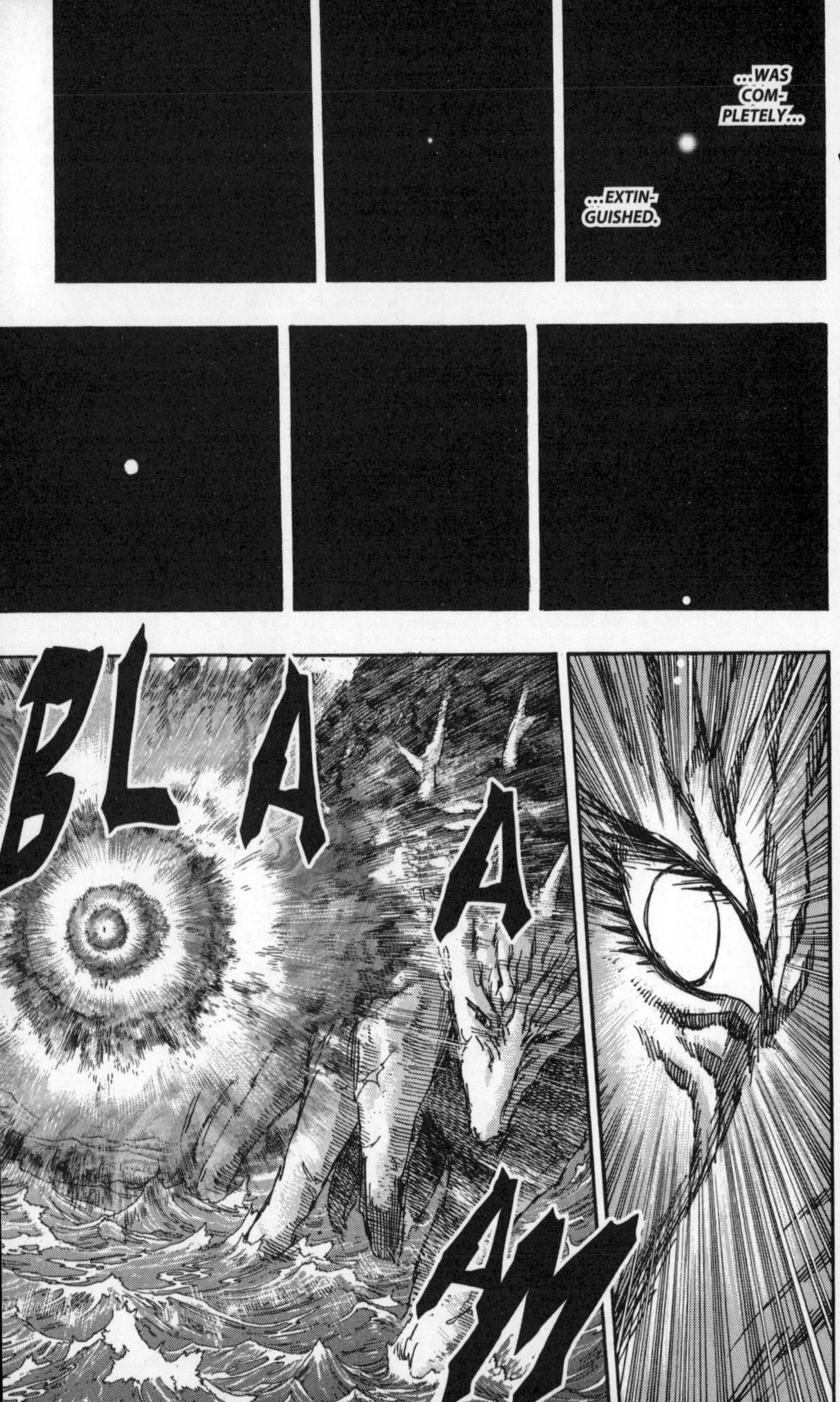
...WAS COM-PLETELY...
...EXTIN-GUISHED.
BLAAAM

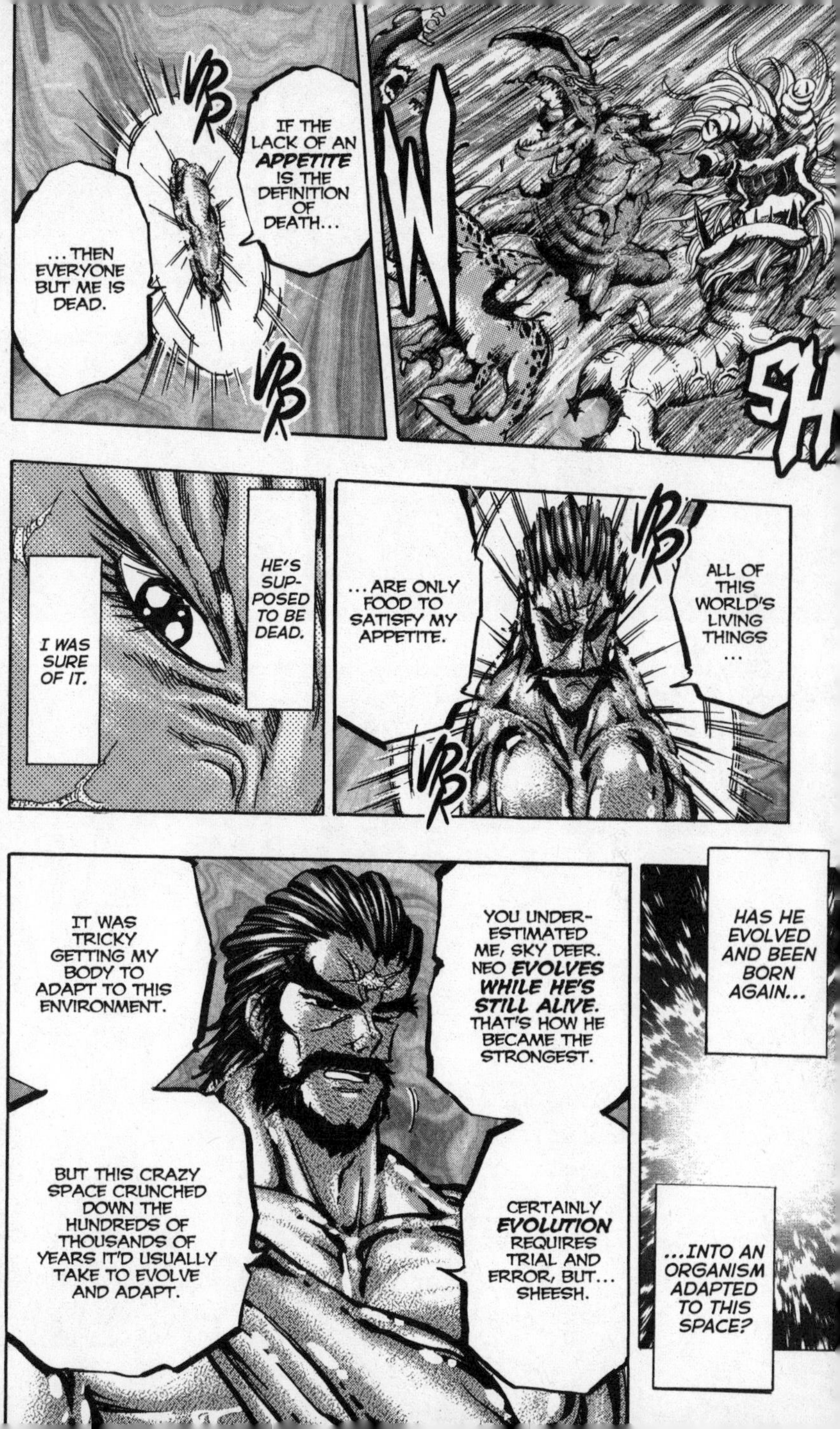
W
SH
VRR
IF THE LACK OF AN APPETITE IS THE DEFINITION OF DEATH...
...THEN EVERYONE BUT ME IS DEAD.
VRR
VRR
ALL OF THIS WORLD'S LIVING THINGS...
...ARE ONLY FOOD TO SATISFY MY APPETITE.
VRR
HE'S SUPPOSED TO BE DEAD.
I WAS SURE OF IT.
HAS HE EVOLVED AND BEEN BORN AGAIN...
...INTO AN ORGANISM ADAPTED TO THIS SPACE?
YOU UNDERESTIMATED ME, SKY DEER. NEO EVOLVES WHILE HE'S STILL ALIVE. THAT'S HOW HE BECAME THE STRONGEST.
IT WAS TRICKY GETTING MY BODY TO ADAPT TO THIS ENVIRONMENT.
CERTAINLY EVOLUTION REQUIRES TRIAL AND ERROR, BUT... SHEESH.
BUT THIS CRAZY SPACE CRUNCHED DOWN THE HUNDREDS OF THOUSANDS OF YEARS IT'D USUALLY TAKE TO EVOLVE AND ADAPT.

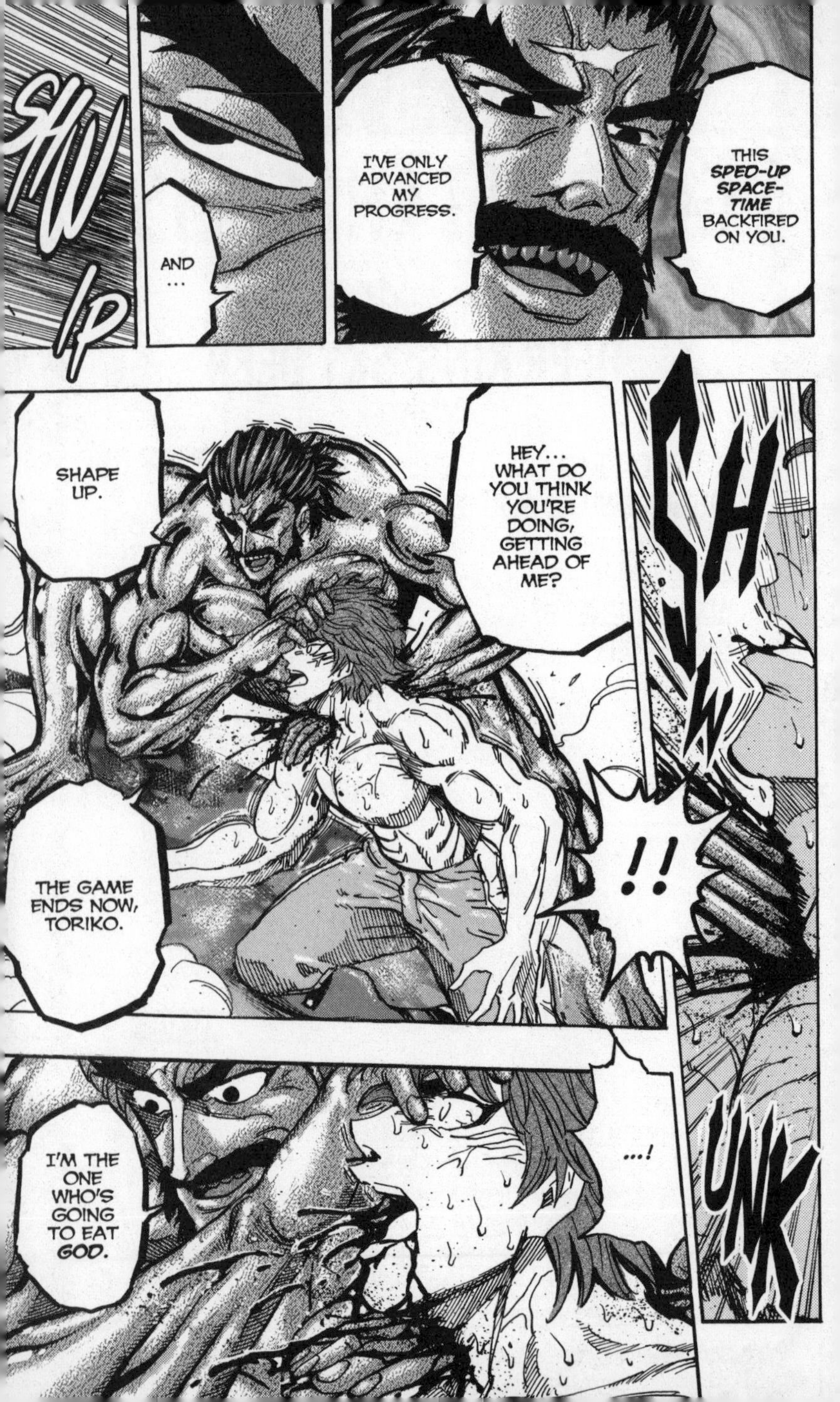
THIS SPED-UP SPACE-TIME BACKFIRED ON YOU.
I'VE ONLY ADVANCED MY PROGRESS.
AND ...
SHWIP
SHWUNK
HEY... WHAT DO YOU THINK YOU'RE DOING, GETTING AHEAD OF ME?
SHAPE UP.
!!
THE GAME ENDS NOW, TORIKO.
...!
I'M THE ONE WHO'S GOING TO EAT GOD.

TORIKO

GOURMET CHECKLIST

Vol. 414

DEER KING: SKY DEER
(MAMMAL)

CAPTURE LEVEL: 6,450
HABITAT: GOURMET WORLD, AREA 5
SIZE: 60,000 M
HEIGHT: 10,000 M
WEIGHT: 8 TRILLION TONS
PRICE: UNKNOWN

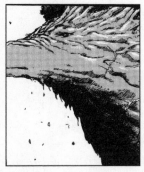

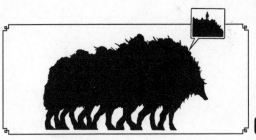

SCALE

ONE OF THE EIGHT KINGS WHO RULES ONE OF THE MAJOR CONTINENTS IN THE GOURMET WORLD. THIS ONE IS THE MOST GENTLE AND PEACEFUL OF THE EIGHT KINGS, BUT ALSO THE LARGEST. THE FOREST GROWING OUT OF ITS HORNS IS KNOWN AS THE "DEN OF MONSTERS" AND IS HOME TO SOME OF THE GOURMET WORLD'S MOST VICIOUS CREATURES WITH CAPTURE LEVELS AVERAGING AROUND 4,000. WHEN ANGERED, THESE MONSTERS ARE SAID TO GATHER AND FIGHT FOR THE DEER KING. BUT THERE ARE TIMES WHEN THE DEER KING WILL FIGHT FOR ITSELF BY TURNING THE SPACE AROUND IT INTO AN AREA OPPOSITE OF A BACK CHANNEL WHERE TIME RAPIDLY PROGRESSES FORWARD AT AROUND 1,000 YEARS A SECOND, KILLING EVERYTHING IN THE IMMEDIATE VICINITY.

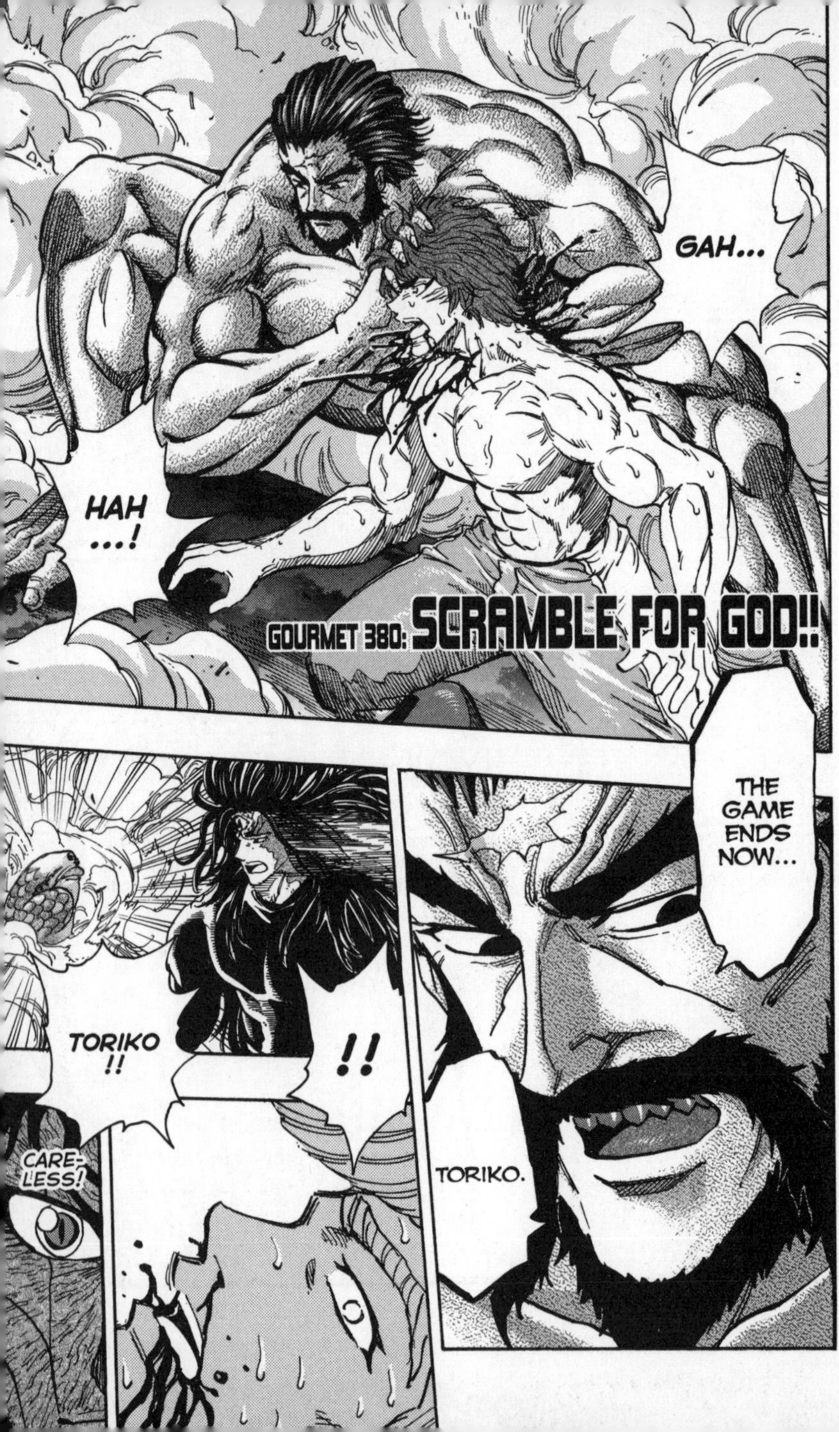
GAH...
HAH ...!
GOURMET 380: SCRAMBLE FOR GOD!!
THE GAME ENDS NOW...
TORIKO.
!!
TORIKO !!
CARE-LESS!

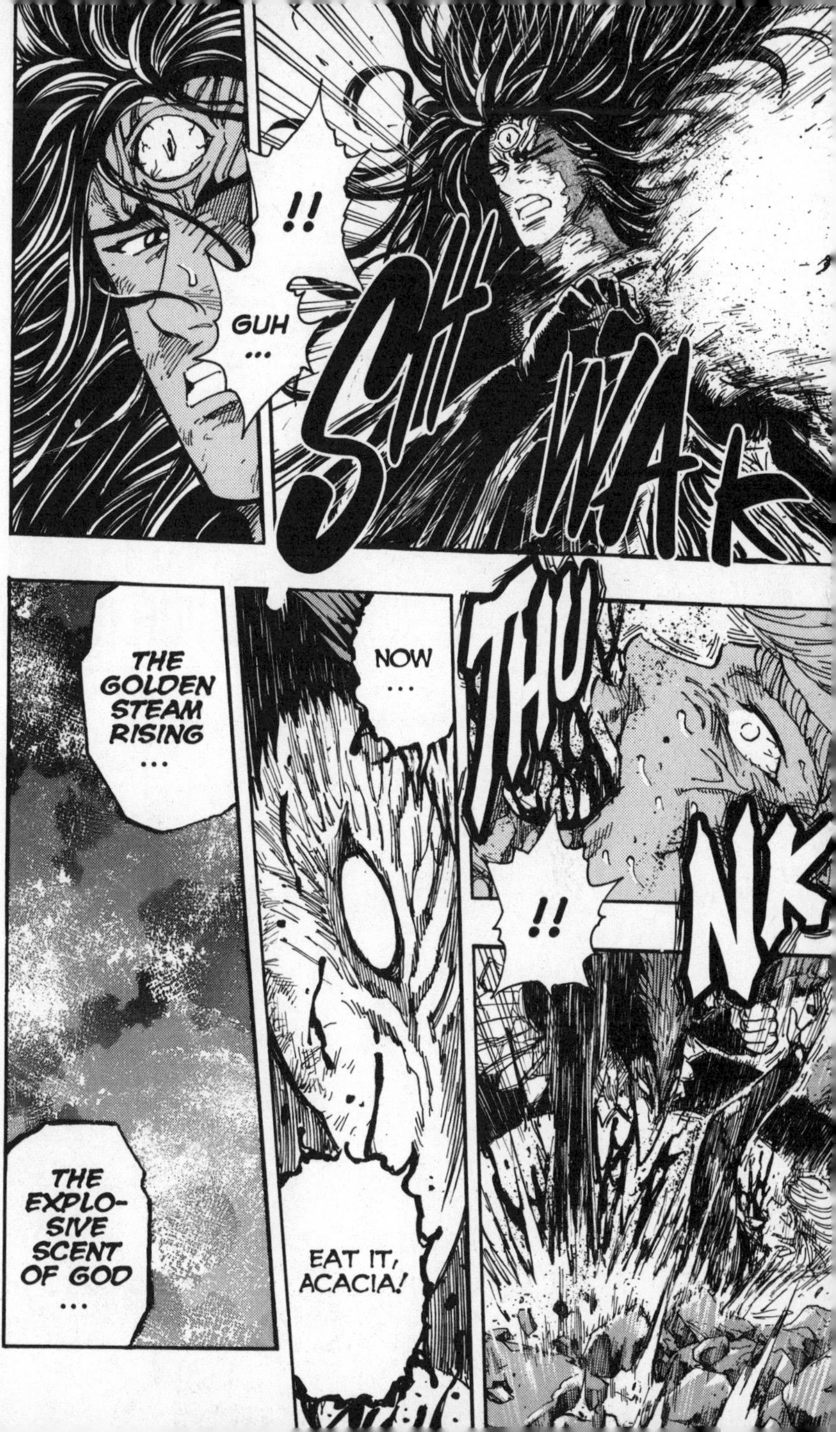

!!
GUH ...
SHWAK
THUNK
!!
NOW ...
EAT IT, ACACIA!
THE GOLDEN STEAM RISING ...
THE EXPLOSIVE SCENT OF GOD ...

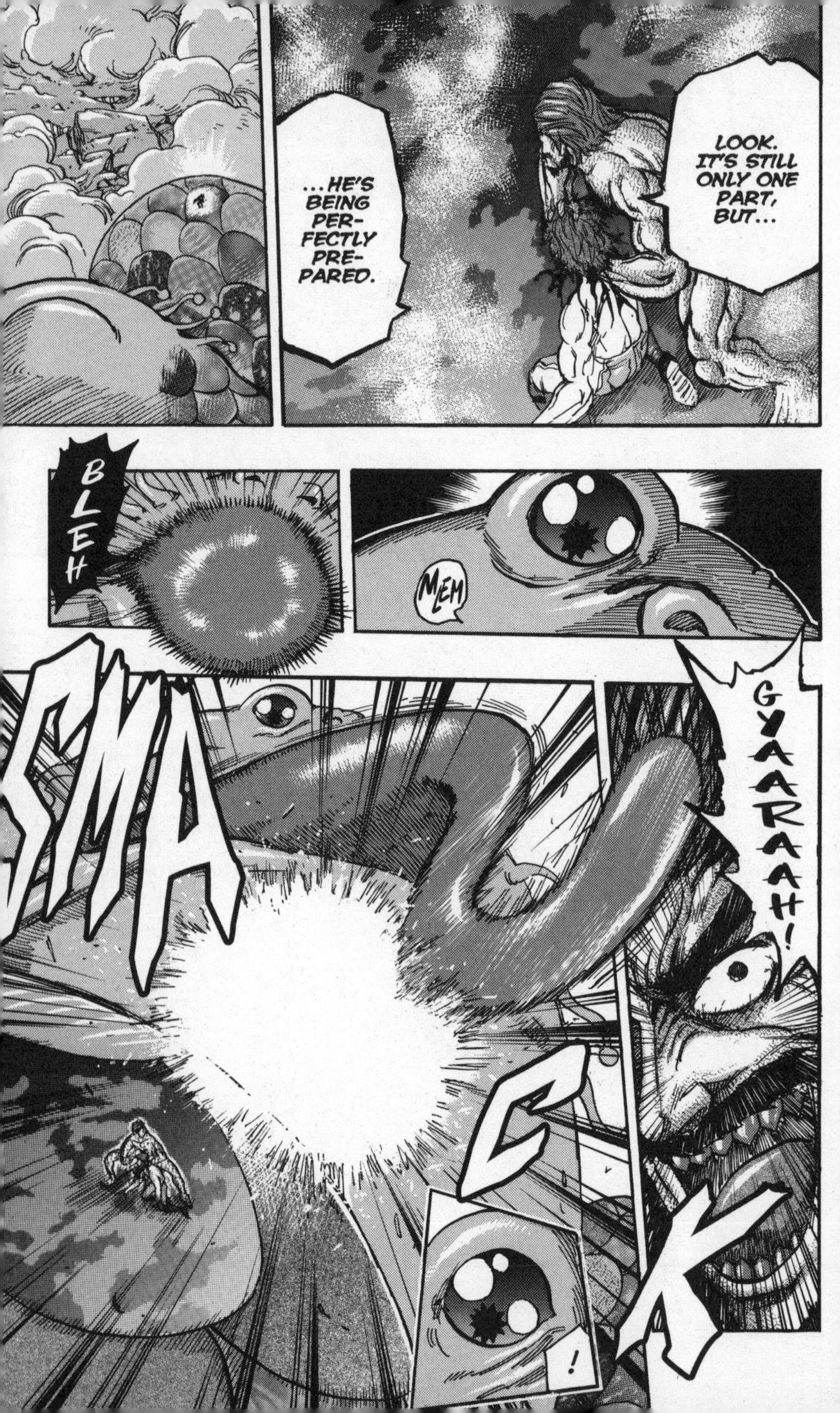
LOOK. IT'S STILL ONLY ONE PART, BUT...
...HE'S BEING PERFECTLY PREPARED.
MLEM
BLEH
GYAAARAAAH!
SMA
CK
!

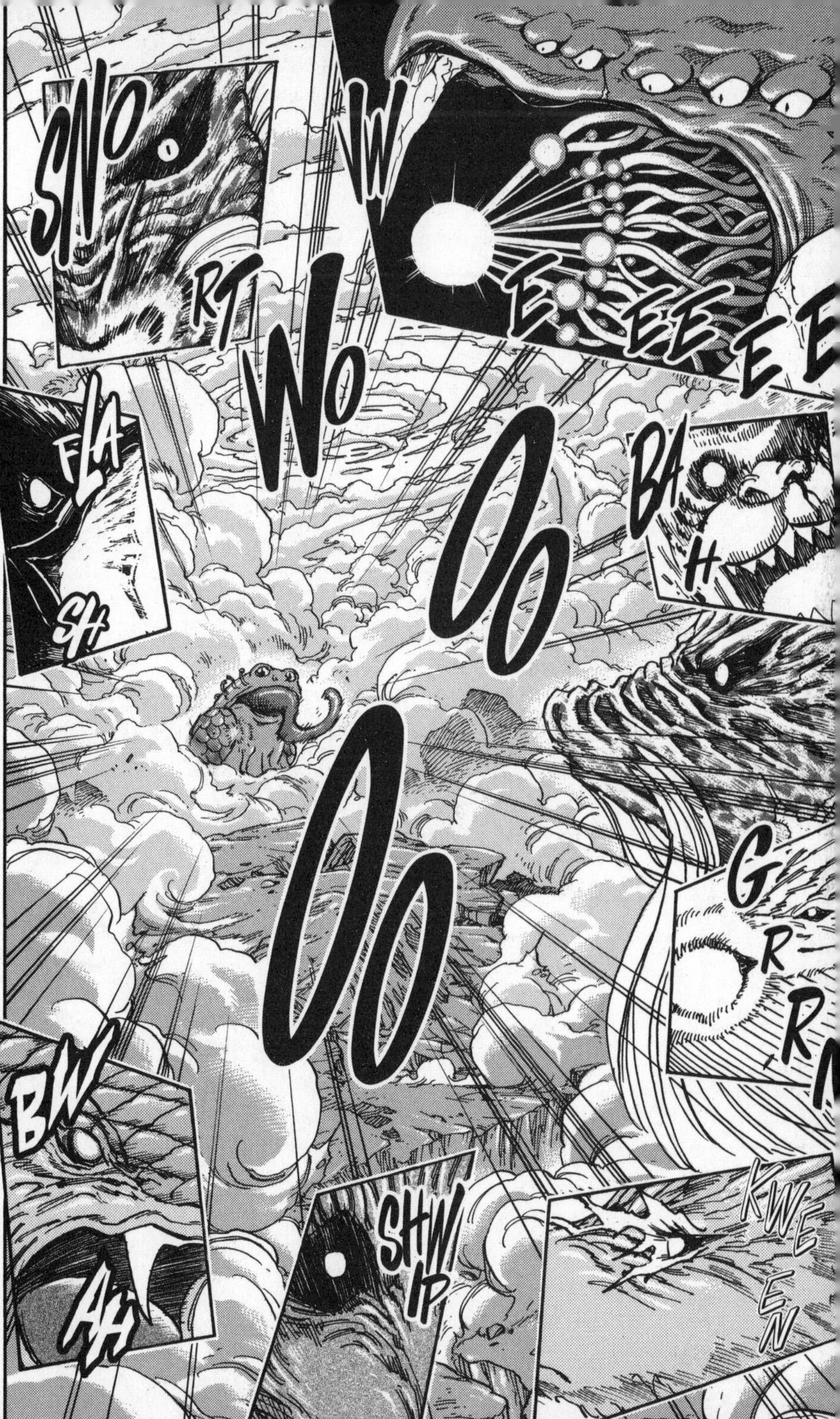

WWEEEEEE
SNORT
WOOOOO
BAH
FLASH
GRR
KWEEN
SHWIP
BWAH

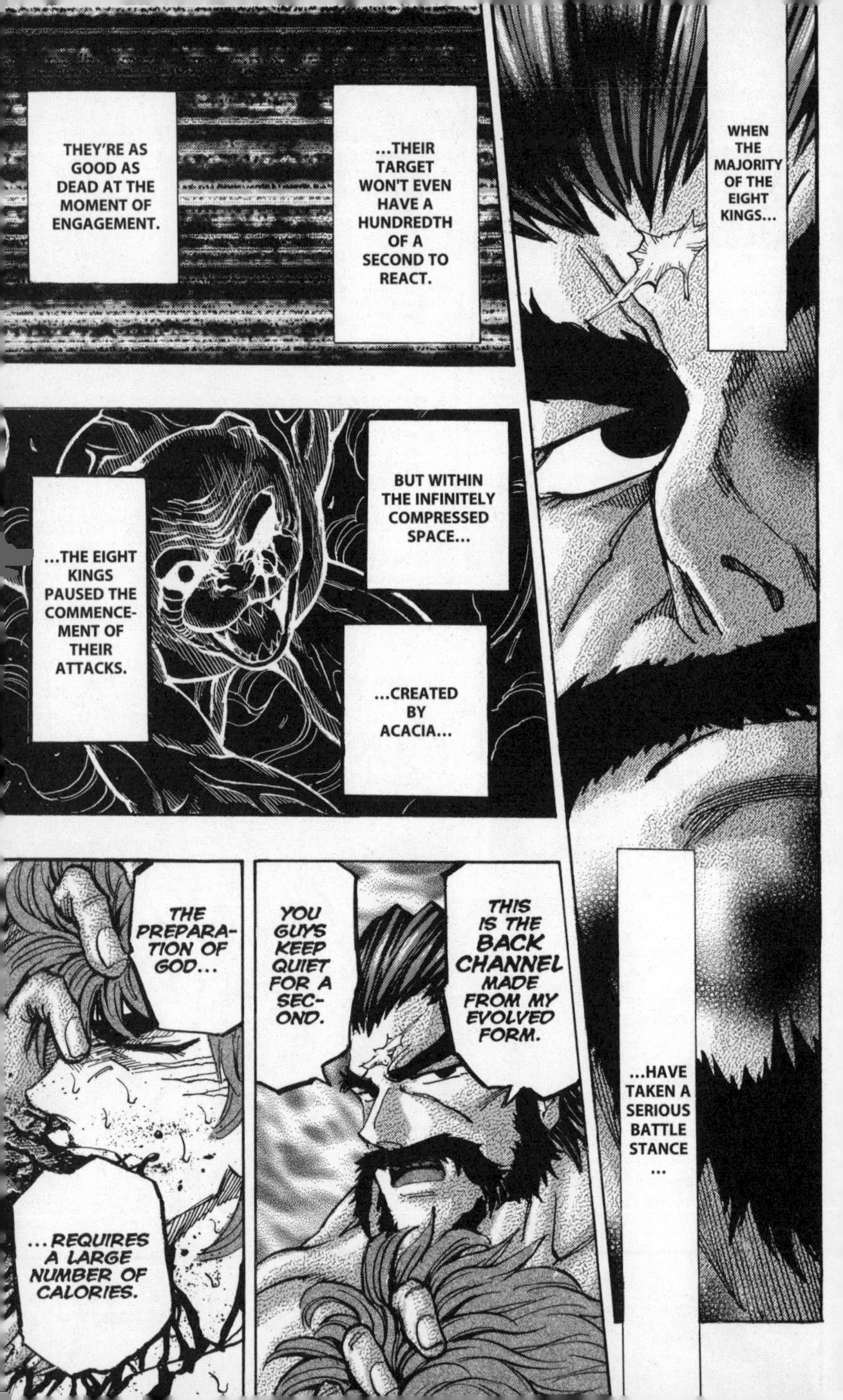
WHEN THE MAJORITY OF THE EIGHT KINGS...
...HAVE TAKEN A SERIOUS BATTLE STANCE...
...THEIR TARGET WON'T EVEN HAVE A HUNDREDTH OF A SECOND TO REACT.
THEY'RE AS GOOD AS DEAD AT THE MOMENT OF ENGAGEMENT.
BUT WITHIN THE INFINITELY COMPRESSED SPACE...
...CREATED BY ACACIA...
...THE EIGHT KINGS PAUSED THE COMMENCEMENT OF THEIR ATTACKS.
THIS IS THE BACK CHANNEL MADE FROM MY EVOLVED FORM.
YOU GUYS KEEP QUIET FOR A SECOND.
THE PREPARATION OF GOD...
...REQUIRES A LARGE NUMBER OF CALORIES.

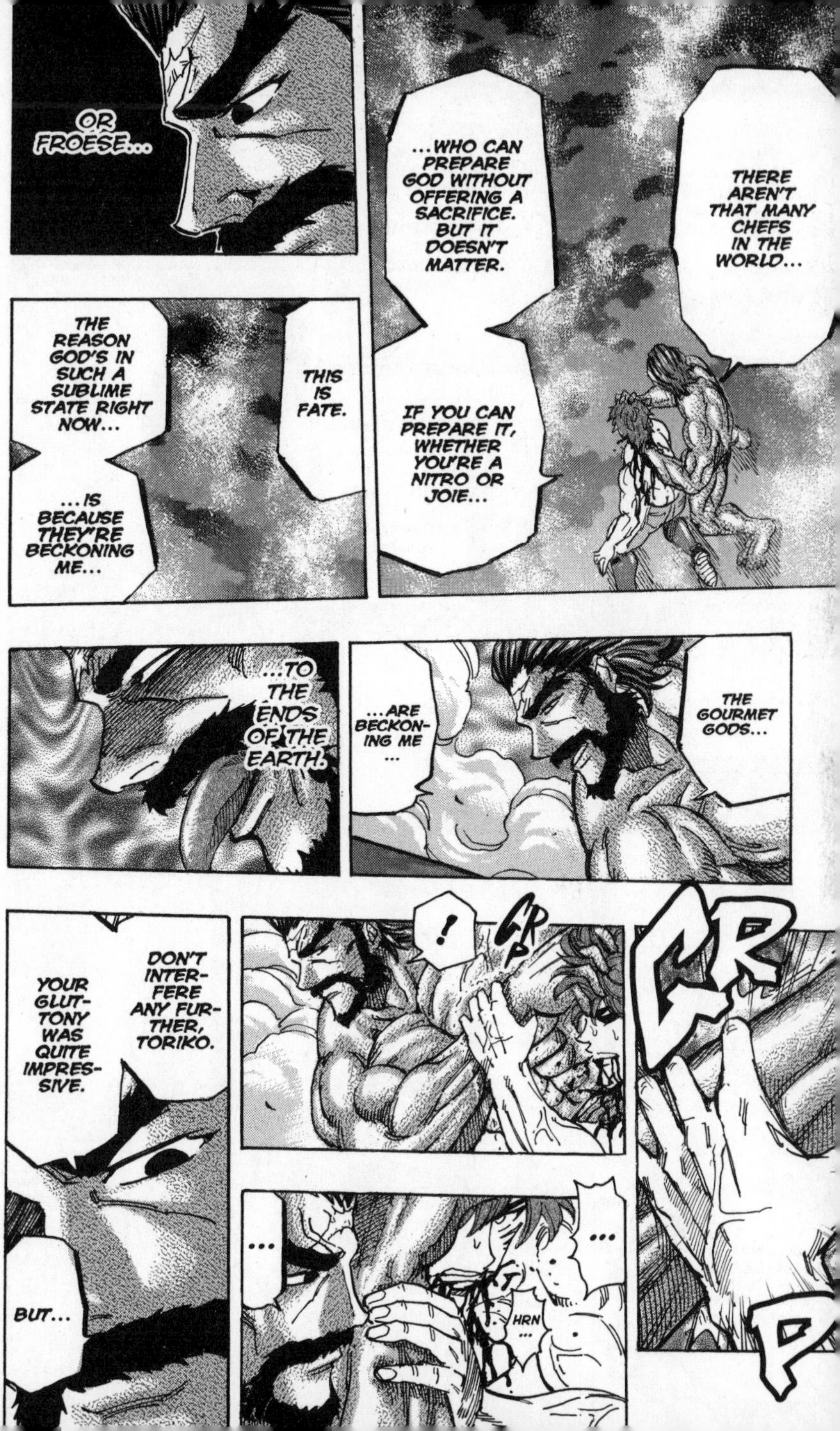
THERE AREN'T THAT MANY CHEFS IN THE WORLD...
...WHO CAN PREPARE GOD WITHOUT OFFERING A SACRIFICE. BUT IT DOESN'T MATTER.
IF YOU CAN PREPARE IT, WHETHER YOU'RE A NITRO OR JOIE...
OR FROESE...
THIS IS FATE.
THE REASON GOD'S IN SUCH A SUBLIME STATE RIGHT NOW...
...IS BECAUSE THEY'RE BECKONING ME...
THE GOURMET GODS...
...ARE BECKONING ME ...
...TO THE ENDS OF THE EARTH.
CRP
CRP
!
...
HRN ...
...
DON'T INTERFERE ANY FURTHER, TORIKO.
YOUR GLUTTONY WAS QUITE IMPRESSIVE.
BUT...

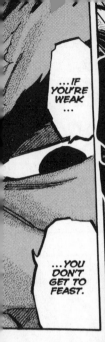
...IF YOU'RE WEAK...

...YOU DON'T GET TO FEAST.

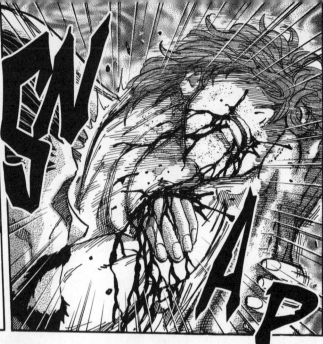

SORRY FOR THE WAIT, GOD.

NOW.

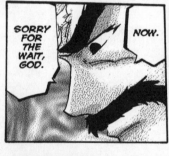

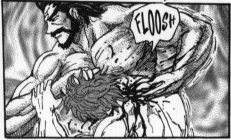
FLOOSH

!

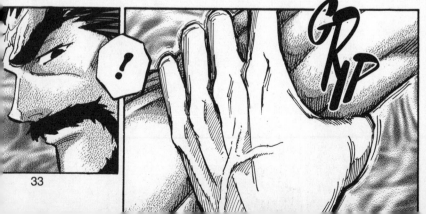
GRYP

33

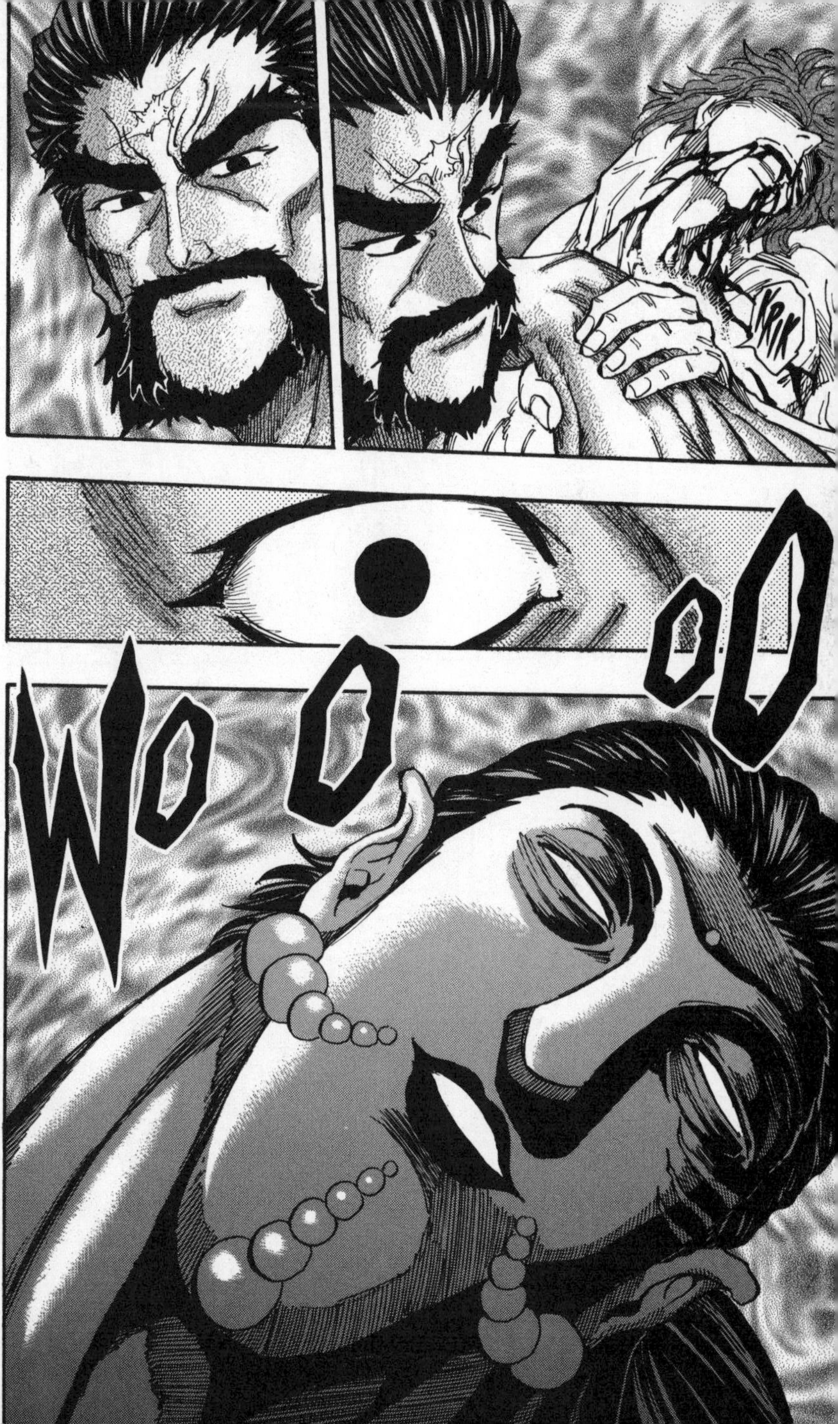
KRIK
WOOOOO

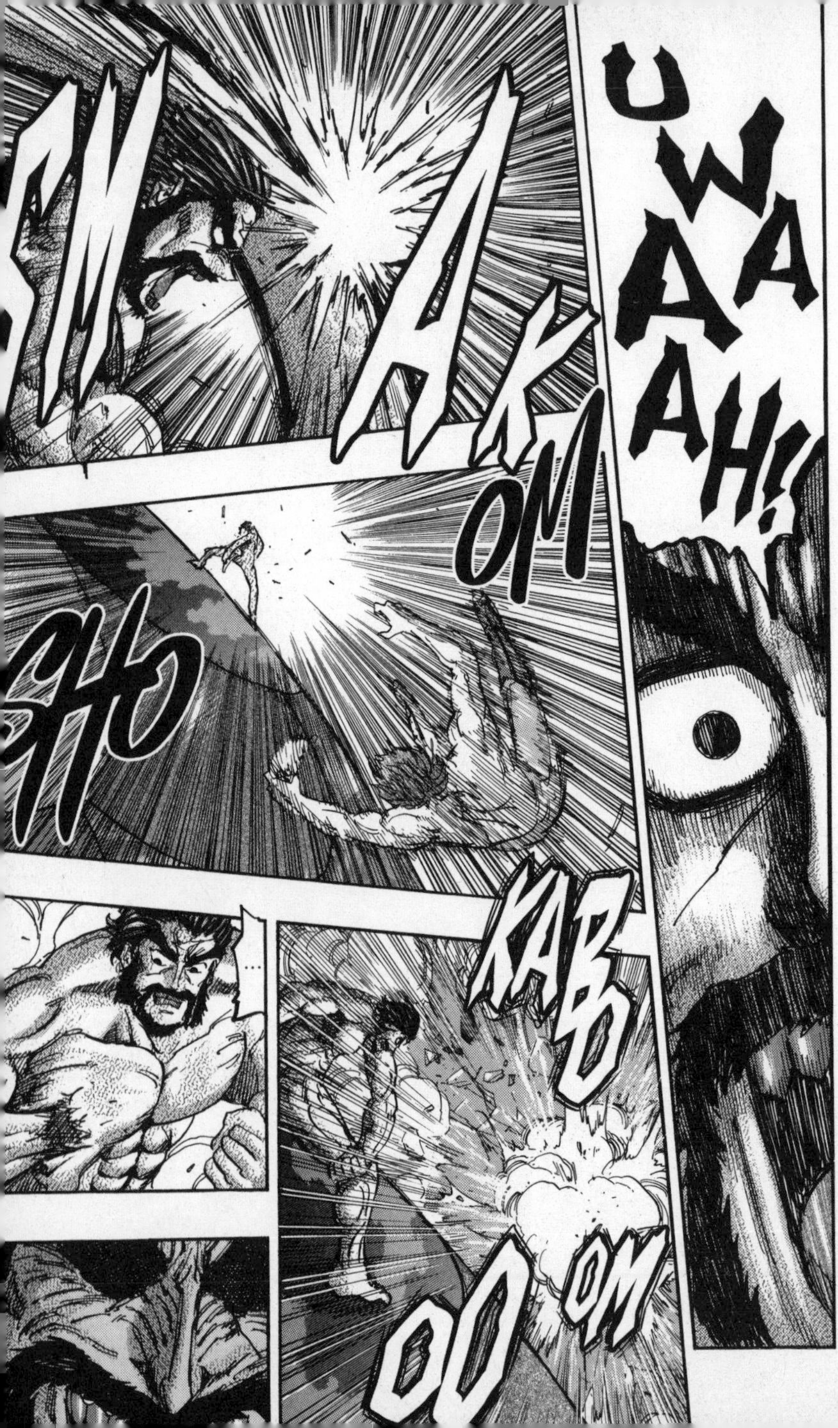
UWAAAH!!
...

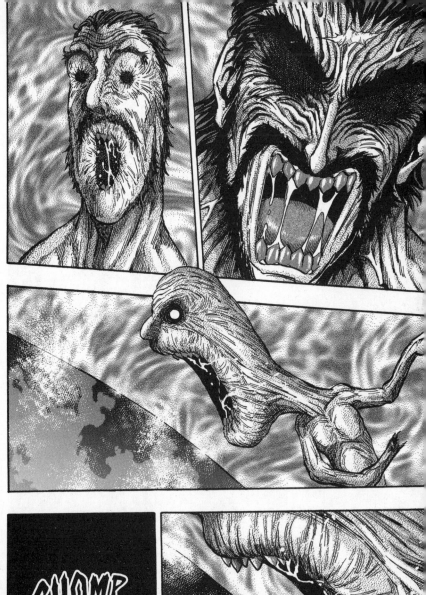
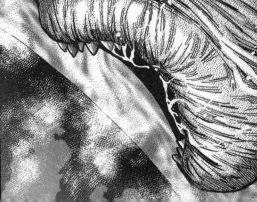
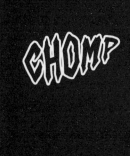

CHOMP

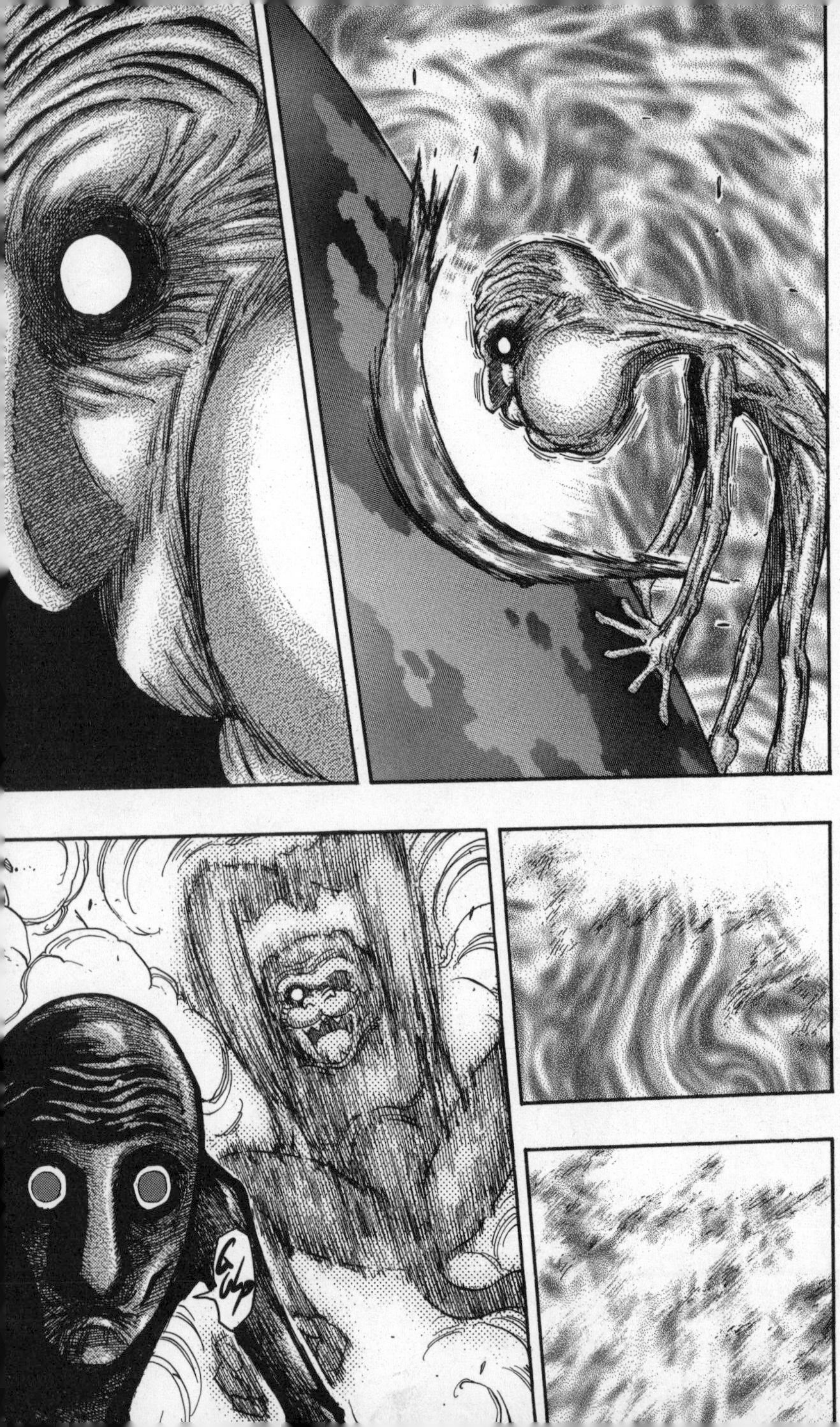
Gulp

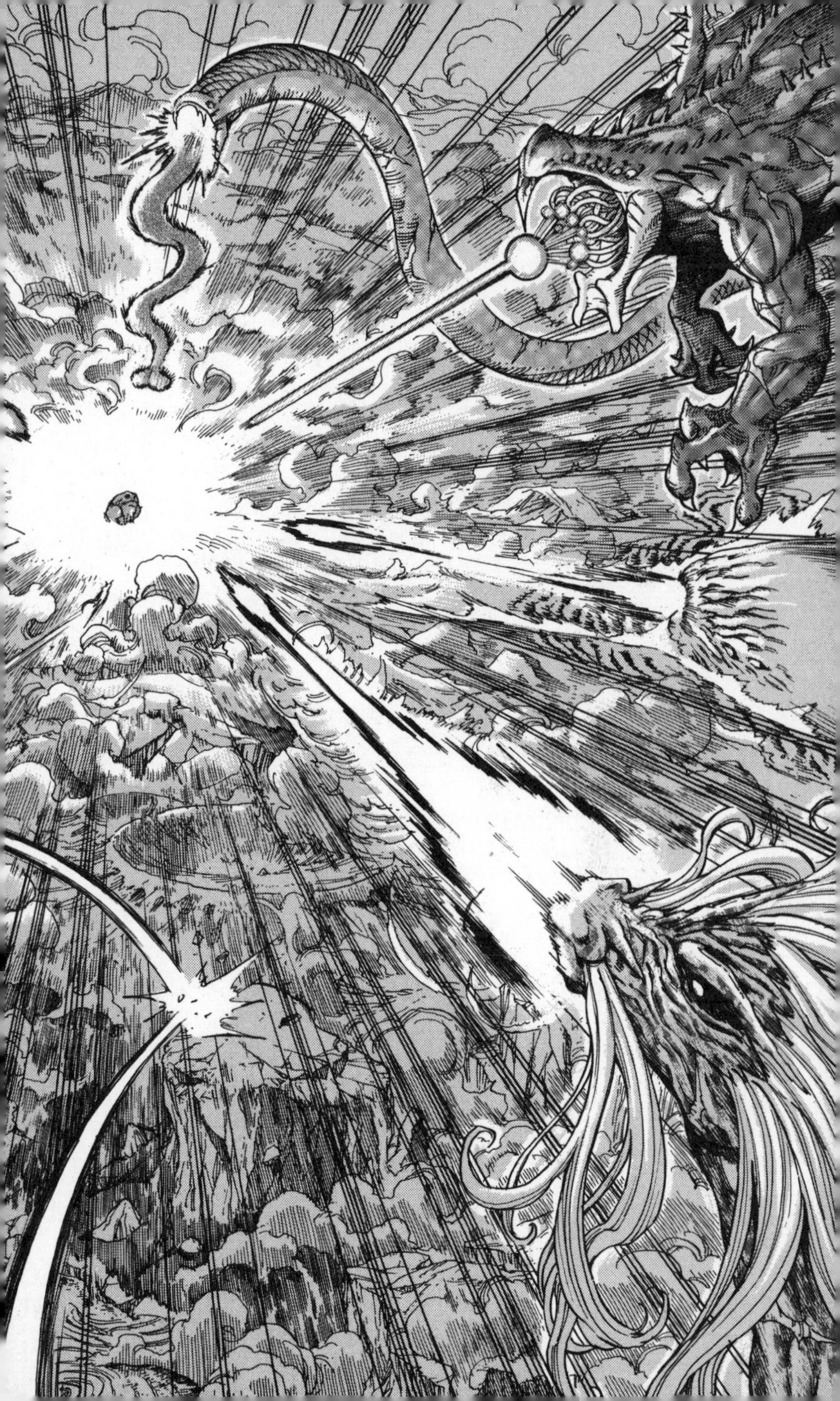

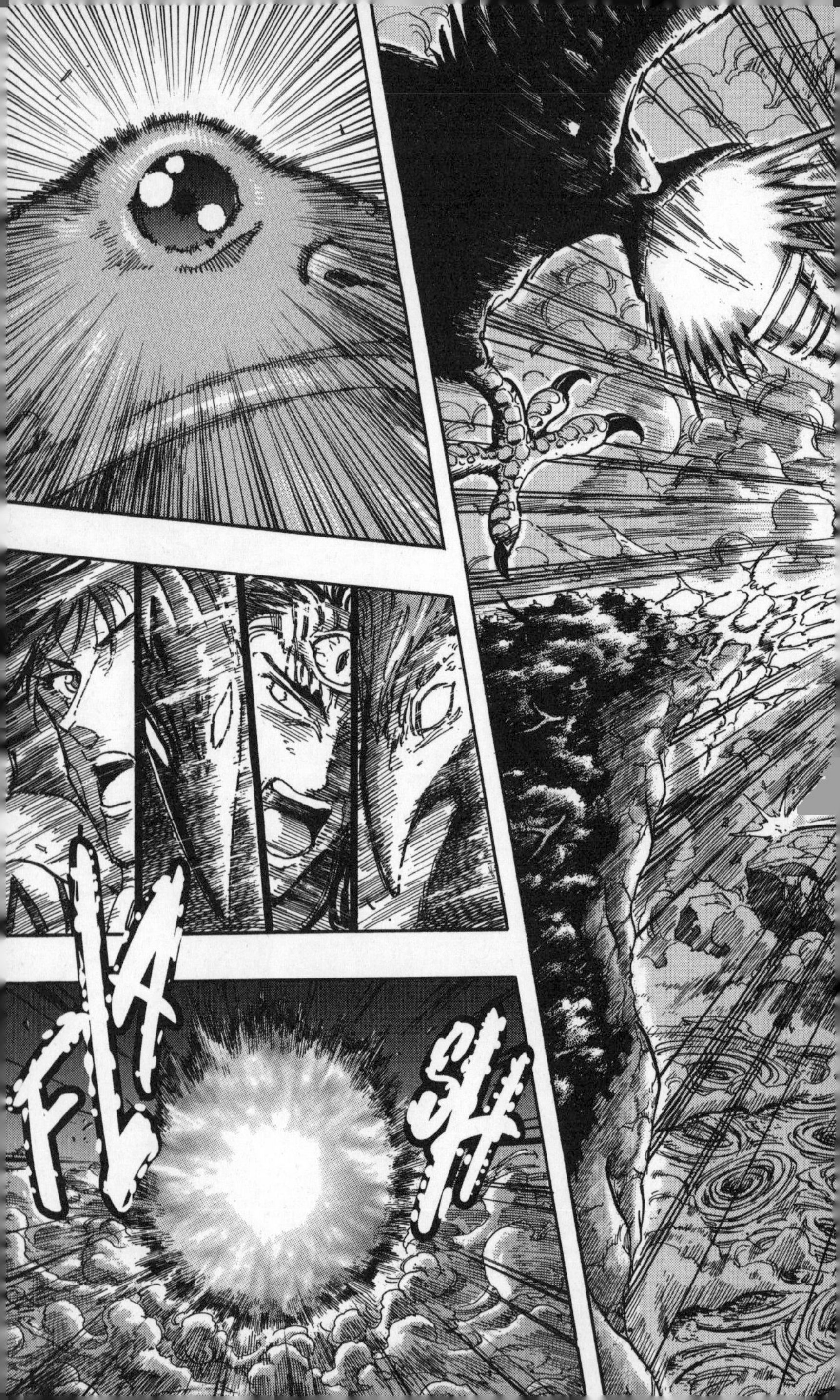
FLASH

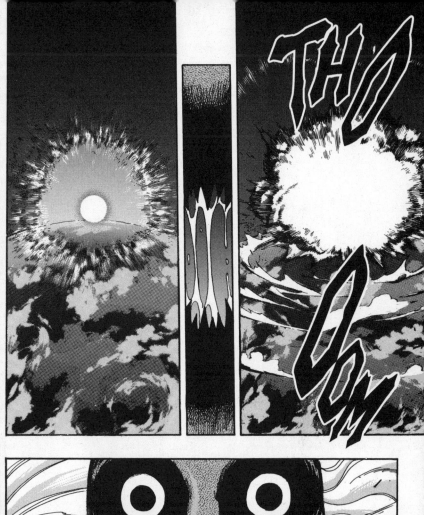

THA
OOM

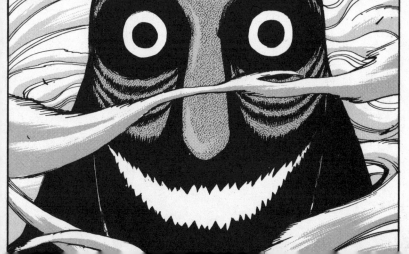

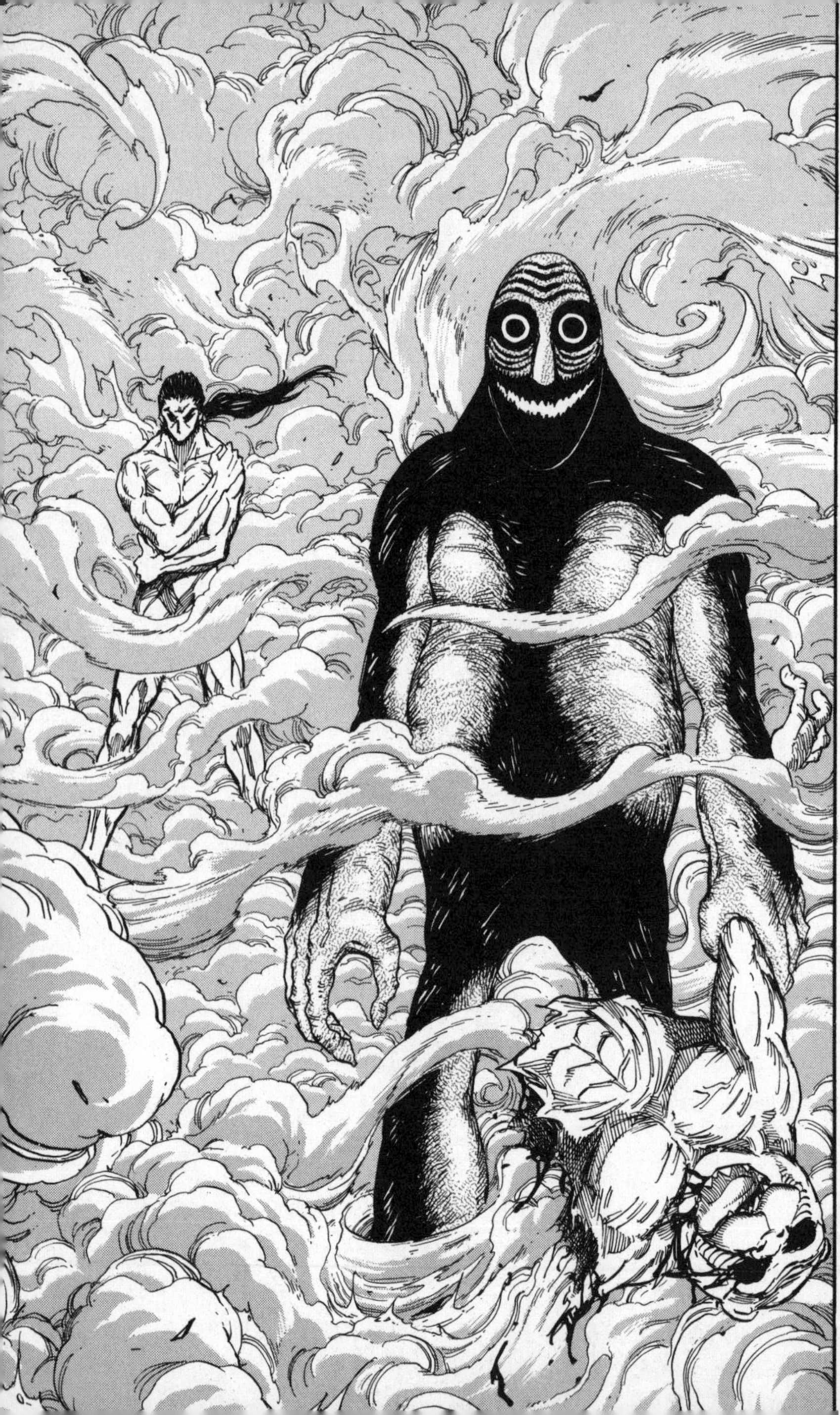

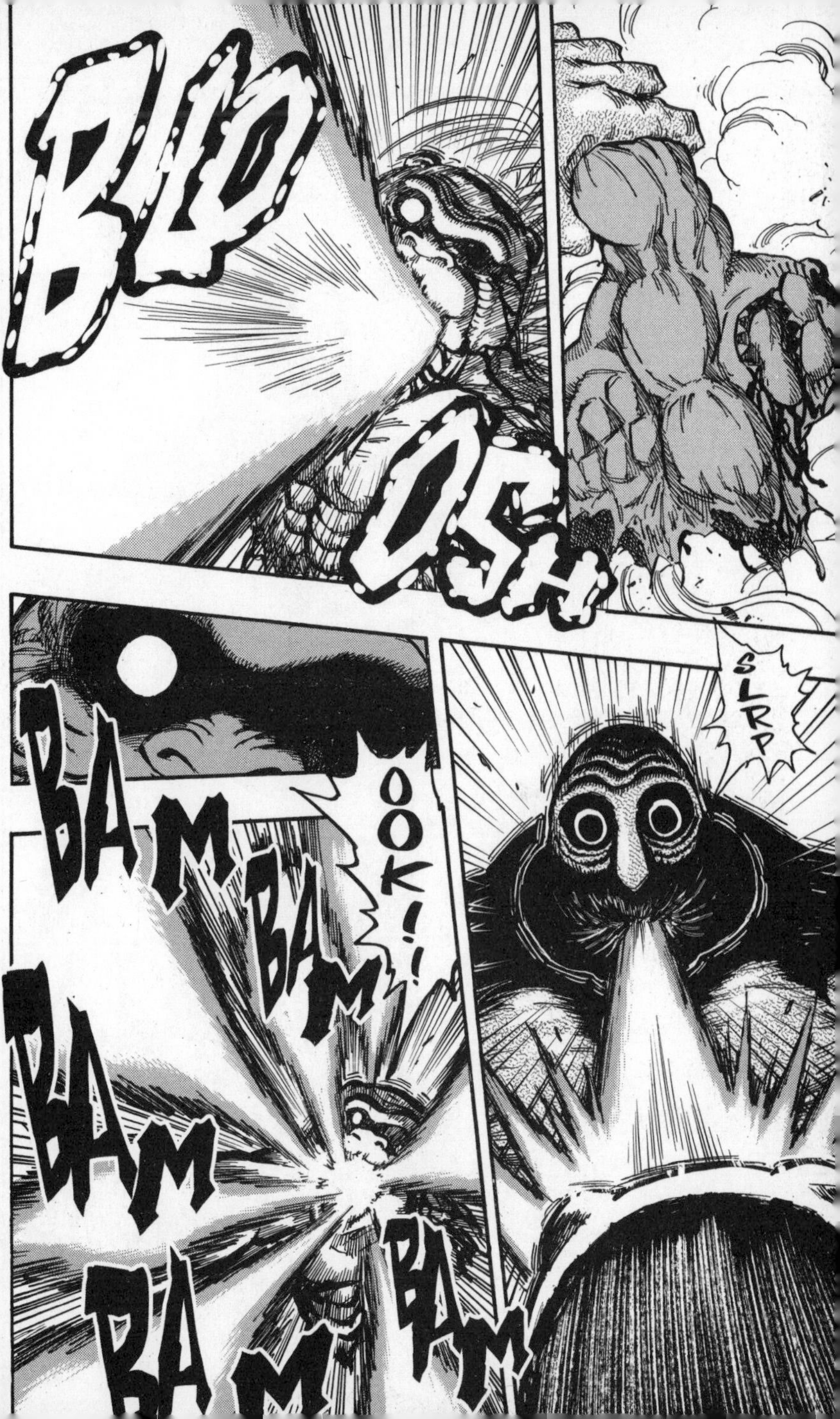
BUO
OSH
SLRP
OOOK!!
BAM
BAM
BAM
BAM
BAM

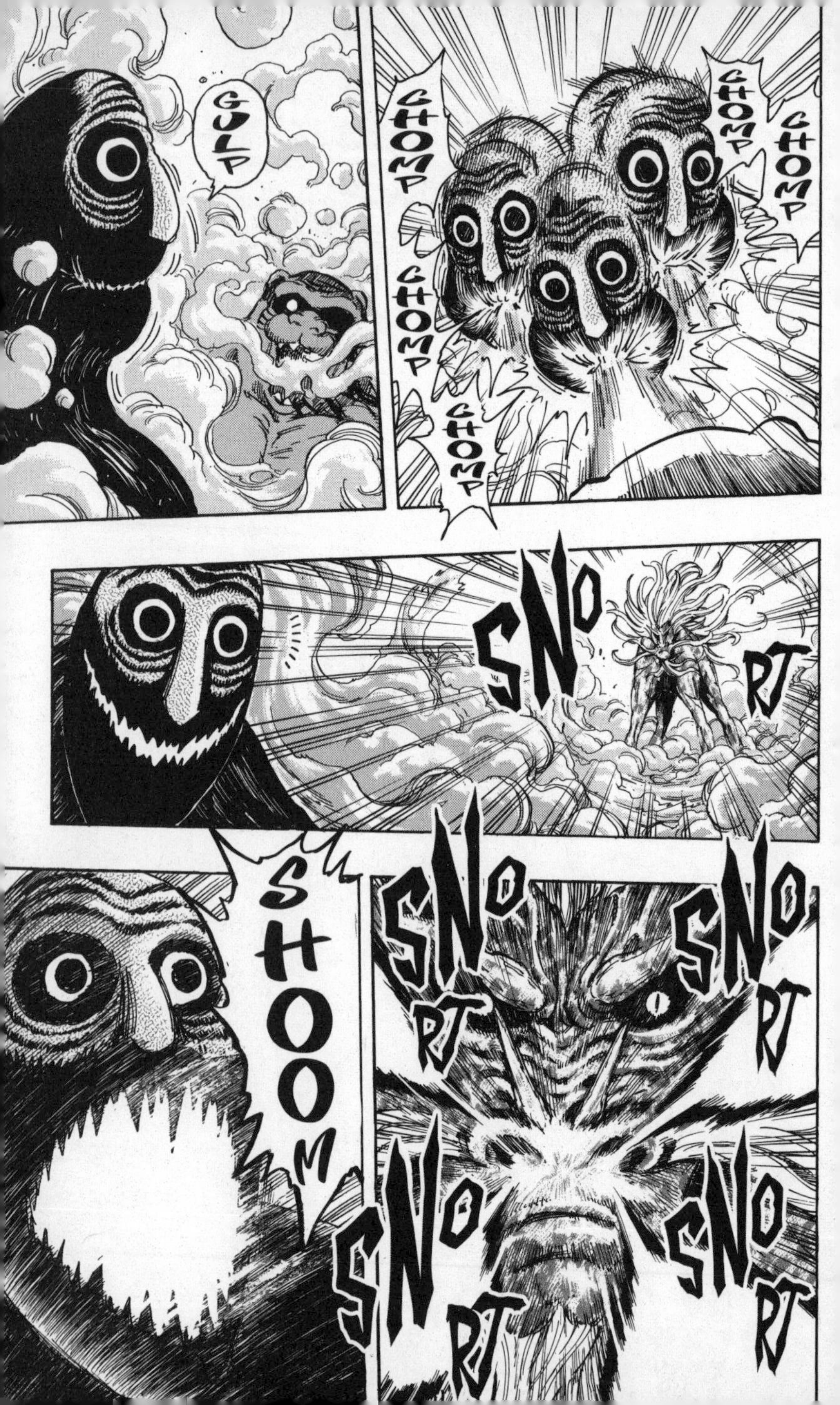
CHOMP
CHOMP
CHOMP
CHOMP
CHOMP
GULP
SNORT
SNORT
SNORT
SNORT
SNORT
SHOOOM

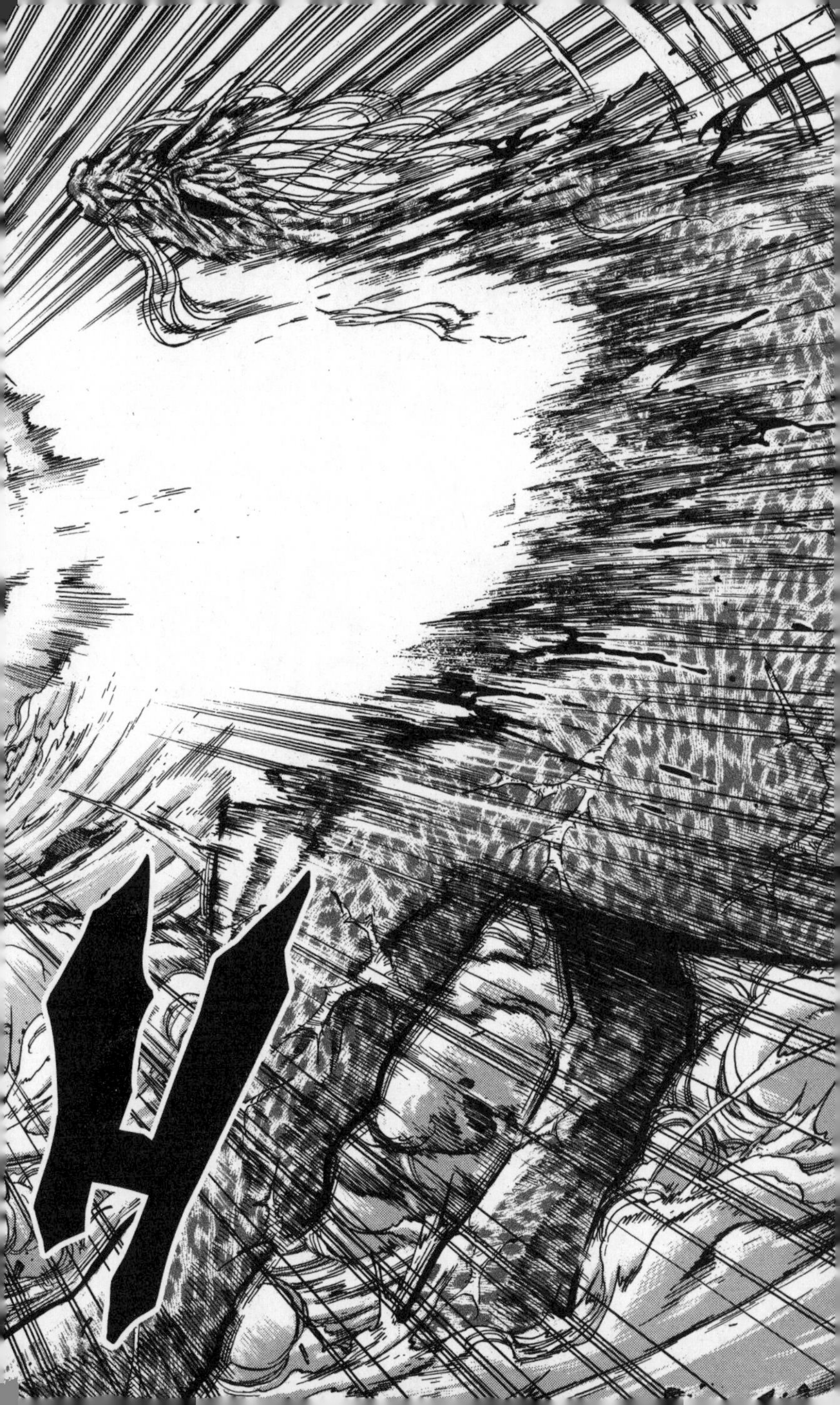

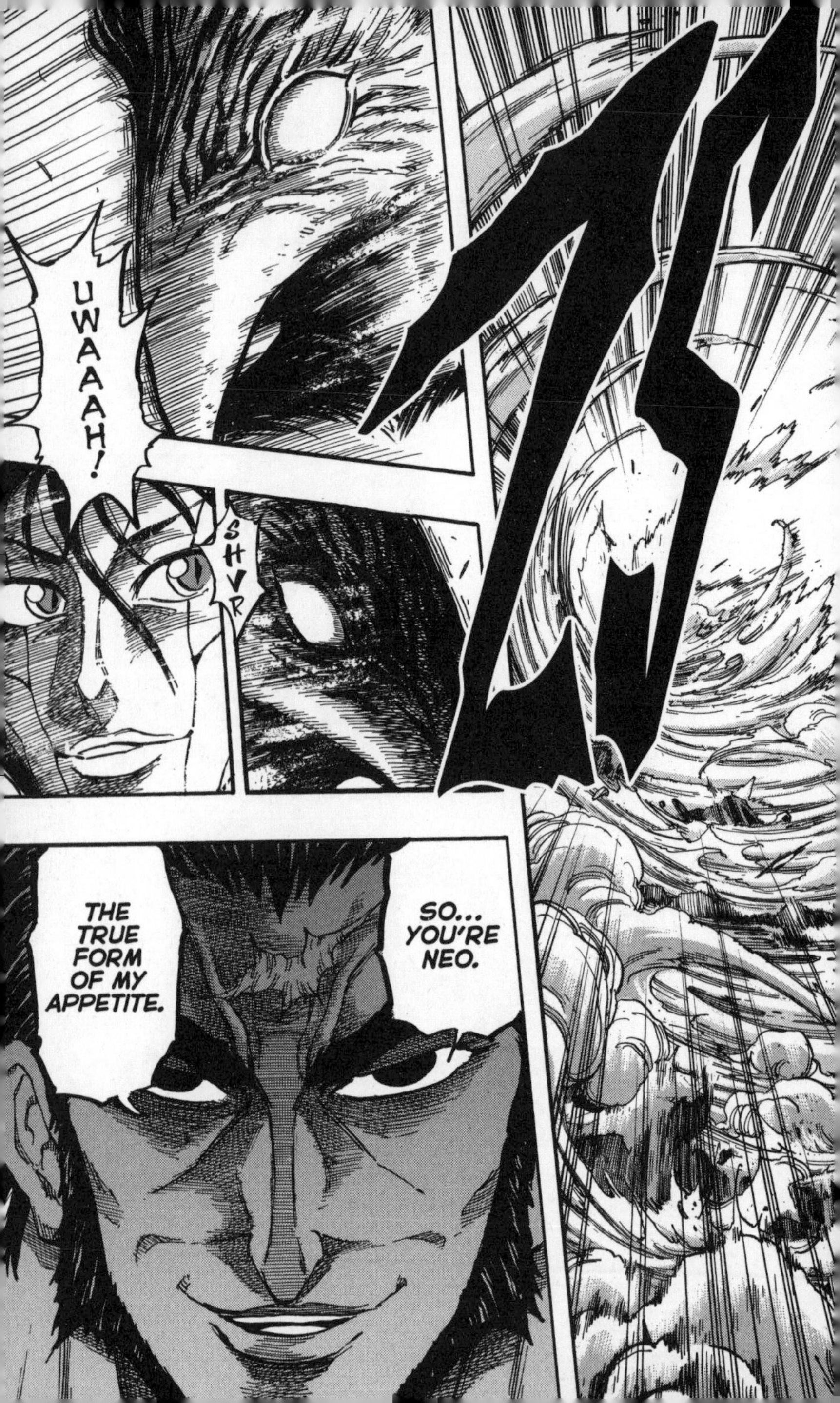
UWAAAAH!
SHVR
SO... YOU'RE NEO.
THE TRUE FORM OF MY APPETITE.

TORIKO

GOURMET CHECKLIST

Vol. 415

SNAKE KING: MOTHER SNAKE
(REPTILE MONSTER)

CAPTURE LEVEL: 6,310
HABITAT: GOURMET WORLD, AREA 4
SIZE: 220,000 KM
HEIGHT: 2,500 M
WEIGHT: 15 QUADRILLION TONS
PRICE: UNKNOWN

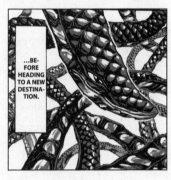

...BEFORE HEADING TO A NEW DESTINATION.

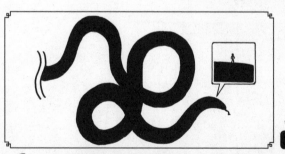

SCALE

ONE OF THE EIGHT KINGS WHO RULES ONE OF THE MAJOR CONTINENTS IN THE GOURMET WORLD. THE SNAKE KING IS THE LONGEST LIVING THING ON EARTH. ITS PREDATORY INSTINCT IS SO POWERFUL THAT IT'S RUMORED THAT JUST LOOKING INTO HER EYES IS ENOUGH TO KILL YOU. SHE CAN TRAVEL BETWEEN EARTH AND SPACE AND IS ONLY BOUND BY THE AREA IN WHICH SHE CAN STRETCH HER BODY. FRIGHTENINGLY ENOUGH, ANYTHING SHE CONSUMES MUST SLOWLY PASS THROUGH HER 220,000 KM-LONG BODY. MANY CREATURES CONSUMED BY HER DON'T EVEN REALIZE THAT THEY ARE BEING DIGESTED!

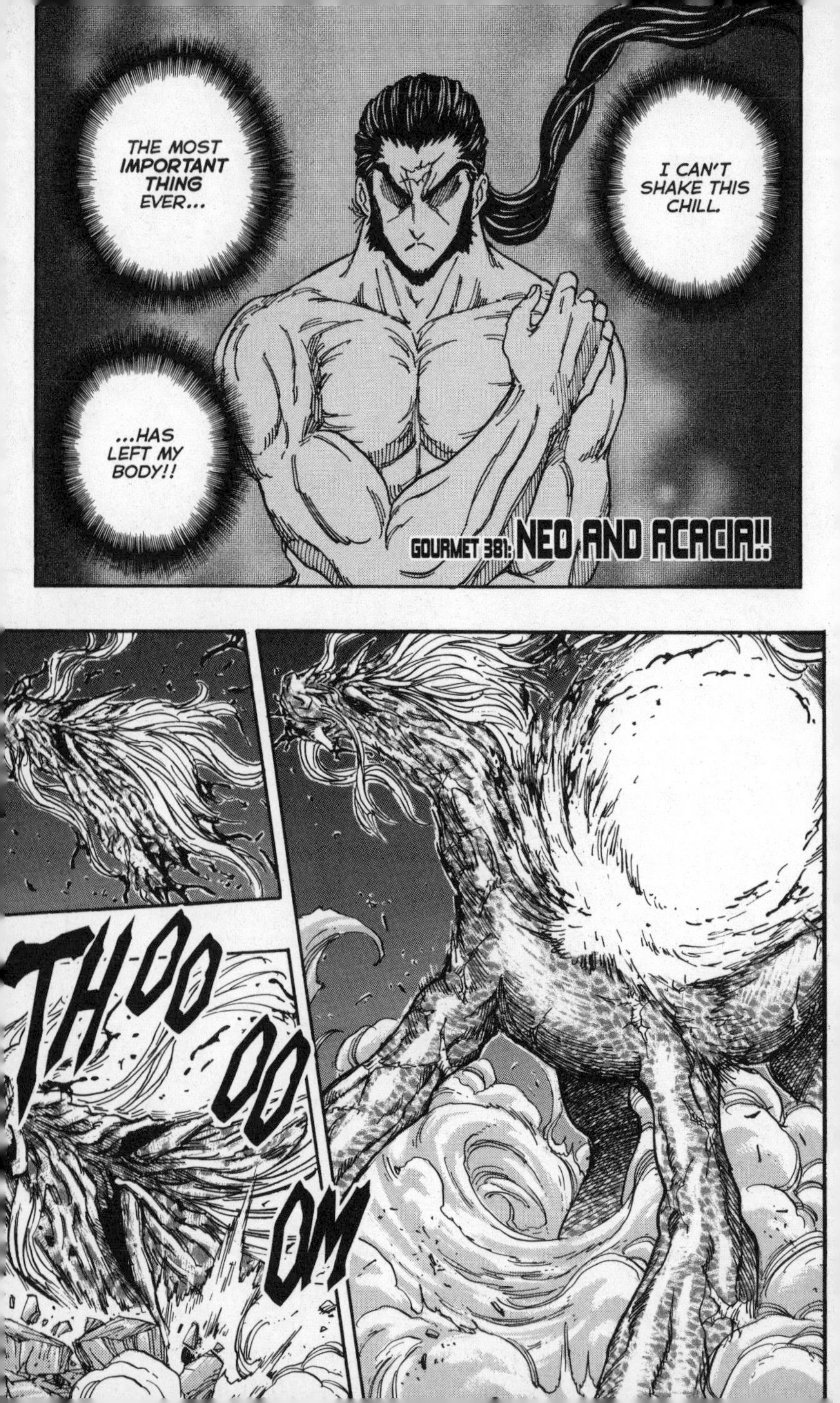
I CAN'T SHAKE THIS CHILL.
THE MOST IMPORTANT THING EVER...
...HAS LEFT MY BODY!!
GOURMET 381: NEO AND ACACIA!!
THOOOOOM

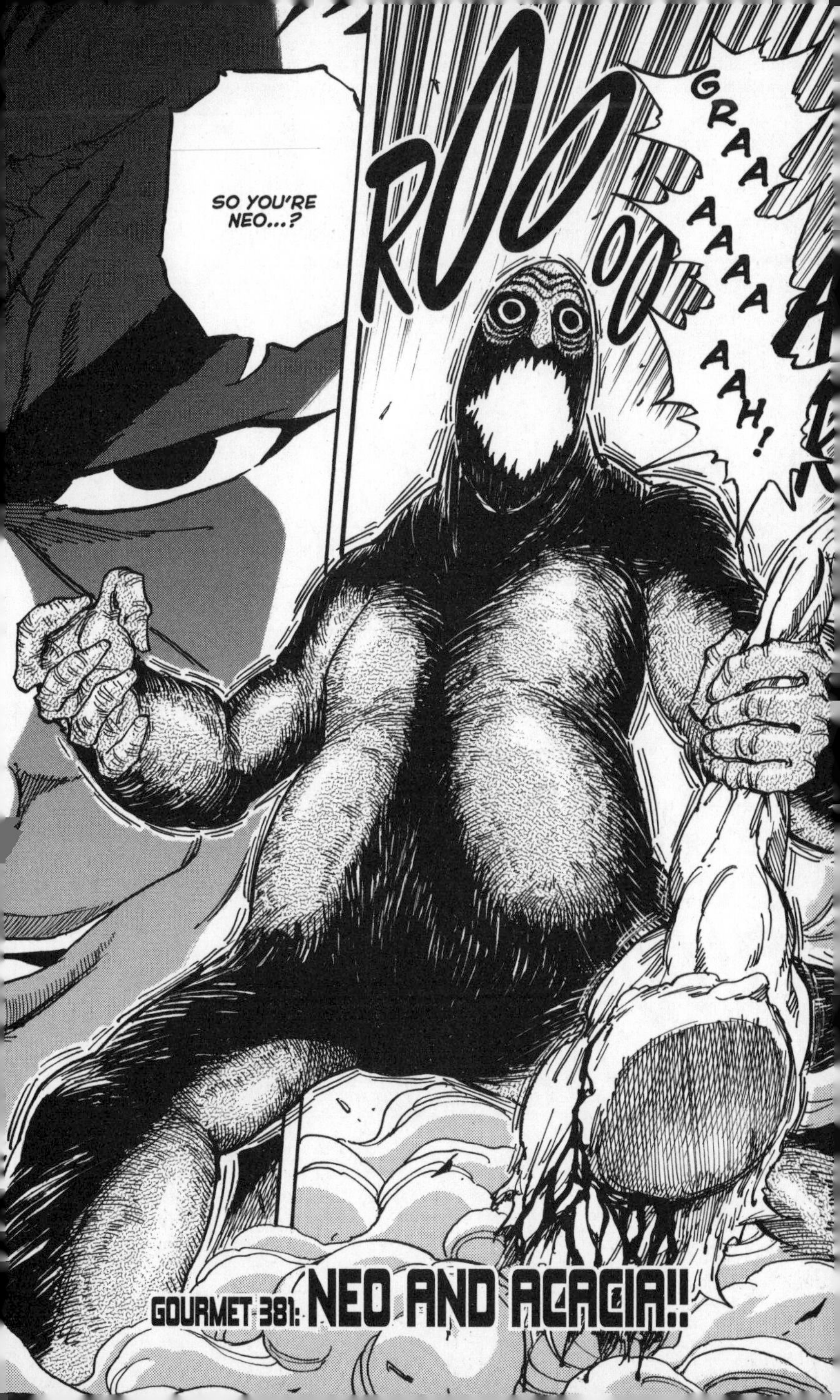
GRAAAAAAAAH!
ROOOO
SO YOU'RE NEO...?
GOURMET 381: NEO AND ACACIA!!

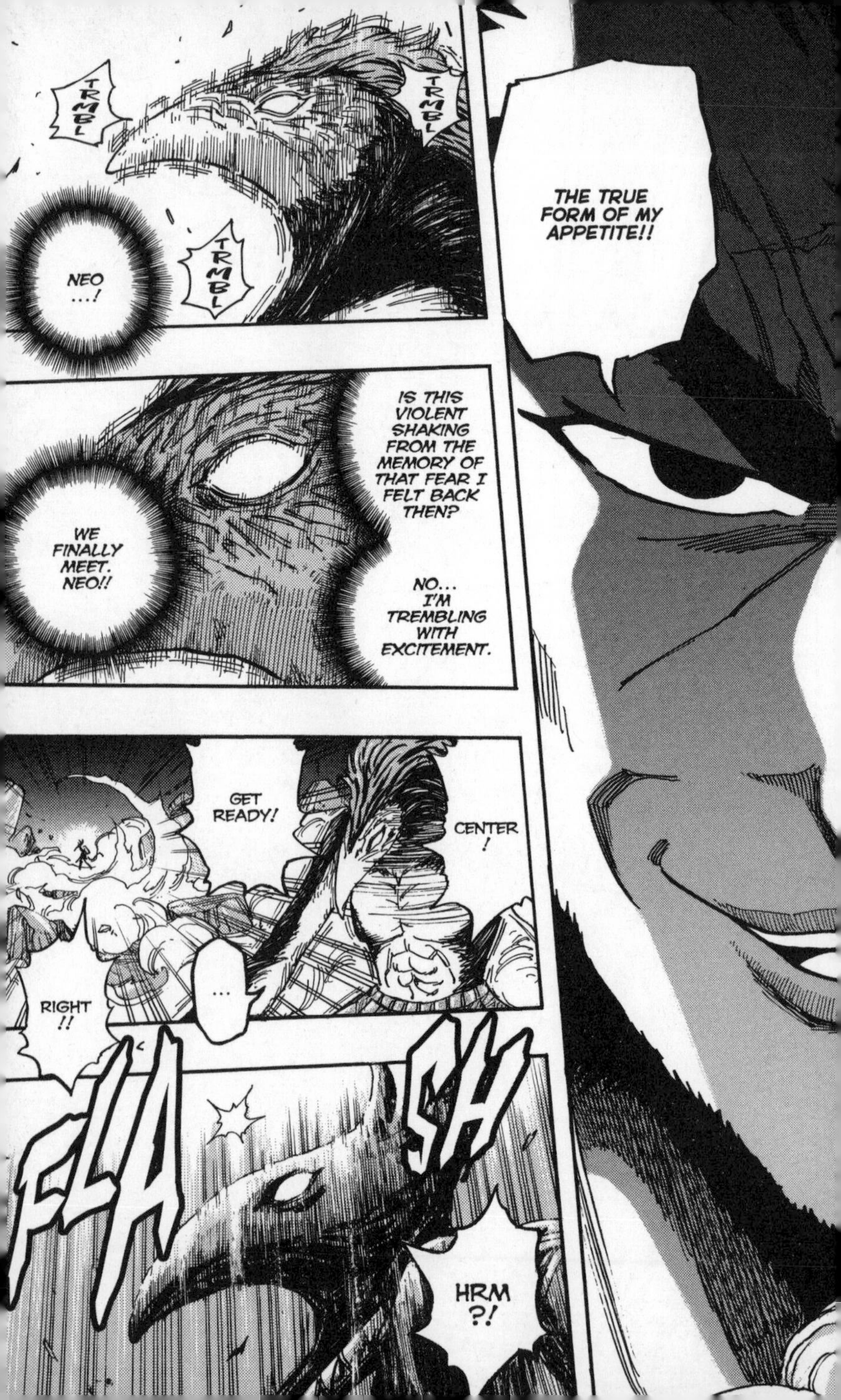
THE TRUE FORM OF MY APPETITE!!
TRMBL
TRMBL
TRMBL
NEO ...!
IS THIS VIOLENT SHAKING FROM THE MEMORY OF THAT FEAR I FELT BACK THEN?
NO... I'M TREMBLING WITH EXCITEMENT.
WE FINALLY MEET. NEO!!
CENTER!
GET READY!
...
RIGHT!!
FLASH
HRM?!

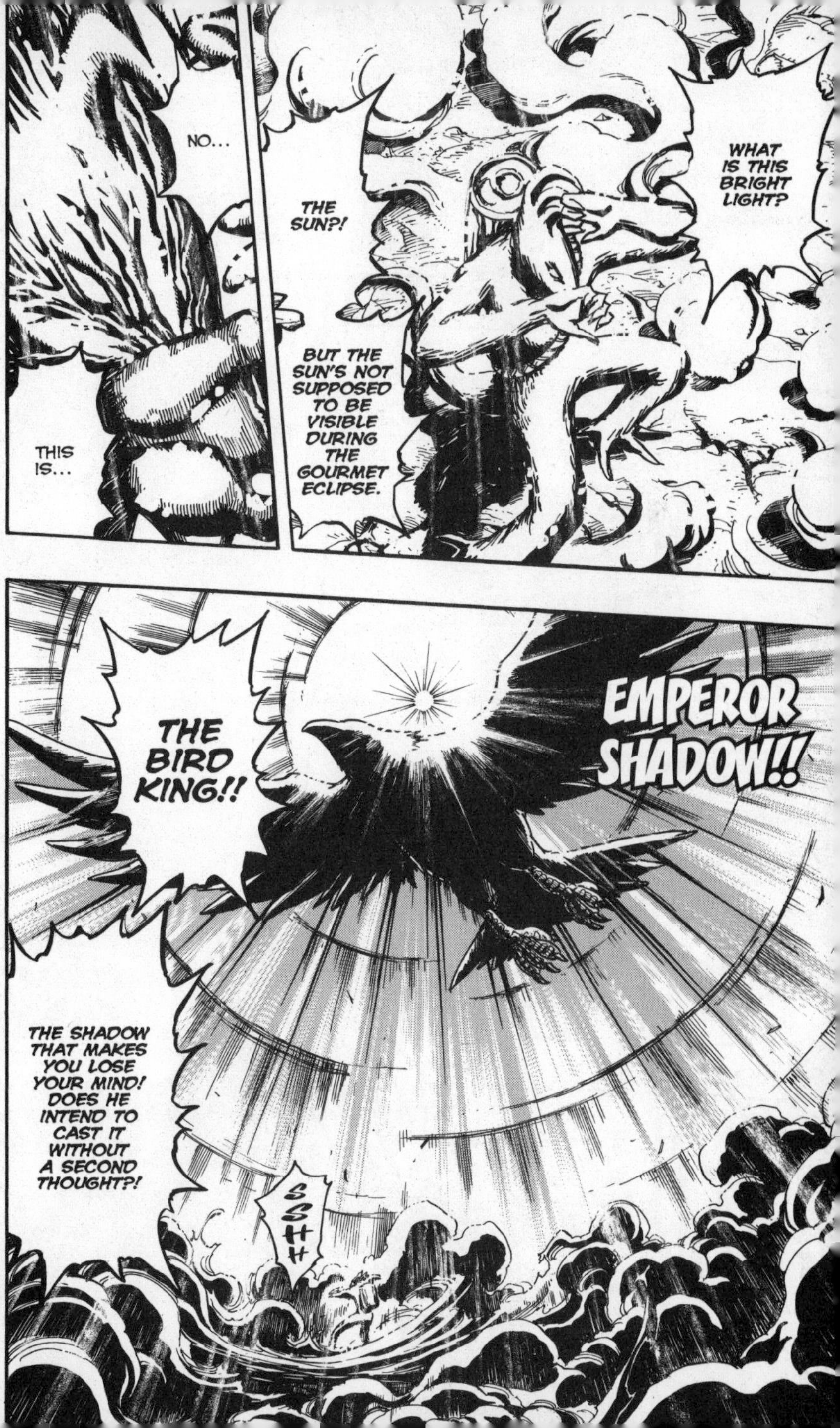
WHAT IS THIS BRIGHT LIGHT?
THE SUN?!
BUT THE SUN'S NOT SUPPOSED TO BE VISIBLE DURING THE GOURMET ECLIPSE.
NO...
THIS IS...
EMPEROR SHADOW!!
THE BIRD KING!!
THE SHADOW THAT MAKES YOU LOSE YOUR MIND! DOES HE INTEND TO CAST IT WITHOUT A SECOND THOUGHT?!
SSHH

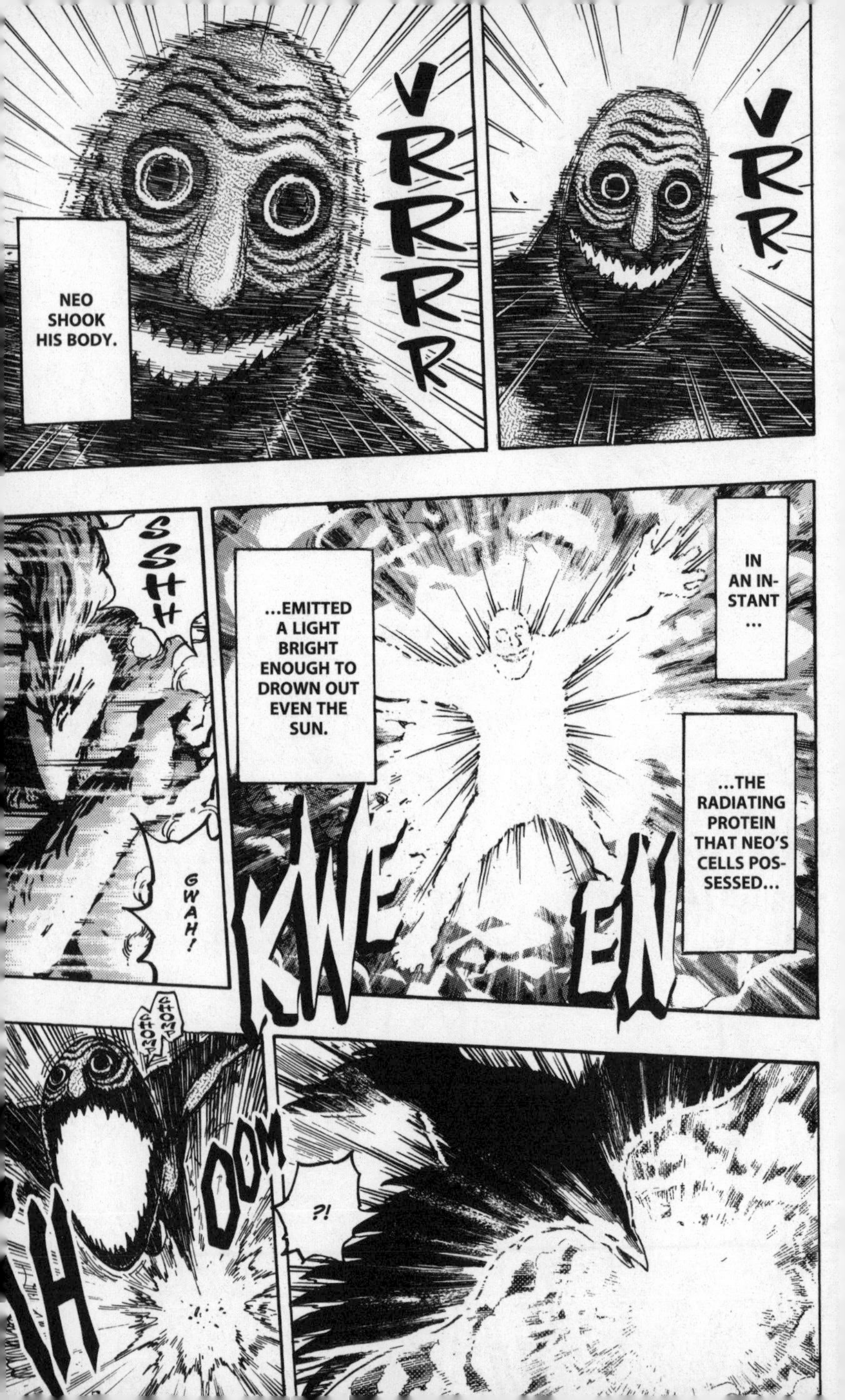
VRR
VRRRR
NEO SHOOK HIS BODY.
IN AN IN-STANT...
...THE RADIATING PROTEIN THAT NEO'S CELLS POS-SESSED...
...EMITTED A LIGHT BRIGHT ENOUGH TO DROWN OUT EVEN THE SUN.
KWEEN
SSHH
GWAH!
?!
CHOMP CHOMP
HOOM

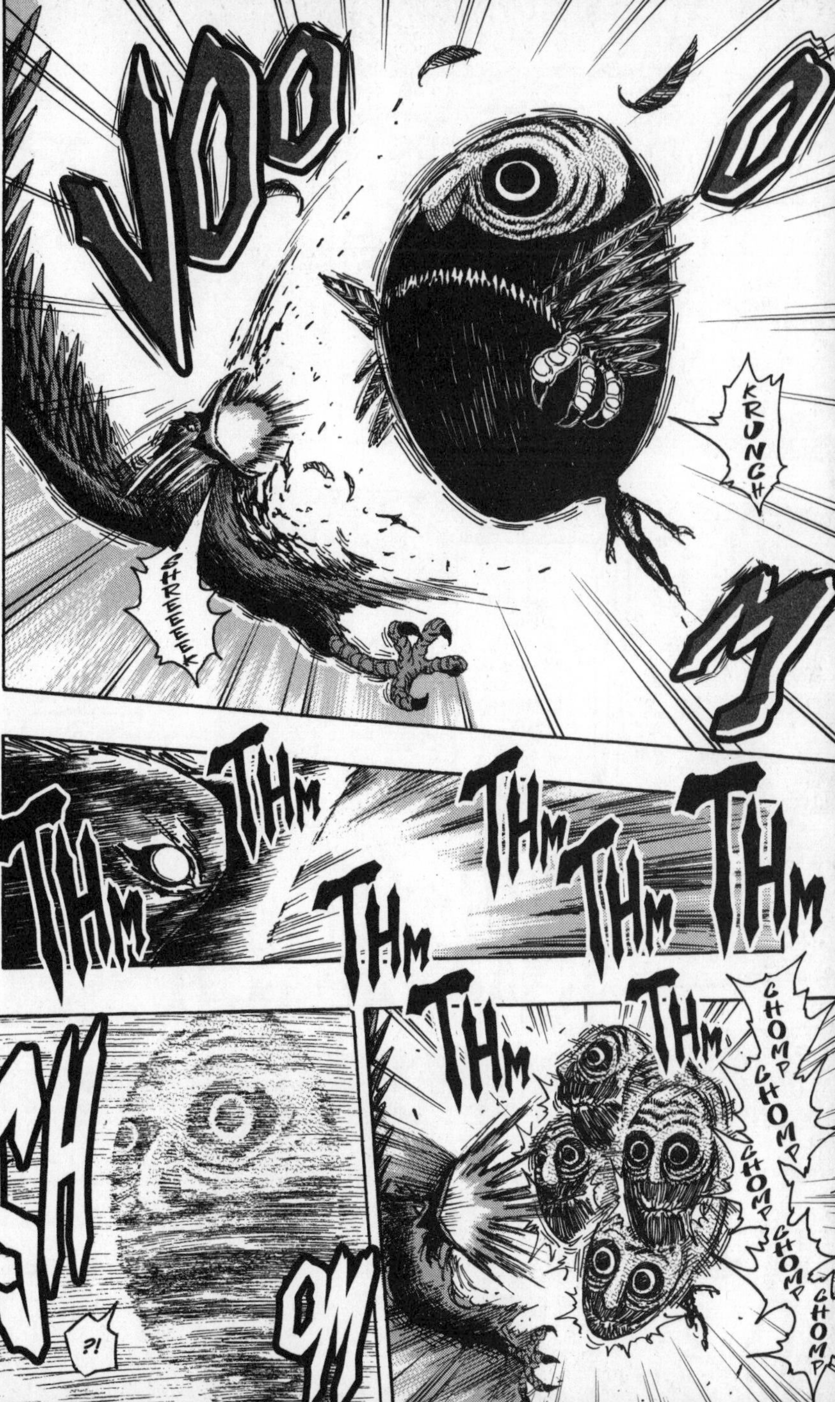
VDOOOM
KRUNCH
SHREEEEK
THM THM THM THM THM THM THM
THM THM
CHOMP CHOMP CHOMP CHOMP CHOMP CHOMP
SHOM
?!

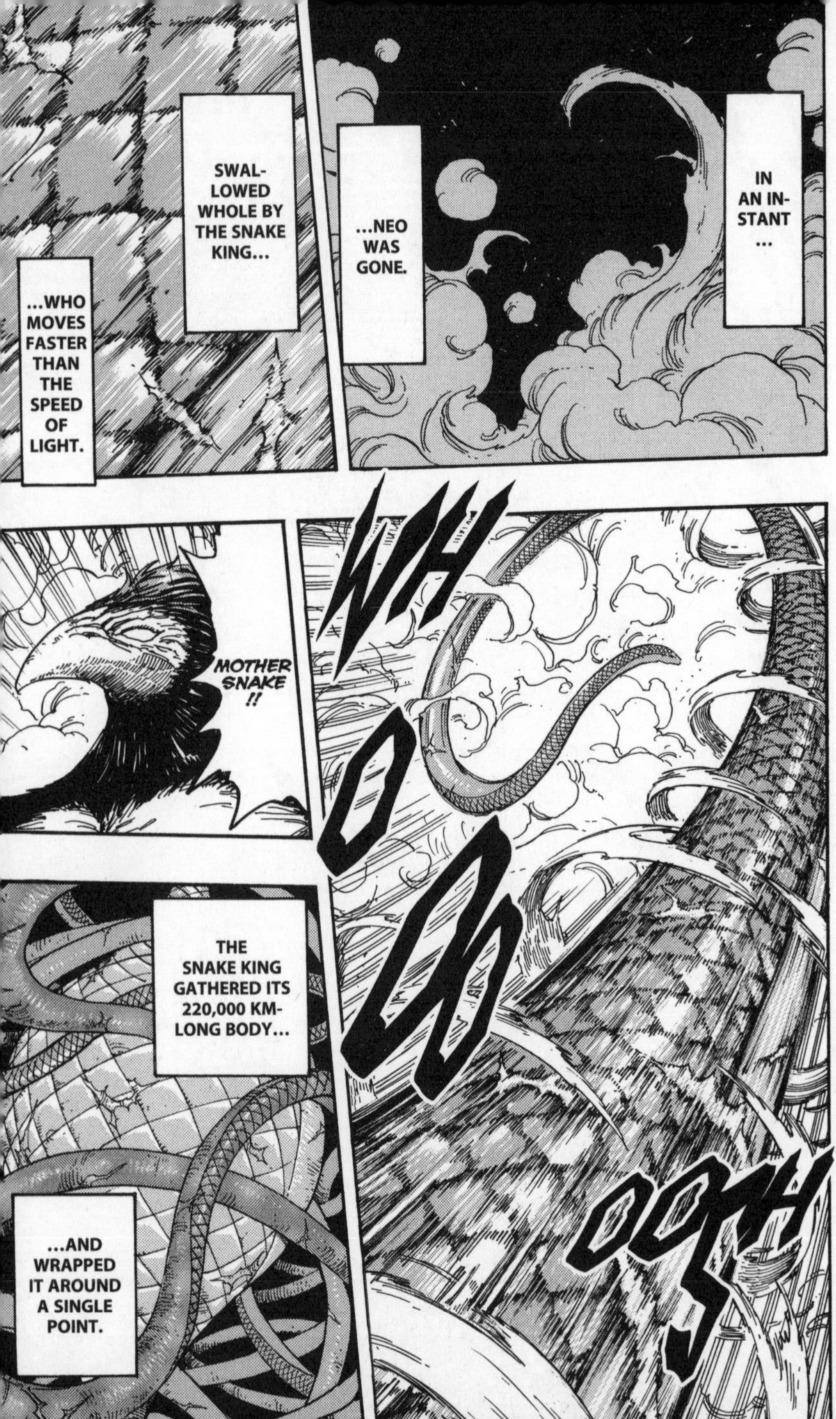
IN AN INSTANT...
...NEO WAS GONE.
SWALLOWED WHOLE BY THE SNAKE KING...
...WHO MOVES FASTER THAN THE SPEED OF LIGHT.
WHOOOOOSH
MOTHER SNAKE!!
THE SNAKE KING GATHERED ITS 220,000 KM-LONG BODY...
...AND WRAPPED IT AROUND A SINGLE POINT.

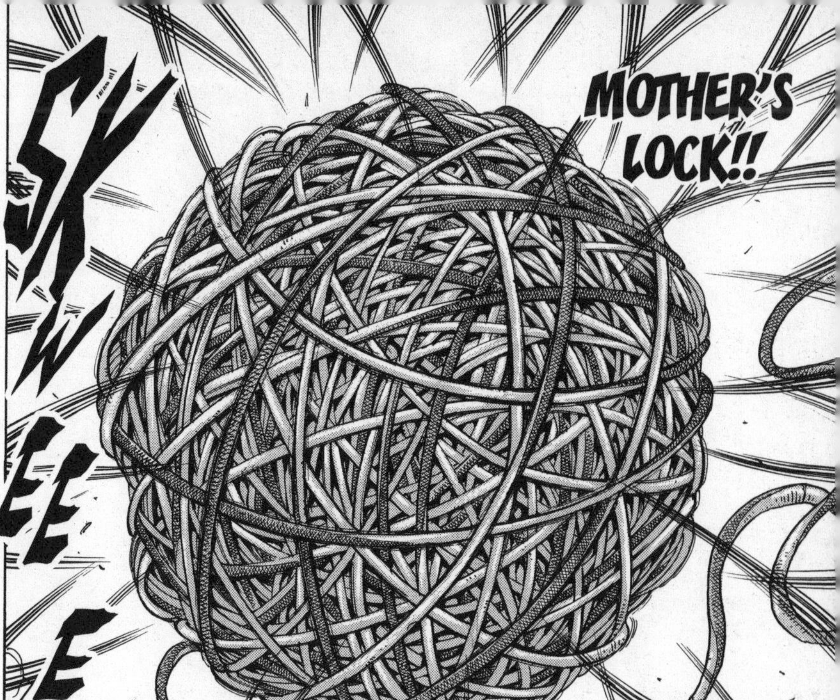
MOTHER'S LOCK!!
SKWEEEEEZ
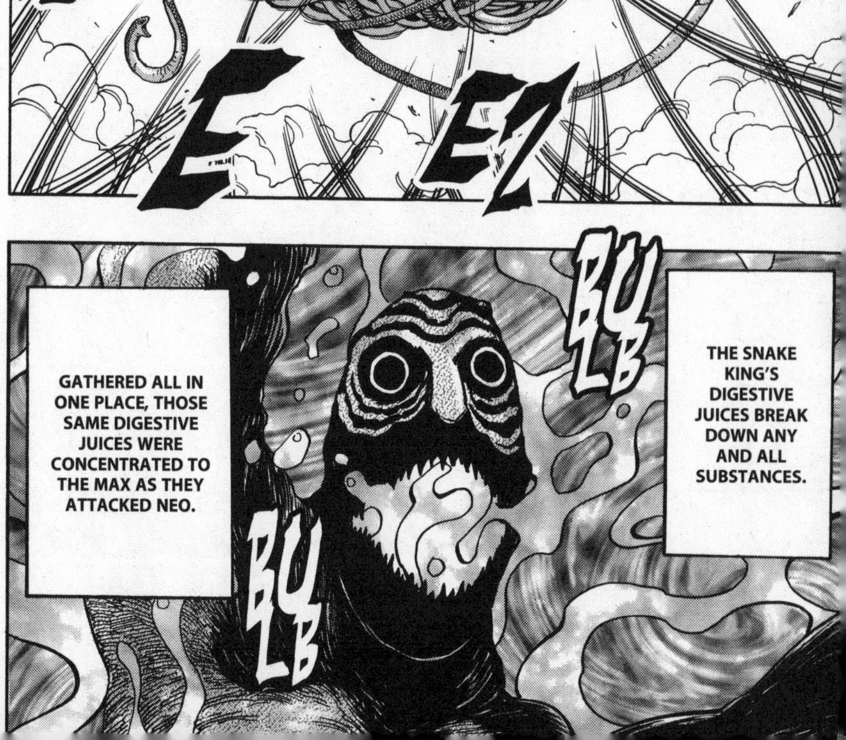
THE SNAKE KING'S DIGESTIVE JUICES BREAK DOWN ANY AND ALL SUBSTANCES.
BUBLUB
GATHERED ALL IN ONE PLACE, THOSE SAME DIGESTIVE JUICES WERE CONCENTRATED TO THE MAX AS THEY ATTACKED NEO.
BUBLUB

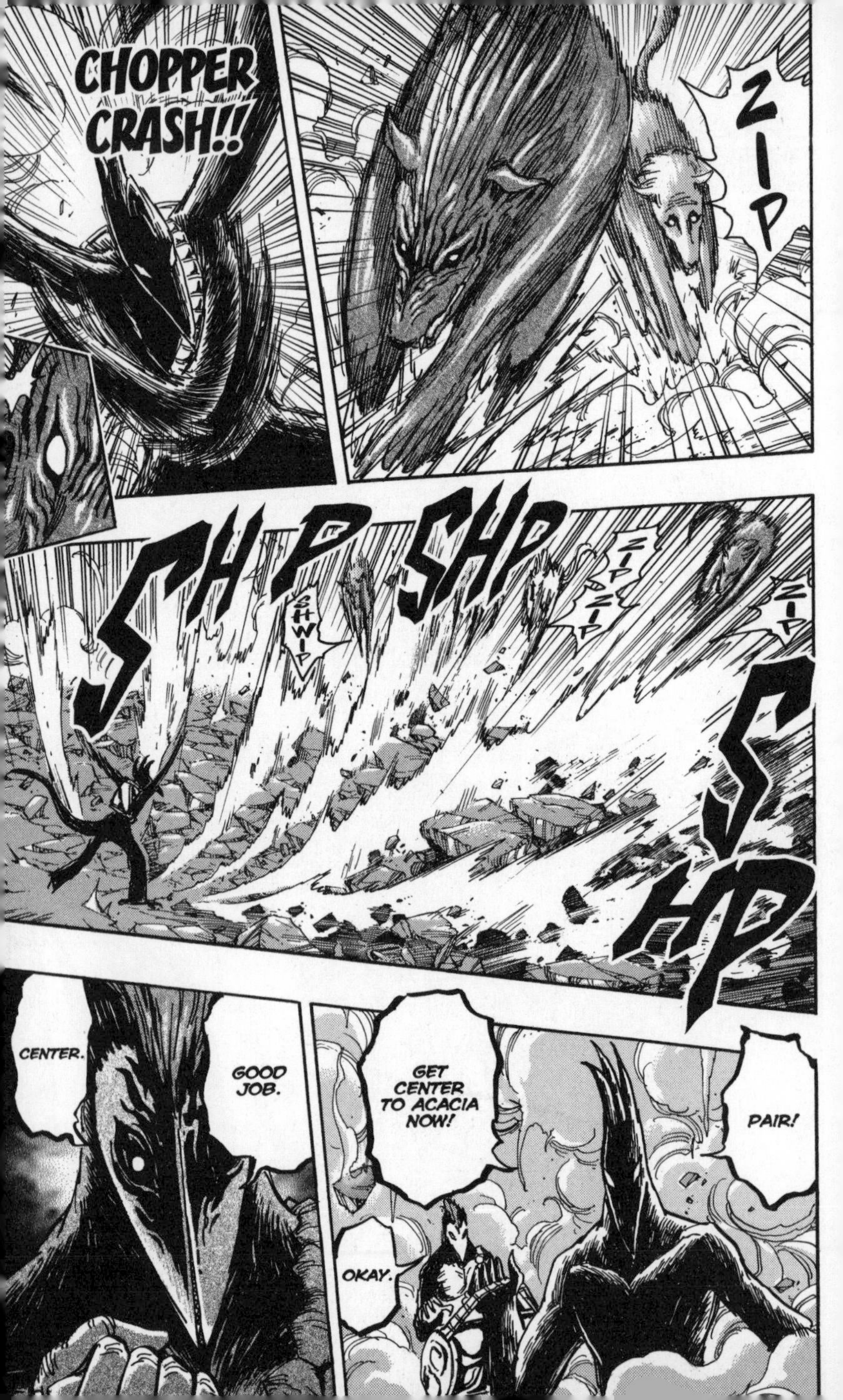
ZIP
CHOPPER CRASH!!
ZIP
SHP
ZIP ZIP
SHP
SHWIP
SHP
PAIR!
GET CENTER TO ACACIA NOW!
OKAY.
GOOD JOB.
CENTER.

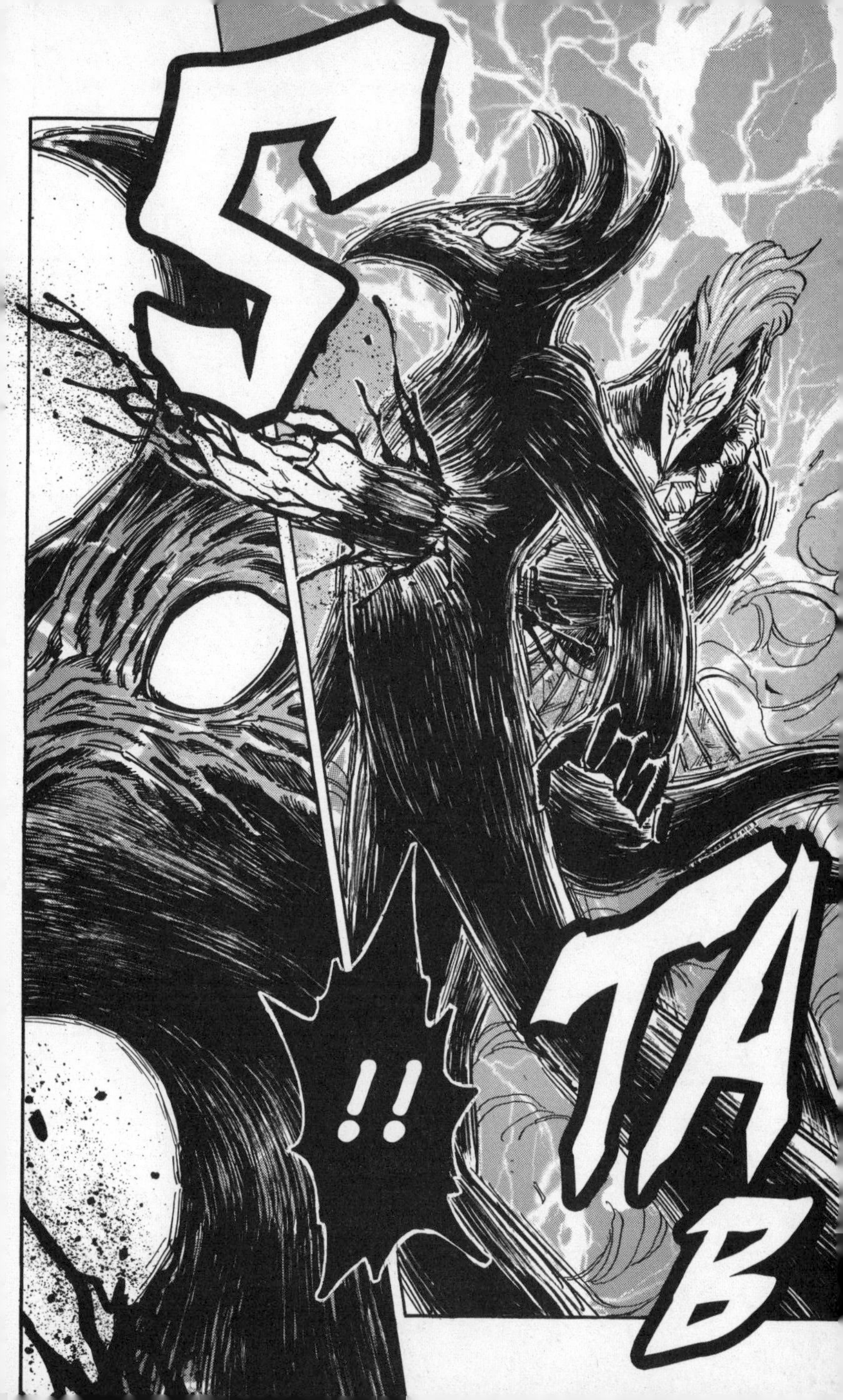
STAB
!!

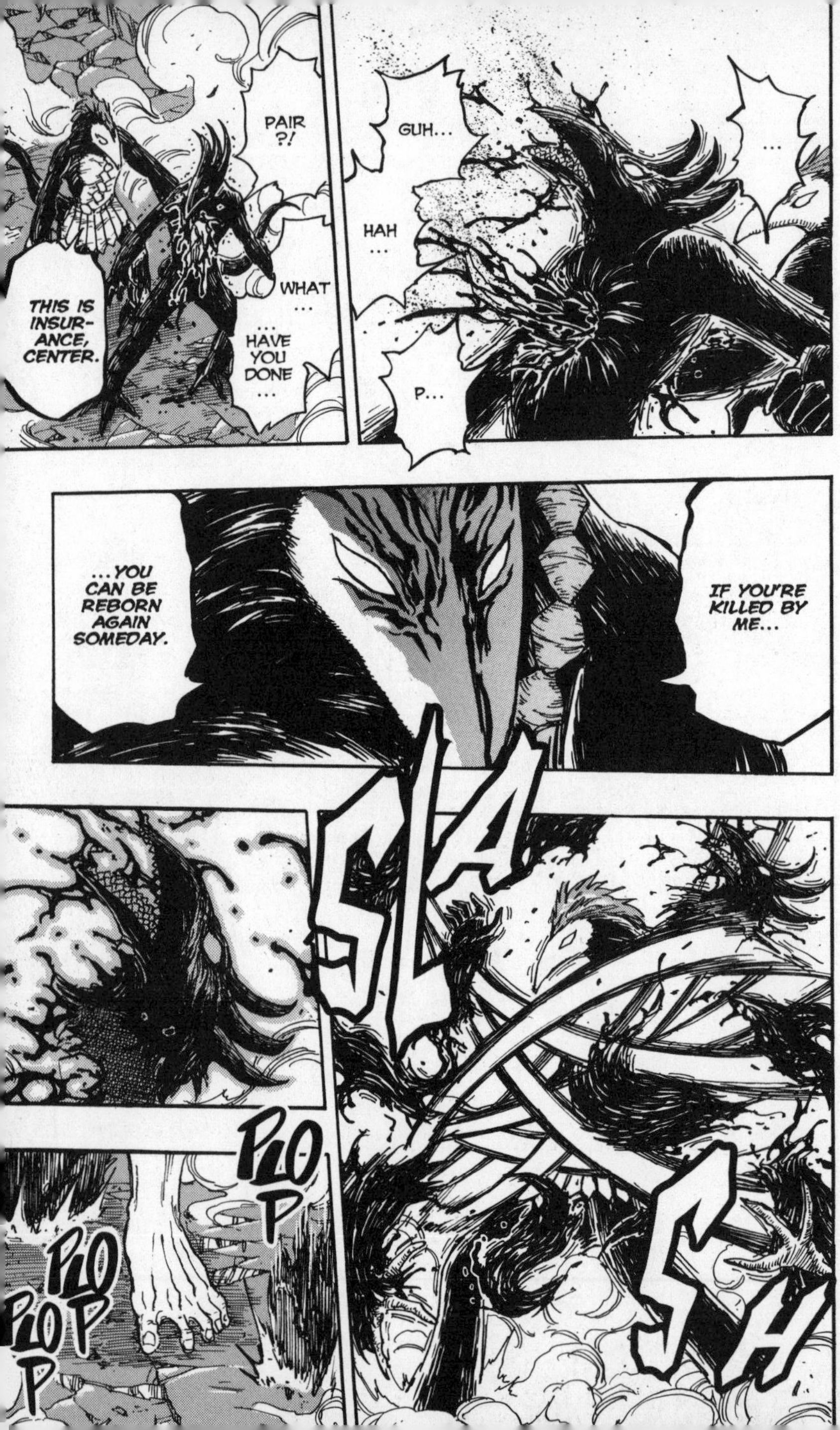
...
GUH... HAH... P...
PAIR?! WHAT... ...HAVE YOU DONE...
THIS IS INSURANCE, CENTER.
IF YOU'RE KILLED BY ME...
...YOU CAN BE REBORN AGAIN SOMEDAY.
SLASH
PLOP
PLOP PLOP

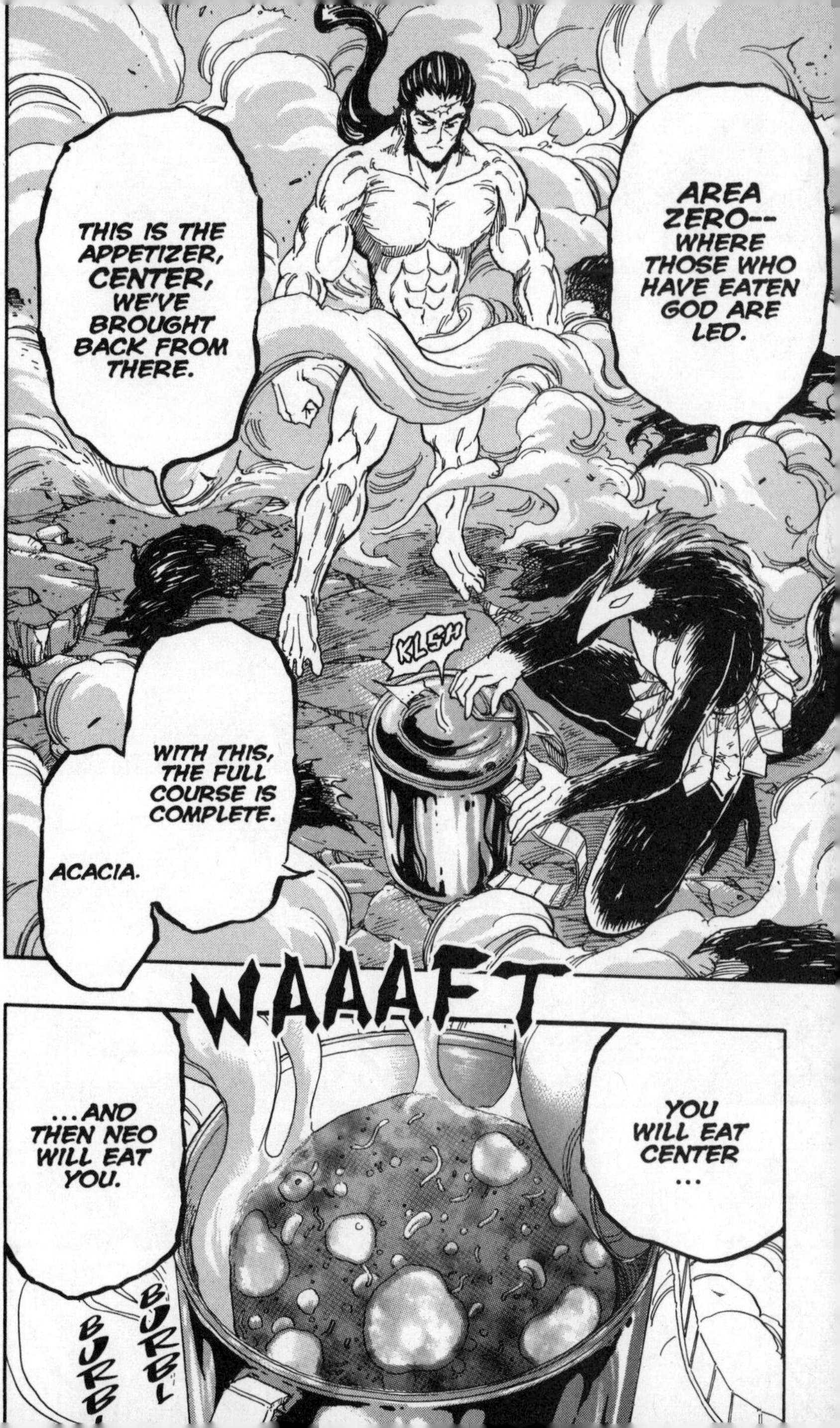
AREA ZERO-- WHERE THOSE WHO HAVE EATEN GOD ARE LED.
THIS IS THE APPETIZER, CENTER, WE'VE BROUGHT BACK FROM THERE.
KLSH
WITH THIS, THE FULL COURSE IS COMPLETE.
ACACIA.
WAAAFT
YOU WILL EAT CENTER ...
...AND THEN NEO WILL EAT YOU.
BURBL
BURBL

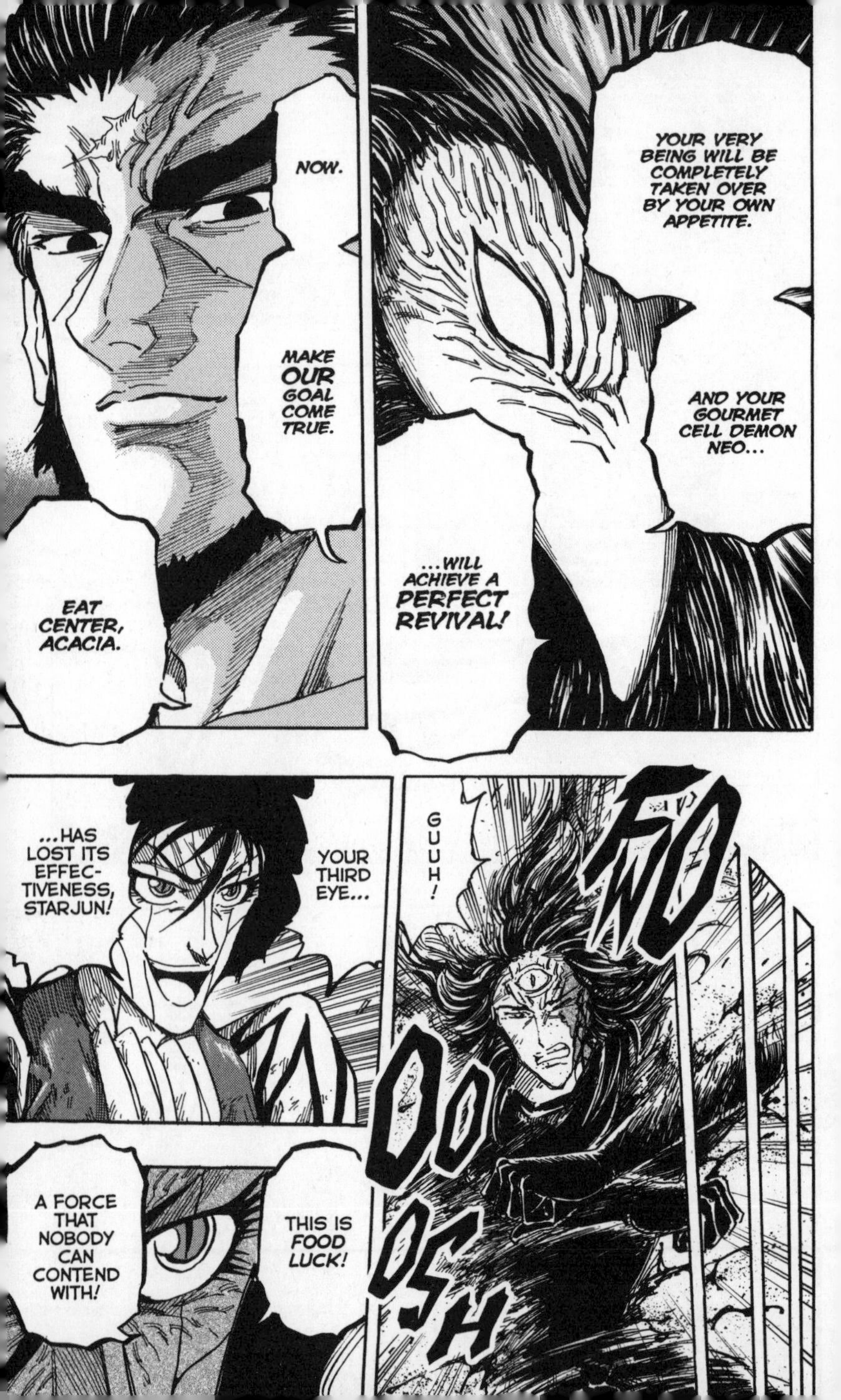
YOUR VERY BEING WILL BE COMPLETELY TAKEN OVER BY YOUR OWN APPETITE.
AND YOUR GOURMET CELL DEMON NEO...
...WILL ACHIEVE A PERFECT REVIVAL!
NOW.
MAKE OUR GOAL COME TRUE.
EAT CENTER, ACACIA.
GUUH!
FWOOOOSH
YOUR THIRD EYE...
...HAS LOST ITS EFFEC-TIVENESS, STARJUN!
THIS IS FOOD LUCK!
A FORCE THAT NOBODY CAN CONTEND WITH!

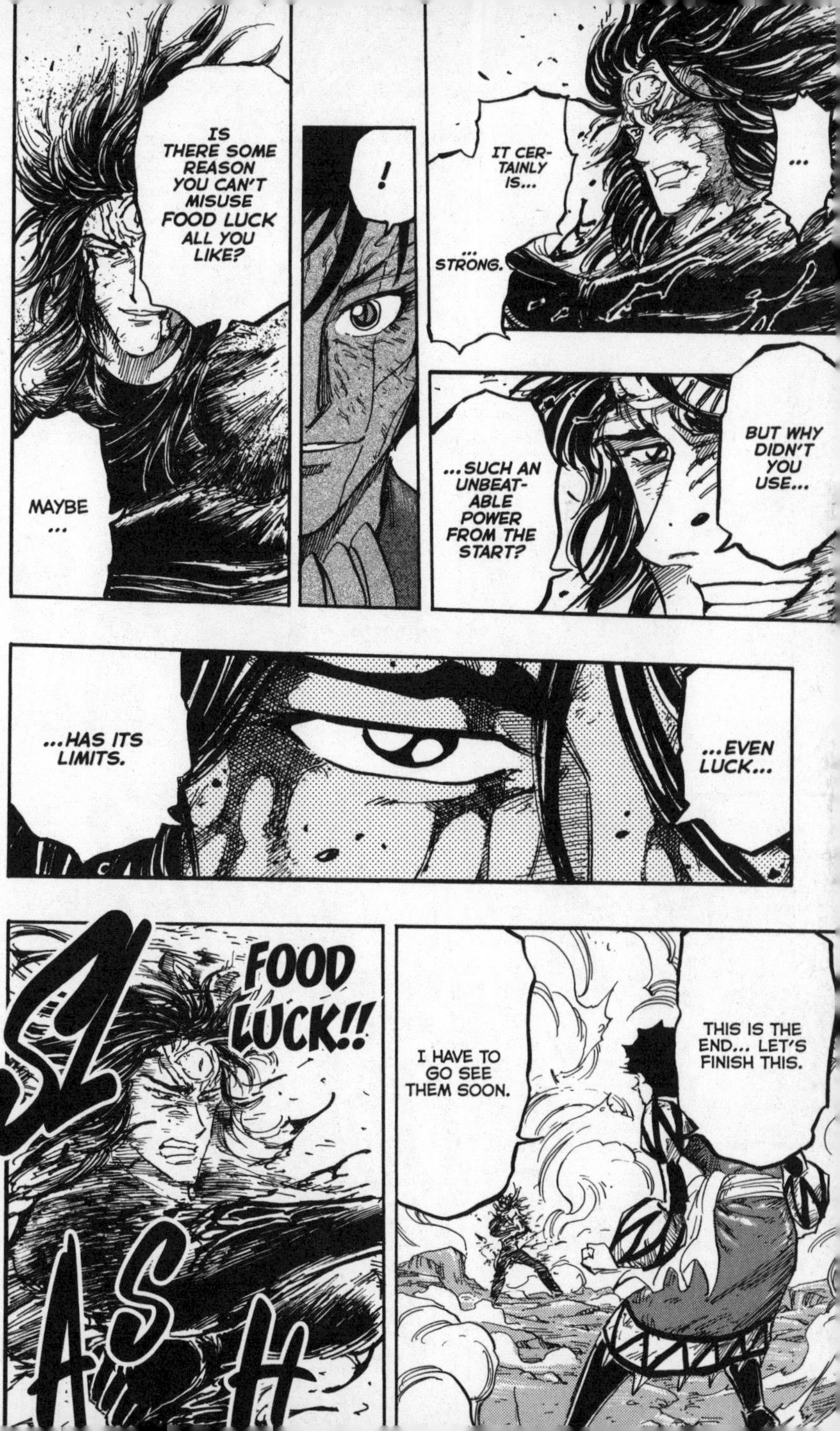
...
IT CER-TAINLY IS...
...STRONG.
BUT WHY DIDN'T YOU USE...
...SUCH AN UNBEAT-ABLE POWER FROM THE START?
!
IS THERE SOME REASON YOU CAN'T MISUSE FOOD LUCK ALL YOU LIKE?
MAYBE ...
...EVEN LUCK...
...HAS ITS LIMITS.
THIS IS THE END... LET'S FINISH THIS.
I HAVE TO GO SEE THEM SOON.
FOOD LUCK!!

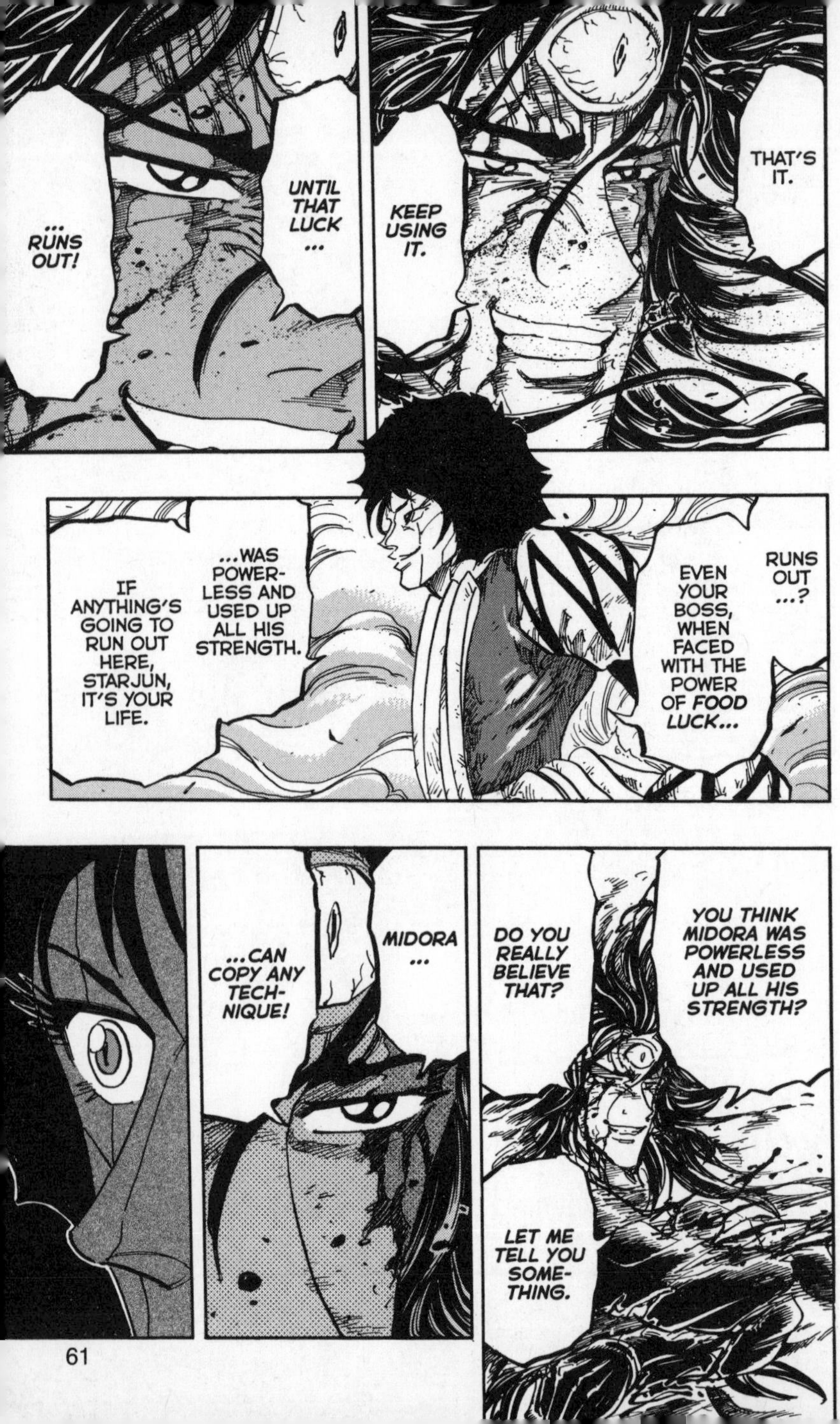
THAT'S IT.
KEEP USING IT.
UNTIL THAT LUCK...
...RUNS OUT!
RUNS OUT...?
EVEN YOUR BOSS, WHEN FACED WITH THE POWER OF *FOOD LUCK*...
...WAS POWERLESS AND USED UP ALL HIS STRENGTH.
IF ANYTHING'S GOING TO RUN OUT HERE, STARJUN, IT'S YOUR LIFE.
YOU THINK MIDORA WAS POWERLESS AND USED UP ALL HIS STRENGTH?
DO YOU REALLY BELIEVE THAT?
LET ME TELL YOU SOMETHING.
MIDORA...
...CAN COPY ANY TECHNIQUE!

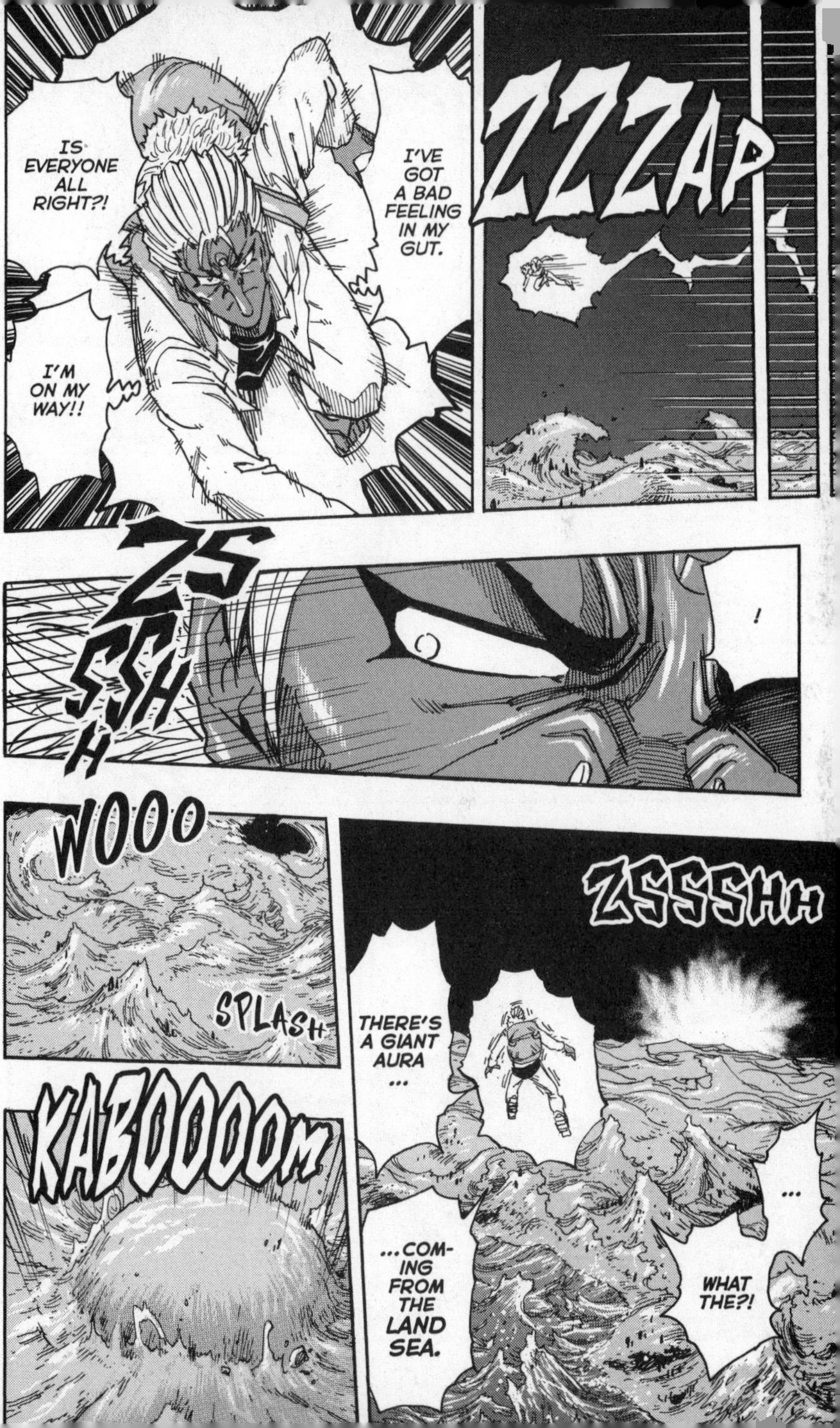
ZZZAP
I'VE GOT A BAD FEELING IN MY GUT.
IS EVERYONE ALL RIGHT?!
I'M ON MY WAY!!
!
ZSSSHH
ZSSSHH
THERE'S A GIANT AURA...
...
...COMING FROM THE LAND SEA.
WHAT THE?!
WOOO
SPLASH
KABOOOOM

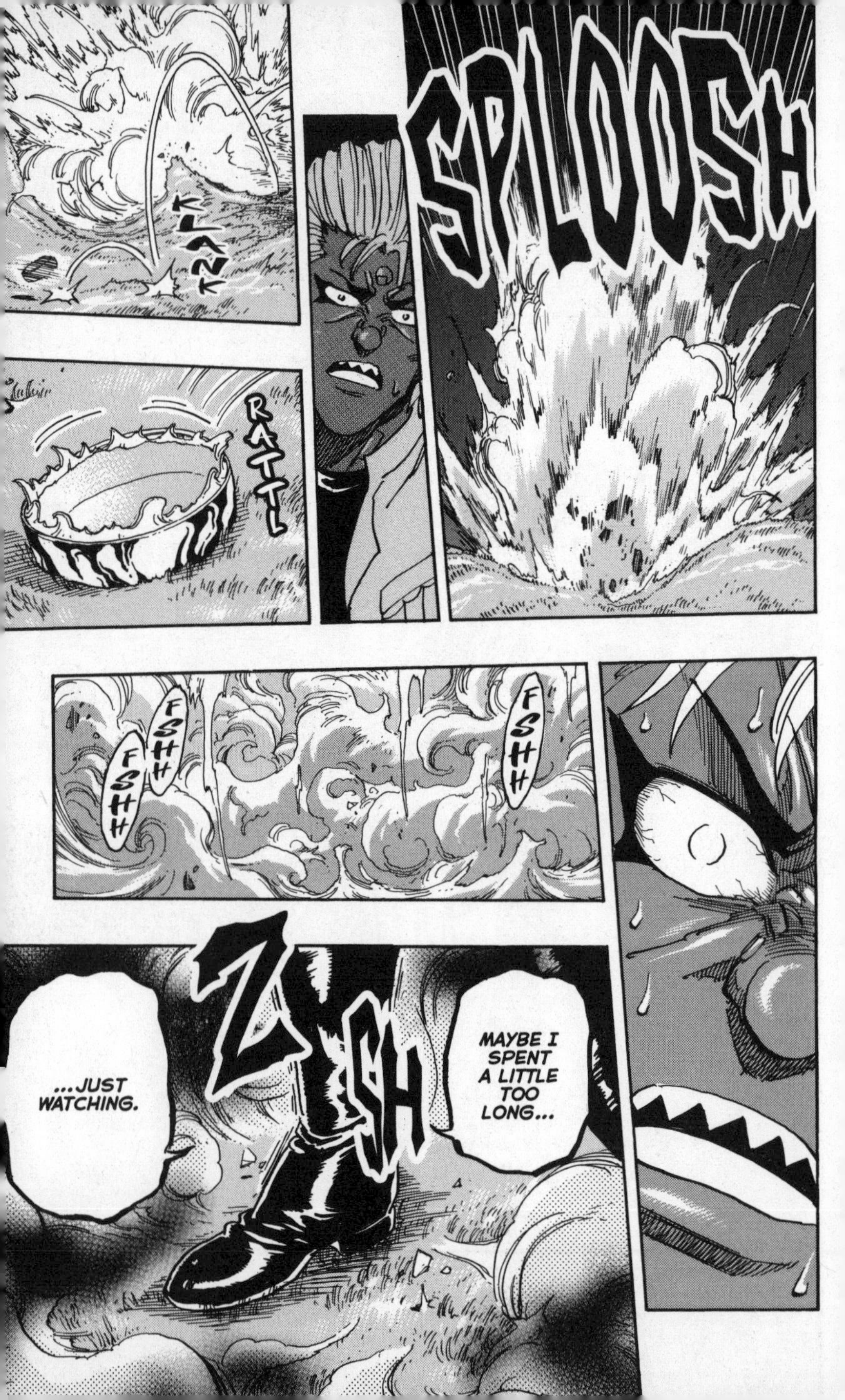
SPLOOSH
KLANK
RATTL
FSHH
FSHH
FSHH
ZGH
MAYBE I SPENT A LITTLE TOO LONG...
...JUST WATCHING.

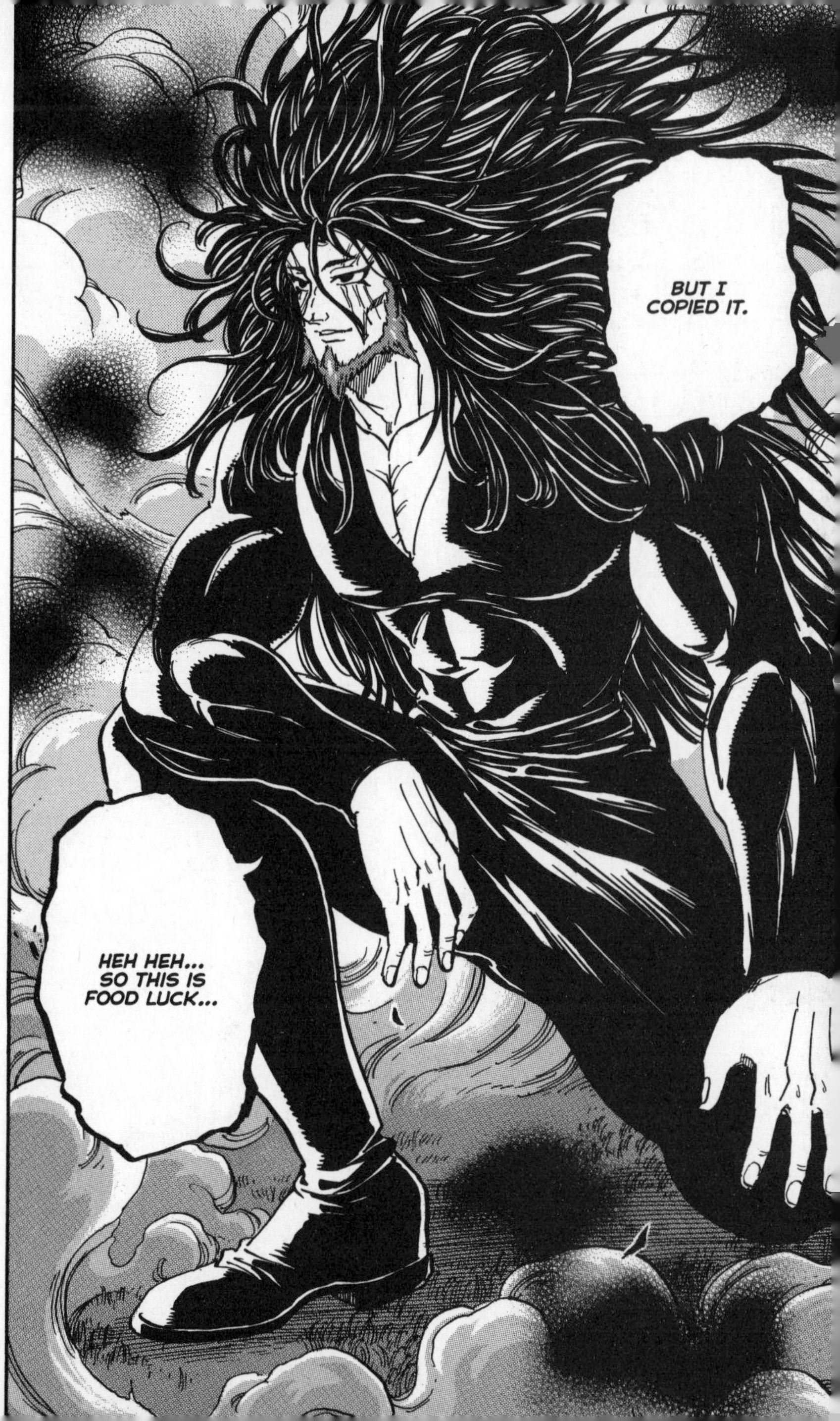
BUT I COPIED IT.
HEH HEH... SO THIS IS FOOD LUCK...

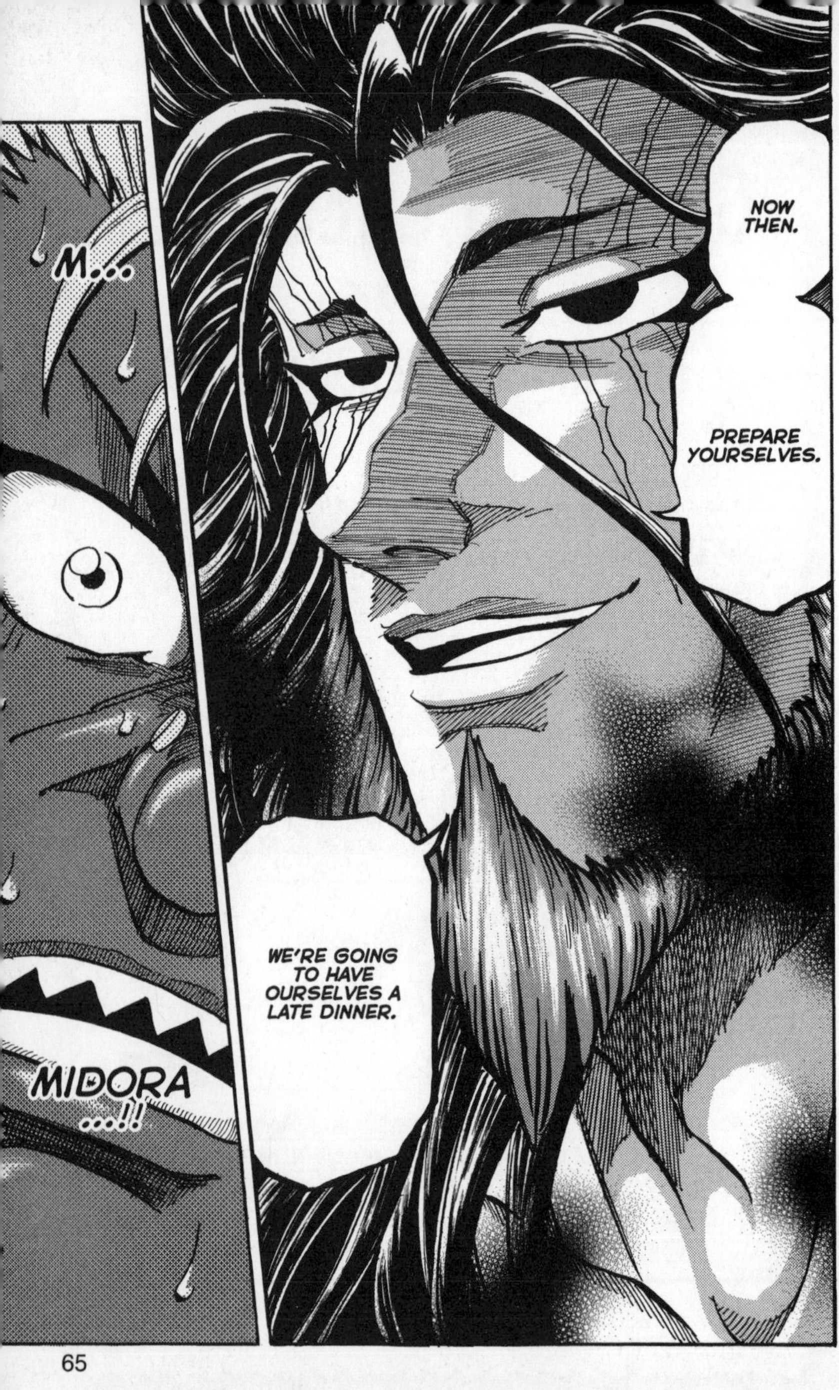
NOW THEN.
PREPARE YOURSELVES.
WE'RE GOING TO HAVE OURSELVES A LATE DINNER.
M...
MIDORA ...!!

TORIKO

GOURMET CHECKLIST

Vol. 416

BIRD KING: EMPEROR CROW

(BIRD)

CAPTURE LEVEL: 6,000

HABITAT: GOURMET WORLD, AREA 3

SIZE: 3,000 M

HEIGHT: ---

WEIGHT: 25 MILLION TONS

PRICE: UNKNOWN

THE BIRD KING!!
EMPEROR SHADOW!!
SSHH

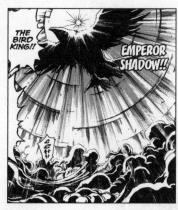

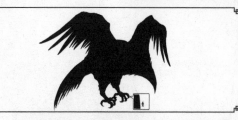

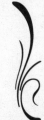

SCALE

ONE OF THE EIGHT KINGS WHO RULES ONE OF THE MAJOR CONTINENTS IN THE GOURMET WORLD. THIS ONE HOLDS ABSOLUTE COMMAND OF ALL THE SKIES IN THE GOURMET WORLD. THOSE WHO ENTER THE BIRD KING'S SHADOW ARE ENGULFED IN DARKNESS AND GO MAD AS THEY ARE SILENTLY AND INSTANTLY DESTROYED. MANY HAVE TRIED TO ESCAPE, BUT ALL HAVE FAILED.

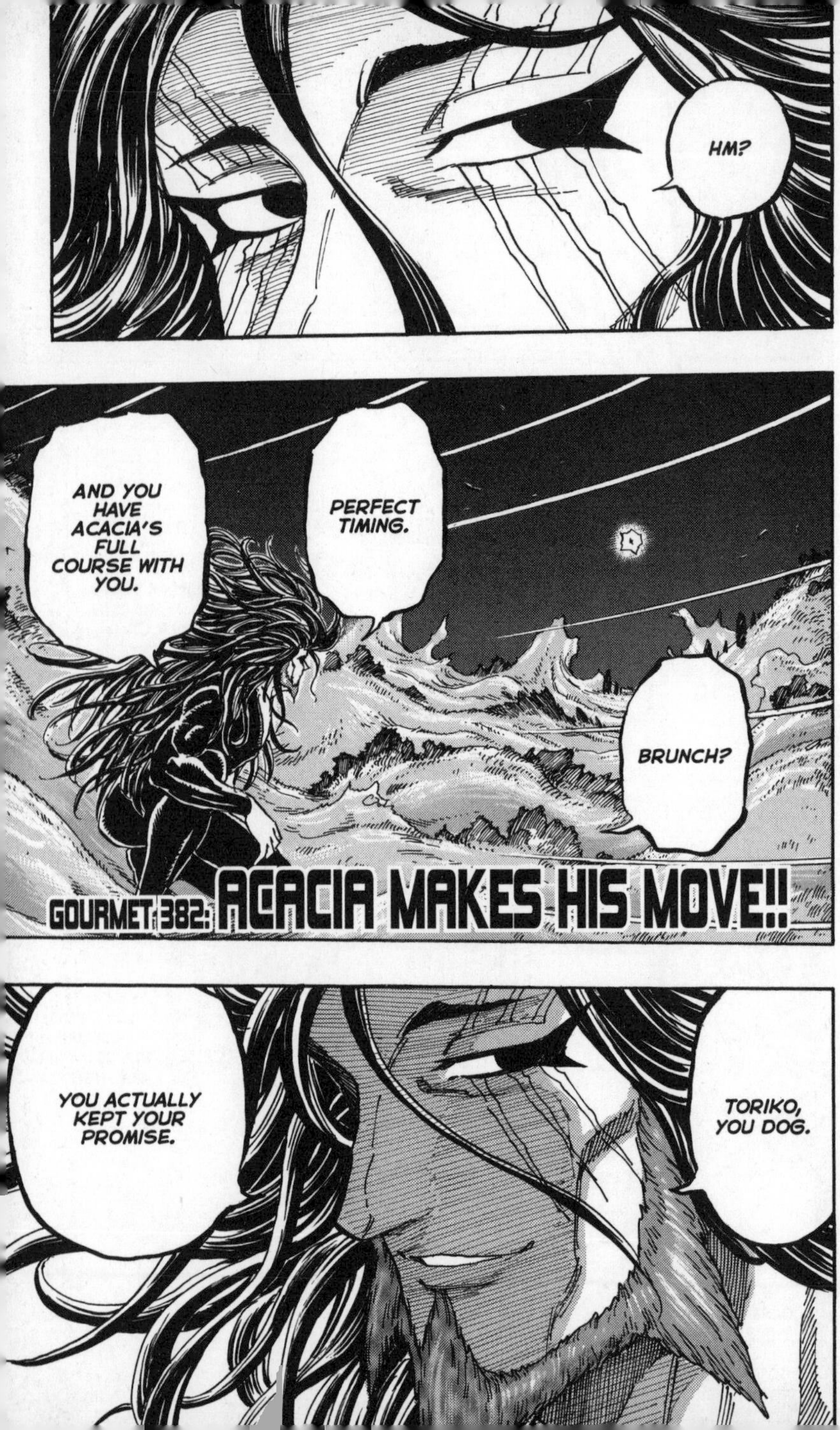
HM?
BRUNCH?
PERFECT TIMING.
AND YOU HAVE ACACIA'S FULL COURSE WITH YOU.
GOURMET 382: ACACIA MAKES HIS MOVE!!
TORIKO, YOU DOG.
YOU ACTUALLY KEPT YOUR PROMISE.

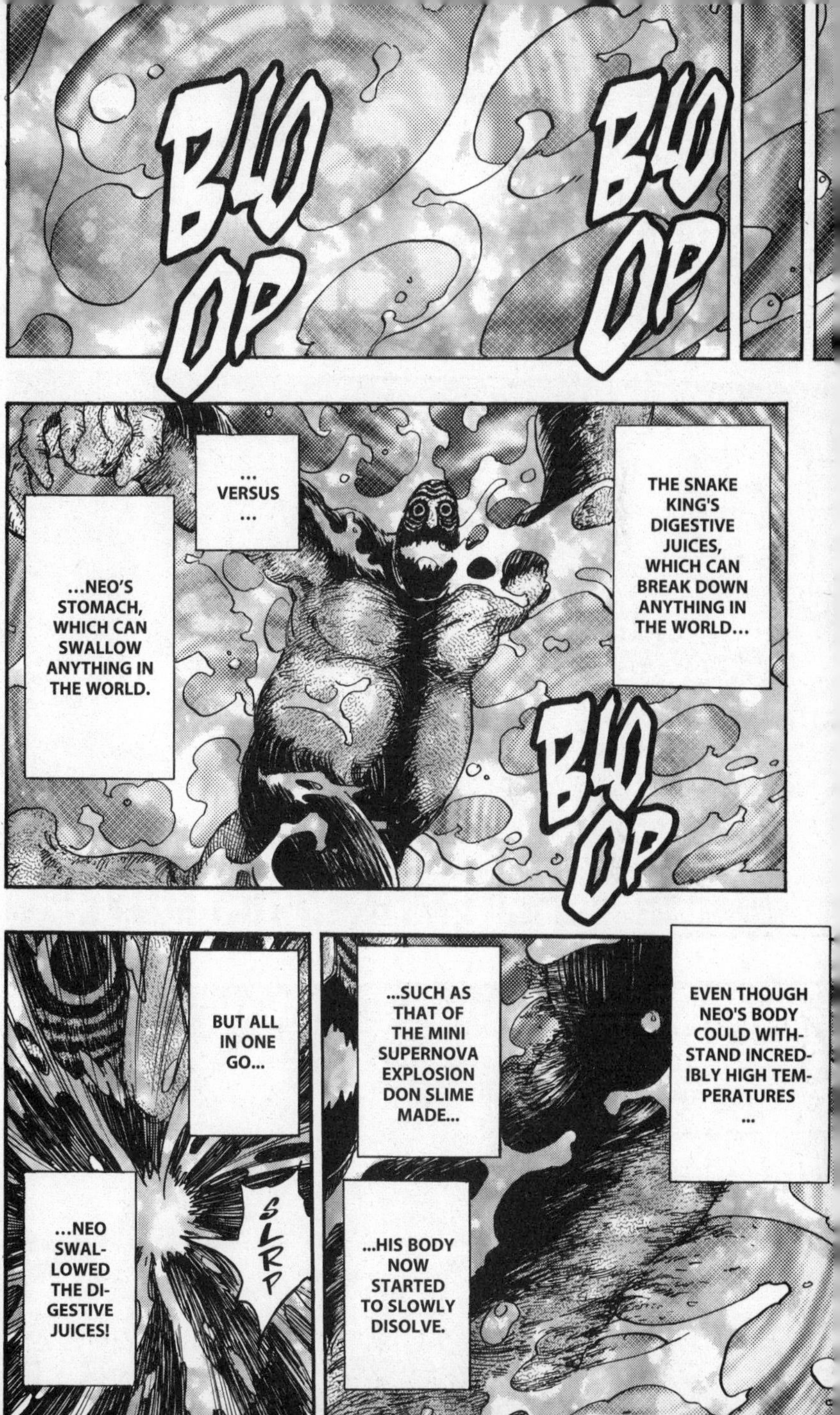
BLOOP
BLOOP
THE SNAKE KING'S DIGESTIVE JUICES, WHICH CAN BREAK DOWN ANYTHING IN THE WORLD...
... VERSUS ...
...NEO'S STOMACH, WHICH CAN SWALLOW ANYTHING IN THE WORLD.
BLOOP
EVEN THOUGH NEO'S BODY COULD WITH-STAND INCRED-IBLY HIGH TEM-PERATURES ...
...SUCH AS THAT OF THE MINI SUPERNOVA EXPLOSION DON SLIME MADE...
...HIS BODY NOW STARTED TO SLOWLY DISOLVE.
BUT ALL IN ONE GO...
SLRP
...NEO SWAL-LOWED THE DI-GESTIVE JUICES!

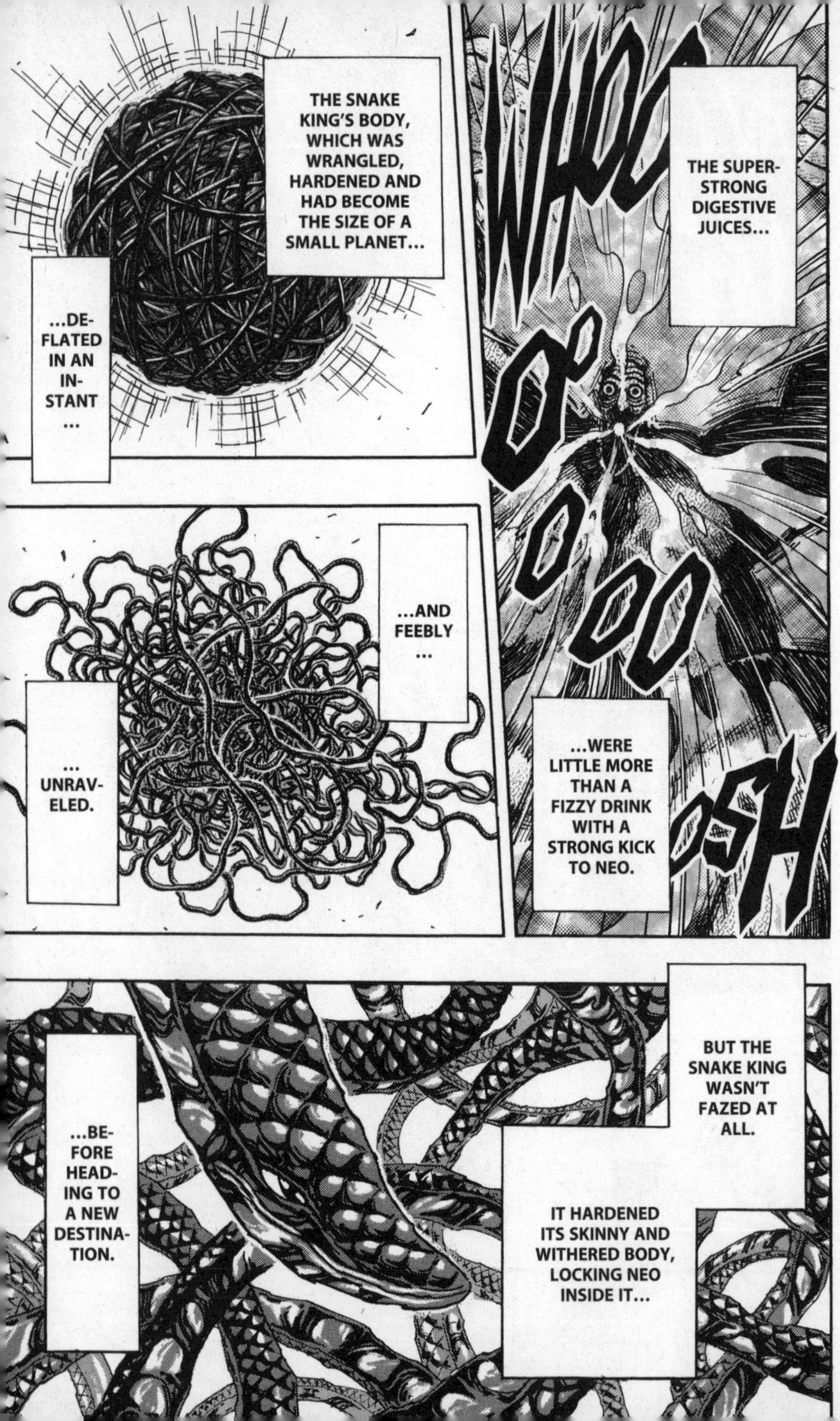
THE SUPER-STRONG DIGESTIVE JUICES...
WHOOOOOOOSH
...WERE LITTLE MORE THAN A FIZZY DRINK WITH A STRONG KICK TO NEO.
THE SNAKE KING'S BODY, WHICH WAS WRANGLED, HARDENED AND HAD BECOME THE SIZE OF A SMALL PLANET...
...DE-FLATED IN AN IN-STANT...
...AND FEEBLY...
...UNRAV-ELED.
BUT THE SNAKE KING WASN'T FAZED AT ALL.
IT HARDENED ITS SKINNY AND WITHERED BODY, LOCKING NEO INSIDE IT...
...BE-FORE HEAD-ING TO A NEW DESTINA-TION.

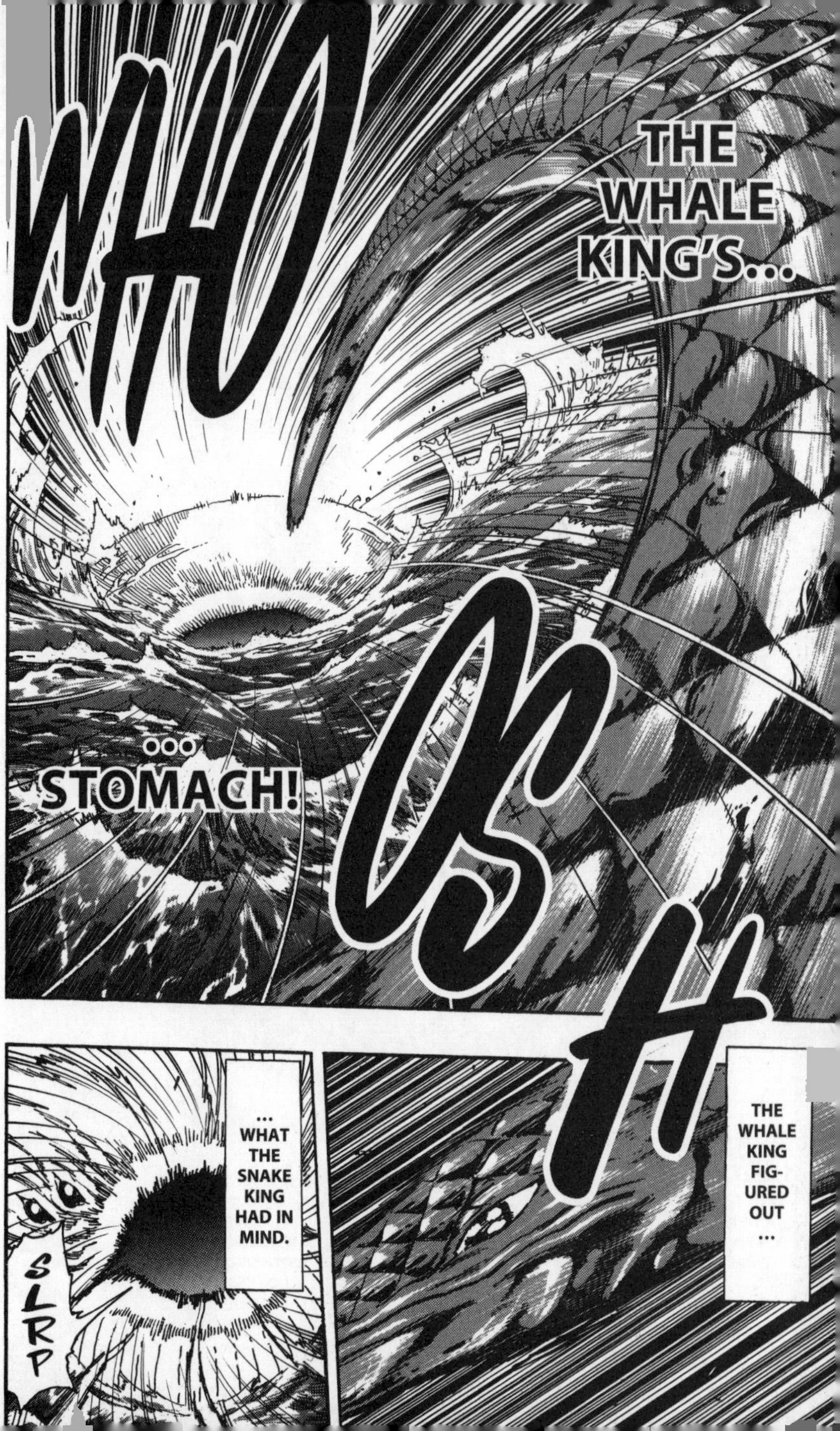
THE WHALE KING'S...
...STOMACH!
THE WHALE KING FIG-URED OUT...
...WHAT THE SNAKE KING HAD IN MIND.
SLRP

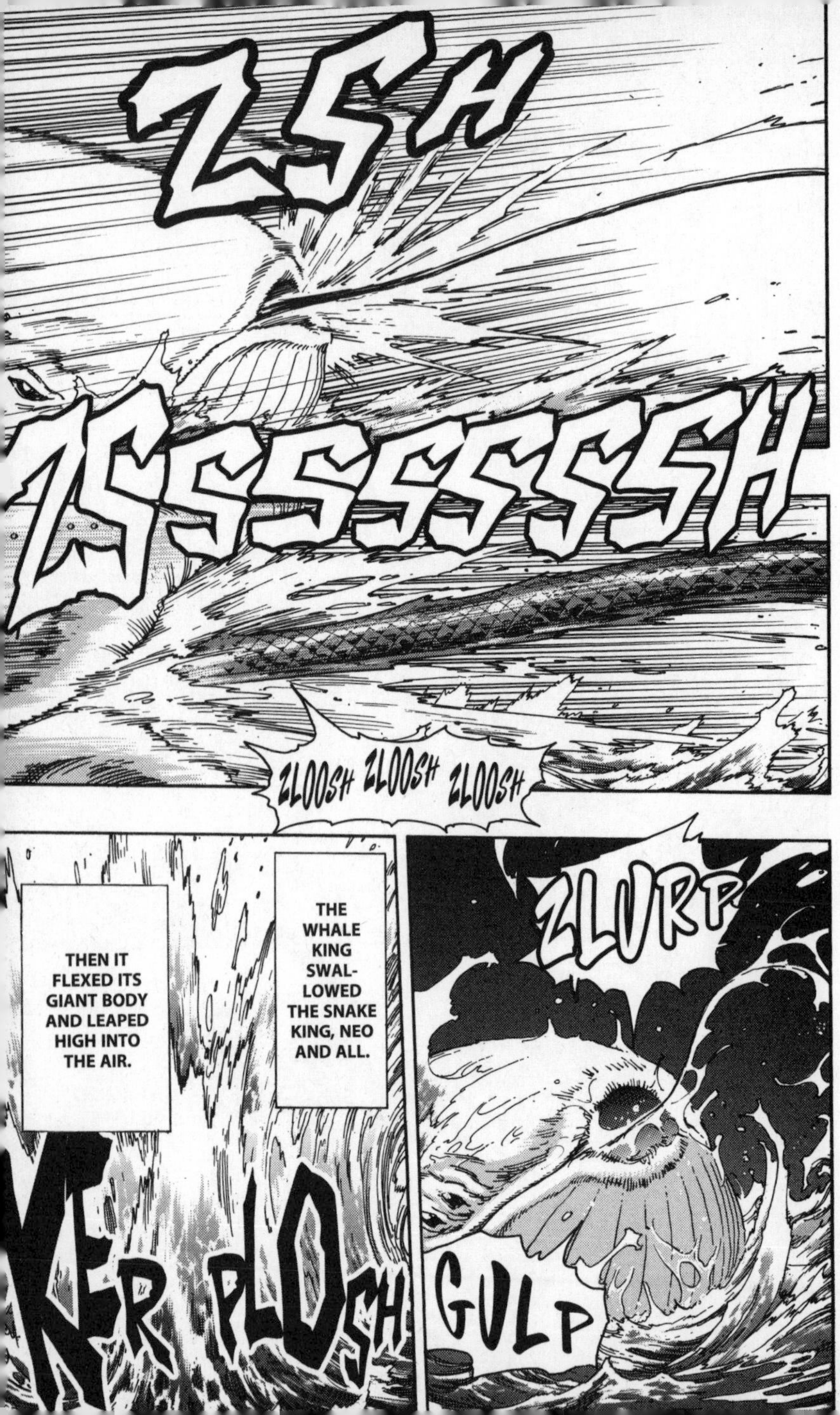
ZSH
ZSSSSSSH
ZLOOSH ZLOOSH ZLOOSH
ZLURP
GULP
THE WHALE KING SWAL-LOWED THE SNAKE KING, NEO AND ALL.
THEN IT FLEXED ITS GIANT BODY AND LEAPED HIGH INTO THE AIR.
KER PLOSH

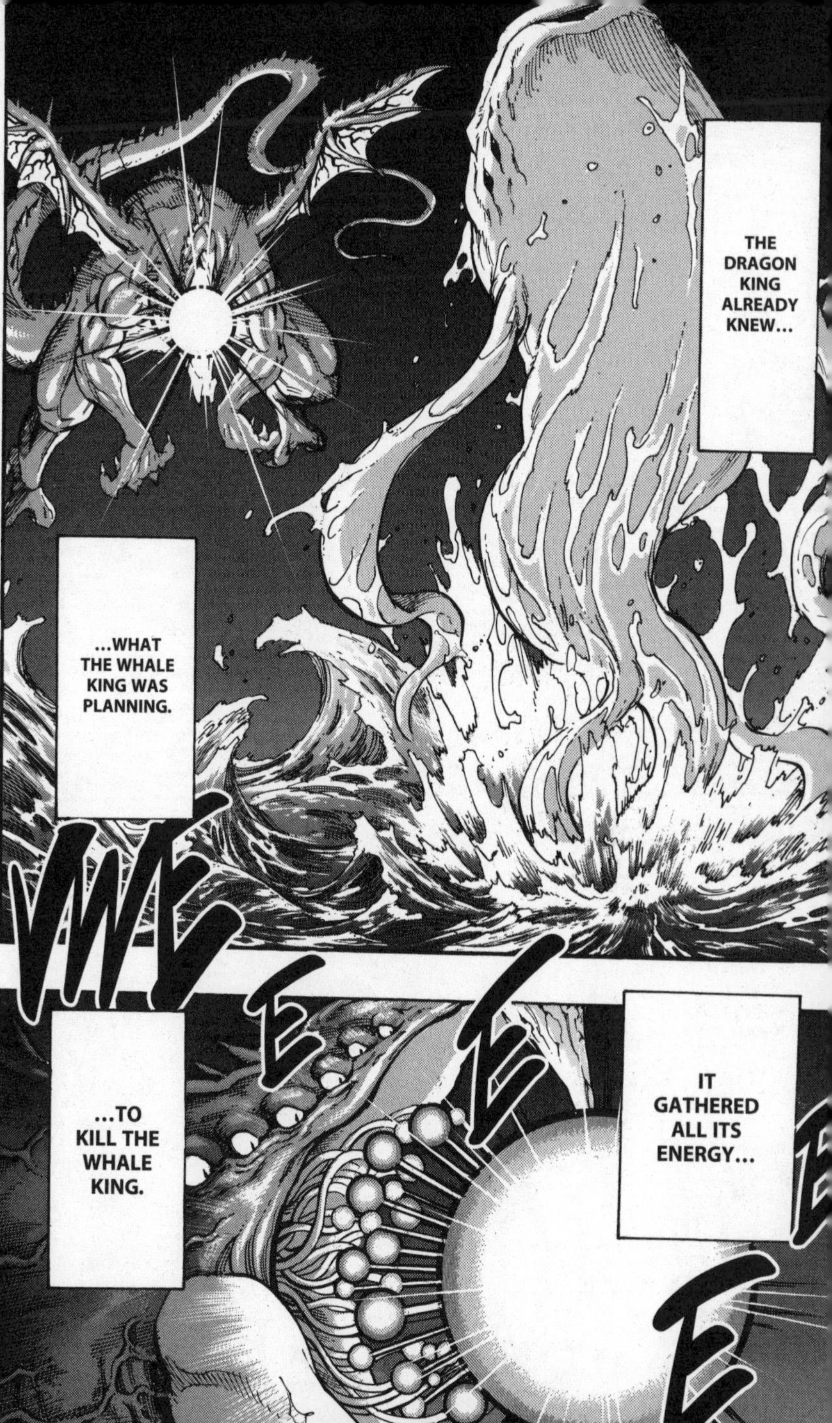
THE DRAGON KING ALREADY KNEW...
...WHAT THE WHALE KING WAS PLANNING.
VWEEEE
IT GATHERED ALL ITS ENERGY...
...TO KILL THE WHALE KING.

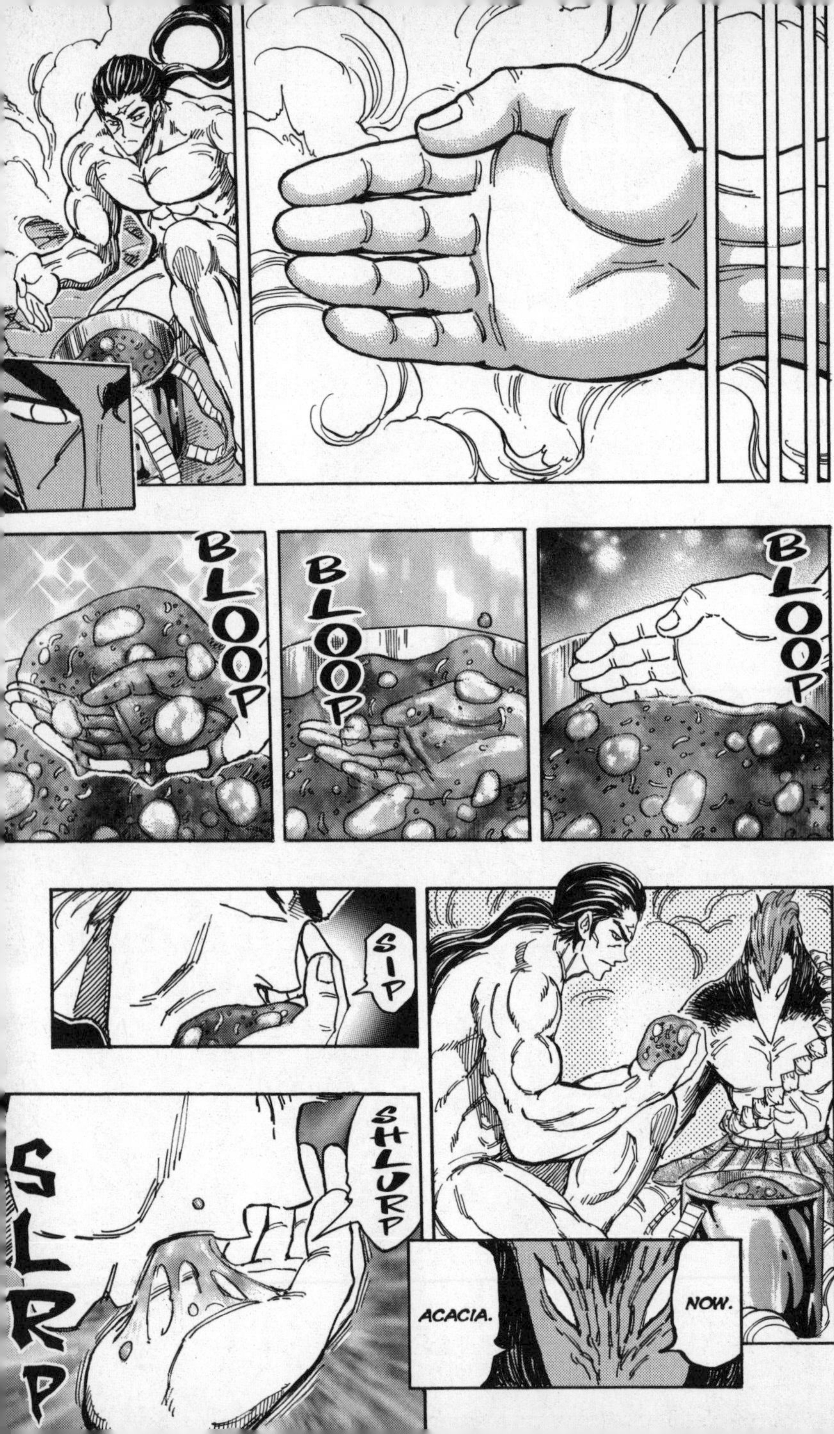
BLOOP
BLOOP
BLOOP
ACACIA.
NOW.
SIP
SHLURP
SLRP

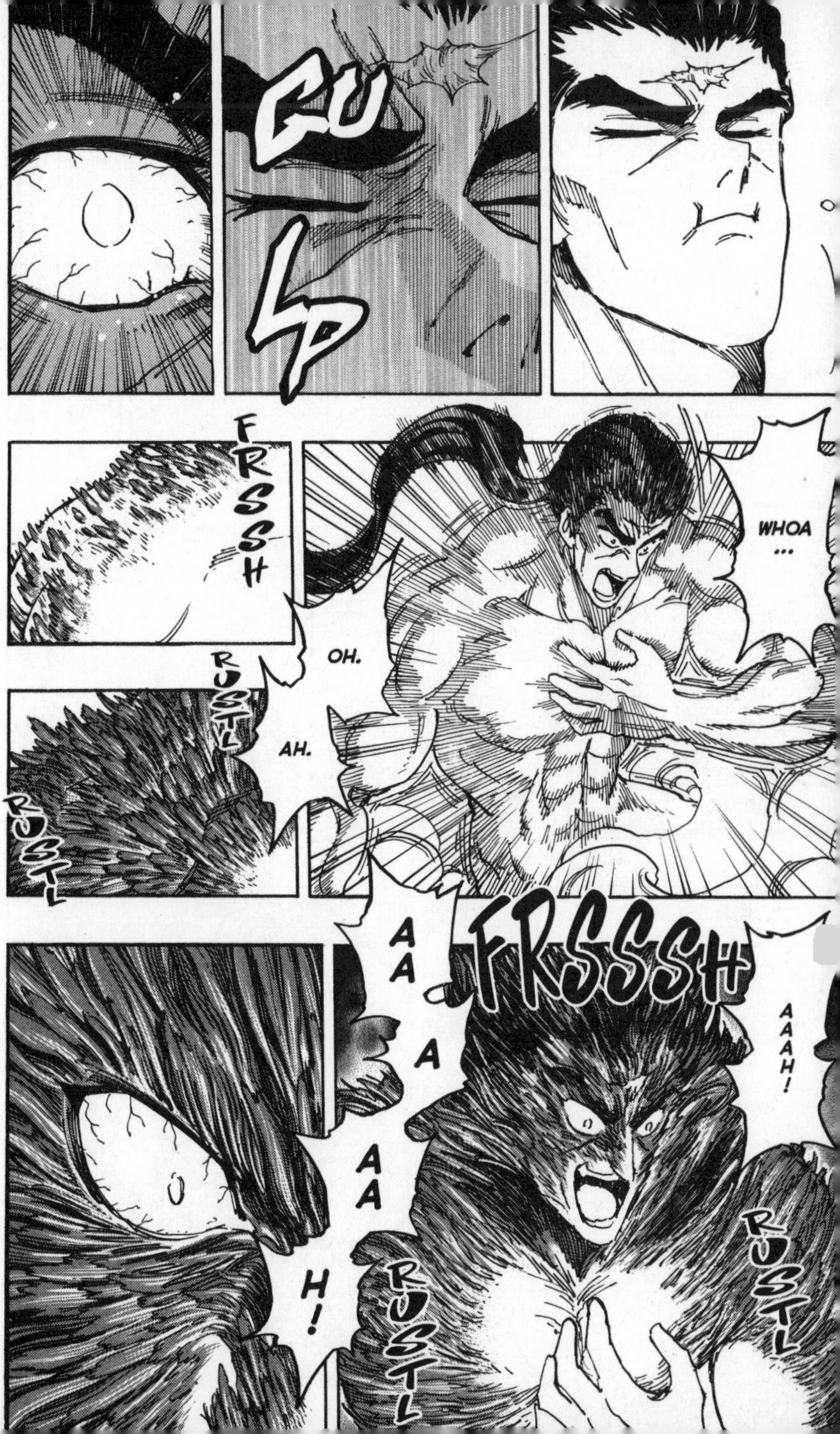

GU
LP
WHOA ...
OH.
AH.
FRSSH
RUSTL
RUSTL
AAAH!
FRSSSH
AAAAAH!
RUSTL
RUSTL

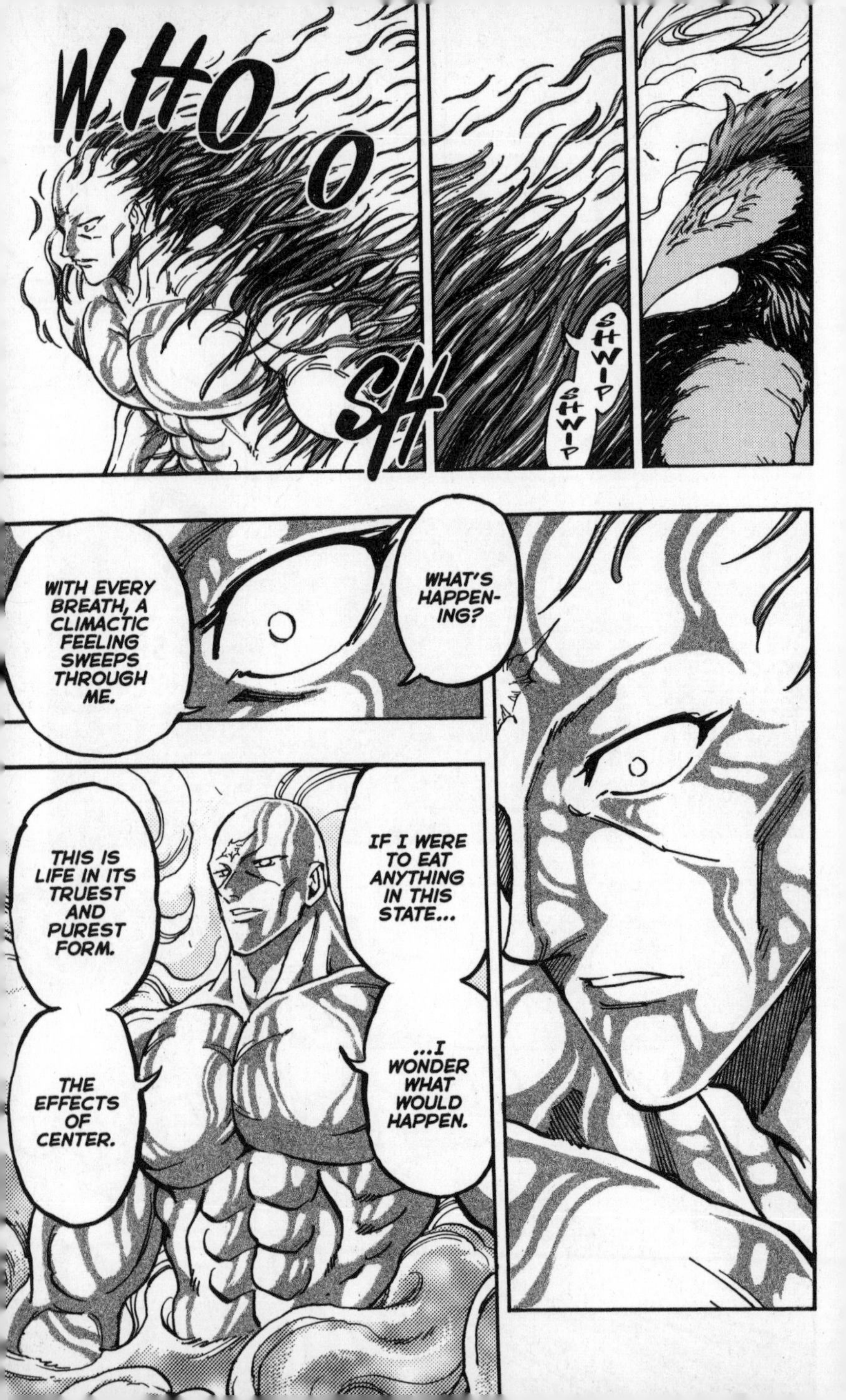
SHWIP
SHWIP
WHOOO
SH
WHAT'S HAPPENING?
WITH EVERY BREATH, A CLIMACTIC FEELING SWEEPS THROUGH ME.
IF I WERE TO EAT ANYTHING IN THIS STATE...
...I WONDER WHAT WOULD HAPPEN.
THIS IS LIFE IN ITS TRUEST AND PUREST FORM.
THE EFFECTS OF CENTER.

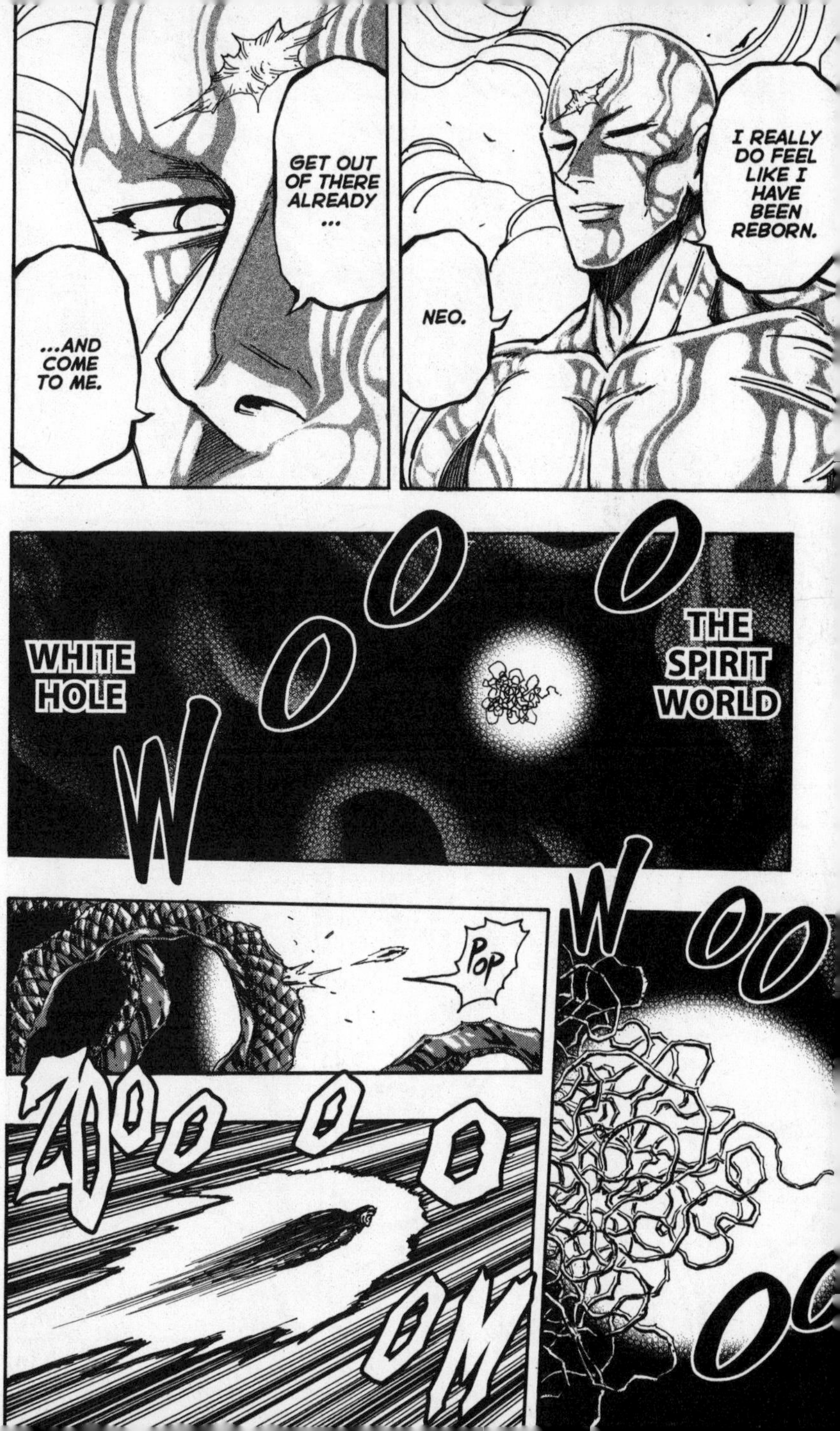
I REALLY DO FEEL LIKE I HAVE BEEN REBORN.
NEO.
GET OUT OF THERE ALREADY ...
...AND COME TO ME.
THE SPIRIT WORLD
WHITE HOLE
WOOOO
WOOO
POP
ZOOOOOOM

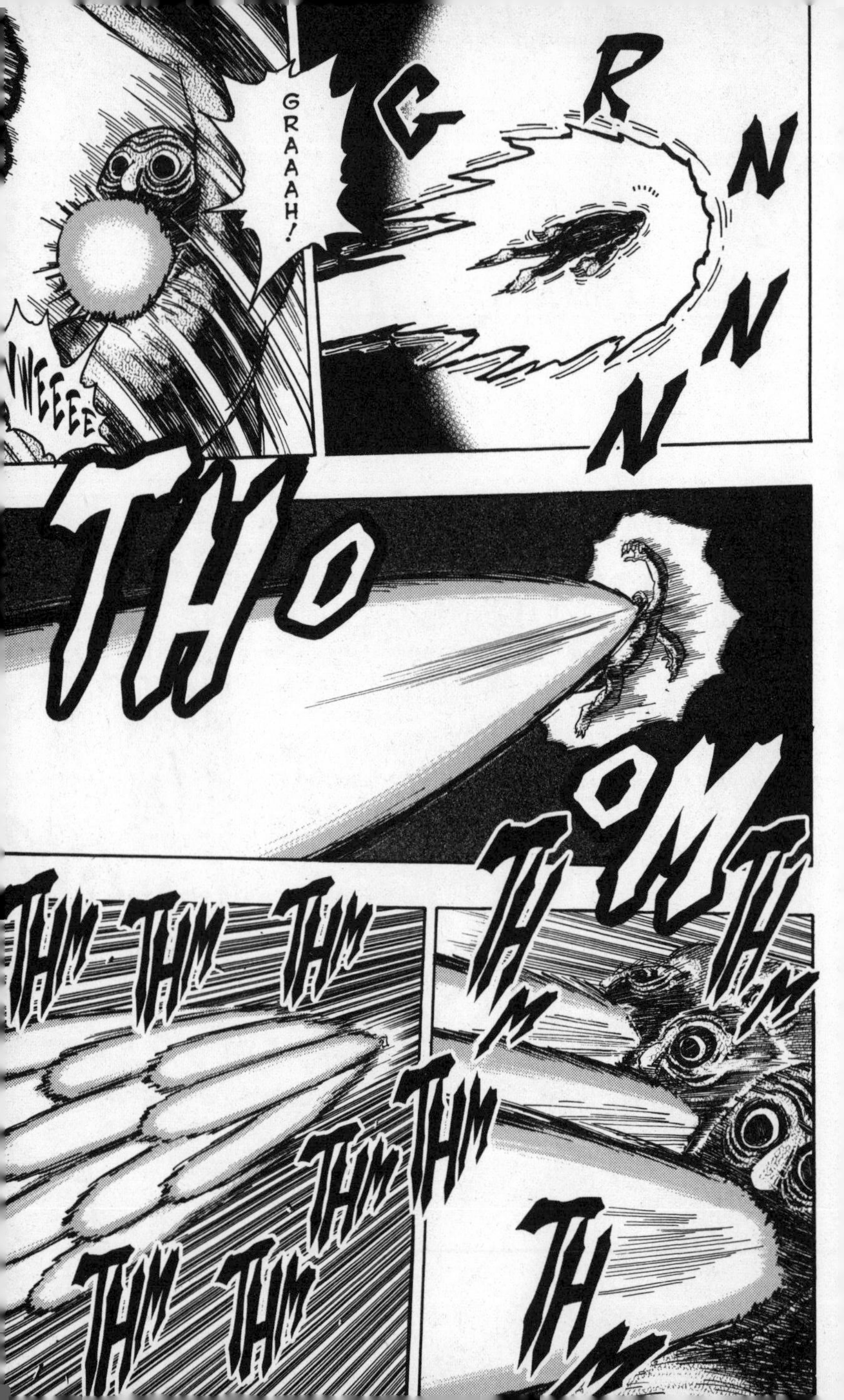
GRRNNNN
GRAAAH!
WEEEEE
THOOM
THM
THM THM THM
THM THM THM THM
THM

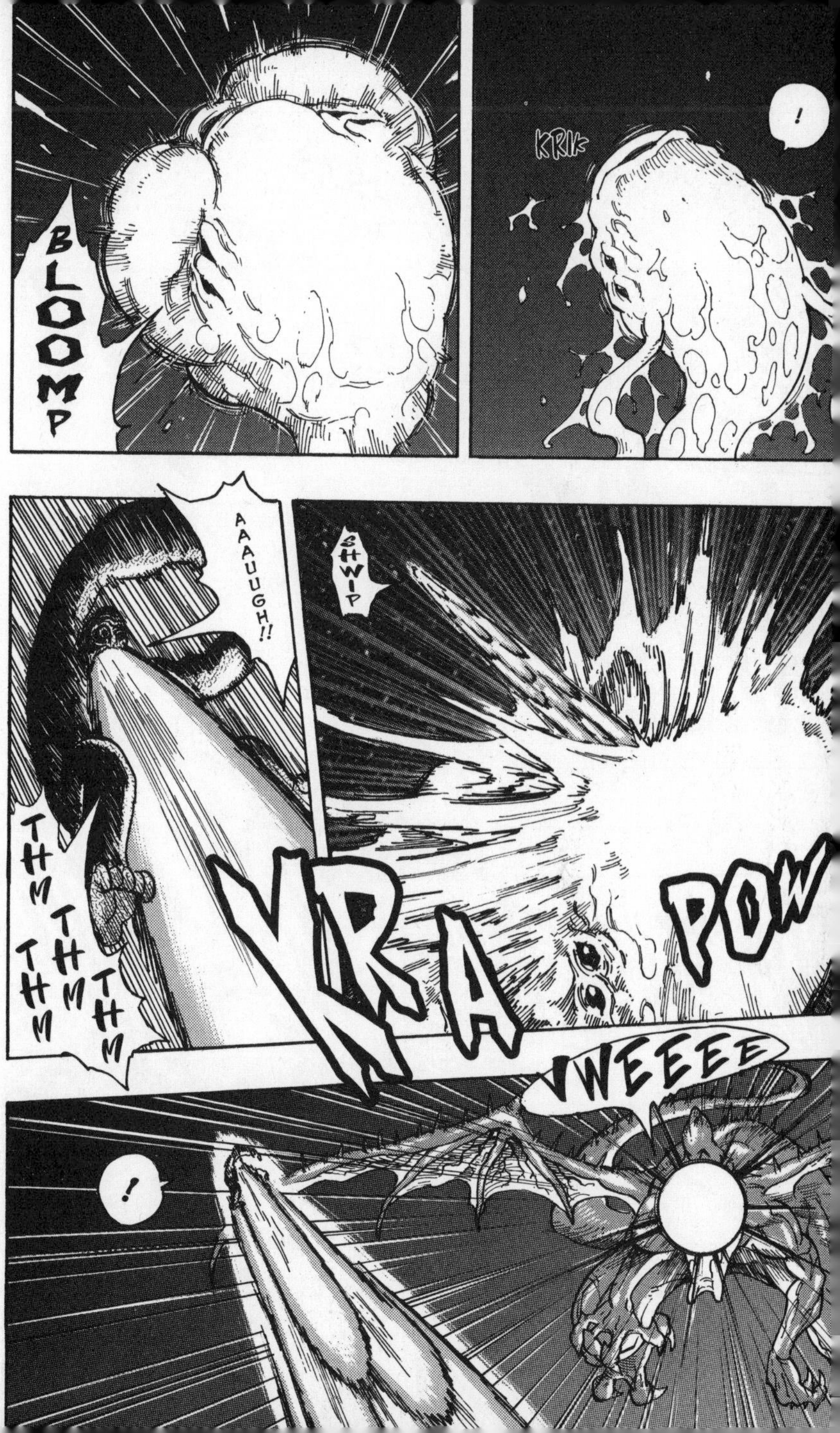
!
KRIK
BLOOMP
SHWIP
VRAPOW
AAAUUGH!!
THM THM THM THM THM THM
VWEEEE
!

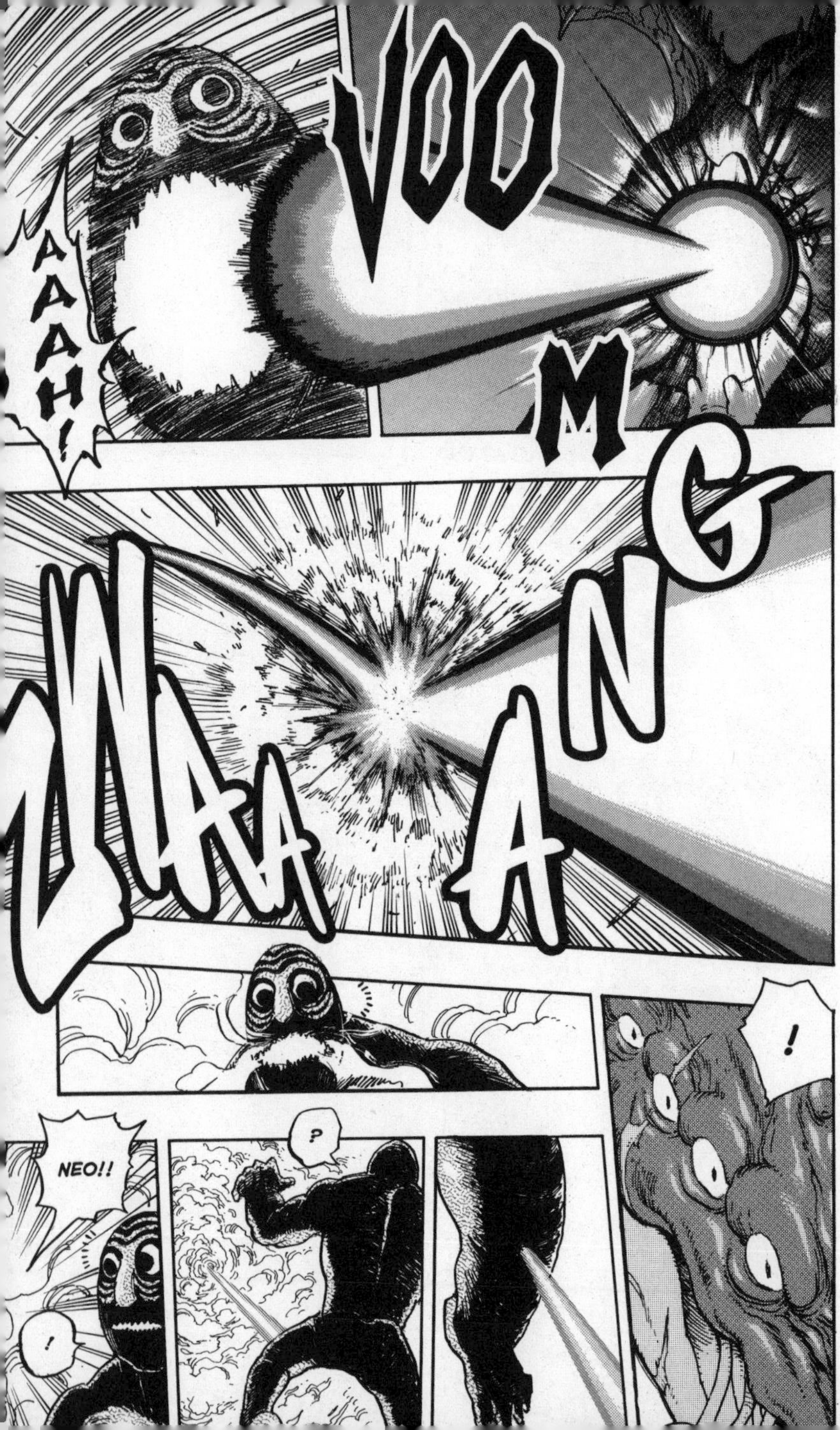
VOOM
AAAH!
ZWAAANG
!
?
NEO!!
!

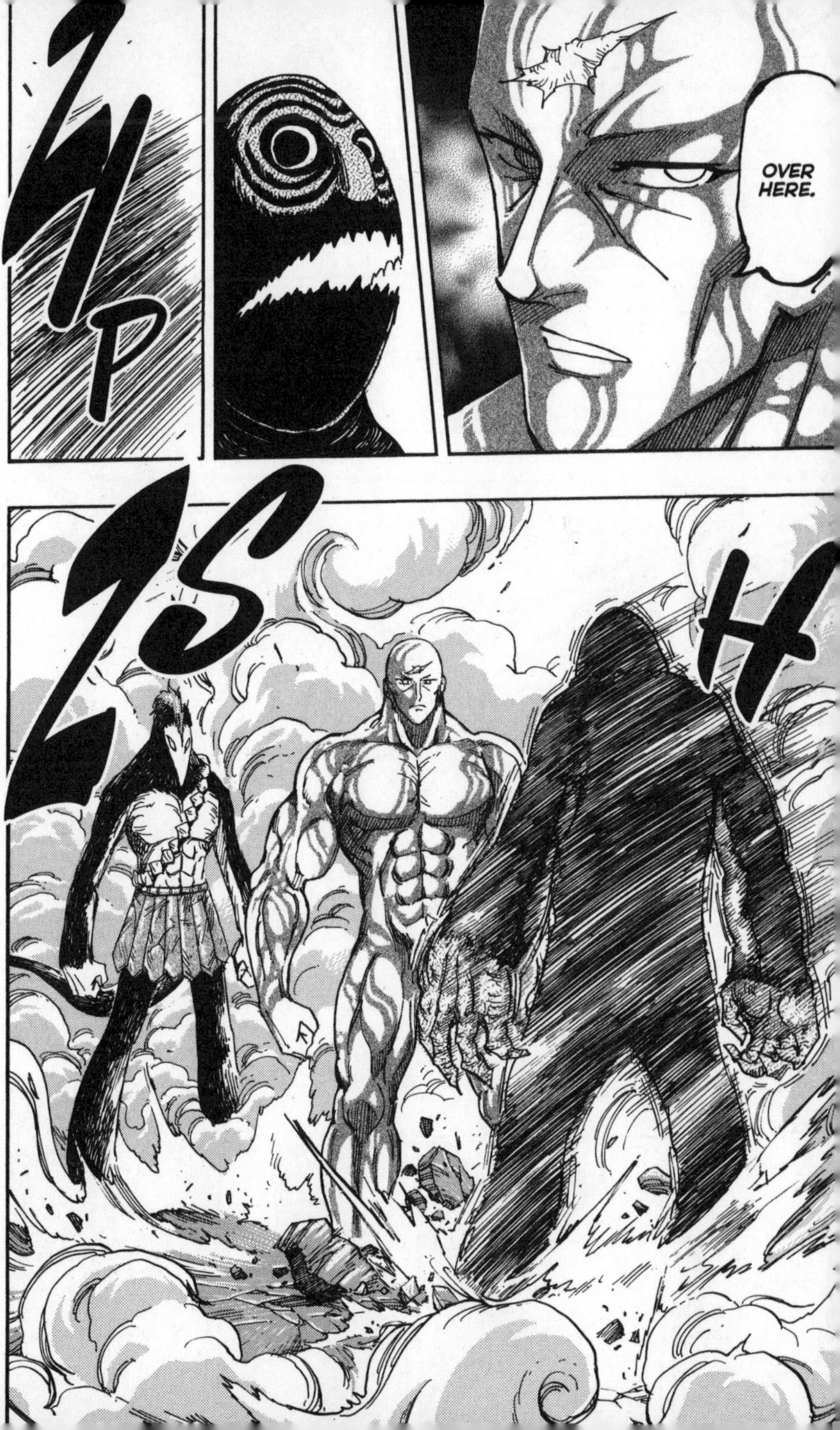
OVER HERE.
ZIP
ZSH

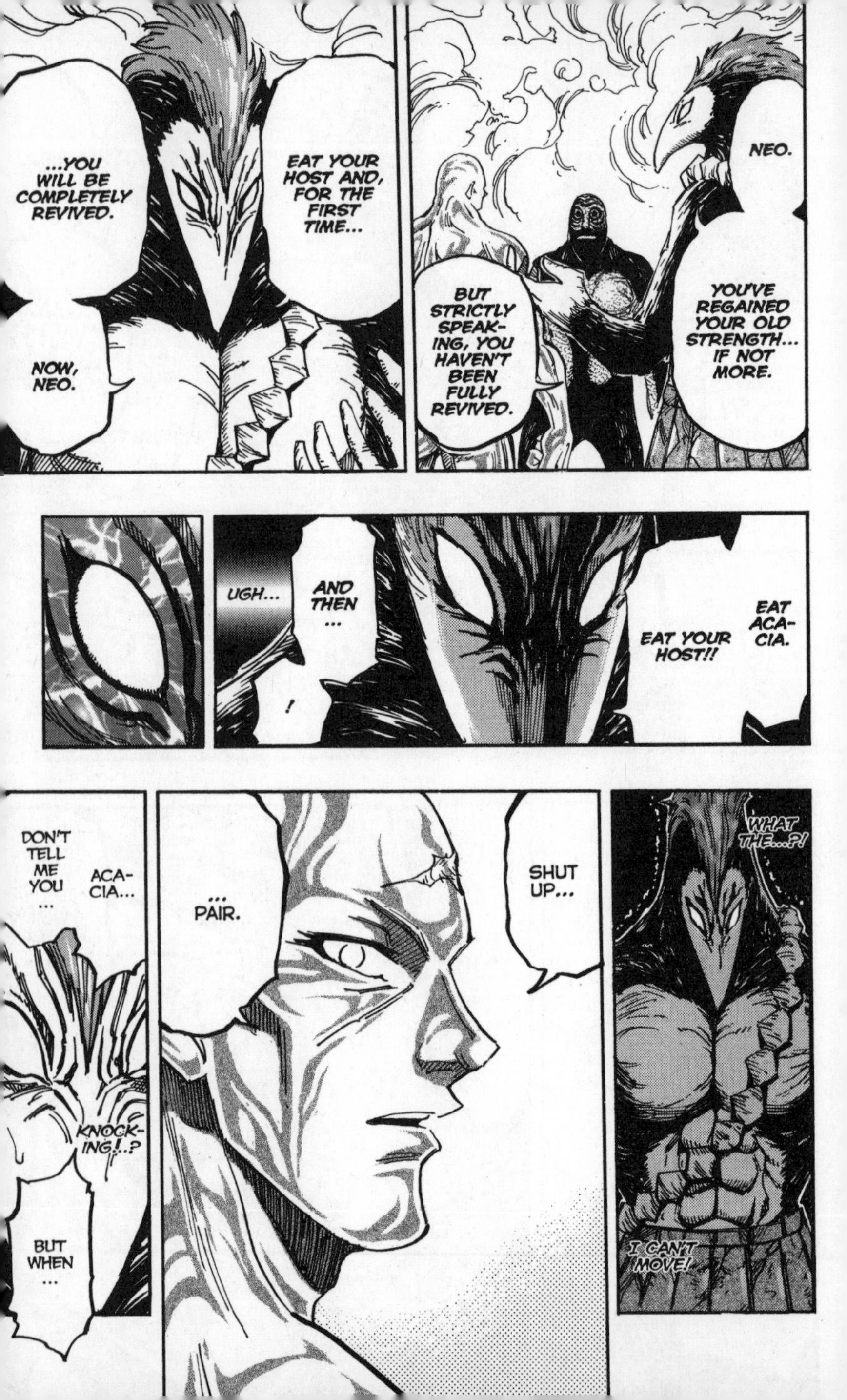
NEO.
YOU'VE REGAINED YOUR OLD STRENGTH... IF NOT MORE.
BUT STRICTLY SPEAKING, YOU HAVEN'T BEEN FULLY REVIVED.
EAT YOUR HOST AND, FOR THE FIRST TIME...
...YOU WILL BE COMPLETELY REVIVED.
NOW, NEO.
EAT ACACIA.
EAT YOUR HOST!!
AND THEN...
UGH...
!
WHAT THE...?!
I CAN'T MOVE!
SHUT UP...
...PAIR.
ACACIA...
DON'T TELL ME YOU...
KNOCKING!..?
BUT WHEN...

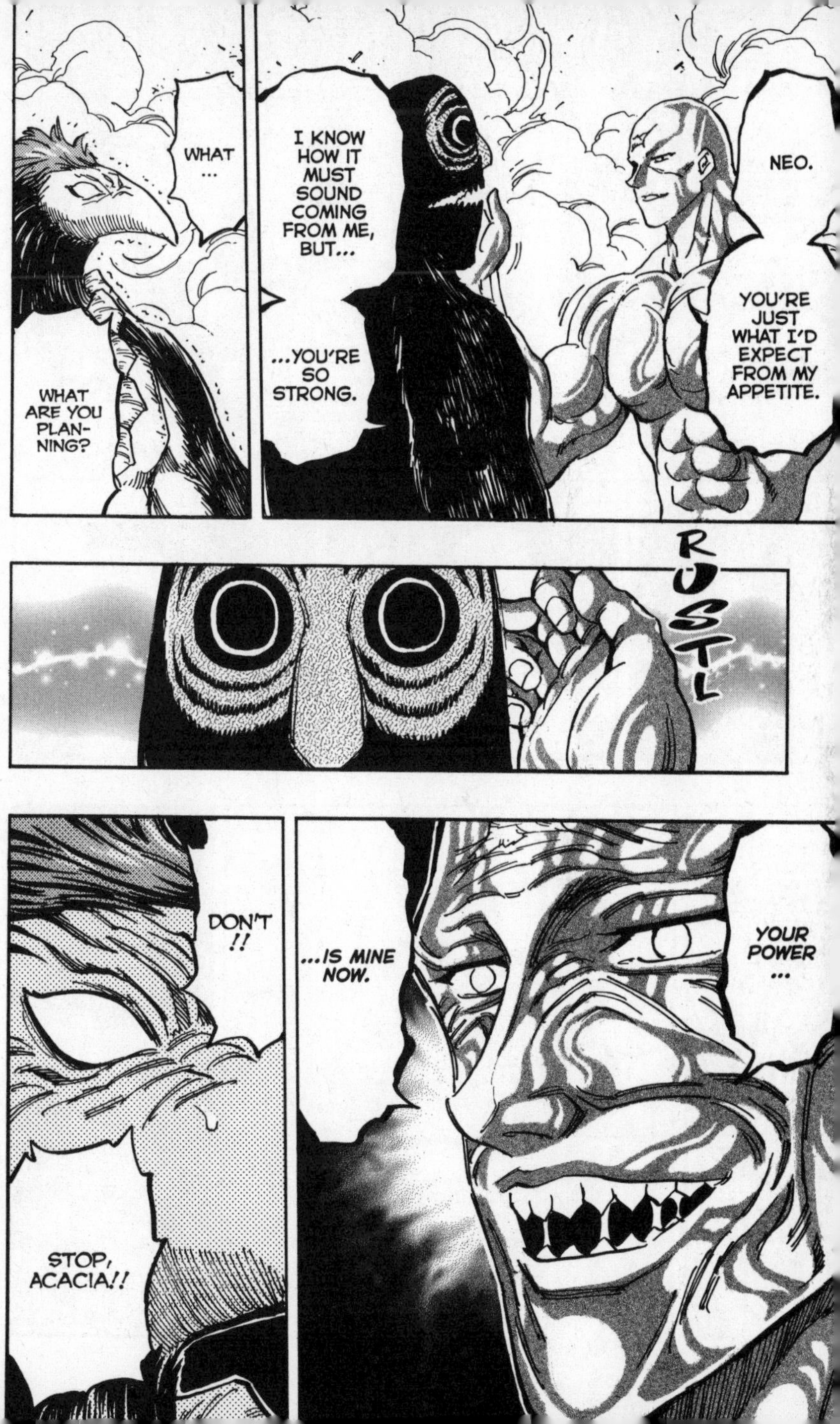
NEO.
YOU'RE JUST WHAT I'D EXPECT FROM MY APPETITE.
I KNOW HOW IT MUST SOUND COMING FROM ME, BUT...
...YOU'RE SO STRONG.
WHAT ...
WHAT ARE YOU PLAN-NING?
RUSTL
YOUR POWER ...
...IS MINE NOW.
DON'T!!
STOP, ACACIA!!

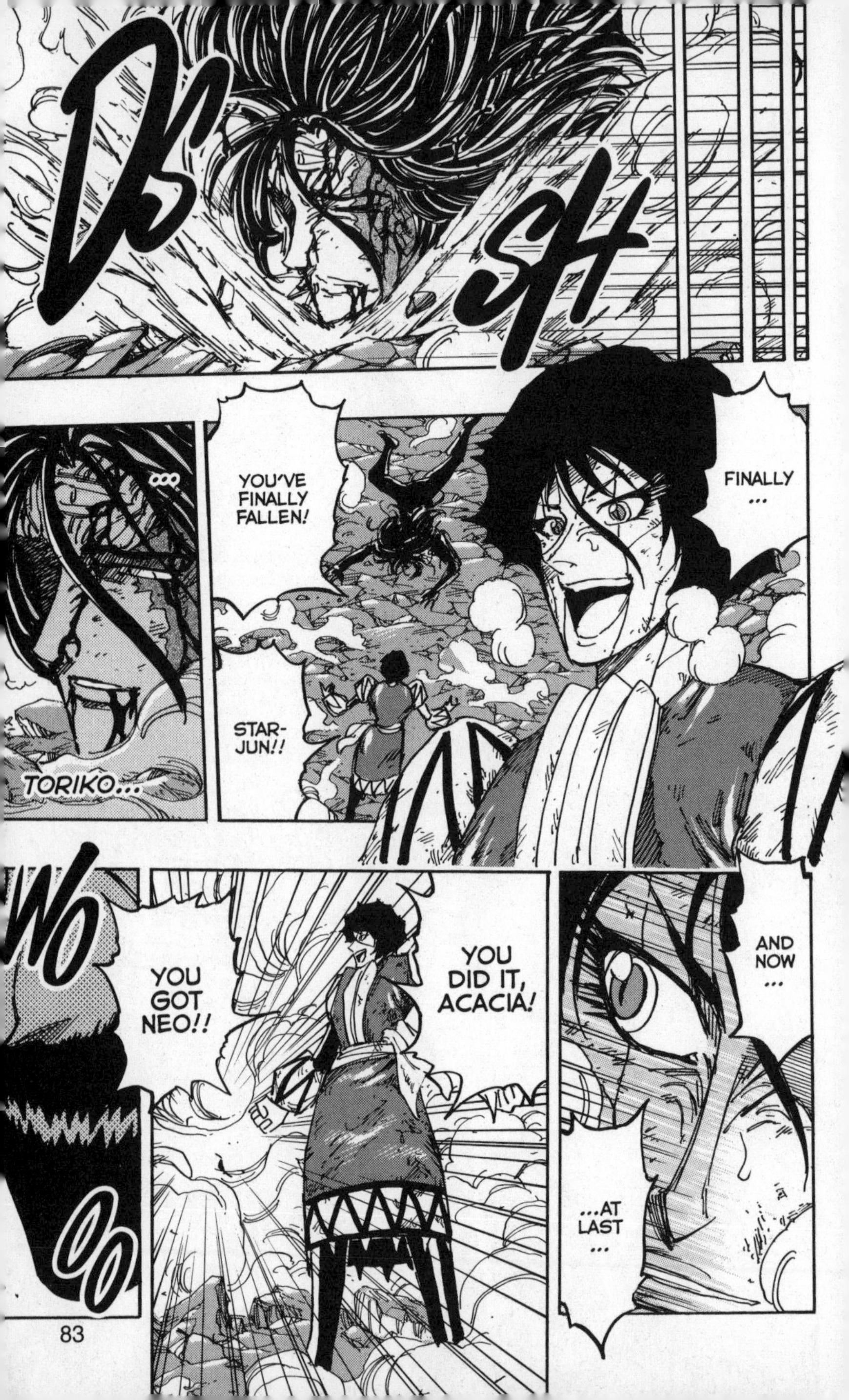
DBSH
FINALLY...
YOU'VE FINALLY FALLEN!
STAR-JUN!!
...
TORIKO...
AND NOW...
...AT LAST...
YOU DID IT, ACACIA!
YOU GOT NEO!!

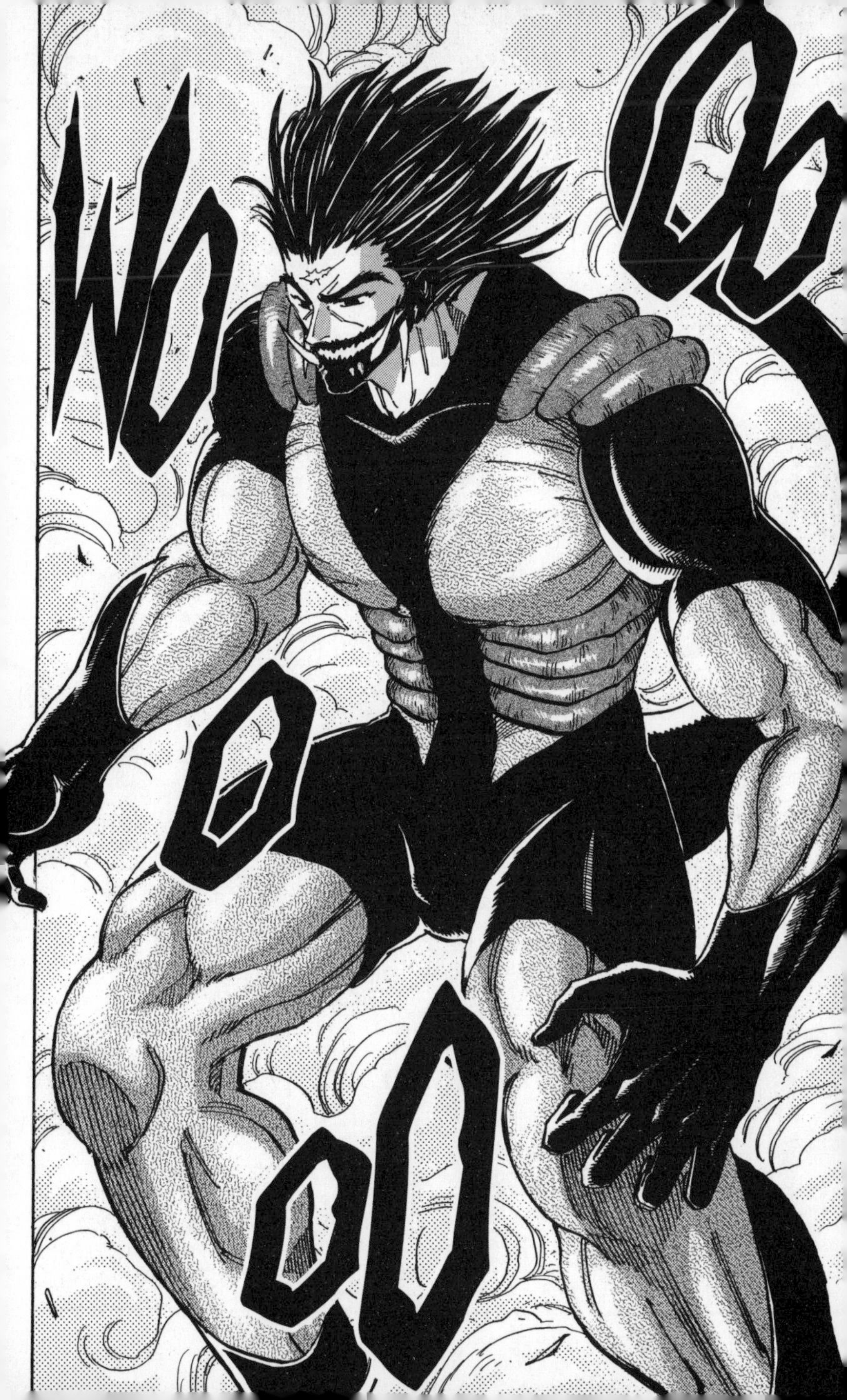
WOOOOO

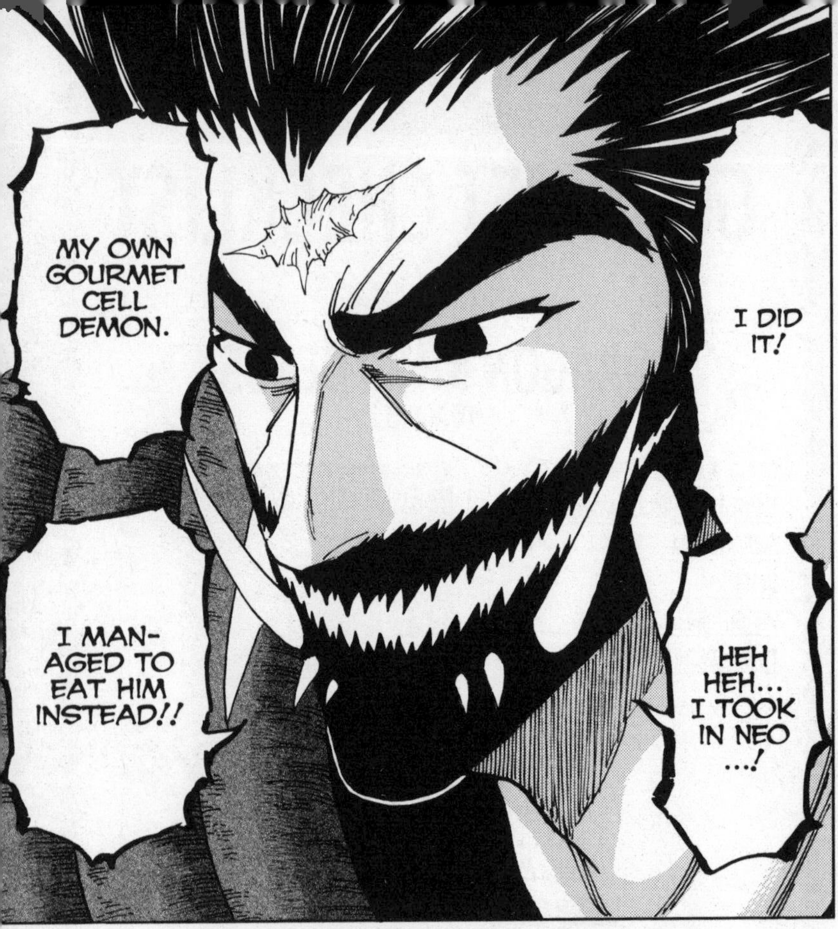
I DID IT!
HEH HEH... I TOOK IN NEO ...!
MY OWN GOURMET CELL DEMON.
I MANAGED TO EAT HIM INSTEAD!!

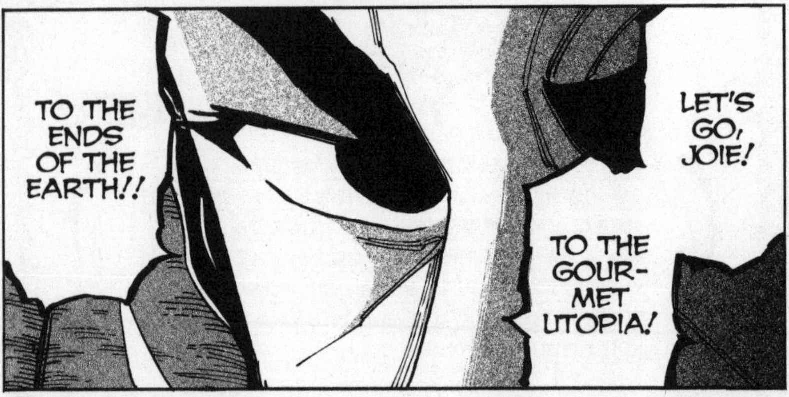
LET'S GO, JOIE!
TO THE GOURMET UTOPIA!
TO THE ENDS OF THE EARTH!!

TORIKO

GOURMET CHECKLIST

Vol. 417

DRAGON KING: DEROS
(DRAGON)

CAPTURE LEVEL: 6,590
HABITAT: GOURMET WORLD, AREA 1
SIZE: 4,000 M
HEIGHT: ---
WEIGHT: 80,000,000 TONS
PRICE: UNKNOWN

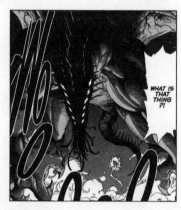

WHAT IS THAT THING ?!

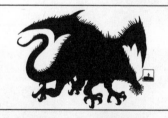

SCALE

ONE OF THE EIGHT KINGS WHO RULES ONE OF THE MAJOR CONTINENTS IN THE GOURMET WORLD. IT'S THE MOST VIOLENT OF ALL THE DRAGONS IN THE GOURMET WORLD. ALL OF THE EIGHT KINGS POSSESS THEIR OWN UNIQUE ABILITIES THAT MAKE THEM POWERFUL, BUT THE DRAGON KING REIGNS SUPREME. ITS FANGS ARE MADE OF THE STRONGEST MATERIAL ON EARTH AND IT CAN STORE AND RELEASE ITS ENERGY IN ITS MOUTH LIKE A LASER BEAM! THIS LASER CAN DESTROY ANY MATERIAL IN EXISTENCE.

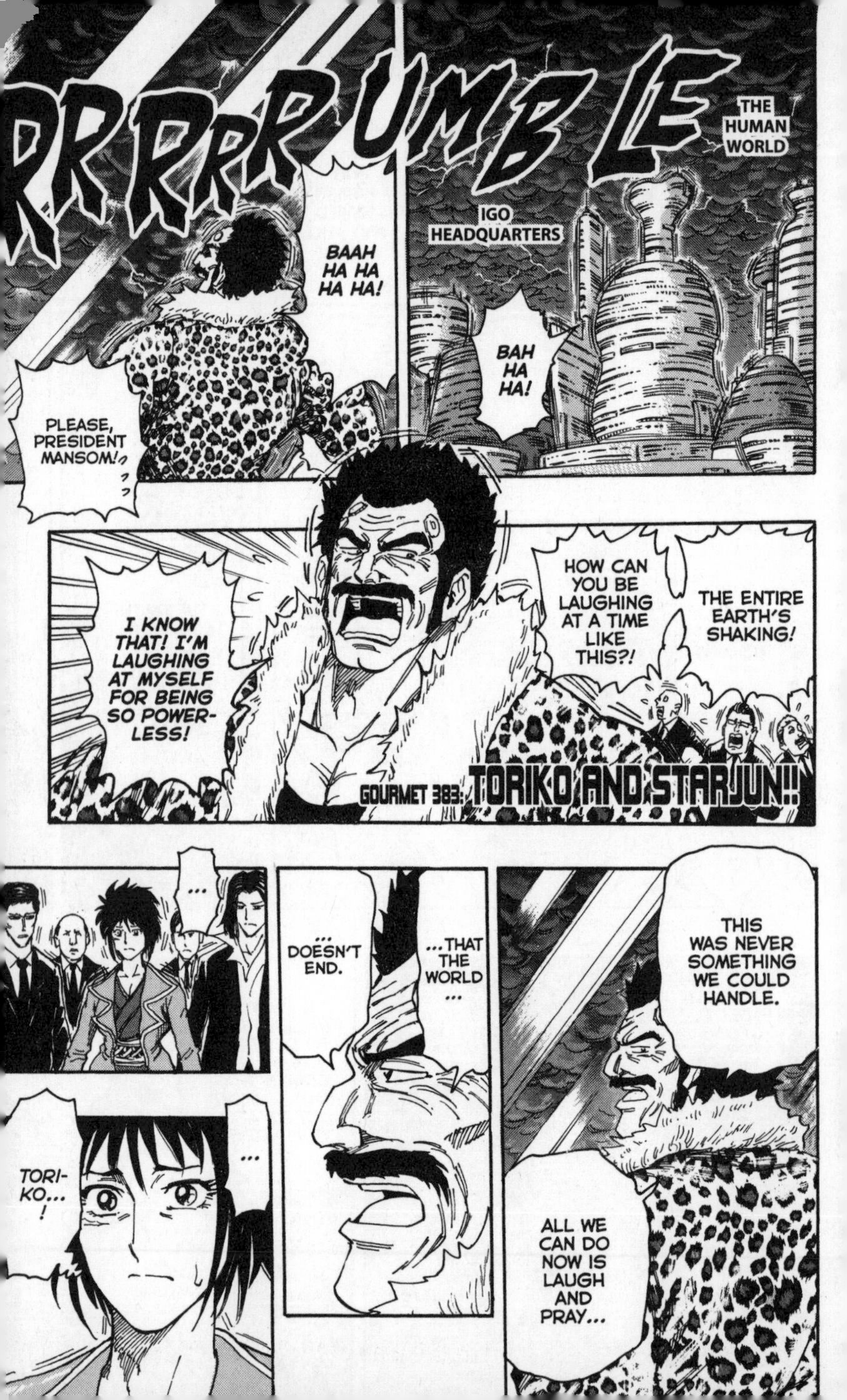
RRRRRUMBLE
THE HUMAN WORLD
IGO HEADQUARTERS
BAH HA HA!
BAAH HA HA HA HA!
PLEASE, PRESIDENT MANSOM!
THE ENTIRE EARTH'S SHAKING!
HOW CAN YOU BE LAUGHING AT A TIME LIKE THIS?!
I KNOW THAT! I'M LAUGHING AT MYSELF FOR BEING SO POWER-LESS!
GOURMET 383: TORIKO AND STARJUN!!
THIS WAS NEVER SOMETHING WE COULD HANDLE.
ALL WE CAN DO NOW IS LAUGH AND PRAY...
...THAT THE WORLD...
...DOESN'T END.
...
...
TORI-KO...!

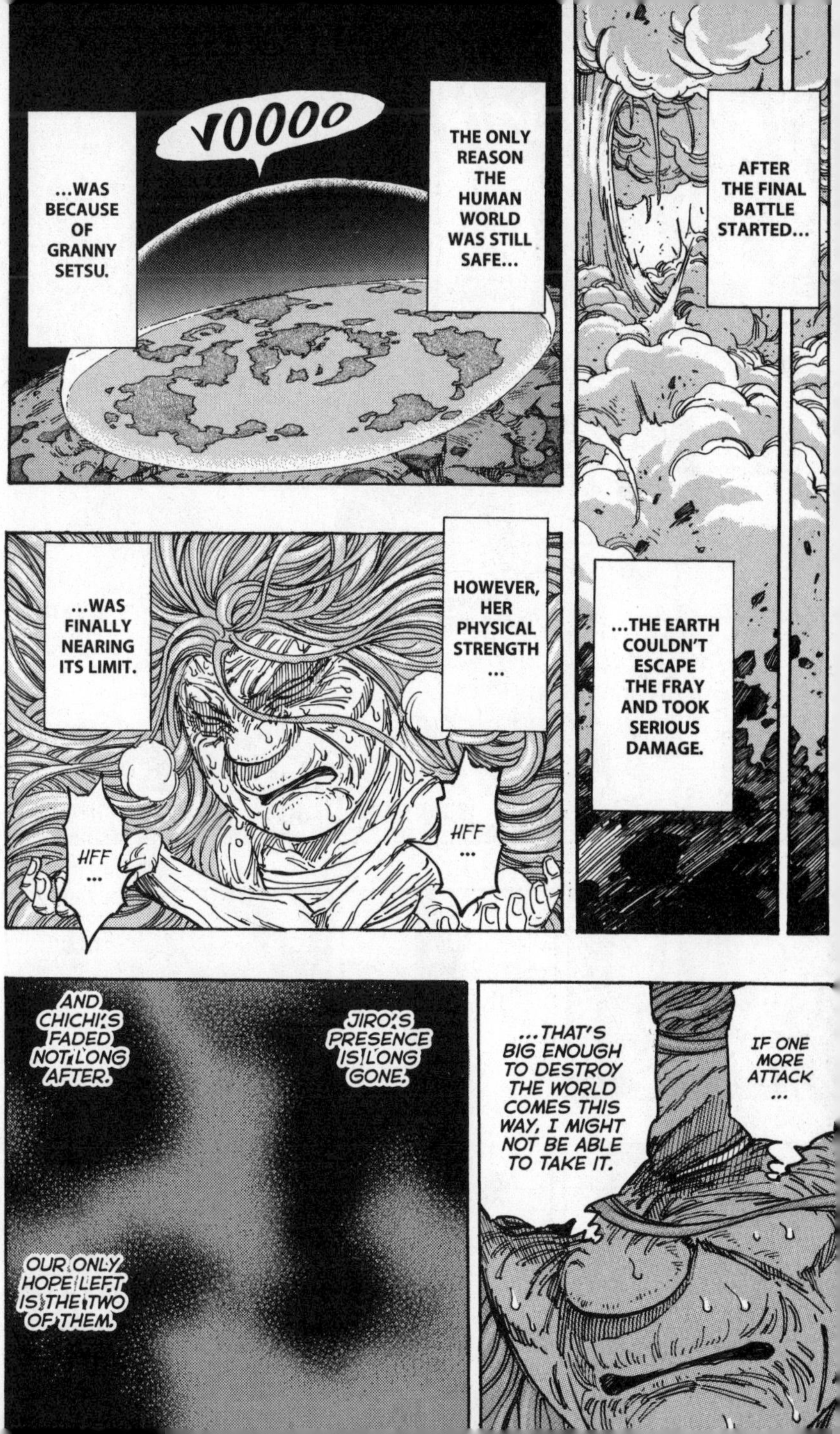
AFTER THE FINAL BATTLE STARTED...
...THE EARTH COULDN'T ESCAPE THE FRAY AND TOOK SERIOUS DAMAGE.
VOOOO
THE ONLY REASON THE HUMAN WORLD WAS STILL SAFE...
...WAS BECAUSE OF GRANNY SETSU.
HOWEVER, HER PHYSICAL STRENGTH...
...WAS FINALLY NEARING ITS LIMIT.
HFF...
HFF...
IF ONE MORE ATTACK...
...THAT'S BIG ENOUGH TO DESTROY THE WORLD COMES THIS WAY, I MIGHT NOT BE ABLE TO TAKE IT.
JIRO'S PRESENCE IS LONG GONE.
AND CHICHI'S FADED NOT LONG AFTER.
OUR ONLY HOPE LEFT IS THE TWO OF THEM.

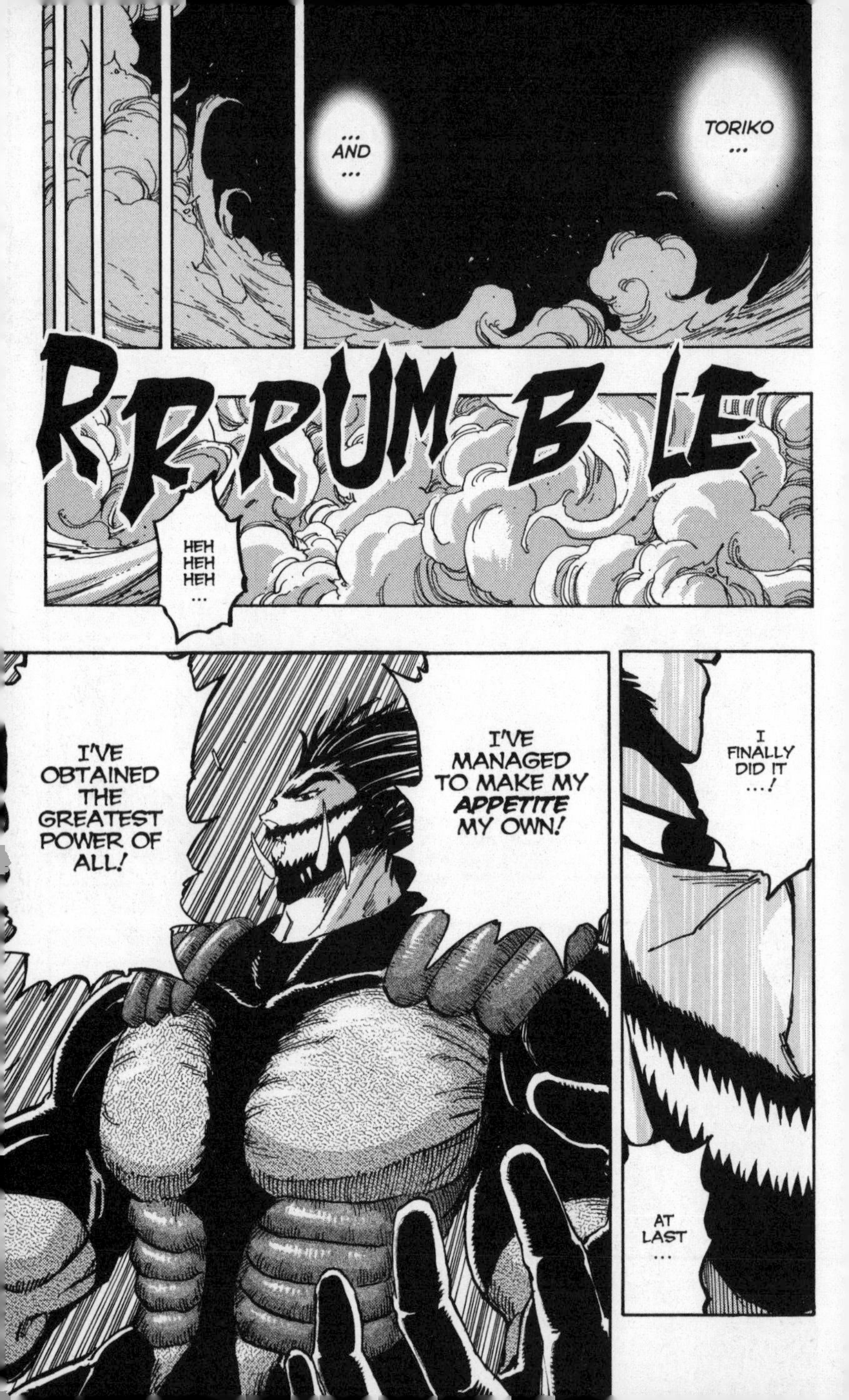
TORIKO ...
... AND ...
RRRUMBLE
HEH HEH HEH ...
I FINALLY DID IT ...!
AT LAST ...
I'VE MANAGED TO MAKE MY *APPETITE* MY OWN!
I'VE OBTAINED THE GREATEST POWER OF ALL!

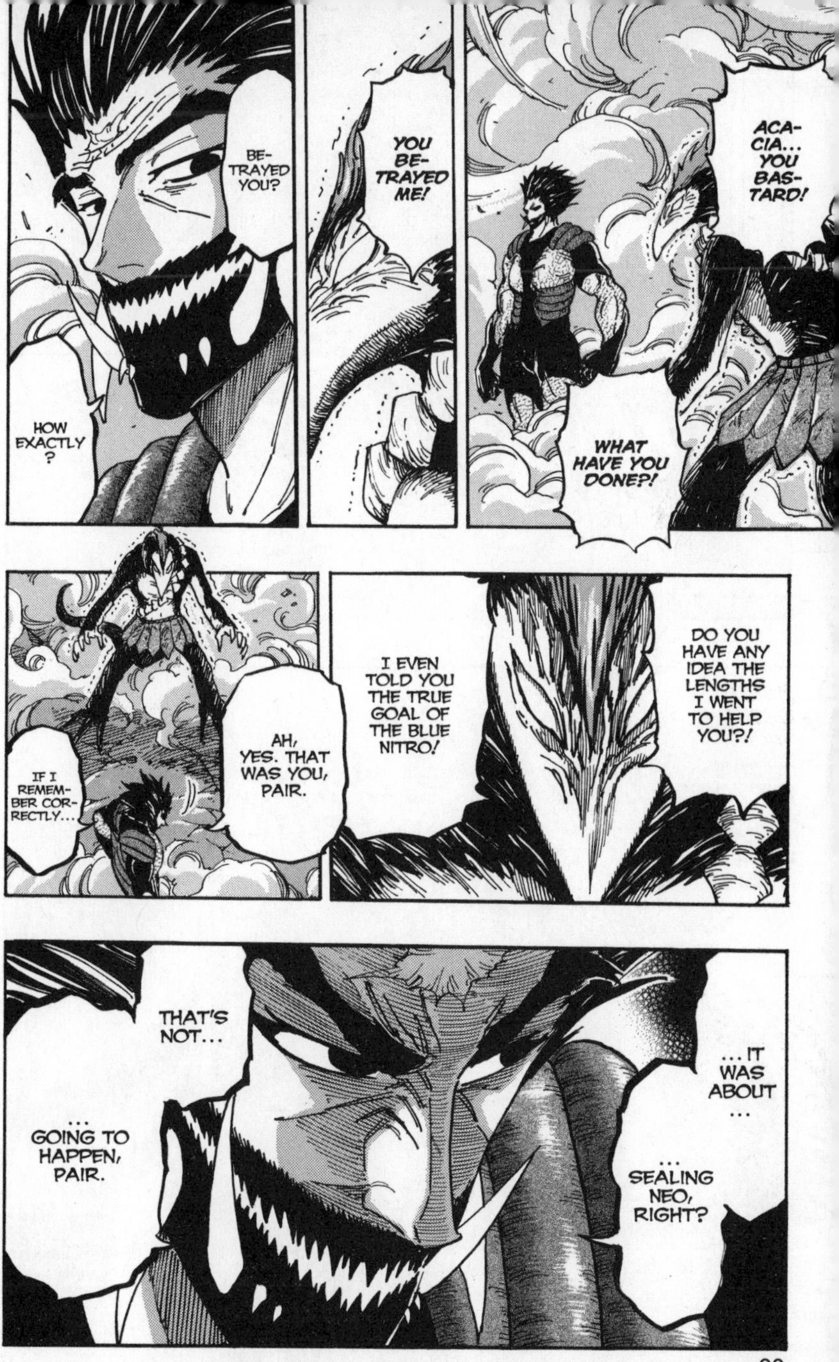
ACA-CIA... YOU BAS-TARD!
WHAT HAVE YOU DONE?!
YOU BE-TRAYED ME!
BE-TRAYED YOU?
HOW EXACTLY?
DO YOU HAVE ANY IDEA THE LENGTHS I WENT TO HELP YOU?!
I EVEN TOLD YOU THE TRUE GOAL OF THE BLUE NITRO!
AH, YES. THAT WAS YOU, PAIR.
IF I REMEM-BER COR-RECTLY...
...IT WAS ABOUT...
...SEALING NEO, RIGHT?
THAT'S NOT...
...GOING TO HAPPEN, PAIR.

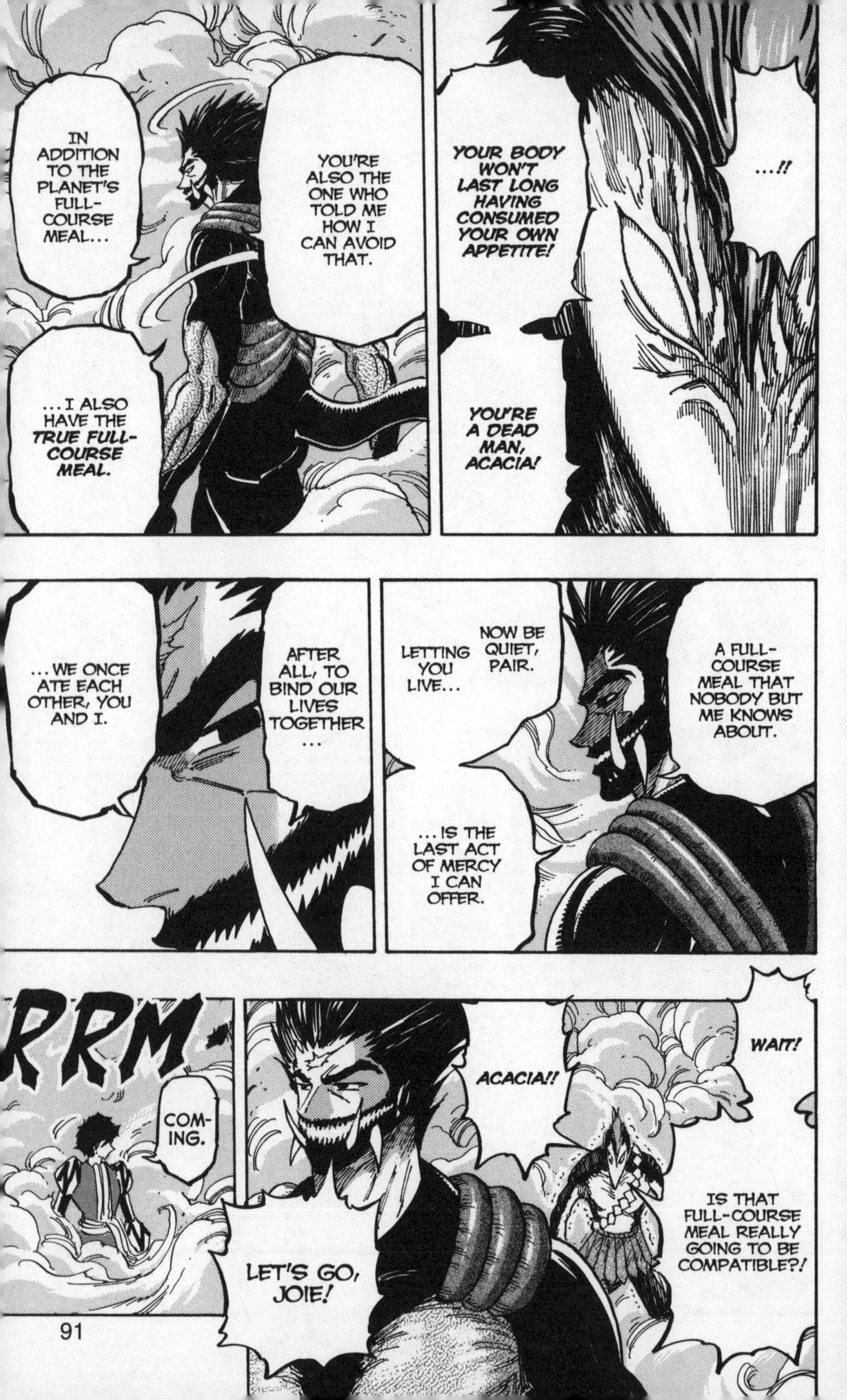
...!!
YOUR BODY WON'T LAST LONG HAVING CONSUMED YOUR OWN APPETITE!
YOU'RE A DEAD MAN, ACACIA!
YOU'RE ALSO THE ONE WHO TOLD ME HOW I CAN AVOID THAT.
IN ADDITION TO THE PLANET'S FULL-COURSE MEAL...
...I ALSO HAVE THE TRUE FULL-COURSE MEAL.
A FULL-COURSE MEAL THAT NOBODY BUT ME KNOWS ABOUT.
NOW BE QUIET, PAIR.
LETTING YOU LIVE...
...IS THE LAST ACT OF MERCY I CAN OFFER.
AFTER ALL, TO BIND OUR LIVES TOGETHER...
...WE ONCE ATE EACH OTHER, YOU AND I.
WAIT!
ACACIA!!
IS THAT FULL-COURSE MEAL REALLY GOING TO BE COMPATIBLE?!
LET'S GO, JOIE!
RRM
COMING.

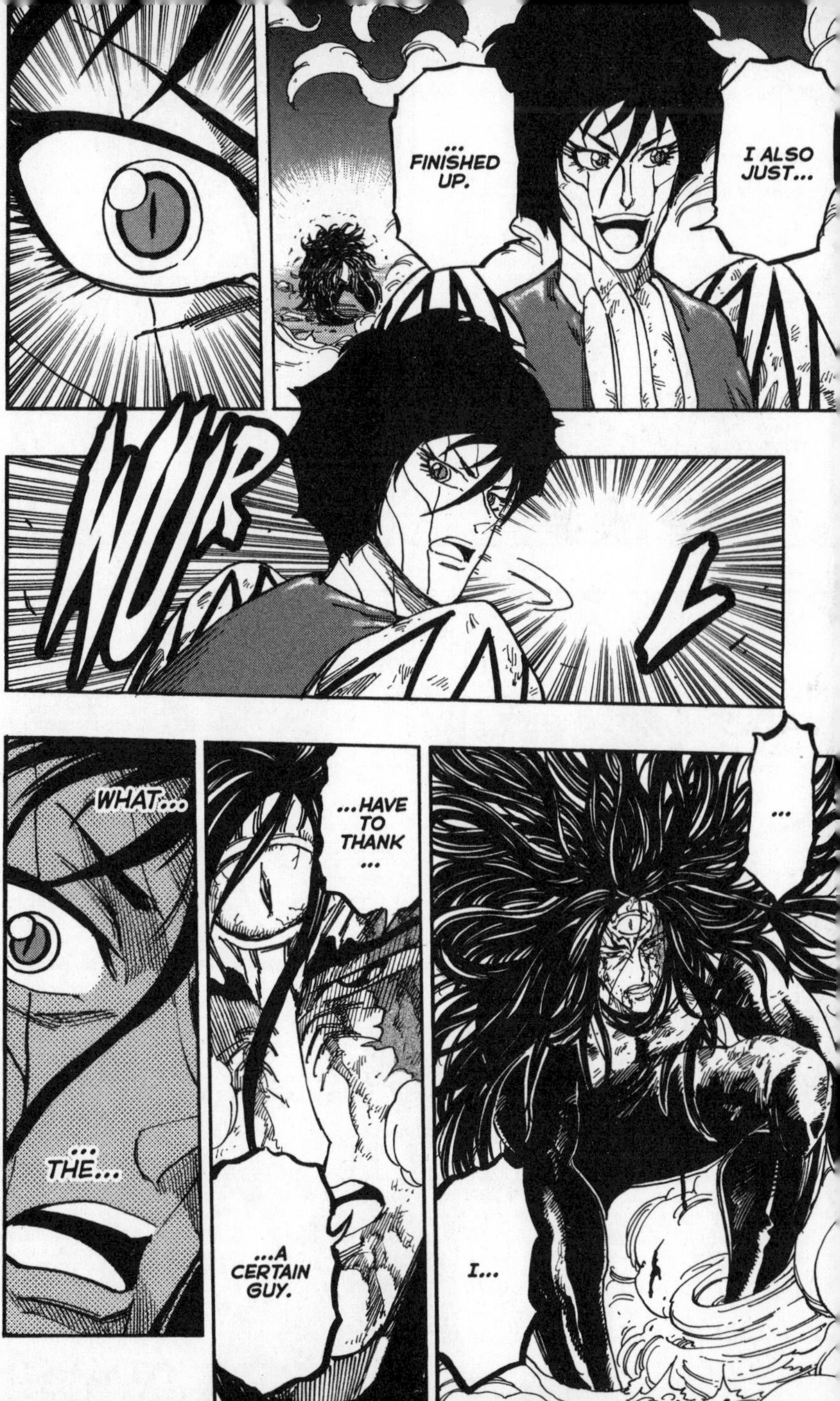
I ALSO JUST...
... FINISHED UP.
...
I...
...HAVE TO THANK ...
...A CERTAIN GUY.
WHAT...
... THE...

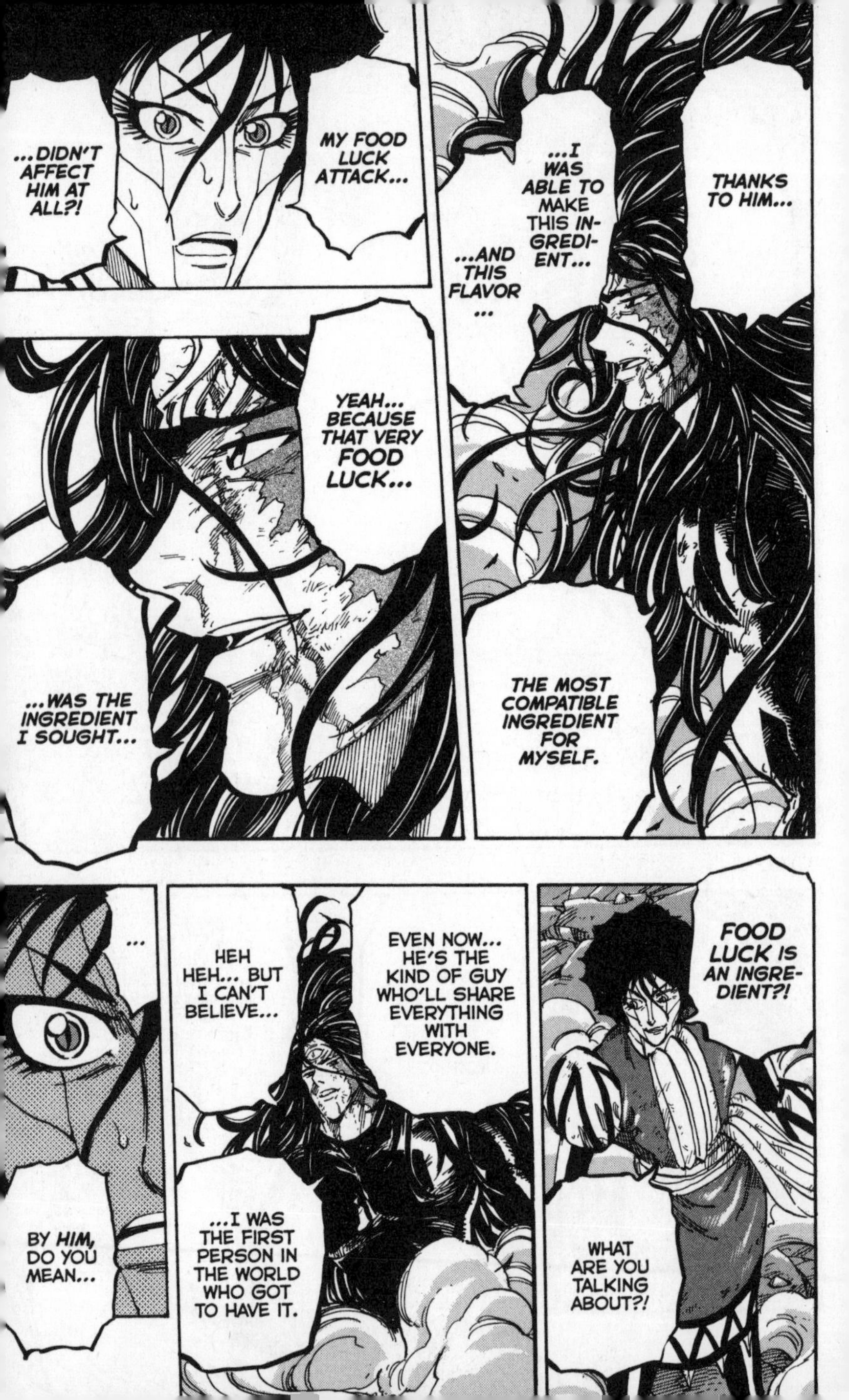
THANKS TO HIM...
...I WAS ABLE TO MAKE THIS INGREDIENT...
...AND THIS FLAVOR...
THE MOST COMPATIBLE INGREDIENT FOR MYSELF.
MY FOOD LUCK ATTACK...
...DIDN'T AFFECT HIM AT ALL?!
YEAH... BECAUSE THAT VERY FOOD LUCK...
...WAS THE INGREDIENT I SOUGHT...
FOOD LUCK IS AN INGREDIENT?!
WHAT ARE YOU TALKING ABOUT?!
EVEN NOW... HE'S THE KIND OF GUY WHO'LL SHARE EVERYTHING WITH EVERYONE.
HEH HEH... BUT I CAN'T BELIEVE...
...I WAS THE FIRST PERSON IN THE WORLD WHO GOT TO HAVE IT.
...
BY HIM, DO YOU MEAN...

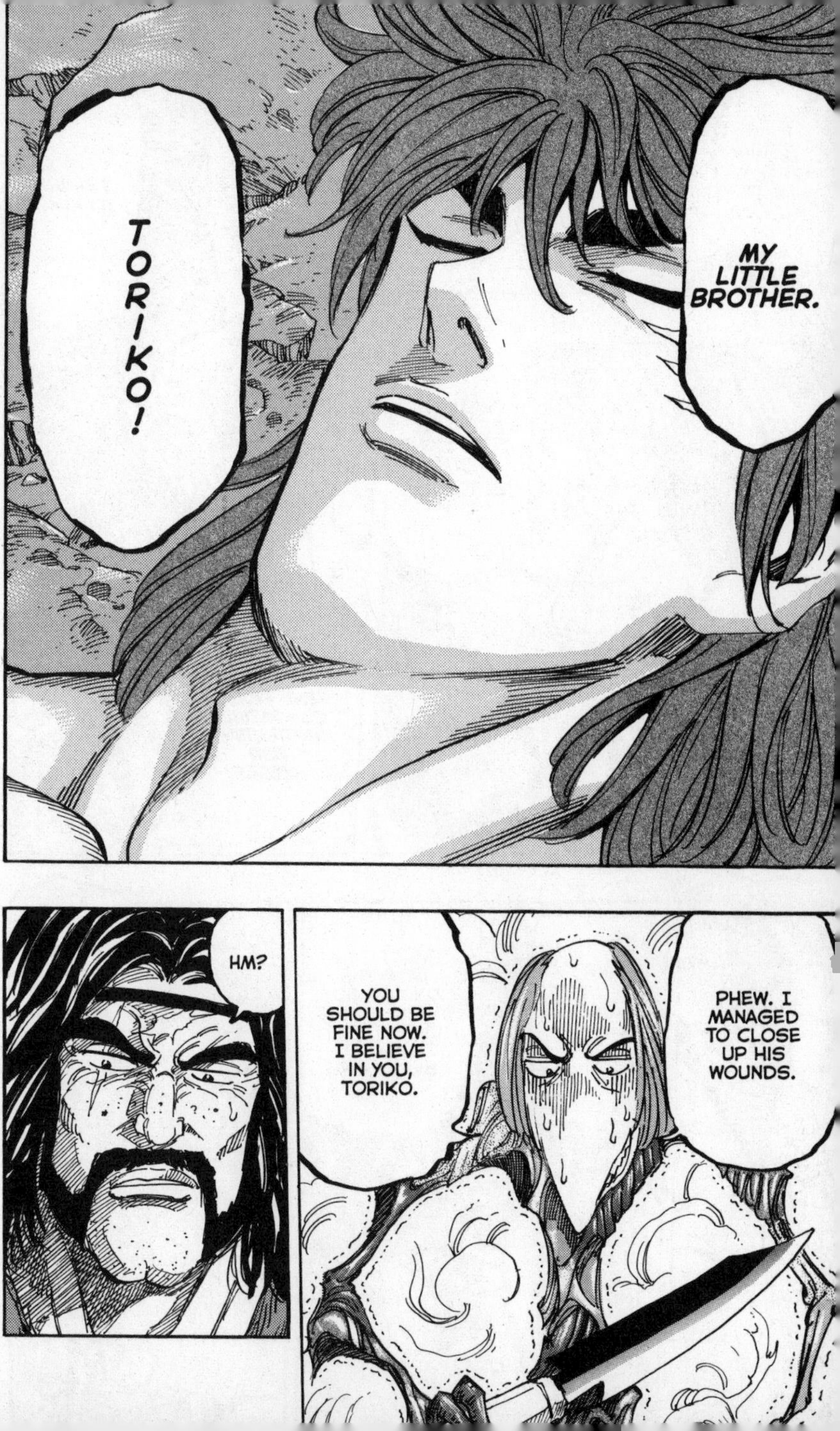
MY LITTLE BROTHER.
TORIKO!
PHEW. I MANAGED TO CLOSE UP HIS WOUNDS.
YOU SHOULD BE FINE NOW. I BELIEVE IN YOU, TORIKO.
HM?

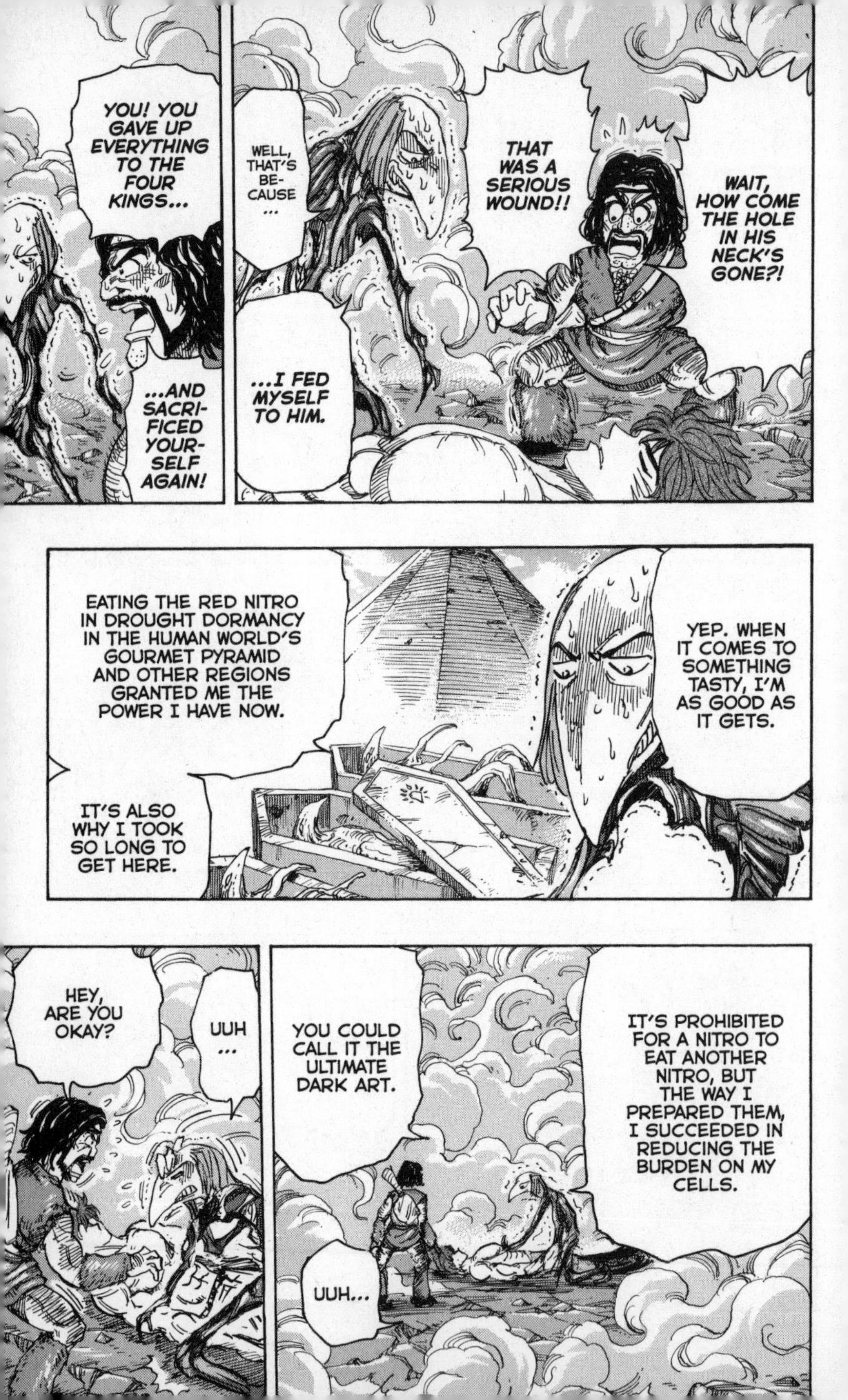
WAIT, HOW COME THE HOLE IN HIS NECK'S GONE?!
THAT WAS A SERIOUS WOUND!!
WELL, THAT'S BE-CAUSE ...
...I FED MYSELF TO HIM.
YOU! YOU GAVE UP EVERYTHING TO THE FOUR KINGS...
...AND SACRIFICED YOURSELF AGAIN!
YEP. WHEN IT COMES TO SOMETHING TASTY, I'M AS GOOD AS IT GETS.
EATING THE RED NITRO IN DROUGHT DORMANCY IN THE HUMAN WORLD'S GOURMET PYRAMID AND OTHER REGIONS GRANTED ME THE POWER I HAVE NOW.
IT'S ALSO WHY I TOOK SO LONG TO GET HERE.
IT'S PROHIBITED FOR A NITRO TO EAT ANOTHER NITRO, BUT THE WAY I PREPARED THEM, I SUCCEEDED IN REDUCING THE BURDEN ON MY CELLS.
YOU COULD CALL IT THE ULTIMATE DARK ART.
UUH...
UUH ...
HEY, ARE YOU OKAY?

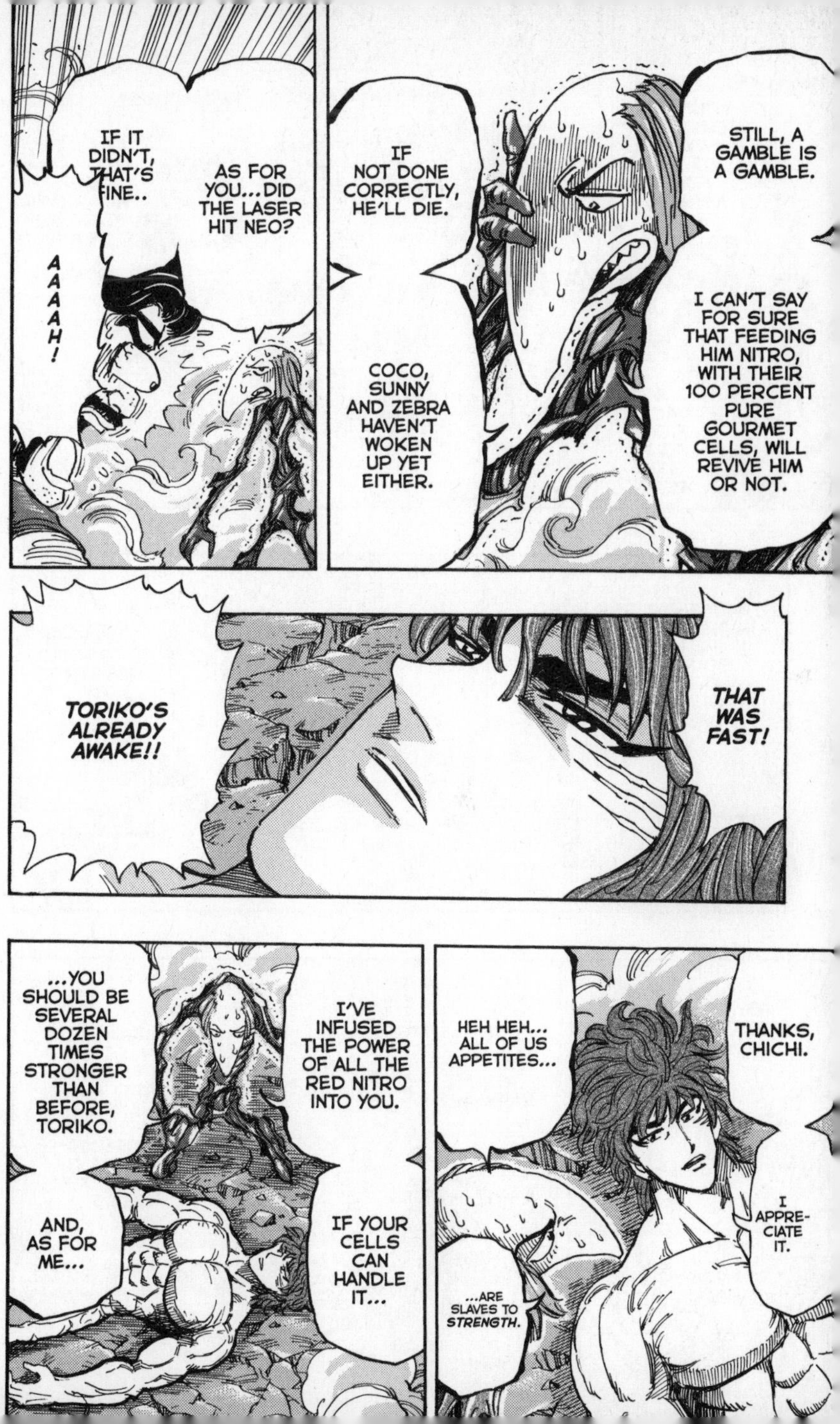
STILL, A GAMBLE IS A GAMBLE.
I CAN'T SAY FOR SURE THAT FEEDING HIM NITRO, WITH THEIR 100 PERCENT PURE GOURMET CELLS, WILL REVIVE HIM OR NOT.
IF NOT DONE CORRECTLY, HE'LL DIE.
COCO, SUNNY AND ZEBRA HAVEN'T WOKEN UP YET EITHER.
AS FOR YOU...DID THE LASER HIT NEO?
IF IT DIDN'T, THAT'S FINE..
AAAAAH!
THAT WAS FAST!
TORIKO'S ALREADY AWAKE!!
THANKS, CHICHI.
HEH HEH... ALL OF US APPETITES...
I APPRECIATE IT.
...ARE SLAVES TO STRENGTH.
I'VE INFUSED THE POWER OF ALL THE RED NITRO INTO YOU.
...YOU SHOULD BE SEVERAL DOZEN TIMES STRONGER THAN BEFORE, TORIKO.
IF YOUR CELLS CAN HANDLE IT...
AND, AS FOR ME...

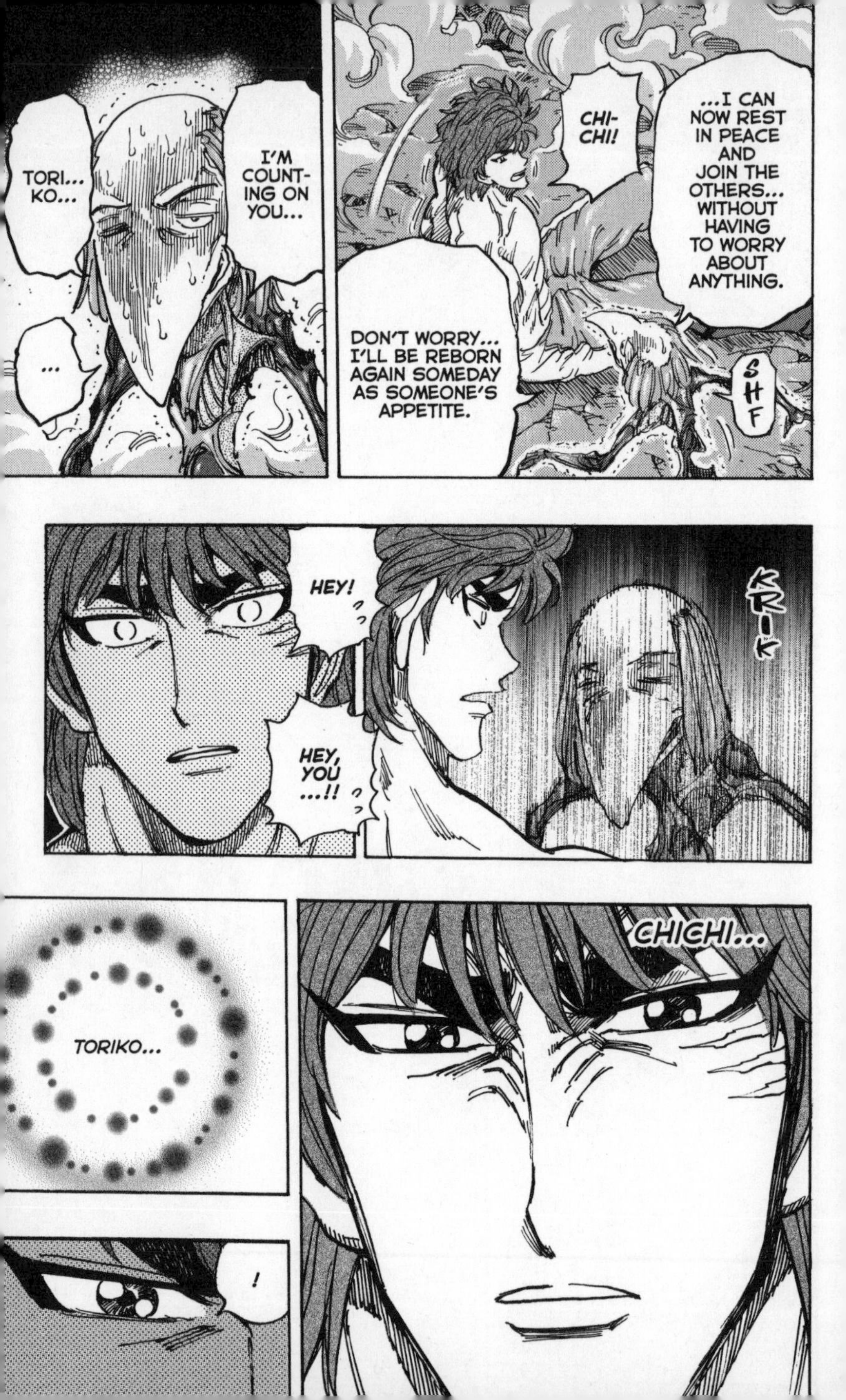
...I CAN NOW REST IN PEACE AND JOIN THE OTHERS... WITHOUT HAVING TO WORRY ABOUT ANYTHING.
CHI-CHI!
SHF
DON'T WORRY... I'LL BE REBORN AGAIN SOMEDAY AS SOMEONE'S APPETITE.
I'M COUNTING ON YOU...
TORI... KO...
...
KRIK
HEY!
HEY, YOU ...!!
CHICHI...
TORIKO...
!

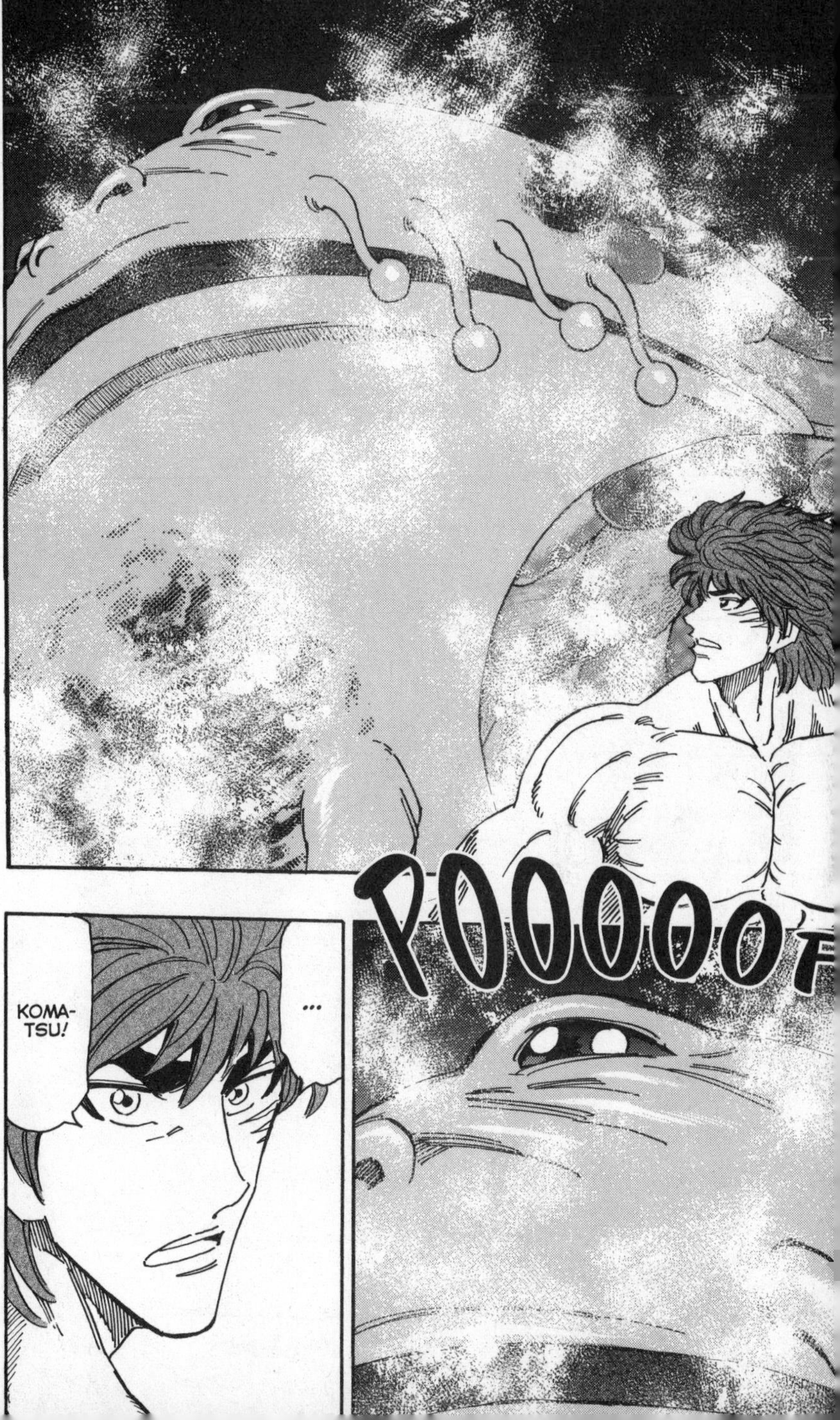
POOOOOF
...
KOMA-TSU!

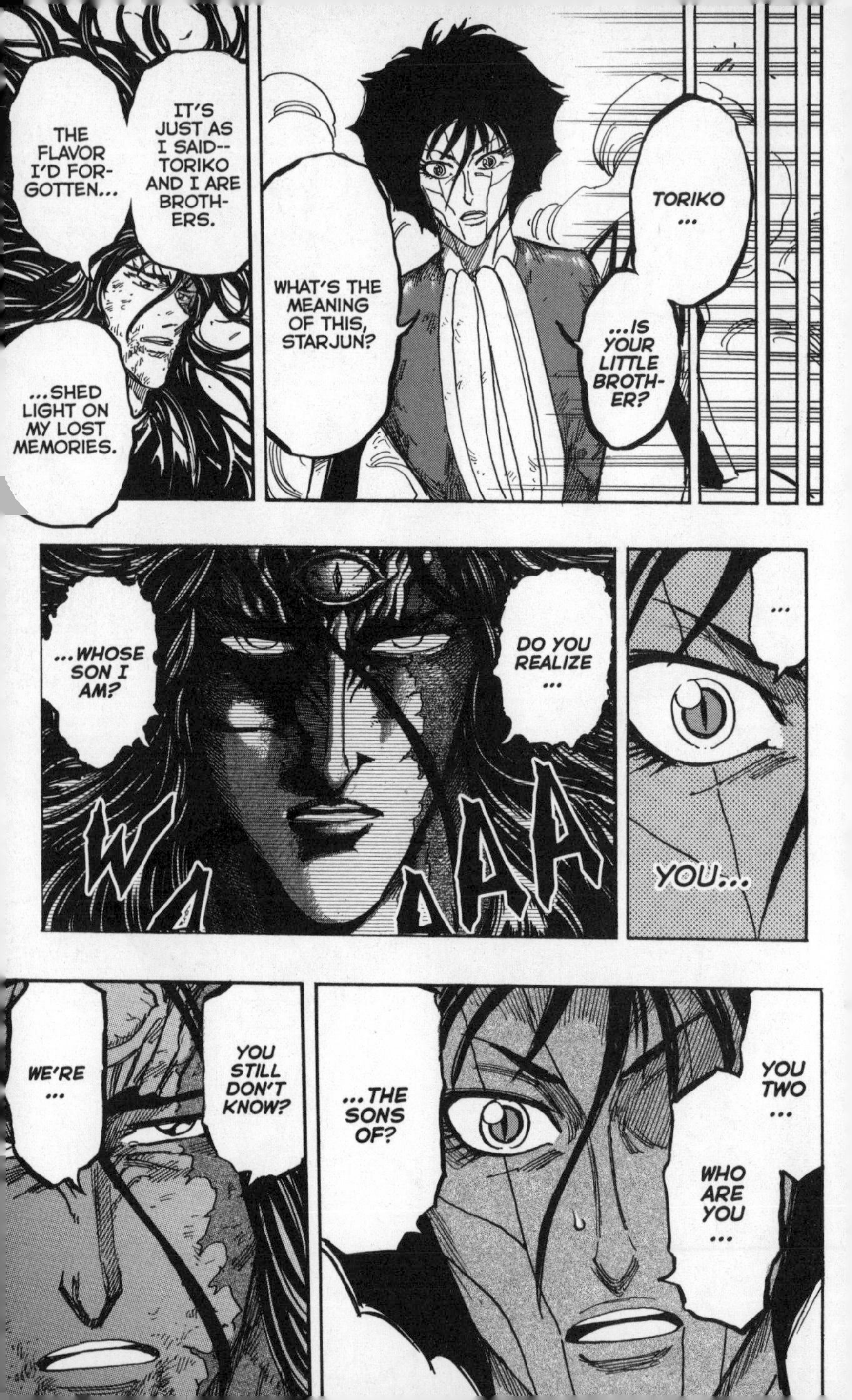
TORIKO ...
...IS YOUR LITTLE BROTHER?
WHAT'S THE MEANING OF THIS, STARJUN?
IT'S JUST AS I SAID-- TORIKO AND I ARE BROTHERS.
THE FLAVOR I'D FORGOTTEN...
...SHED LIGHT ON MY LOST MEMORIES.
...
YOU...
DO YOU REALIZE ...
...WHOSE SON I AM?
WAAA
YOU TWO ...
WHO ARE YOU ...
...THE SONS OF?
YOU STILL DON'T KNOW?
WE'RE ...

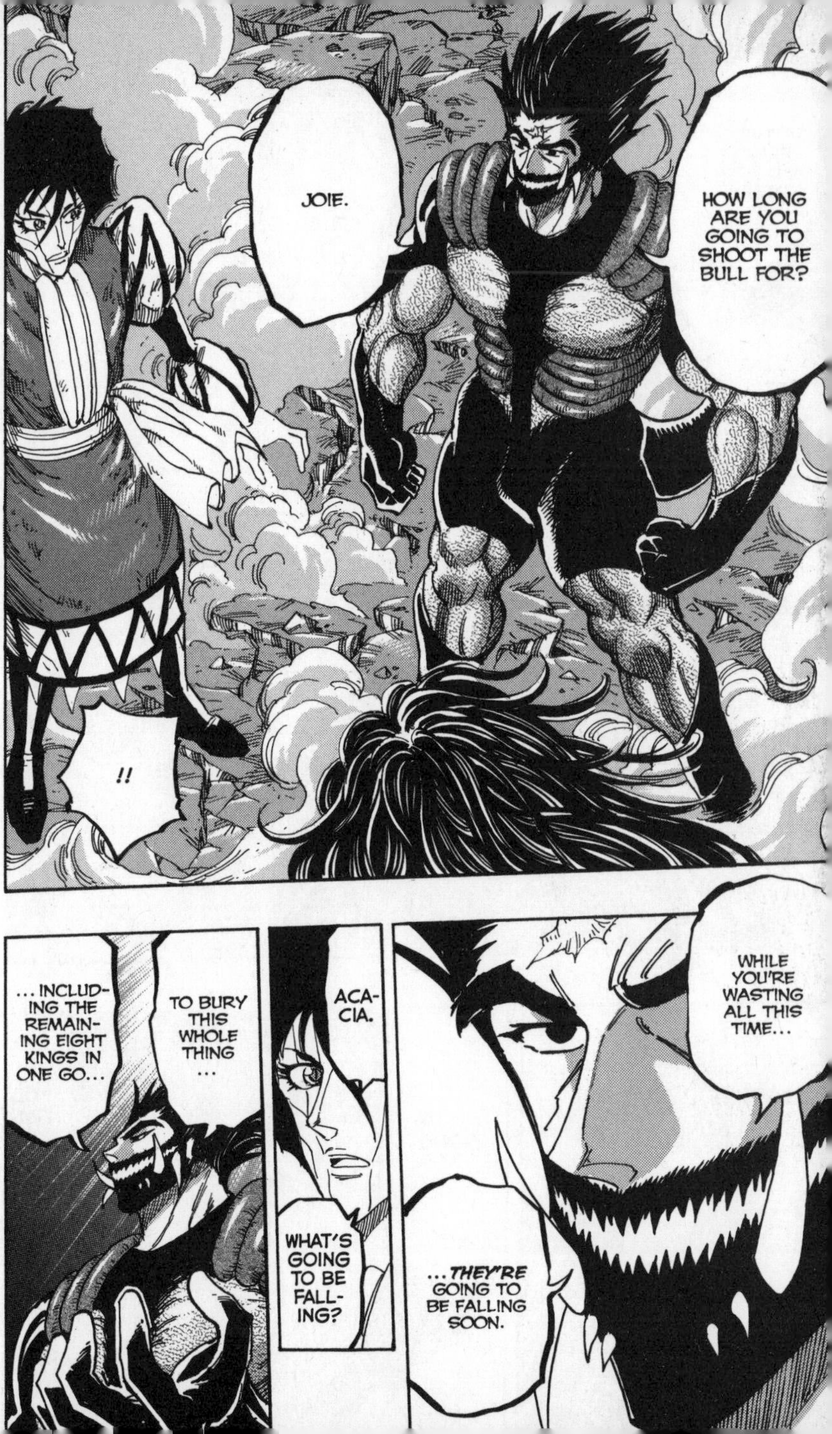

HOW LONG ARE YOU GOING TO SHOOT THE BULL FOR?
JOIE.
!!
WHILE YOU'RE WASTING ALL THIS TIME...
...*THEY'RE* GOING TO BE FALLING SOON.
ACACIA.
WHAT'S GOING TO BE FALLING?
TO BURY THIS WHOLE THING...
...INCLUDING THE REMAINING EIGHT KINGS IN ONE GO...

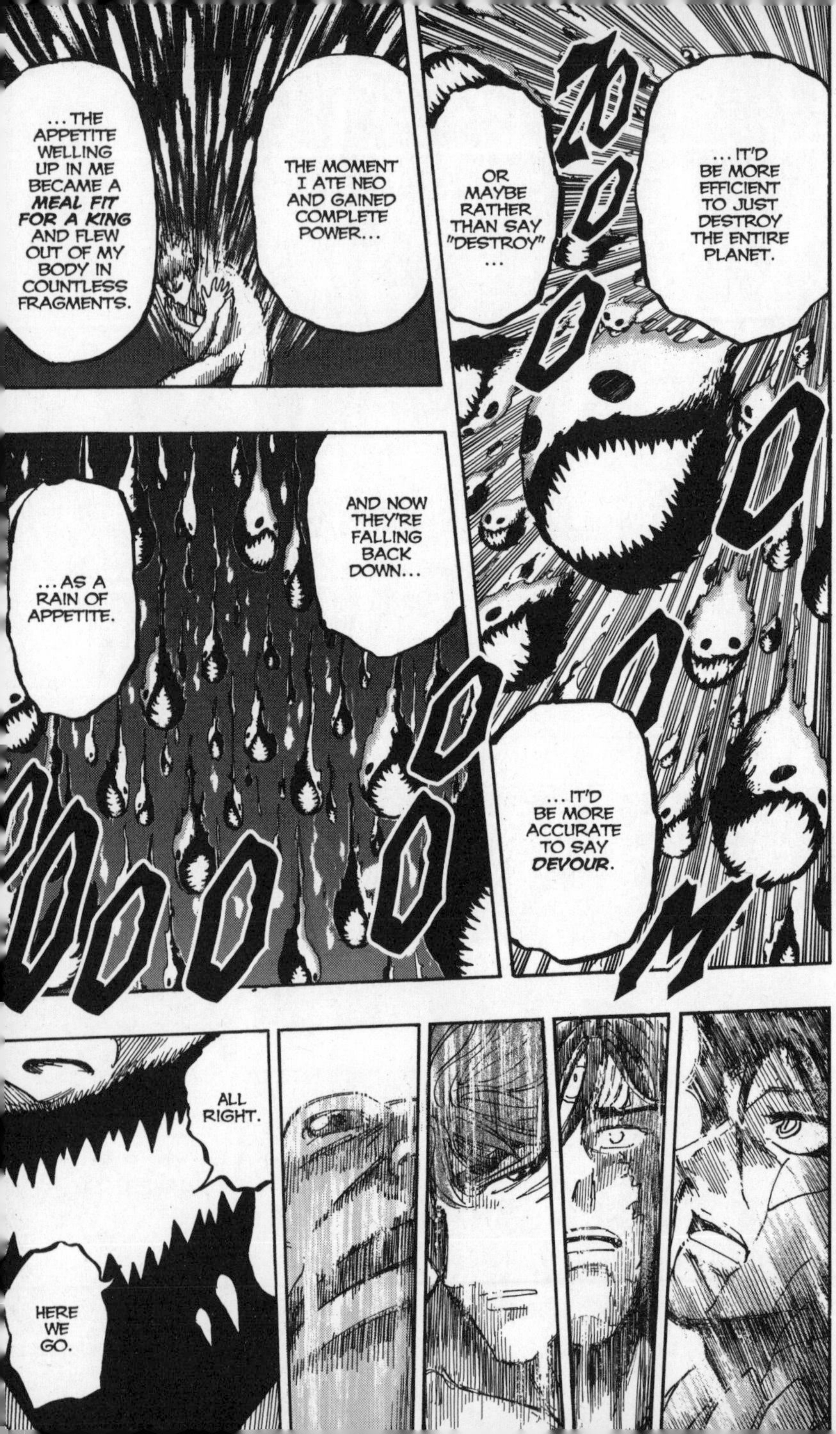
...IT'D BE MORE EFFICIENT TO JUST DESTROY THE ENTIRE PLANET.
OR MAYBE RATHER THAN SAY "DESTROY" ...
...IT'D BE MORE ACCURATE TO SAY *DEVOUR*.
ZOOOOOOOOOOOOOOOOM
THE MOMENT I ATE NEO AND GAINED COMPLETE POWER...
...THE APPETITE WELLING UP IN ME BECAME A ***MEAL FIT FOR A KING*** AND FLEW OUT OF MY BODY IN COUNTLESS FRAGMENTS.
AND NOW THEY'RE FALLING BACK DOWN...
...AS A RAIN OF APPETITE.
ALL RIGHT.
HERE WE GO.

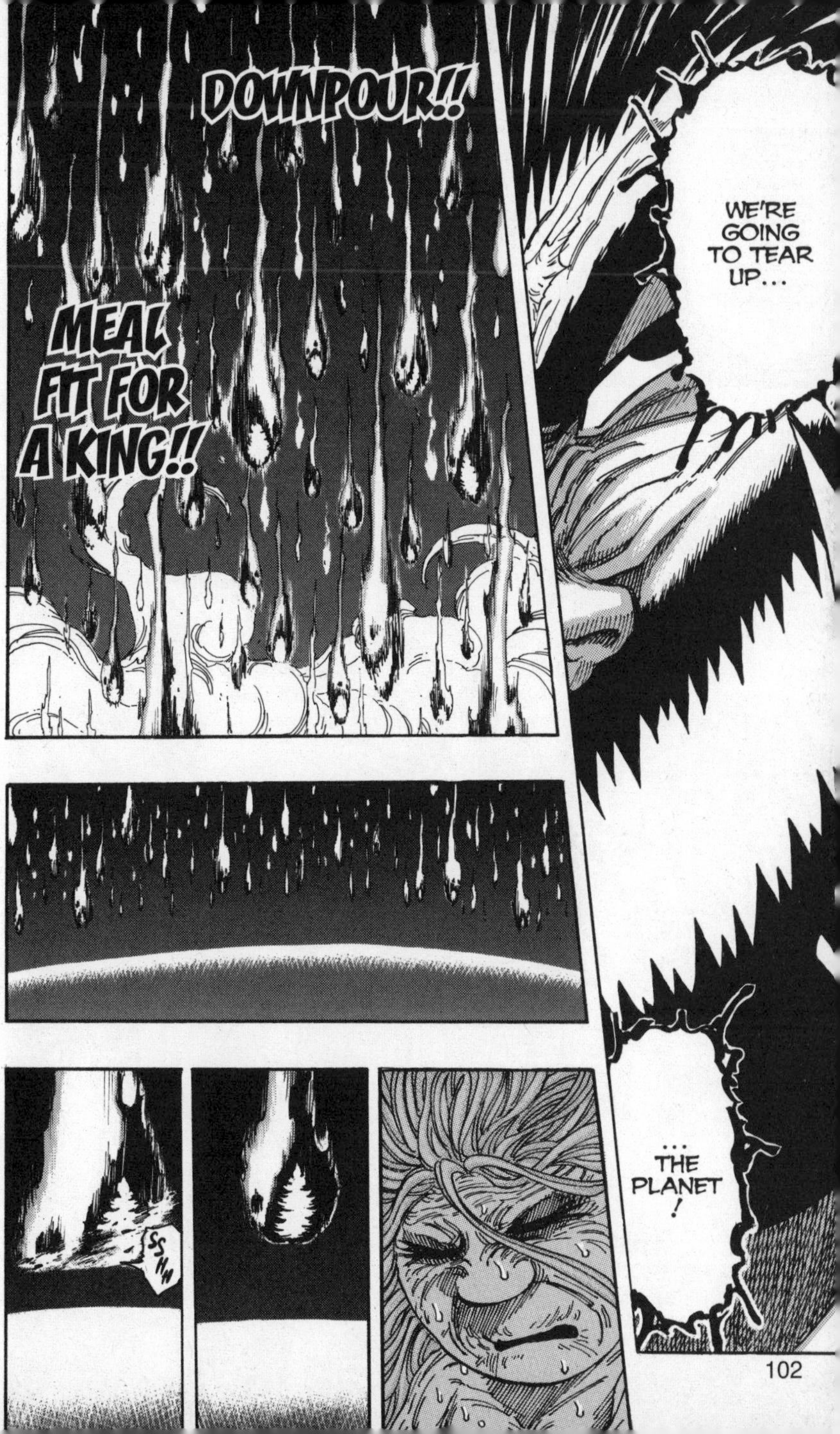
WE'RE GOING TO TEAR UP...
...THE PLANET!
DOWNPOUR!!
MEAL FIT FOR A KING!!
SSHH

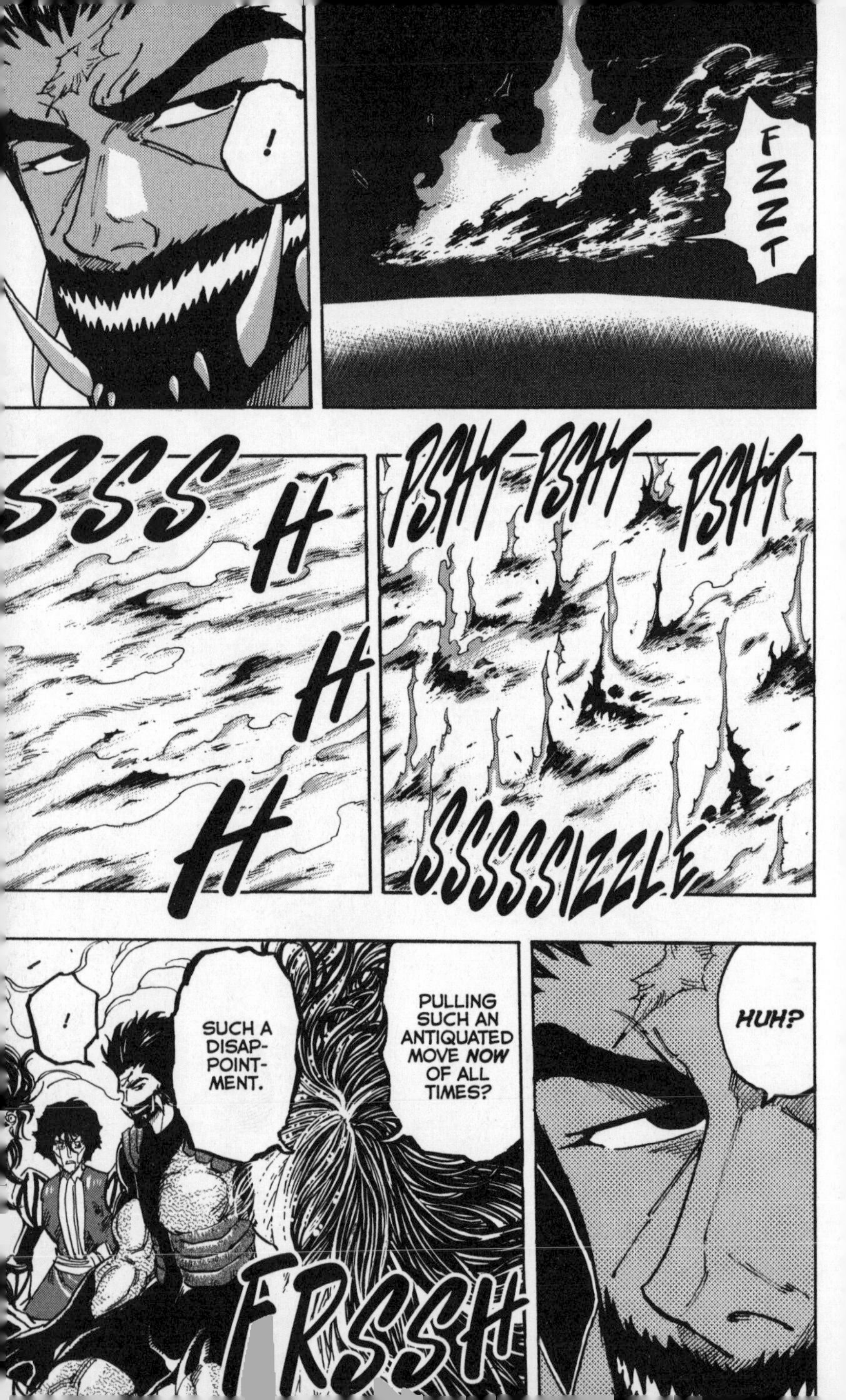
FZZT
!
PSHT PSHT PSHT
SSSSIZZLE
SSSHHH
HUH?
PULLING SUCH AN ANTIQUATED MOVE *NOW* OF ALL TIMES?
SUCH A DISAPPOINTMENT.
!
FRSSH

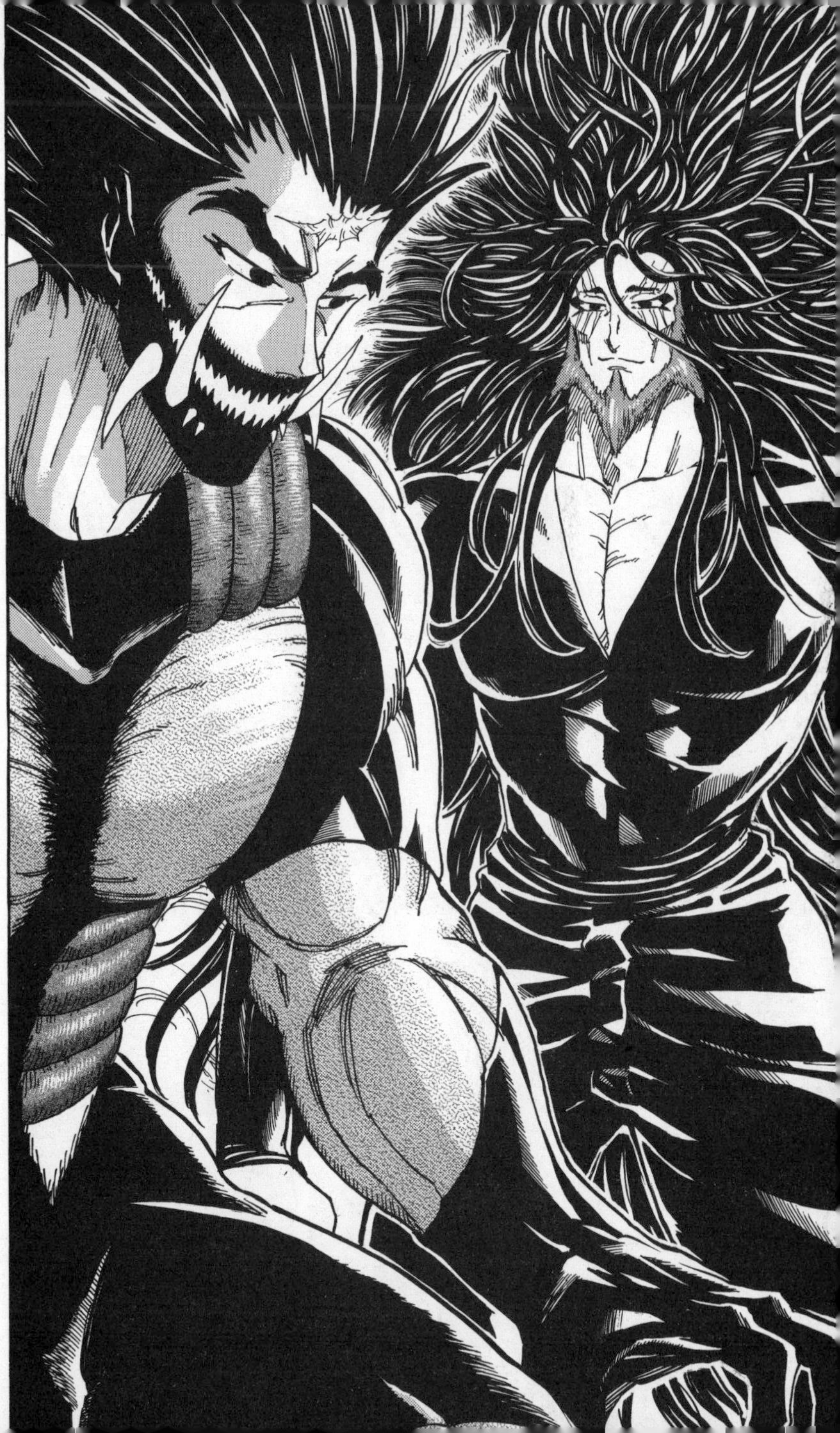

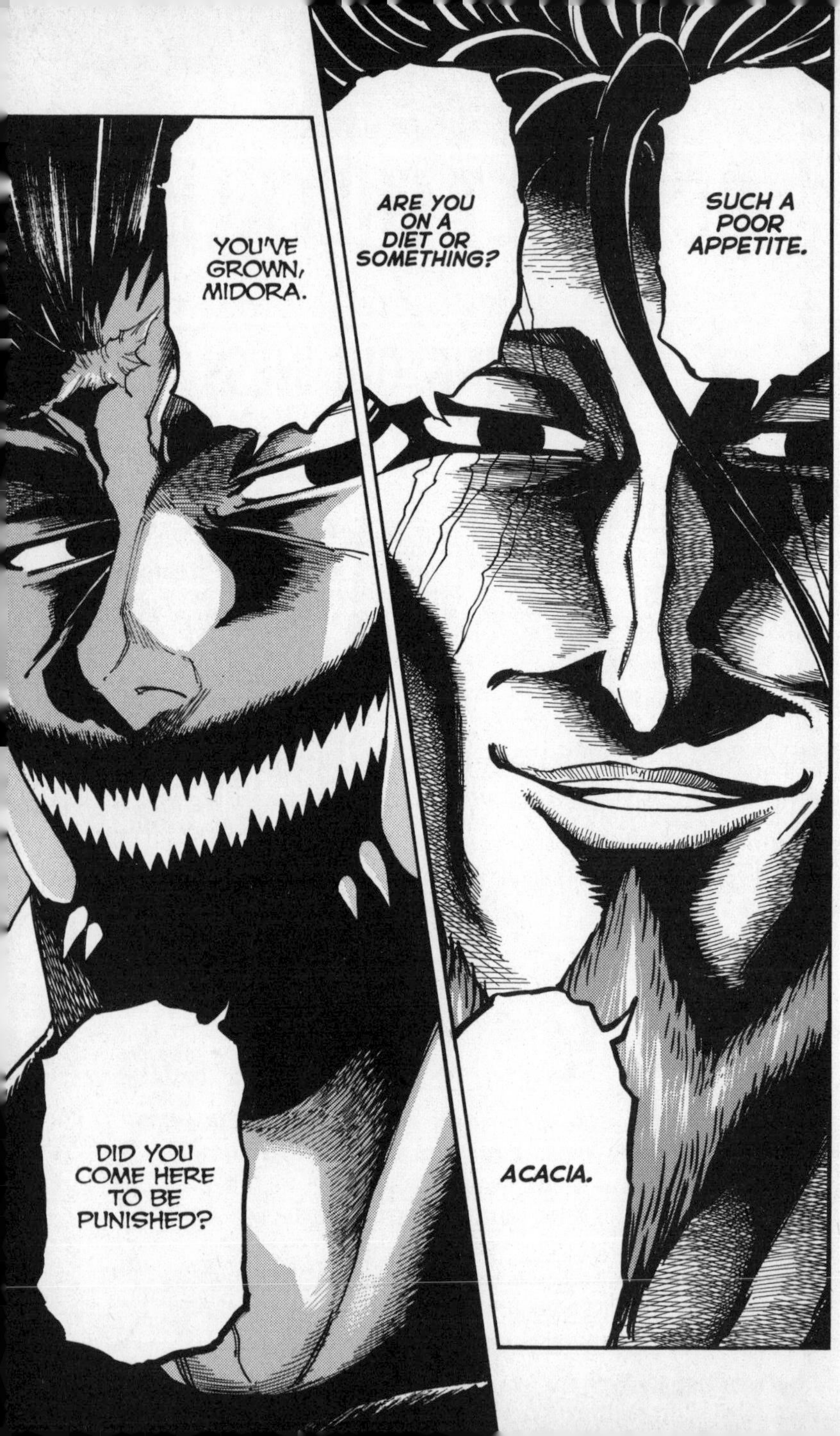
SUCH A POOR APPETITE.
ARE YOU ON A DIET OR SOMETHING?
ACACIA.
YOU'VE GROWN, MIDORA.
DID YOU COME HERE TO BE PUNISHED?

TORIKO

GOURMET CHECKLIST

Vol. 418

WOLF KING: GUINNESS
(BATTLE WOLF)

CAPTURE LEVEL: 6,550
HABITAT: GOURMET WORLD, AREA 2
SIZE: 100 M
HEIGHT: 55 M
WEIGHT: 20,000 TONS
PRICE: UNKNOWN

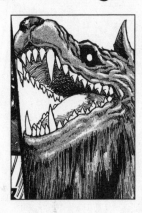

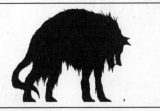

SCALE

ONE OF THE EIGHT KINGS WHO RULES ONE OF THE MAJOR CONTINENTS IN THE GOURMET WORLD. THIS ONE IN PARTICULAR EXCELS IN COMBAT AND IS THE ALPHA MALE WHO COMMANDS ALL OF THE BATTLE WOLVES. HIS COMBAT ABILITY IS WELL-BALANCED BETWEEN OFFENSE, DEFENSE AND AGILITY AND HE PROBABLY HAS THE MOST BATTLE EXPERIENCE OUT OF ANY OF THE EIGHT KINGS. IN ADDITION TO STOMPING ON AND BITING ITS PREY, IT CAN ALSO GATHER DATA ON ITS TARGETS THROUGH SMELL AND USES KNOCKING ABILITIES TO KNOCK OUT TARGETS. ITS SPECIAL SENSE OF SMELL ALLOWS IT TO EFFECTIVELY COMMUNICATE INFORMATION TO THE REST OF ITS PACK.

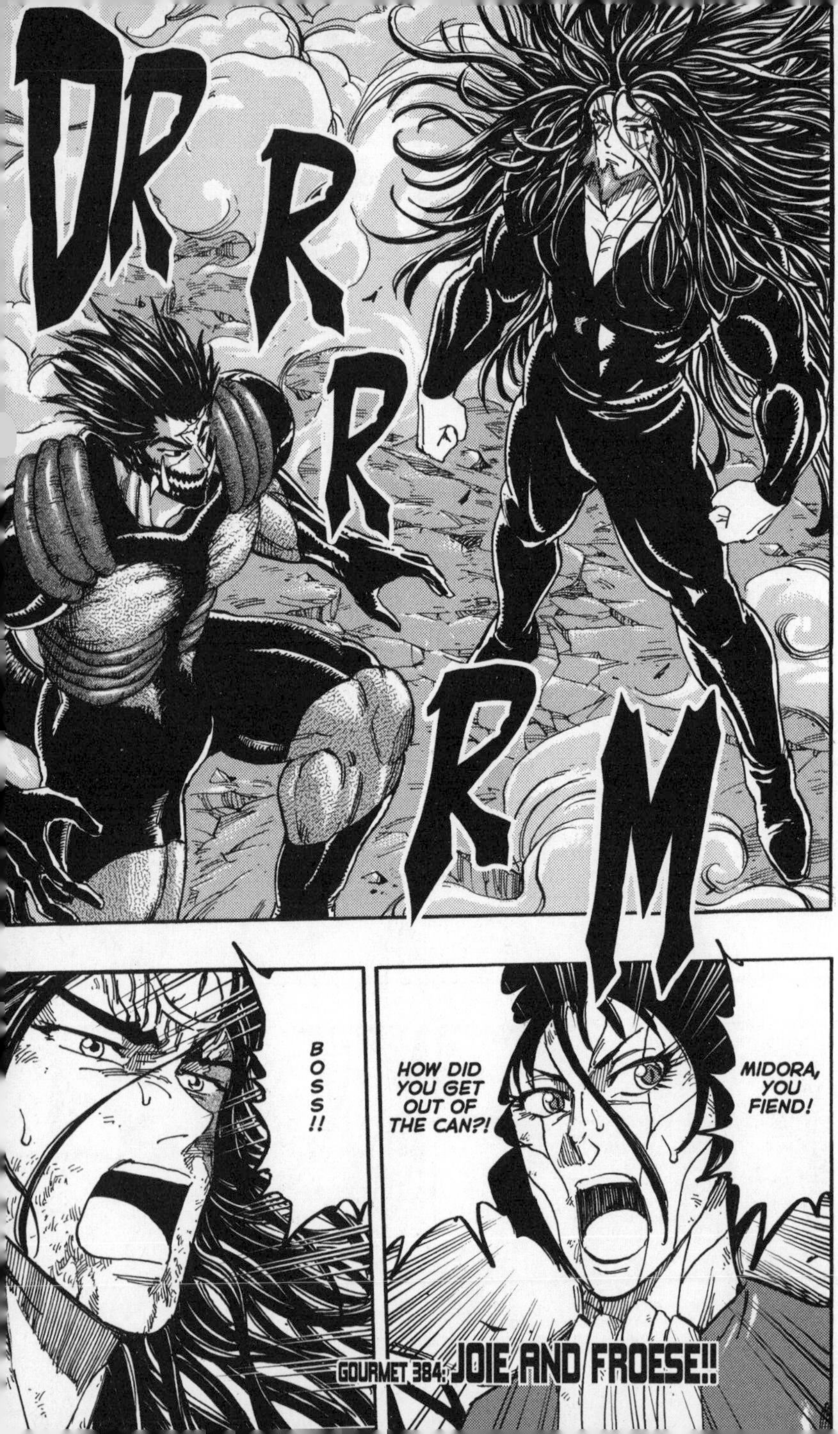
DRRRRM
MIDORA, YOU FIEND!
HOW DID YOU GET OUT OF THE CAN?!
BOSS!!
GOURMET 384: JOIE AND FROESE!!

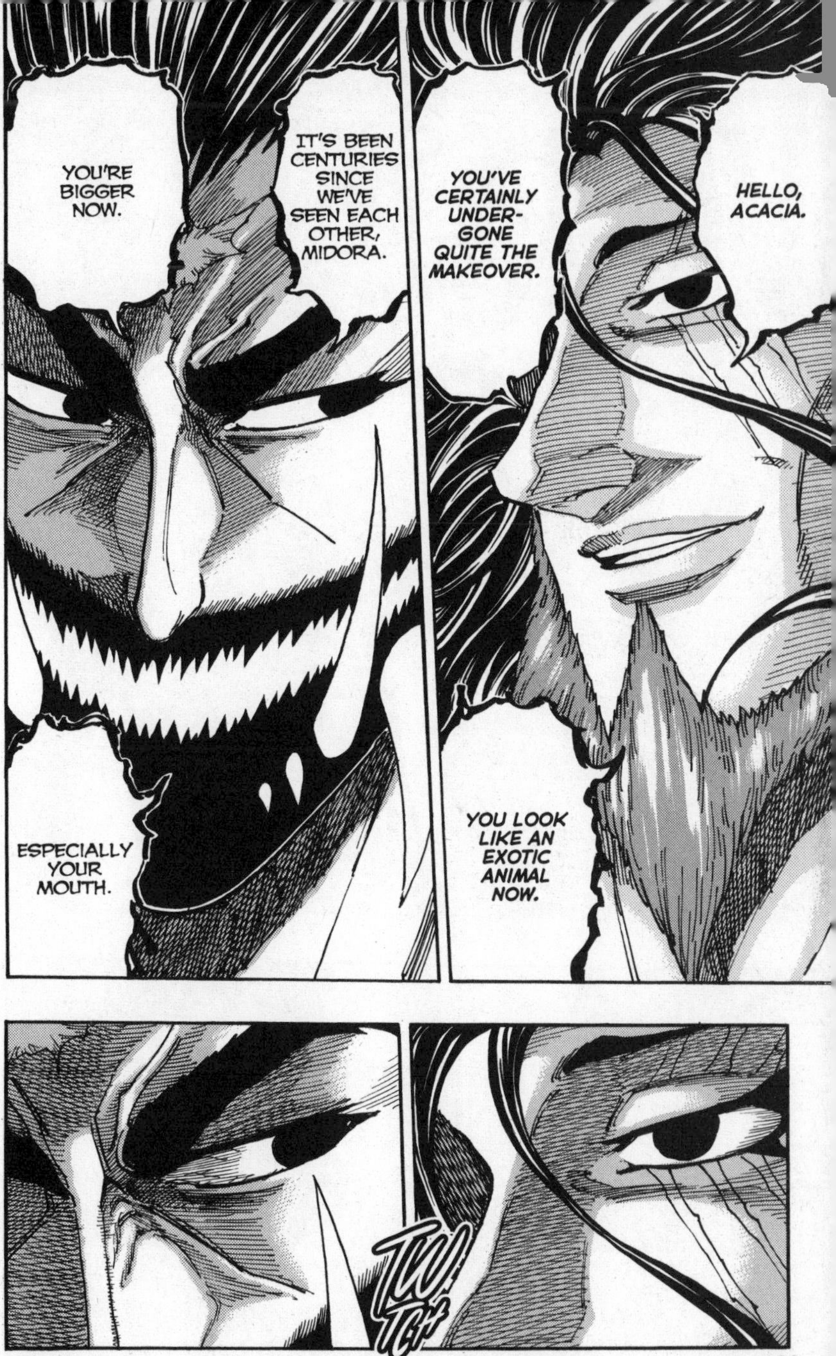
HELLO, ACACIA.
YOU'VE CERTAINLY UNDER-GONE QUITE THE MAKEOVER.
YOU LOOK LIKE AN EXOTIC ANIMAL NOW.
IT'S BEEN CENTURIES SINCE WE'VE SEEN EACH OTHER, MIDORA.
YOU'RE BIGGER NOW.
ESPECIALLY YOUR MOUTH.

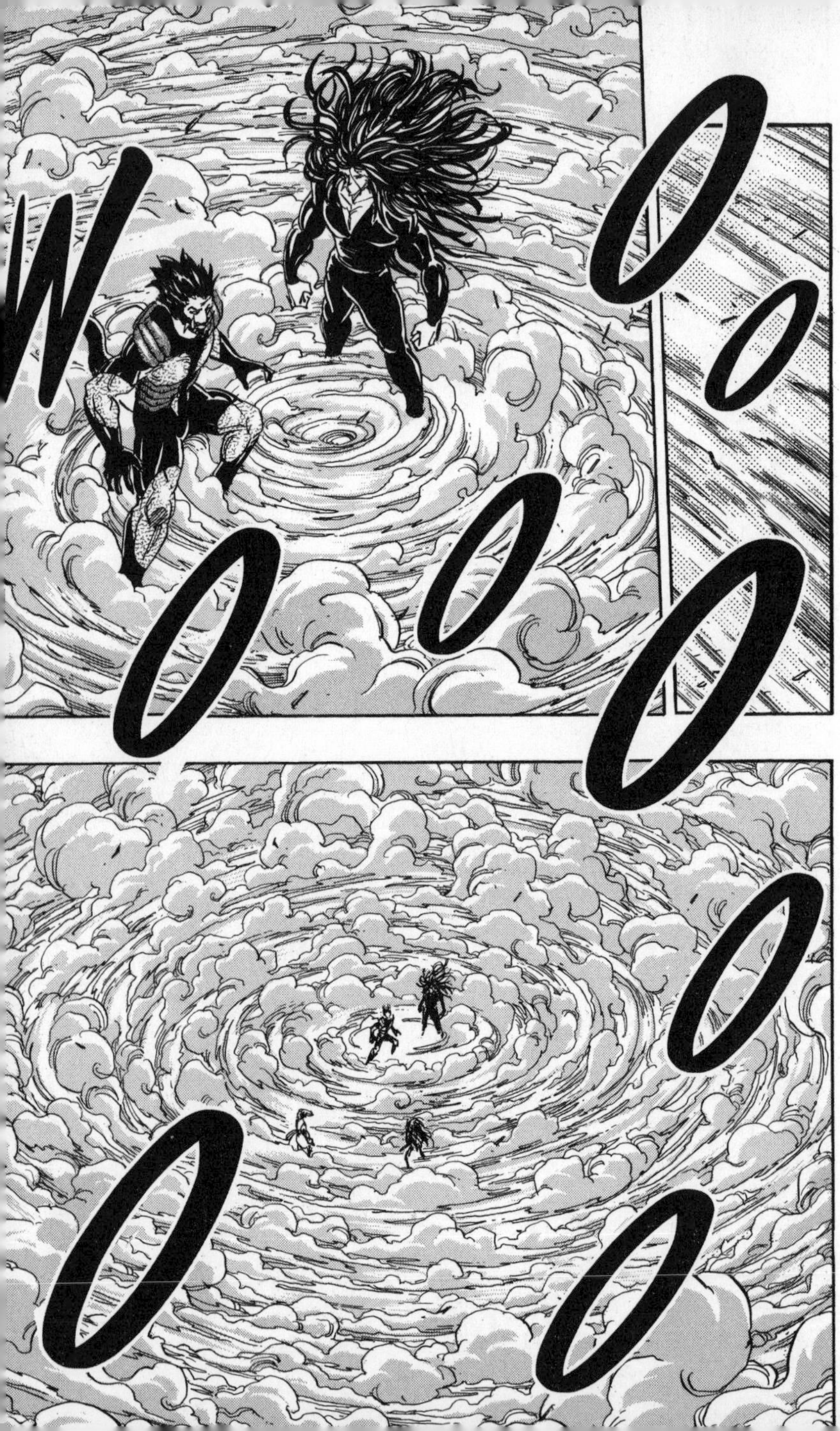
WOOOOOOOO

GOURMET 384: JOIE AND FROESE!!

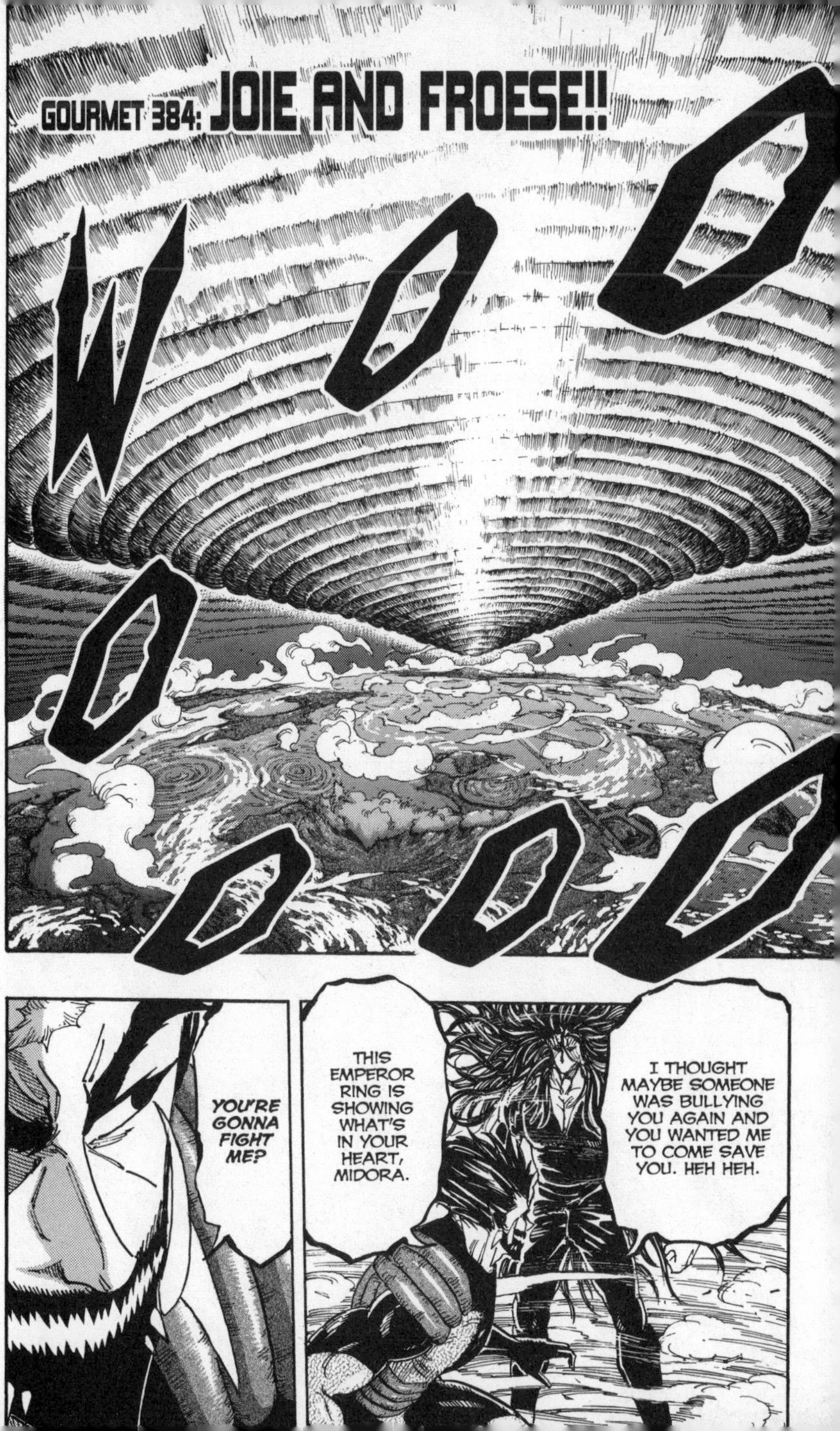
WOOOOOOOOO
I THOUGHT MAYBE SOMEONE WAS BULLYING YOU AGAIN AND YOU WANTED ME TO COME SAVE YOU. HEH HEH.
THIS EMPEROR RING IS SHOWING WHAT'S IN YOUR HEART, MIDORA.
YOU'RE GONNA FIGHT ME?

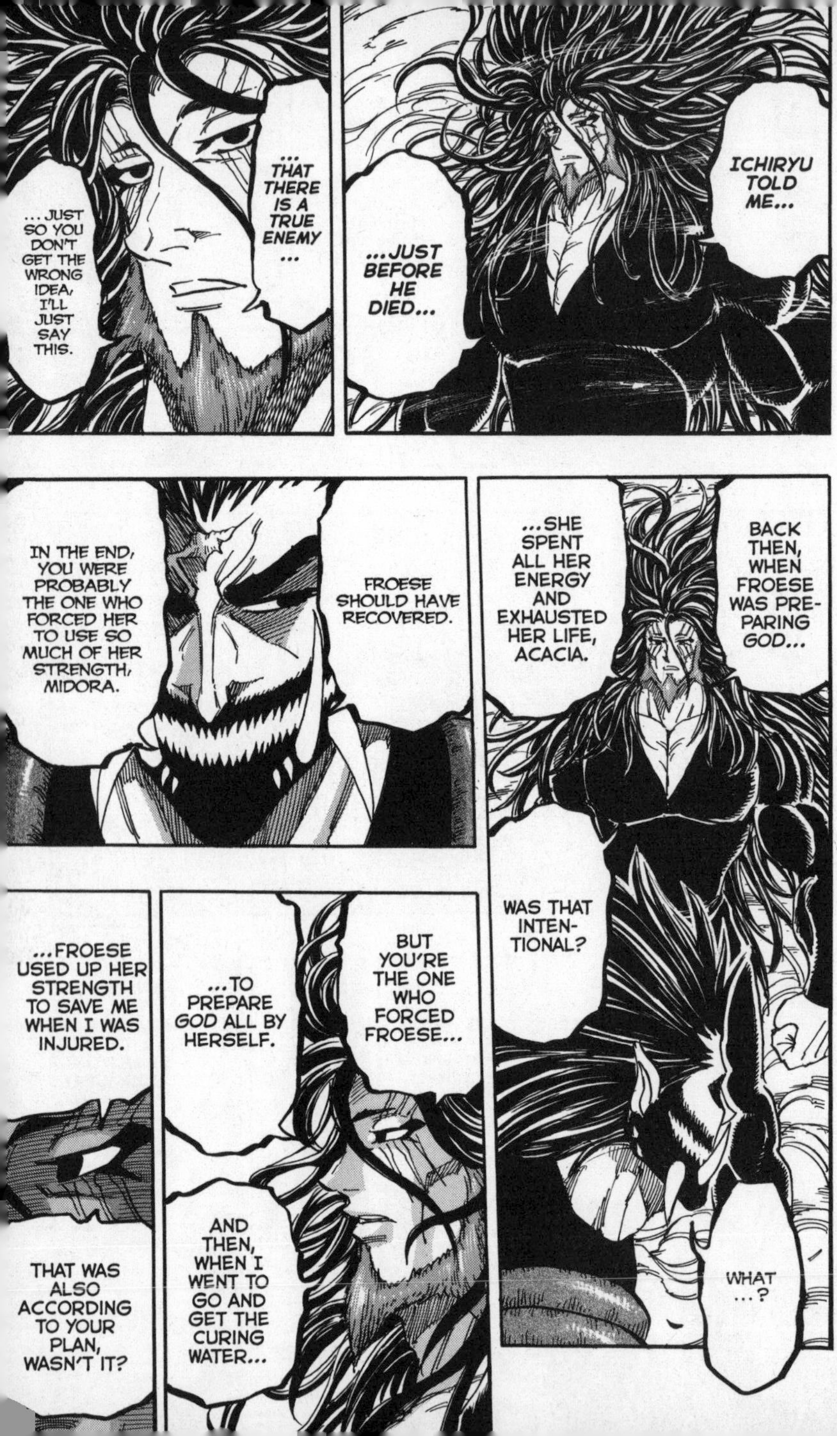
ICHIRYU TOLD ME...
...JUST BEFORE HE DIED...
...THAT THERE IS A TRUE ENEMY...
...JUST SO YOU DON'T GET THE WRONG IDEA, I'LL JUST SAY THIS.
BACK THEN, WHEN FROESE WAS PRE-PARING *GOD*...
...SHE SPENT ALL HER ENERGY AND EXHAUSTED HER LIFE, ACACIA.
FROESE SHOULD HAVE RECOVERED.
IN THE END, YOU WERE PROBABLY THE ONE WHO FORCED HER TO USE SO MUCH OF HER STRENGTH, MIDORA.
WAS THAT INTEN-TIONAL?
WHAT ...?
BUT YOU'RE THE ONE WHO FORCED FROESE...
...TO PREPARE *GOD* ALL BY HERSELF.
...FROESE USED UP HER STRENGTH TO SAVE ME WHEN I WAS INJURED.
AND THEN, WHEN I WENT TO GO AND GET THE CURING WATER...
THAT WAS ALSO ACCORDING TO YOUR PLAN, WASN'T IT?

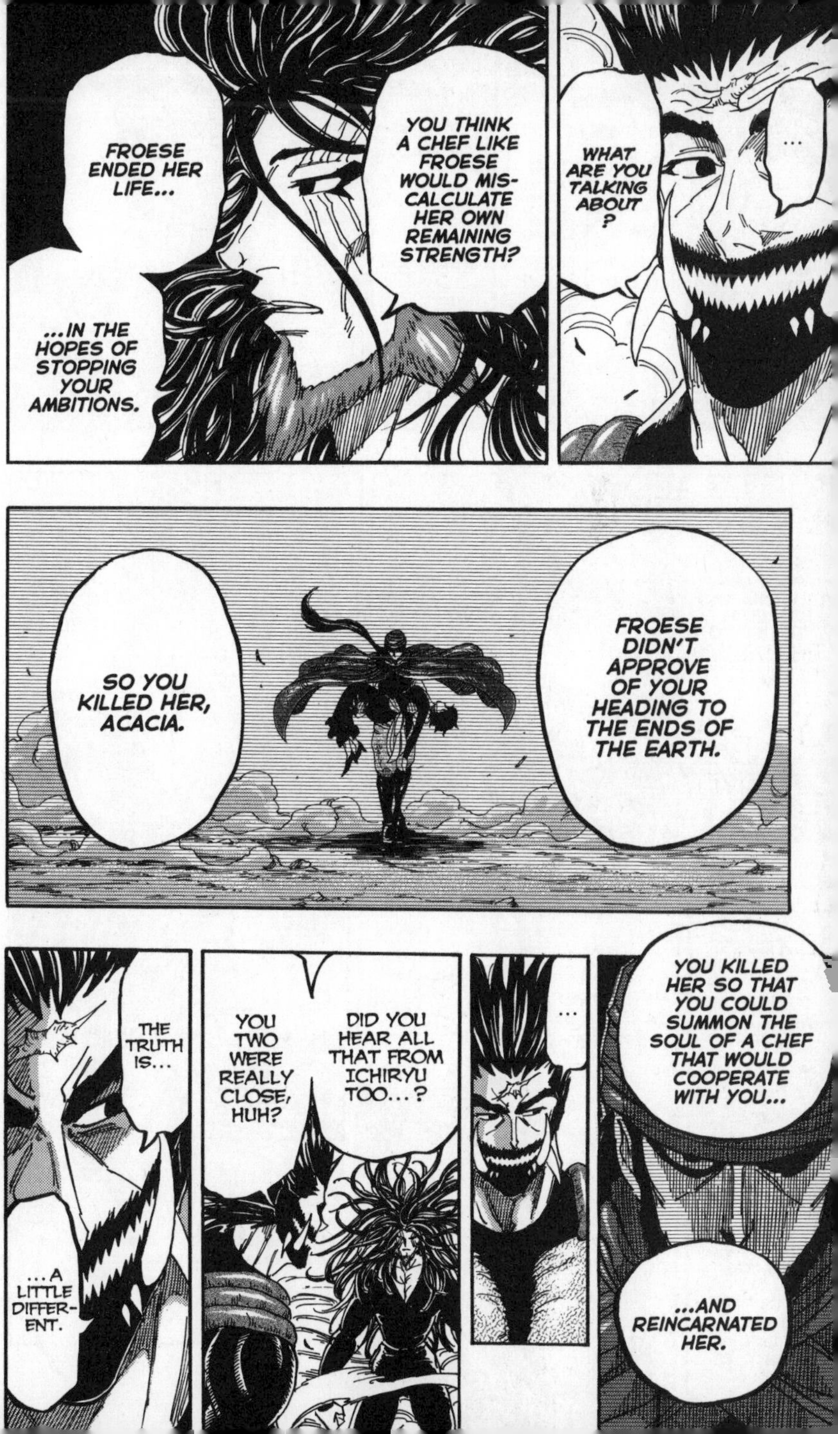
...
WHAT ARE YOU TALKING ABOUT?
YOU THINK A CHEF LIKE FROESE WOULD MIS-CALCULATE HER OWN REMAINING STRENGTH?
FROESE ENDED HER LIFE...
...IN THE HOPES OF STOPPING YOUR AMBITIONS.
FROESE DIDN'T APPROVE OF YOUR HEADING TO THE ENDS OF THE EARTH.
SO YOU KILLED HER, ACACIA.
YOU KILLED HER SO THAT YOU COULD SUMMON THE SOUL OF A CHEF THAT WOULD COOPERATE WITH YOU...
...AND REINCARNATED HER.
...
DID YOU HEAR ALL THAT FROM ICHIRYU TOO...?
YOU TWO WERE REALLY CLOSE, HUH?
THE TRUTH IS...
...A LITTLE DIFFER-ENT.

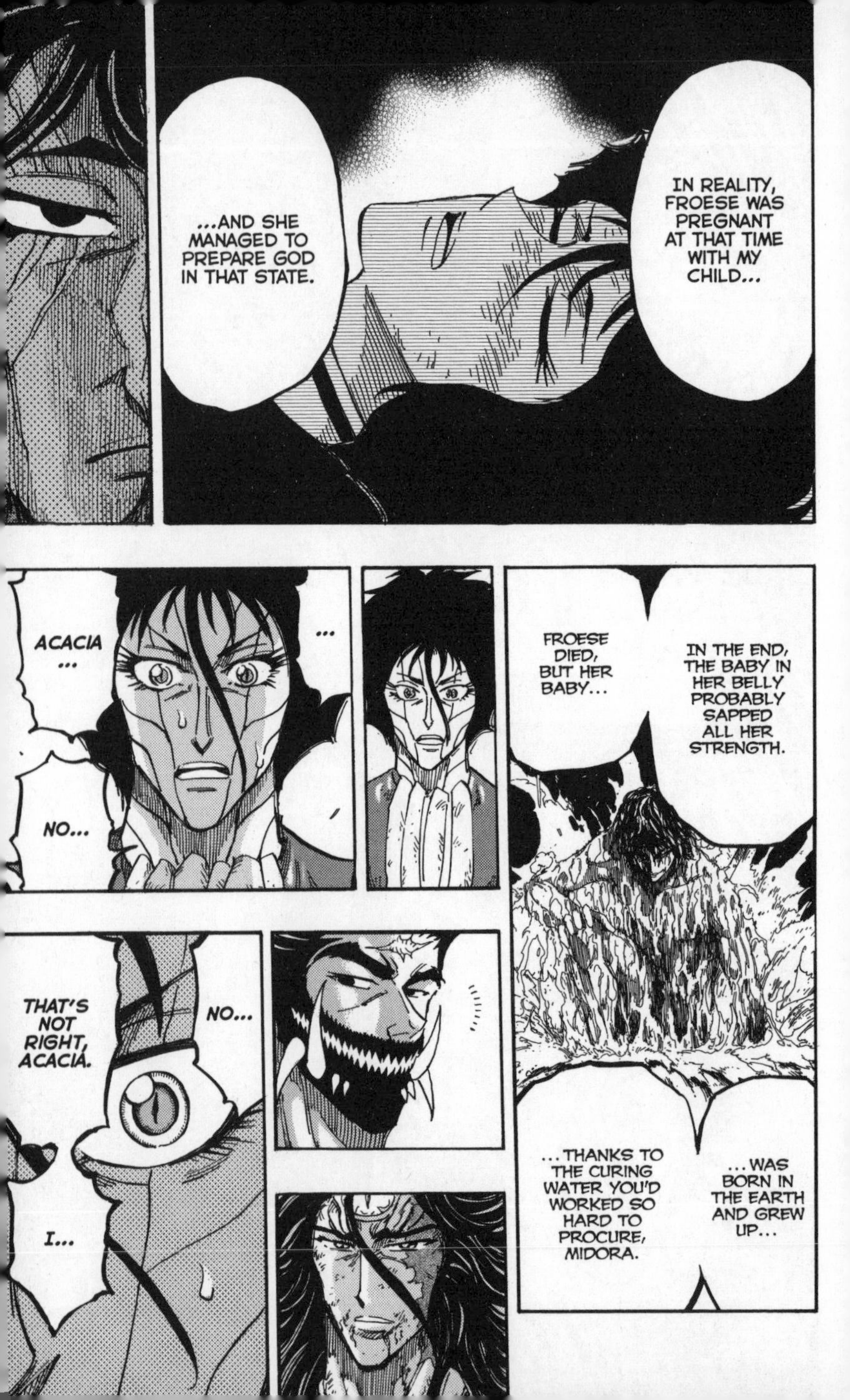
IN REALITY, FROESE WAS PREGNANT AT THAT TIME WITH MY CHILD...
...AND SHE MANAGED TO PREPARE GOD IN THAT STATE.
IN THE END, THE BABY IN HER BELLY PROBABLY SAPPED ALL HER STRENGTH.
FROESE DIED, BUT HER BABY...
...WAS BORN IN THE EARTH AND GREW UP...
...THANKS TO THE CURING WATER YOU'D WORKED SO HARD TO PROCURE, MIDORA.
...
ACACIA ...
NO...
NO...
THAT'S NOT RIGHT, ACACIA.
I...

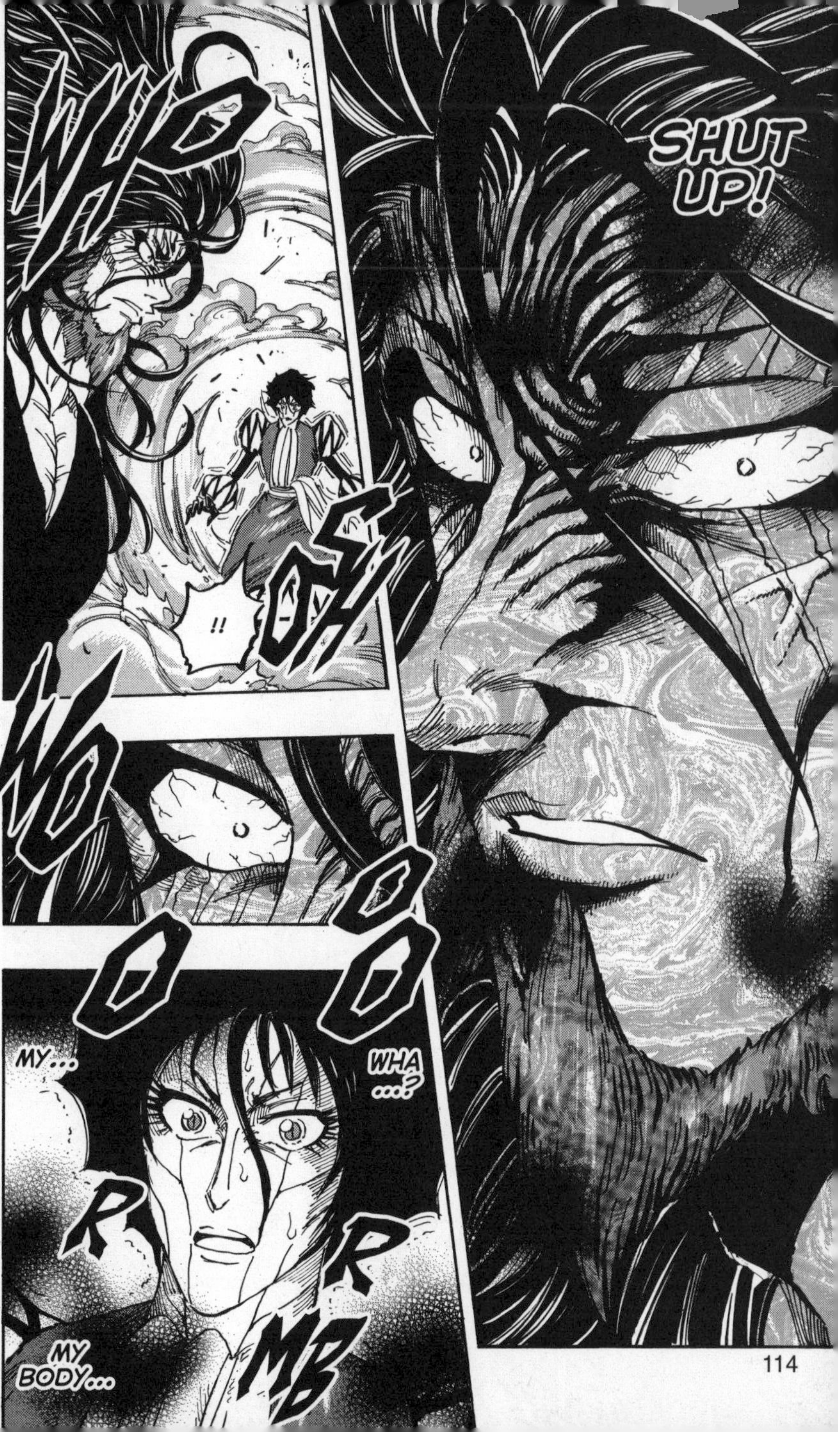
SHUT UP!
!!
WHA...?
MY...
MY BODY...

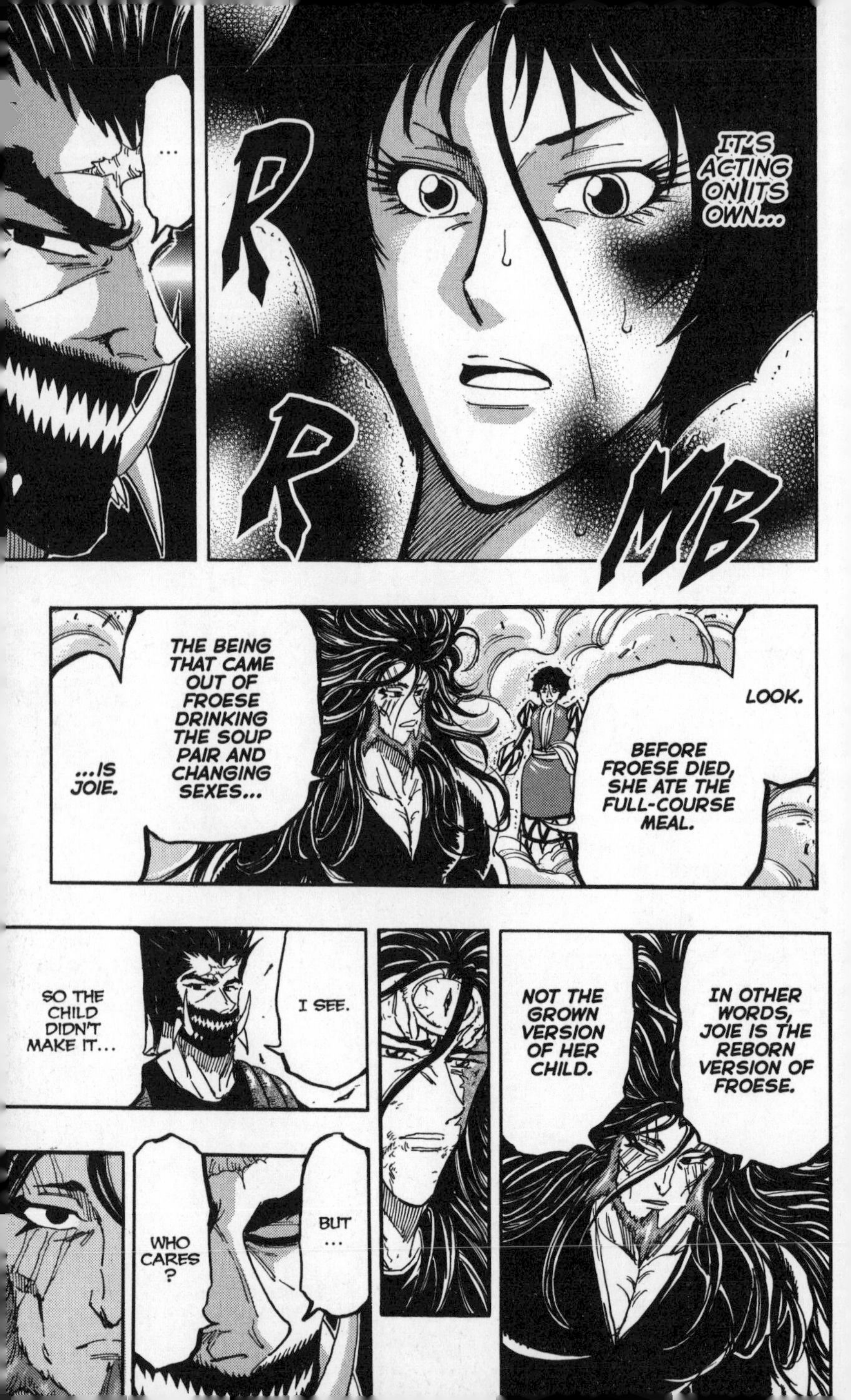
IT'S ACTING ON ITS OWN...
RRMB
...
LOOK.
BEFORE FROESE DIED, SHE ATE THE FULL-COURSE MEAL.
THE BEING THAT CAME OUT OF FROESE DRINKING THE SOUP PAIR AND CHANGING SEXES...
...IS JOIE.
IN OTHER WORDS, JOIE IS THE REBORN VERSION OF FROESE.
NOT THE GROWN VERSION OF HER CHILD.
I SEE.
SO THE CHILD DIDN'T MAKE IT...
BUT...
WHO CARES?

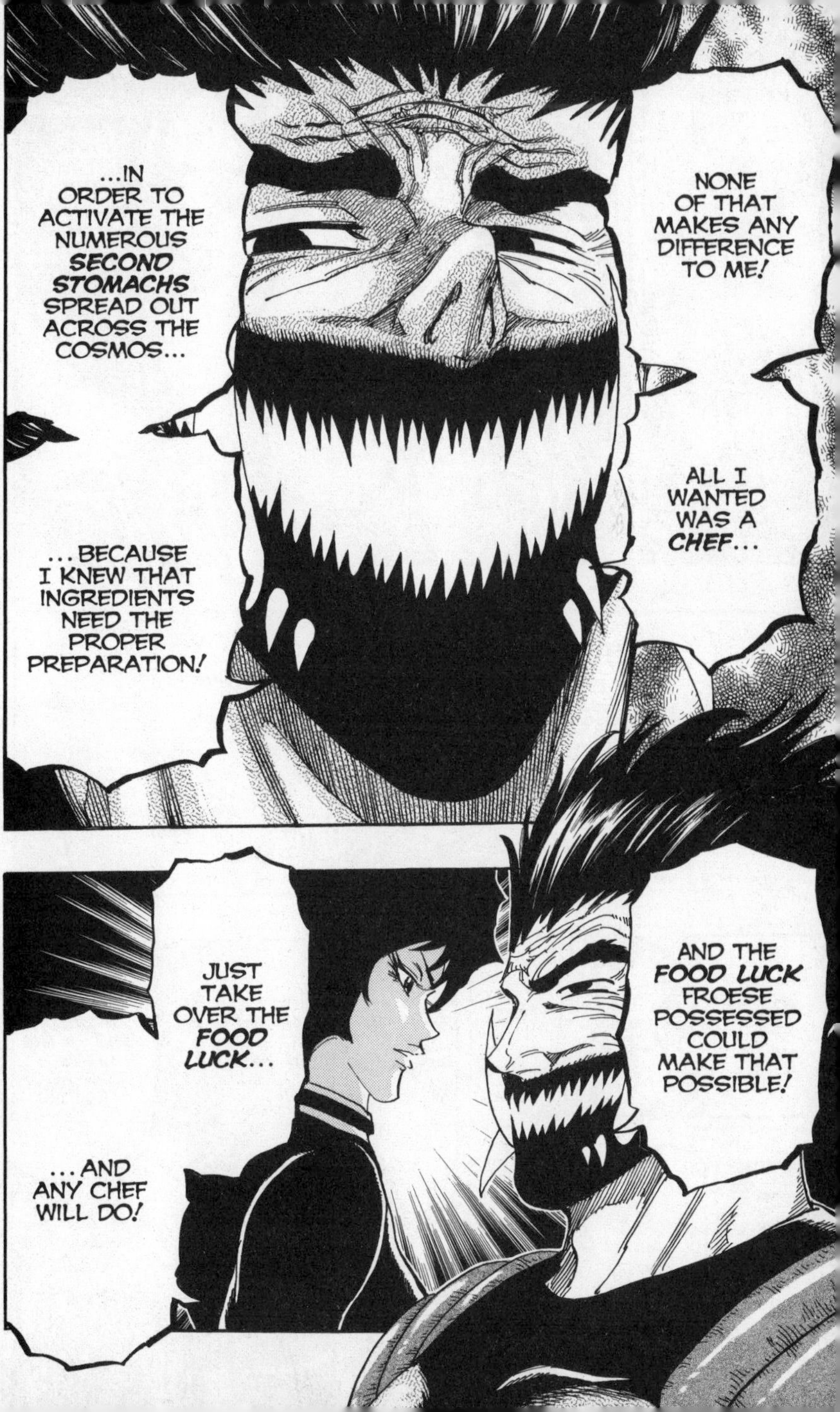
NONE OF THAT MAKES ANY DIFFERENCE TO ME!
ALL I WANTED WAS A *CHEF*...
...IN ORDER TO ACTIVATE THE NUMEROUS *SECOND STOMACHS* SPREAD OUT ACROSS THE COSMOS...
...BECAUSE I KNEW THAT INGREDIENTS NEED THE PROPER PREPARATION!
AND THE *FOOD LUCK* FROESE POSSESSED COULD MAKE THAT POSSIBLE!
JUST TAKE OVER THE *FOOD LUCK*...
...AND ANY CHEF WILL DO!

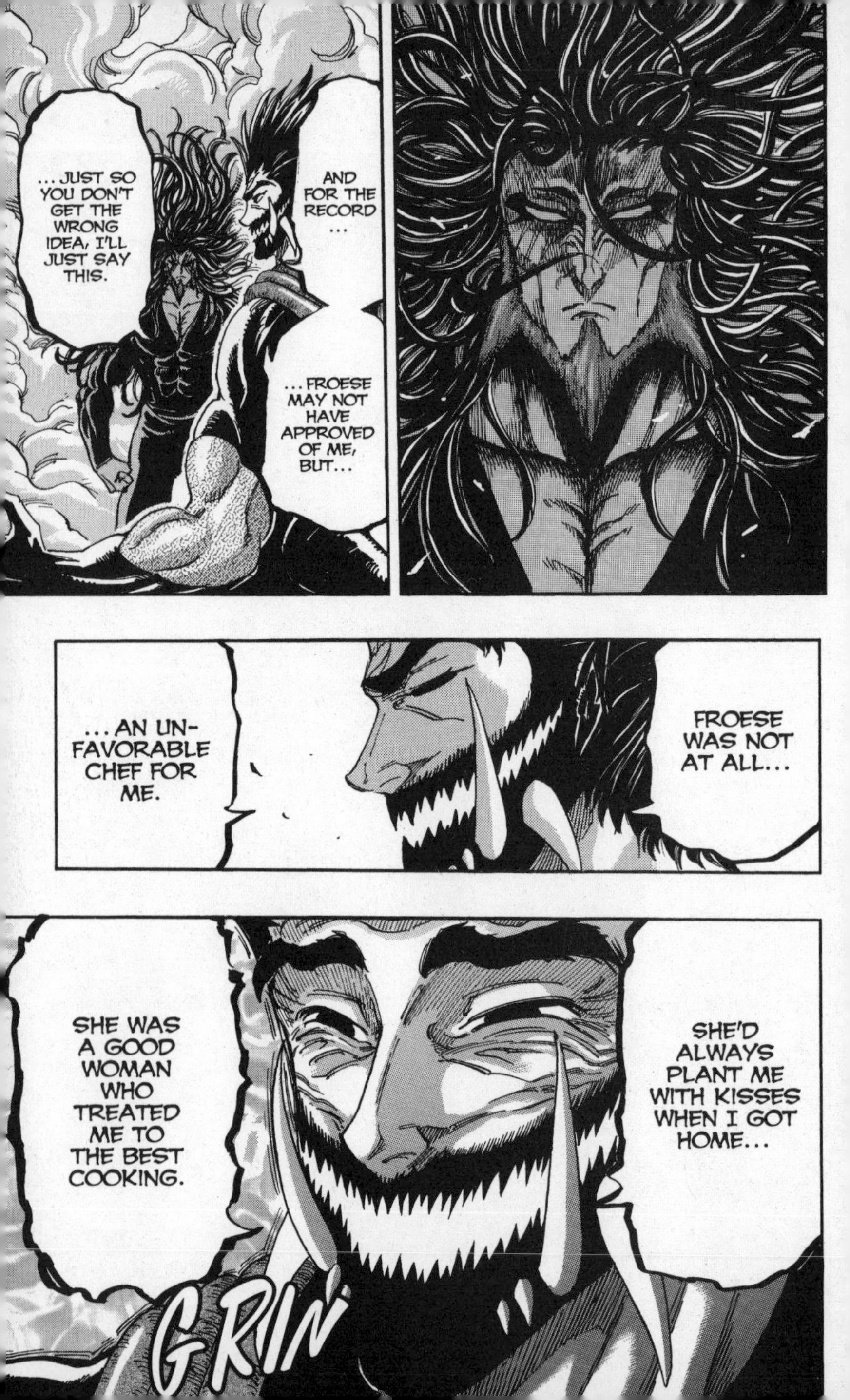
AND FOR THE RECORD...
...JUST SO YOU DON'T GET THE WRONG IDEA, I'LL JUST SAY THIS.
...FROESE MAY NOT HAVE APPROVED OF ME, BUT...
FROESE WAS NOT AT ALL...
...AN UN-FAVORABLE CHEF FOR ME.
SHE'D ALWAYS PLANT ME WITH KISSES WHEN I GOT HOME...
SHE WAS A GOOD WOMAN WHO TREATED ME TO THE BEST COOKING.
GRIN

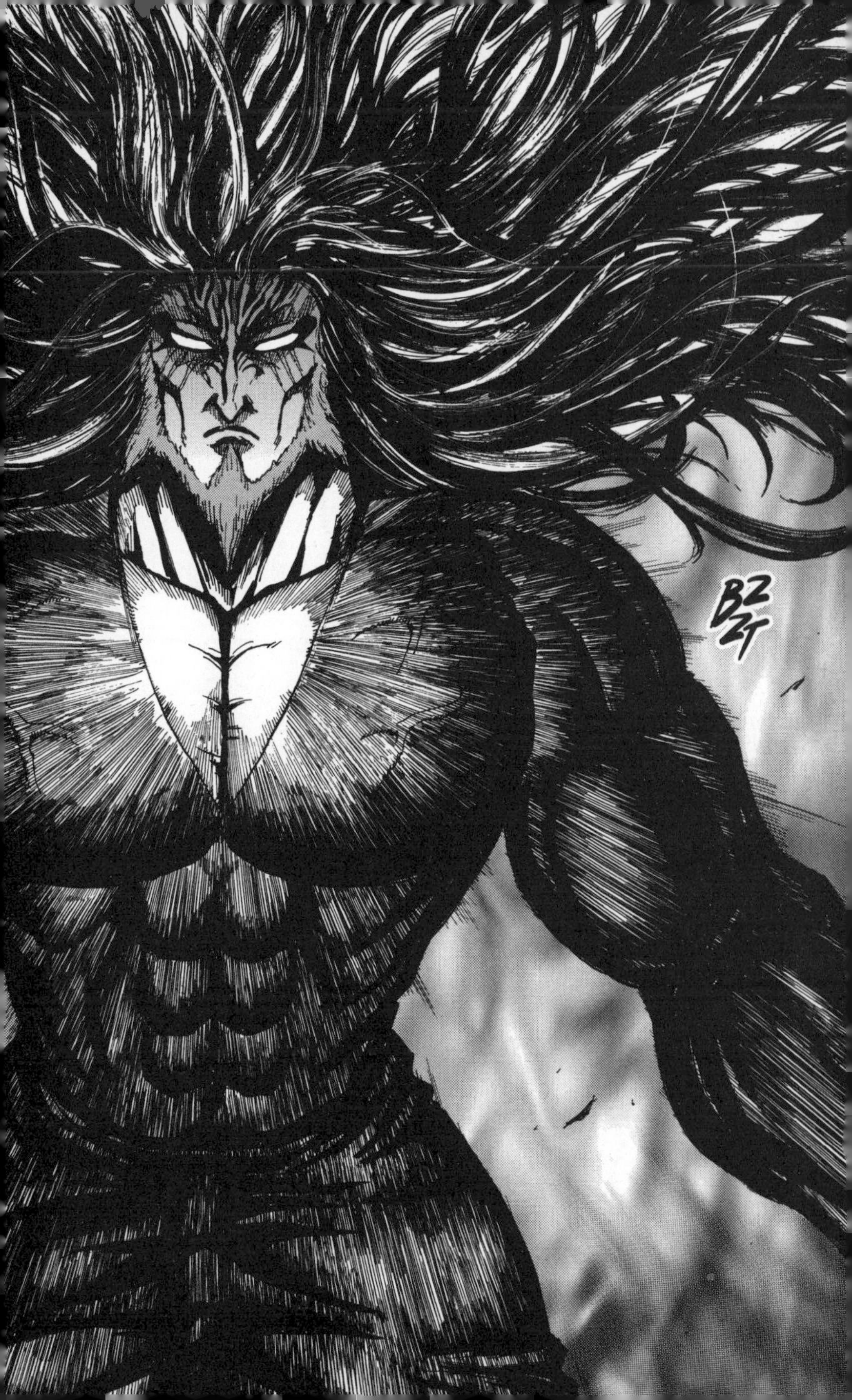
BZZT

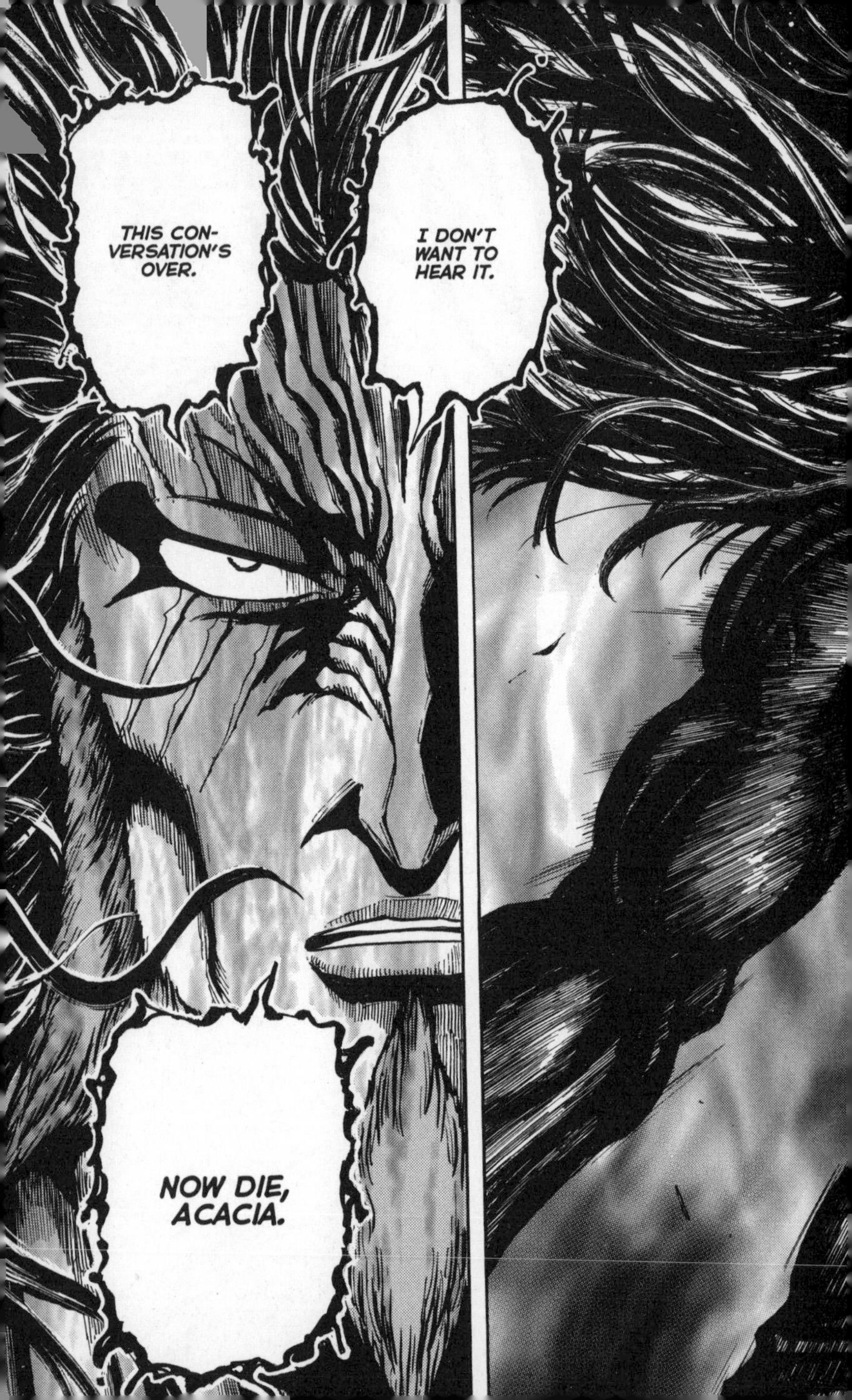
I DON'T WANT TO HEAR IT.
THIS CON-VERSATION'S OVER.
NOW DIE, ACACIA.

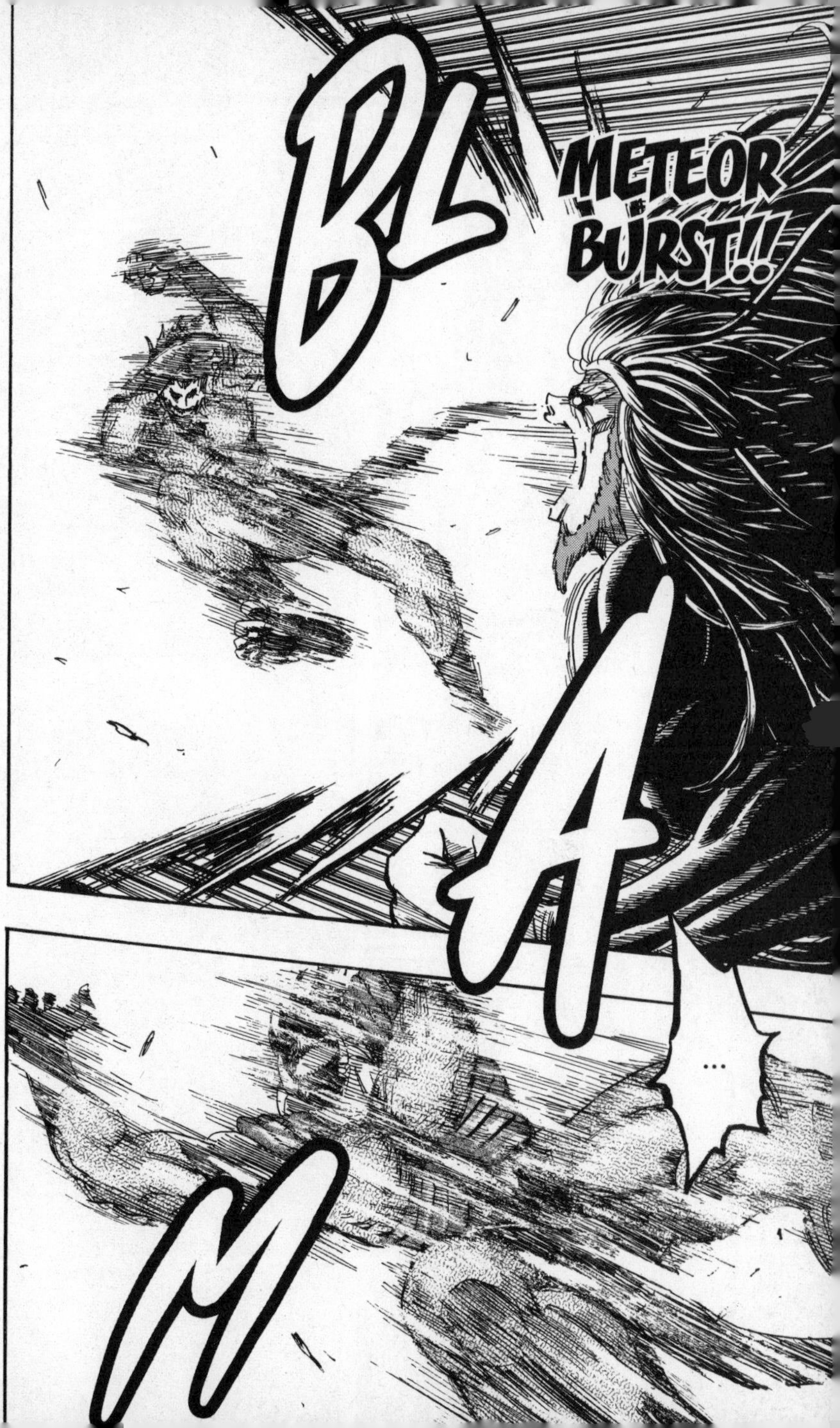
METEOR BURST!!
BLAM
...

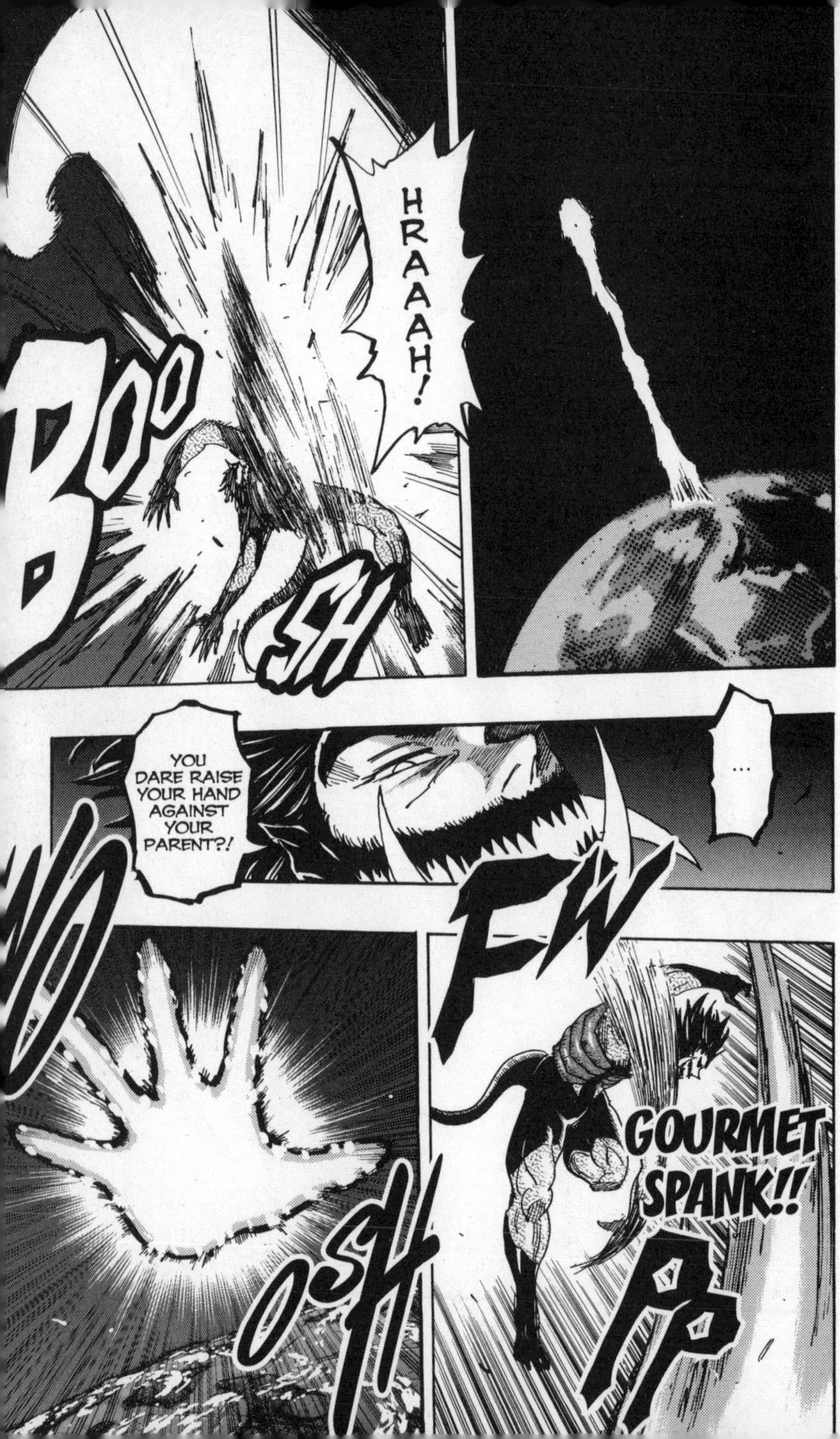
HRAAAH!
SH
...
YOU DARE RAISE YOUR HAND AGAINST YOUR PARENT?!
FW
GOURMET SPANK!!
OSH

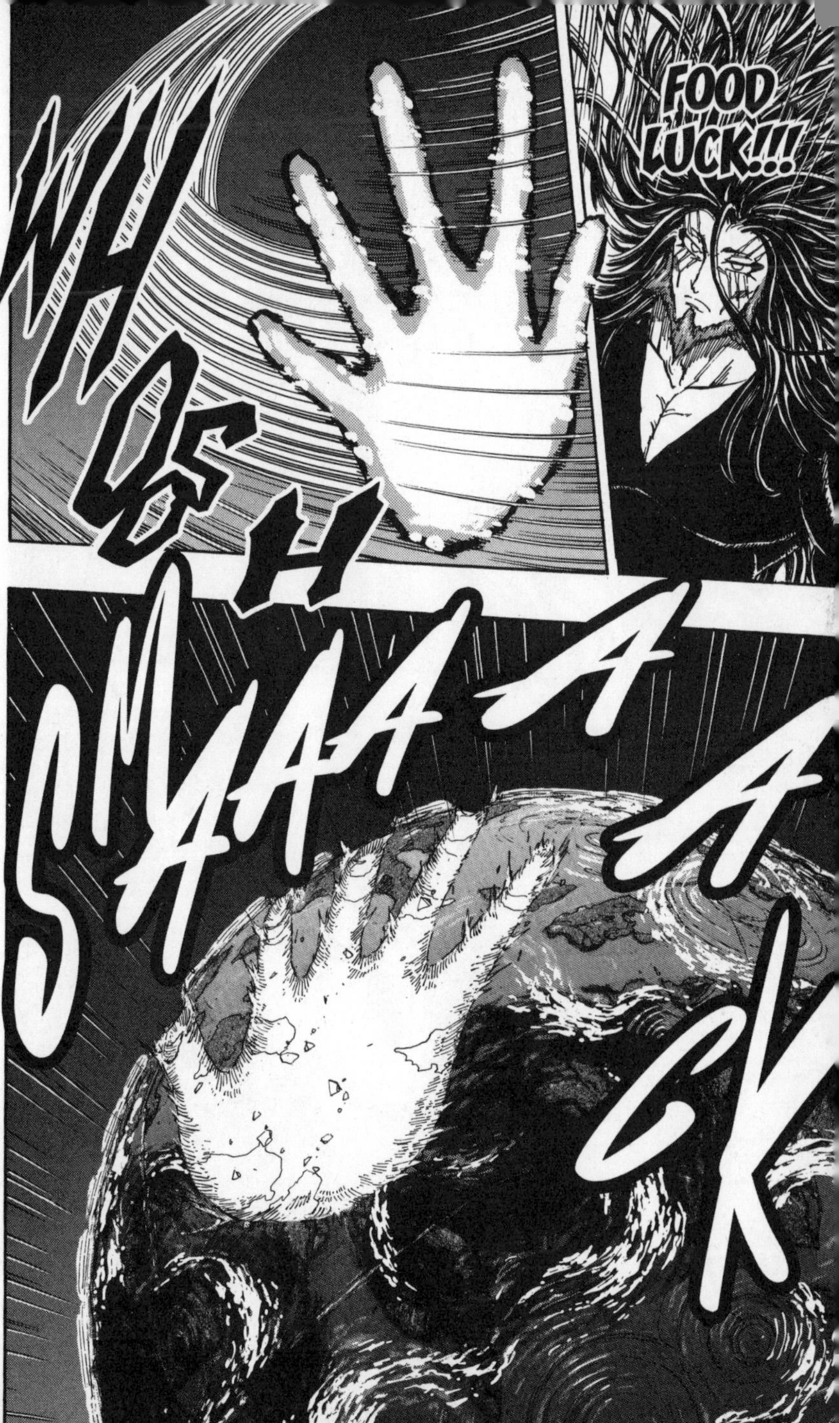
FOOD LUCK!!!
WHOOSH
SMAAAACK

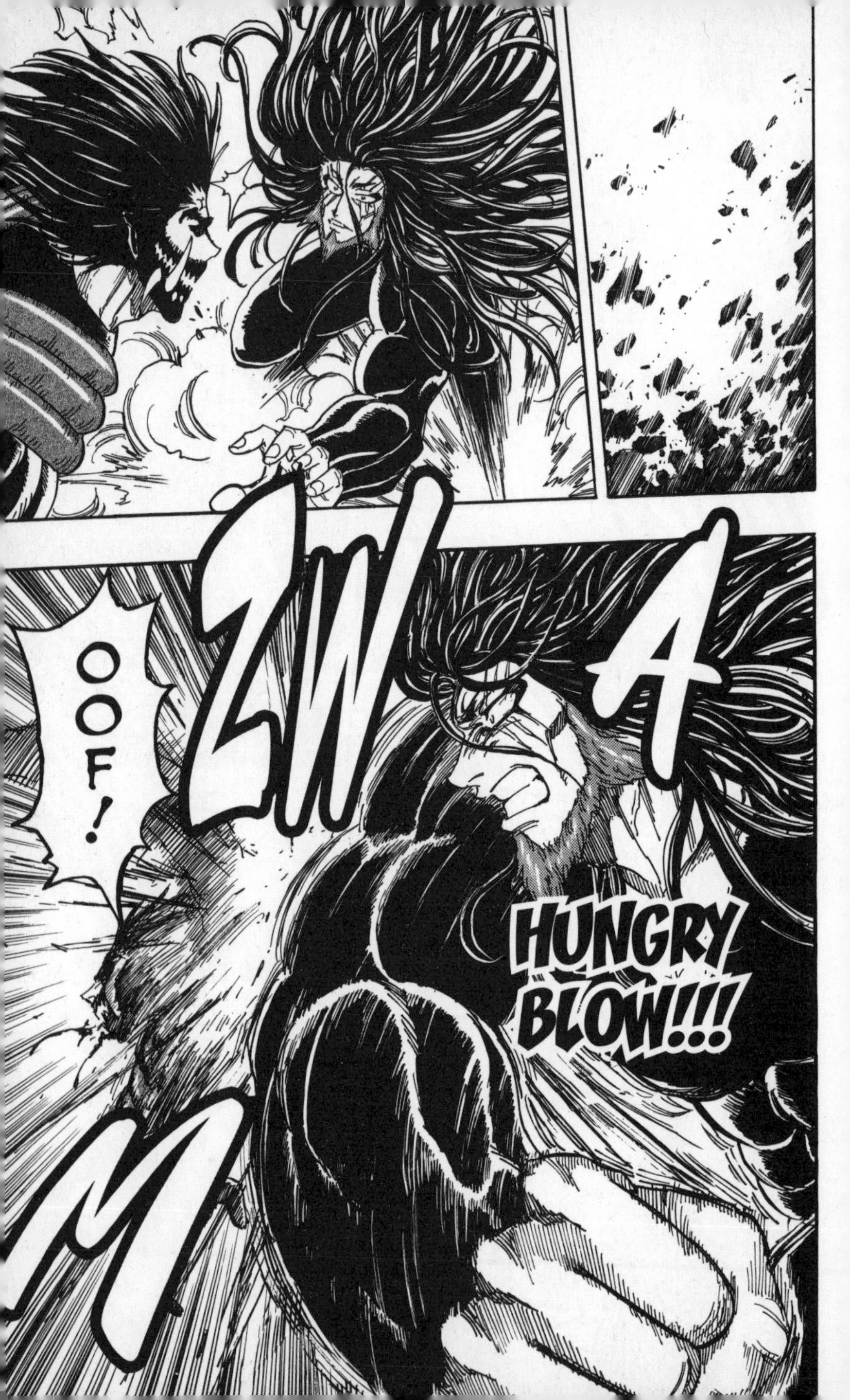
ZWAM
HUNGRY BLOW!!!
OOF!

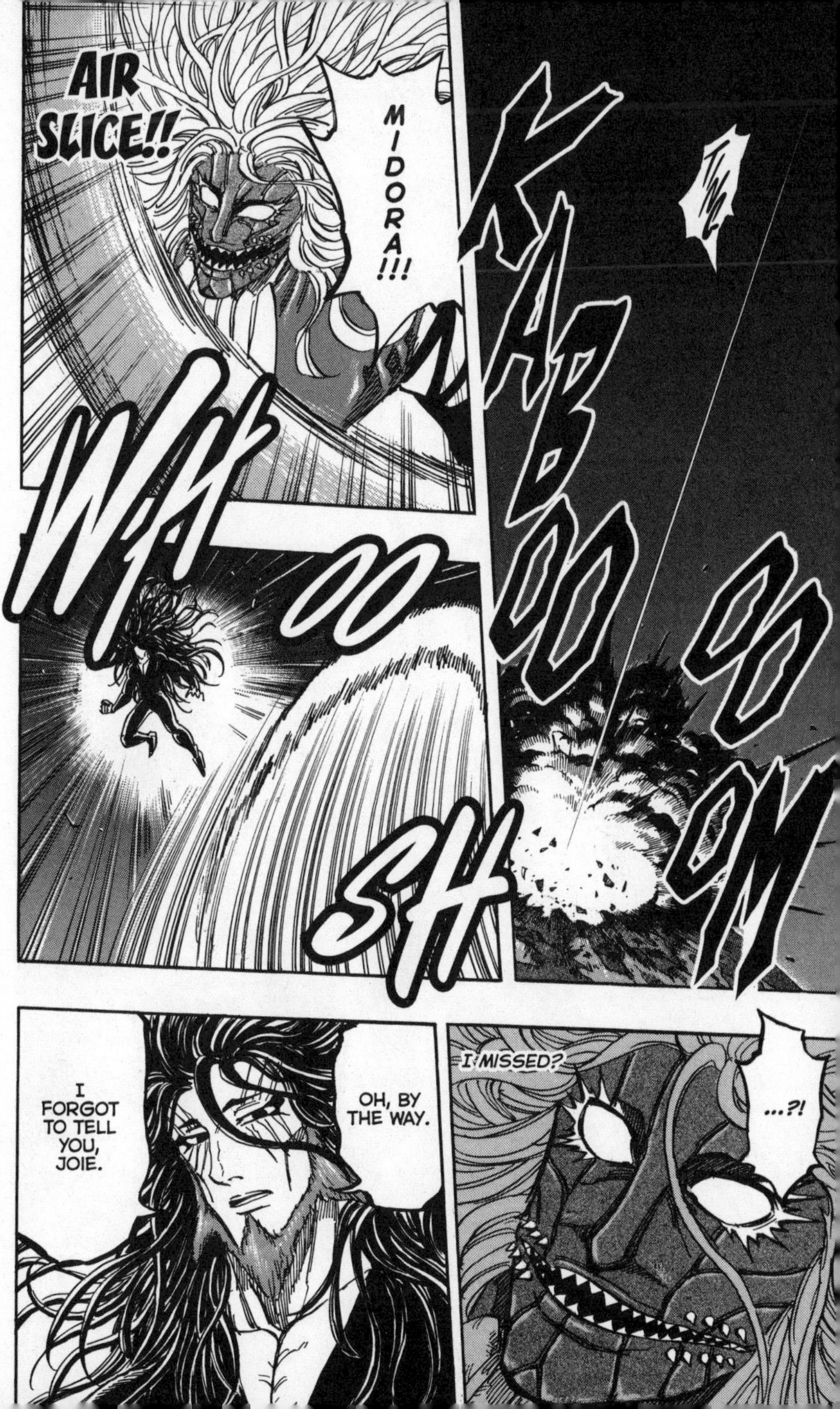
TNG
KABOOOOOM
MIDORA!!!
AIR SLICE!!
WHOOOSH
...?!
I MISSED?
OH, BY THE WAY.
I FORGOT TO TELL YOU, JOIE.

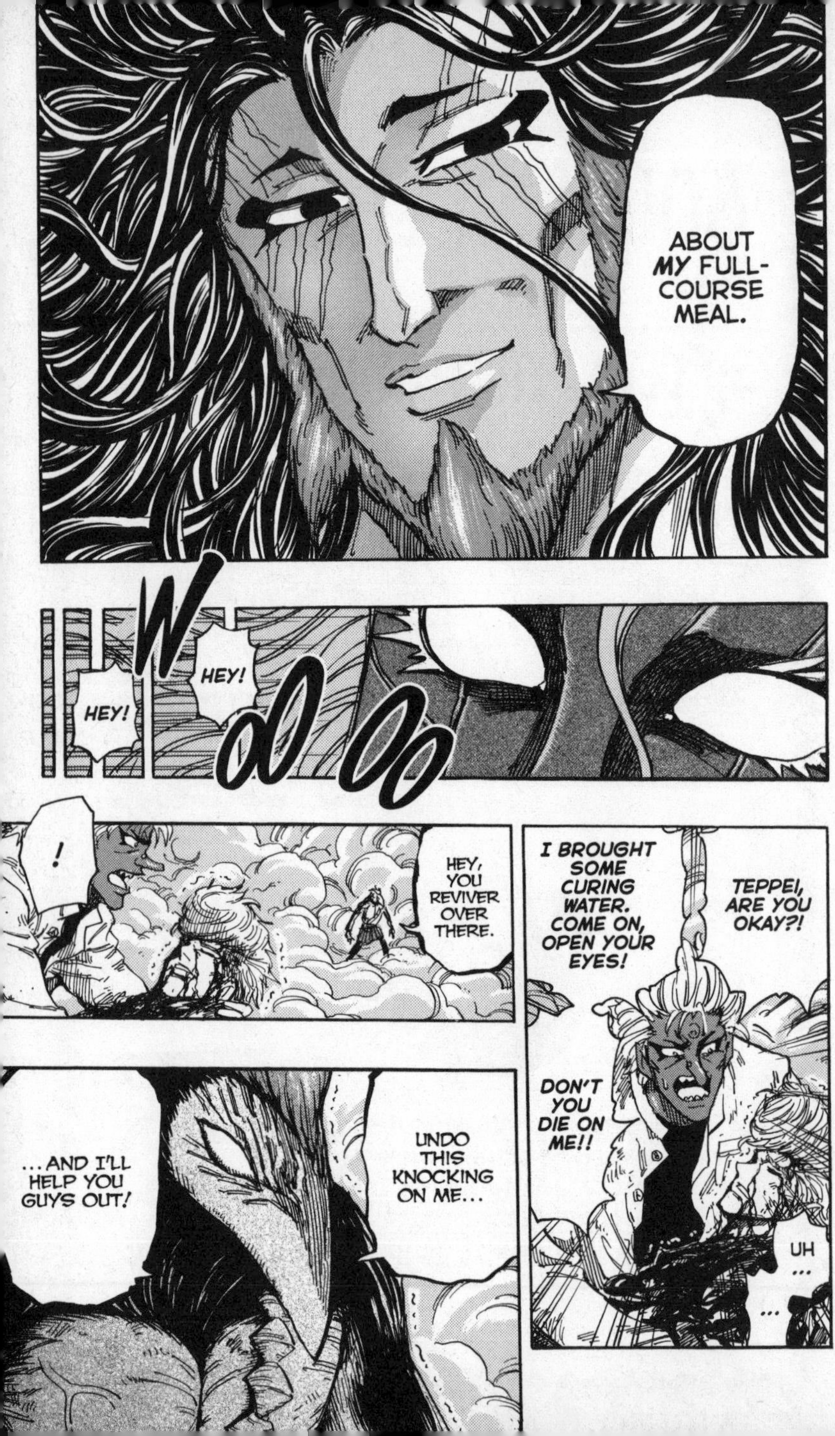
ABOUT MY FULL-COURSE MEAL.
WOOO
HEY!
HEY!
TEPPEI, ARE YOU OKAY?!
I BROUGHT SOME CURING WATER. COME ON, OPEN YOUR EYES!
DON'T YOU DIE ON ME!!
UH ... ...
HEY, YOU REVIVER OVER THERE.
!
UNDO THIS KNOCKING ON ME...
...AND I'LL HELP YOU GUYS OUT!

TORIKO

GOURMET CHECKLIST

Vol.419

❦ DEVIL PYTHON (WILD BREED) ❧
(REPTILE)

CAPTURE LEVEL: 5,100
HABITAT: THE FOREST IN SKY
DEER'S HORNS
SIZE: 1,200 M
HEIGHT: ---
WEIGHT: 500,000 TONS
PRICE: 1,500,000 YEN PER 100 G

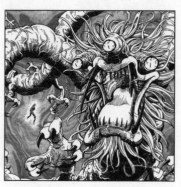

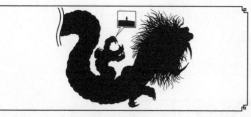

SCALE

A WILD BREED OF DEVIL PYTHON THAT LIVES IN THE FOREST IN THE DEER KING'S HORNS IN AREA 5. THIS FOREST IS ALSO KNOWN AS THE "DEN OF MONSTERS" WITH HORDES OF MONSTERS WHOSE CAPTURE LEVELS AVERAGE AROUND 4,000. WILD DEVIL PYTHONS ARE COMPLETELY DIFFERENT THAN THEIR RELATIVES IN THE HUMAN WORLD AND THOUSANDS OF TIMES STRONGER.

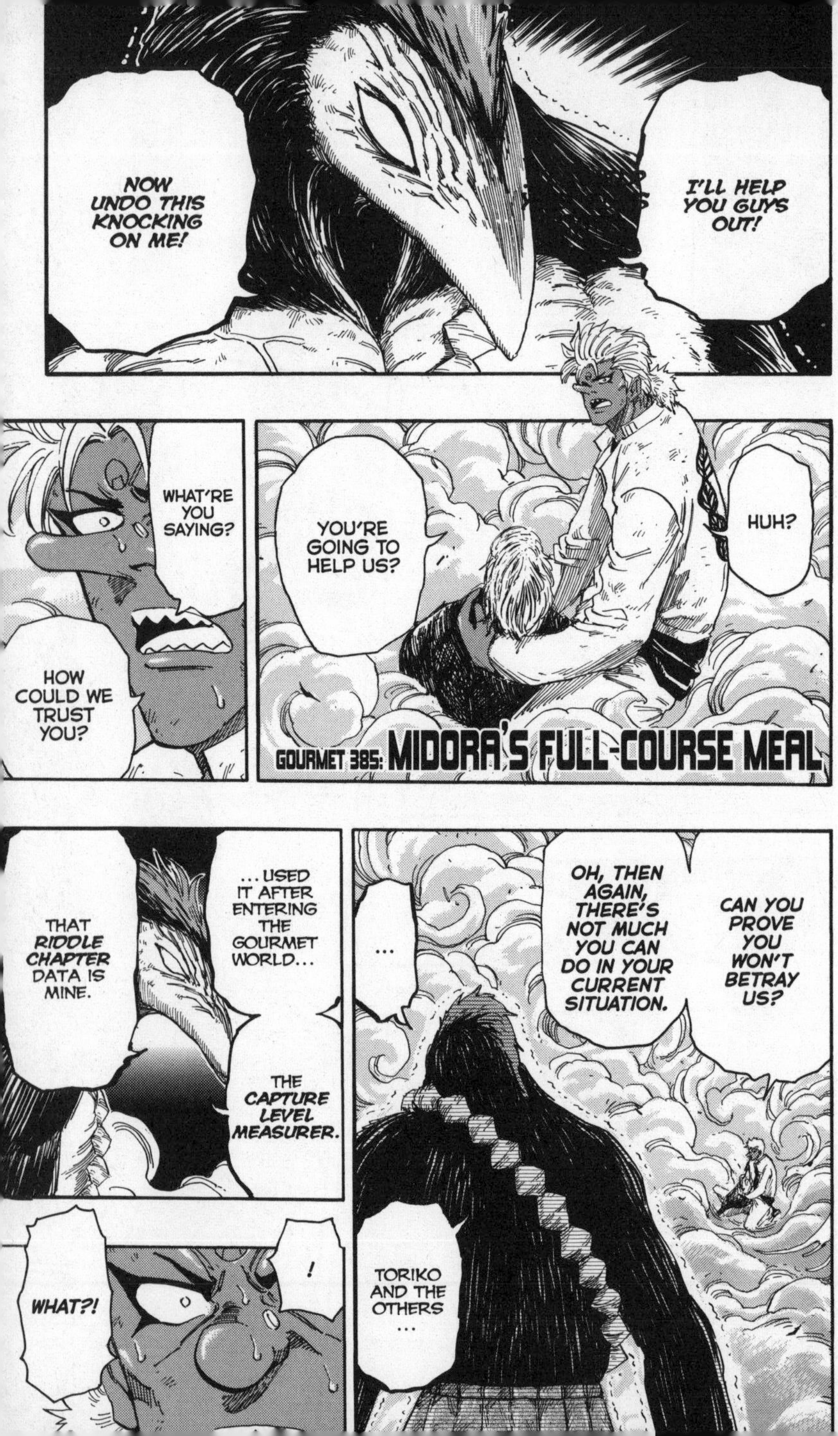
I'LL HELP YOU GUYS OUT!
NOW UNDO THIS KNOCKING ON ME!
HUH?
YOU'RE GOING TO HELP US?
WHAT'RE YOU SAYING?
HOW COULD WE TRUST YOU?
GOURMET 385: MIDORA'S FULL-COURSE MEAL
CAN YOU PROVE YOU WON'T BETRAY US?
OH, THEN AGAIN, THERE'S NOT MUCH YOU CAN DO IN YOUR CURRENT SITUATION.
...
TORIKO AND THE OTHERS ...
...USED IT AFTER ENTERING THE GOURMET WORLD...
THAT RIDDLE CHAPTER DATA IS MINE.
THE CAPTURE LEVEL MEASURER.
!
WHAT?!

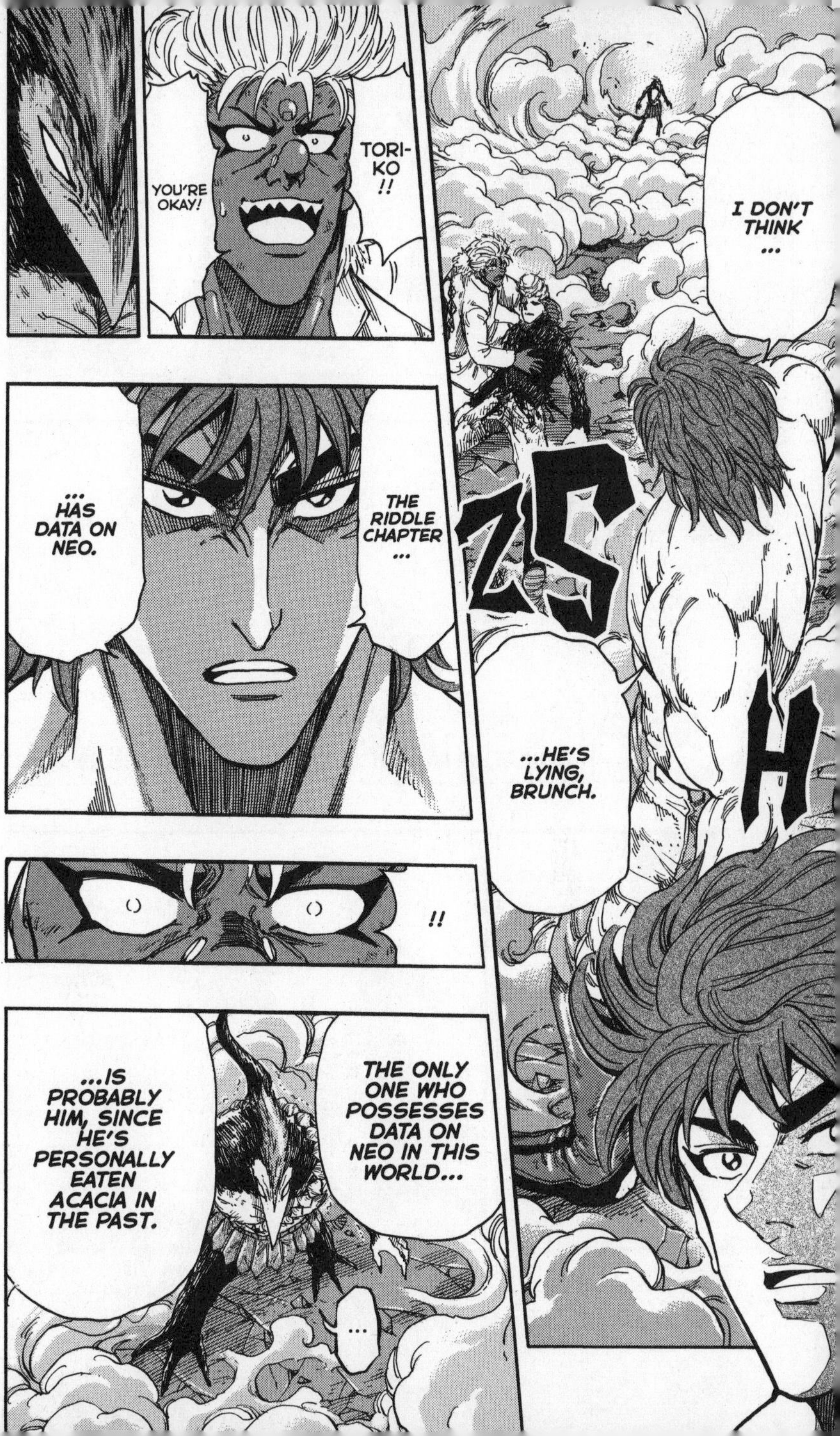
I DON'T THINK ...
ZS
...HE'S LYING, BRUNCH.
H
TORI-KO !!
YOU'RE OKAY!
THE RIDDLE CHAPTER ...
... HAS DATA ON NEO.
!!
THE ONLY ONE WHO POSSESSES DATA ON NEO IN THIS WORLD...
...IS PROBABLY HIM, SINCE HE'S PERSONALLY EATEN ACACIA IN THE PAST.
...

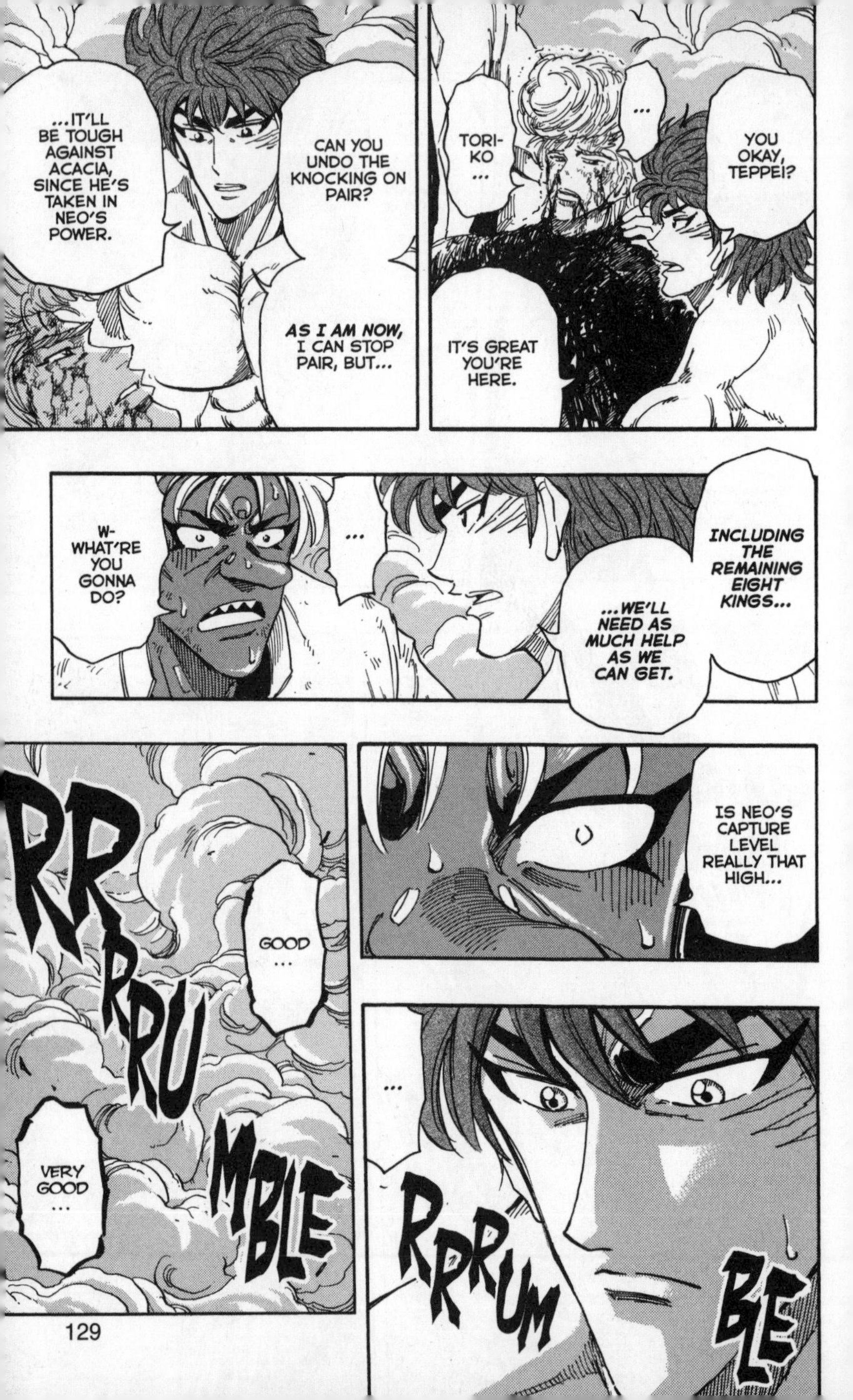
YOU OKAY, TEPPEI?
...
TORI-KO ...
IT'S GREAT YOU'RE HERE.
CAN YOU UNDO THE KNOCKING ON PAIR?
AS I AM NOW, I CAN STOP PAIR, BUT...
...IT'LL BE TOUGH AGAINST ACACIA, SINCE HE'S TAKEN IN NEO'S POWER.
INCLUDING THE REMAINING EIGHT KINGS...
...WE'LL NEED AS MUCH HELP AS WE CAN GET.
...
W-WHAT'RE YOU GONNA DO?
IS NEO'S CAPTURE LEVEL REALLY THAT HIGH...
...
RRRUMBLE
RRRRUMBLE
GOOD ...
VERY GOOD ...

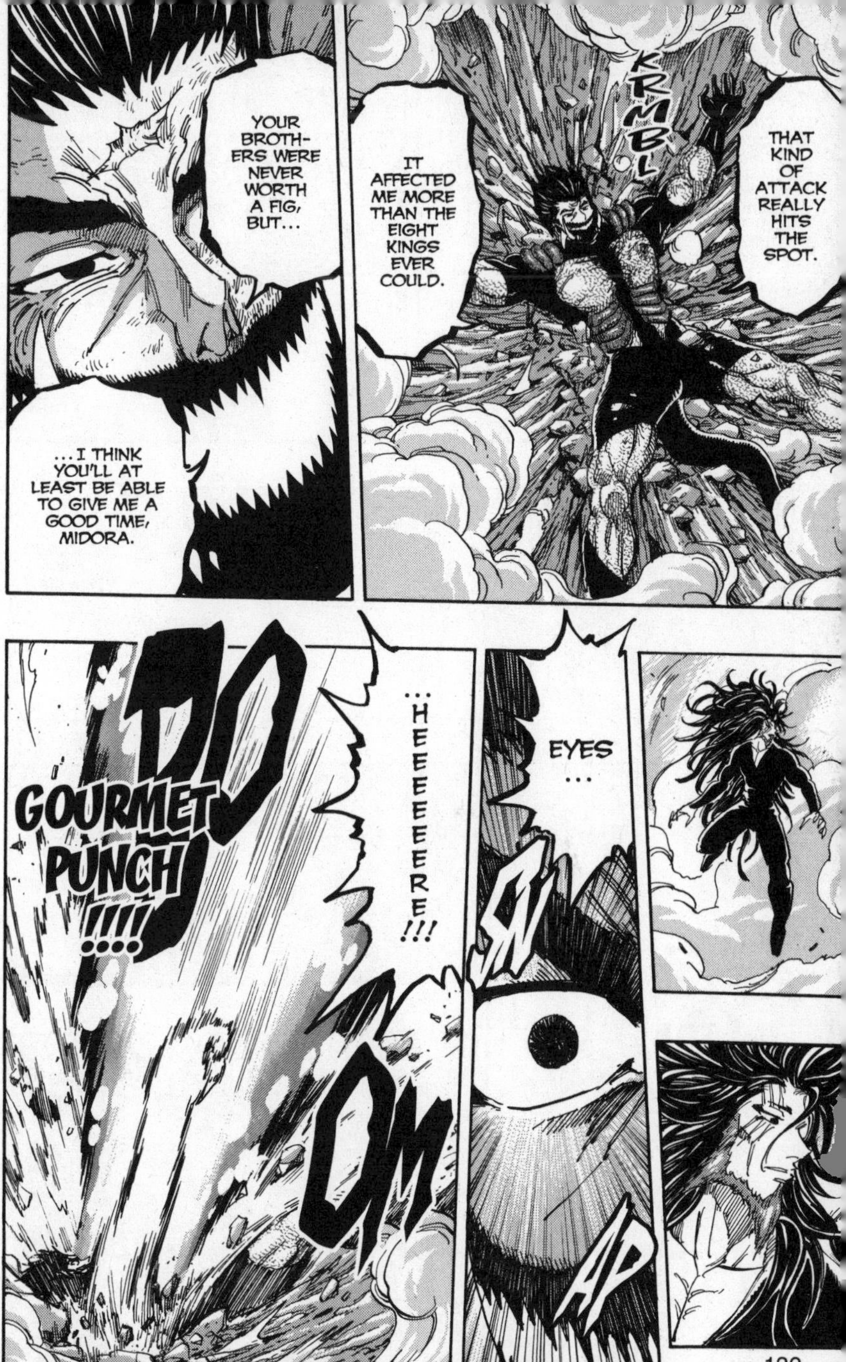
KRMBL
THAT KIND OF ATTACK REALLY HITS THE SPOT.
IT AFFECTED ME MORE THAN THE EIGHT KINGS EVER COULD.
YOUR BROTHERS WERE NEVER WORTH A FIG, BUT...
...I THINK YOU'LL AT LEAST BE ABLE TO GIVE ME A GOOD TIME, MIDORA.
EYES...
..HEEEEEEERE!!!
DO
GOURMET PUNCH!!!!
OM

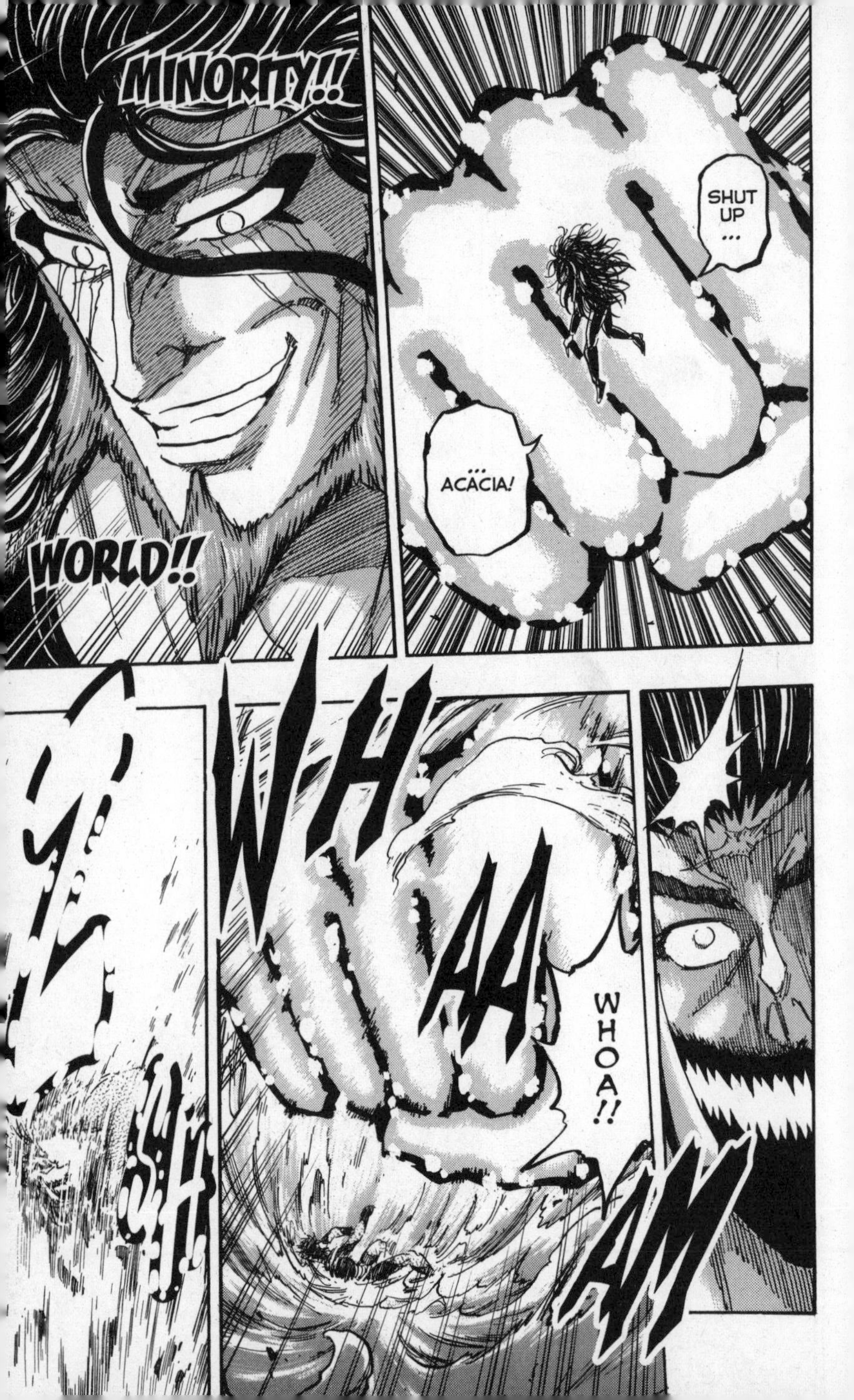

SHUT UP ...
... ACACIA!
MINORITY!!
WORLD!!
WHOA!!
WHAAAM

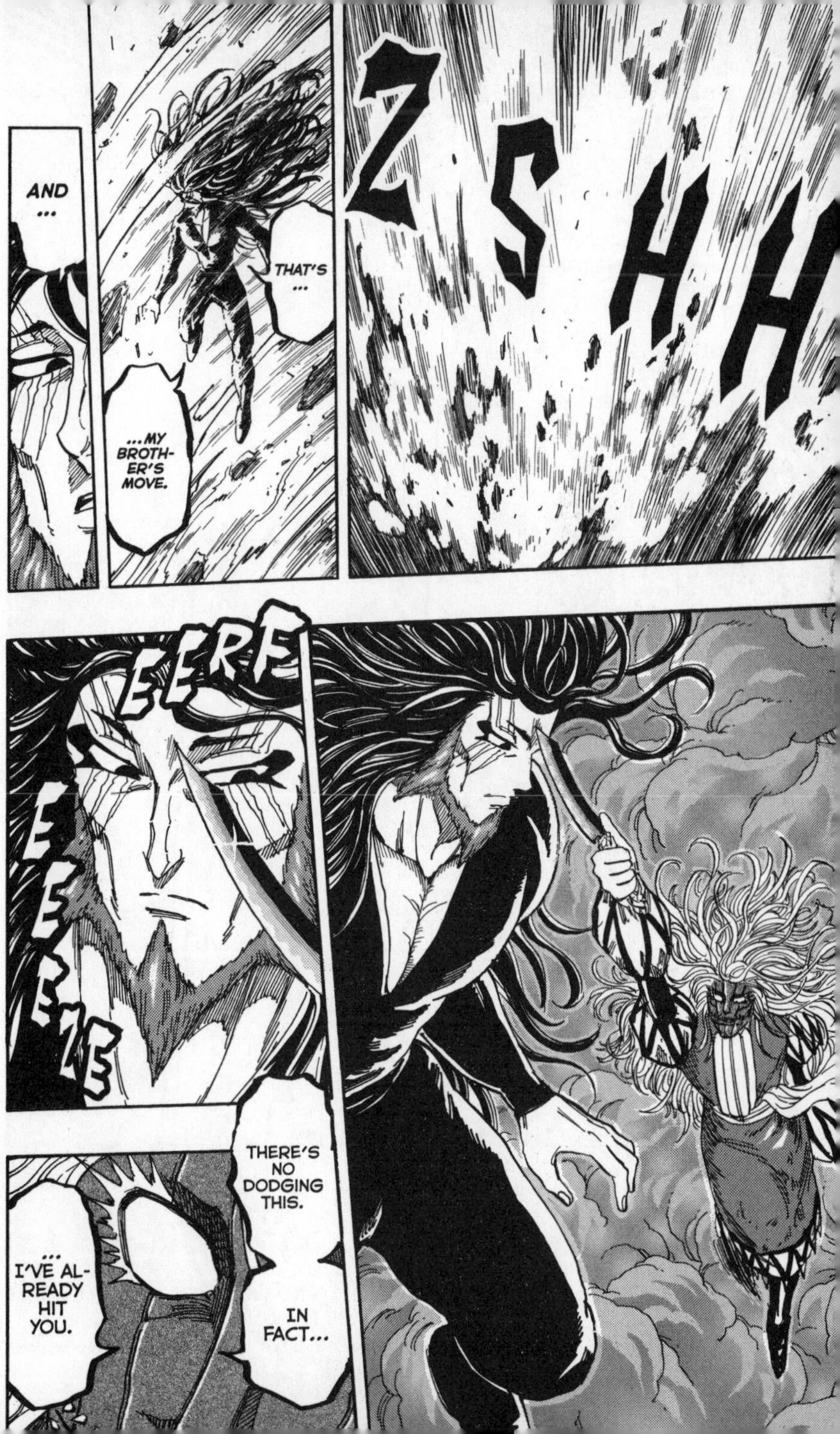
ZSHH
THAT'S...
...MY BROTHER'S MOVE.
AND...
THERE'S NO DODGING THIS.
IN FACT...
EERF
EEEEEE
...I'VE ALREADY HIT YOU.

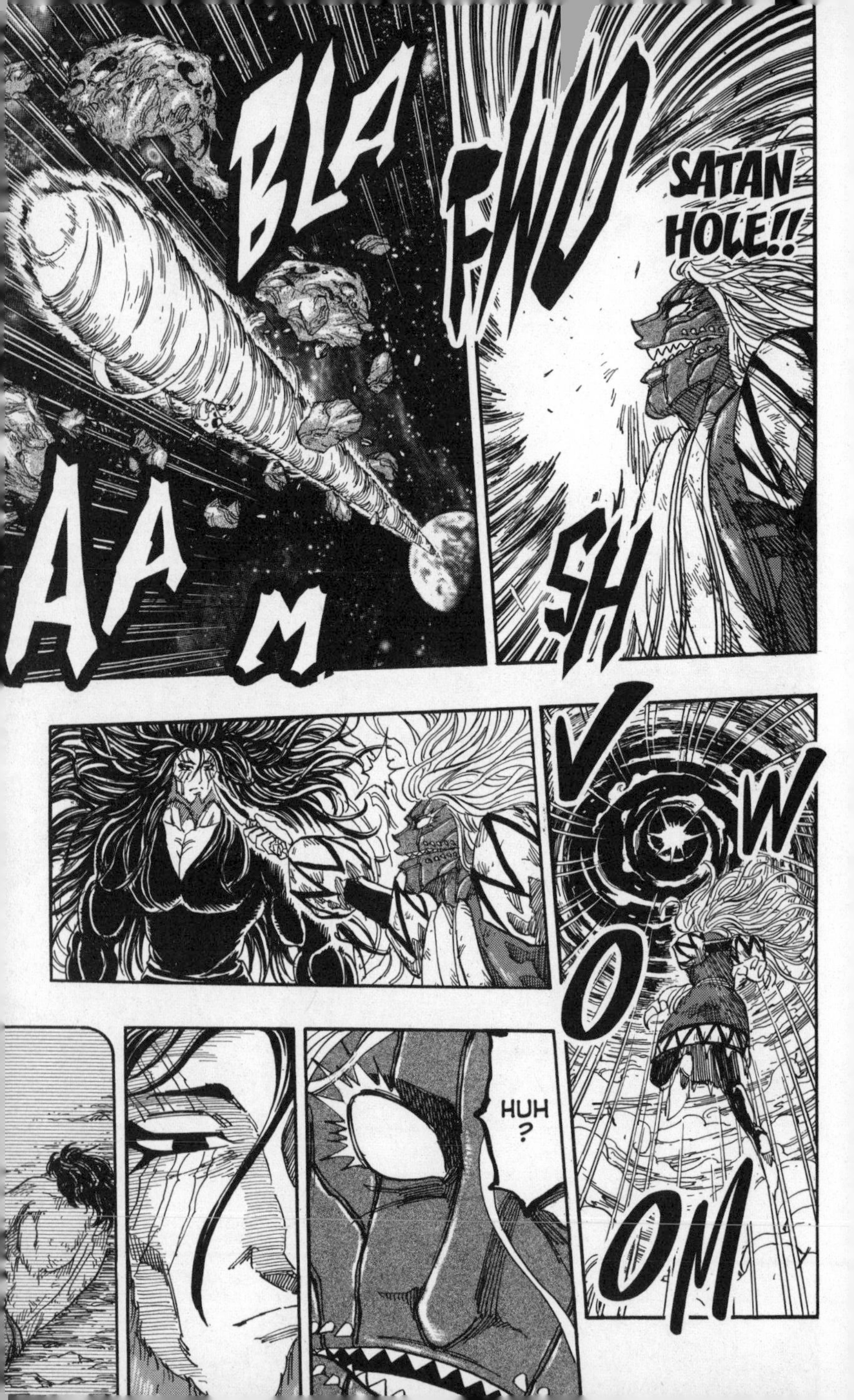
SATAN HOLE!!
FWO
SH
BLA
AAM
V
W
O
OM
HUH?

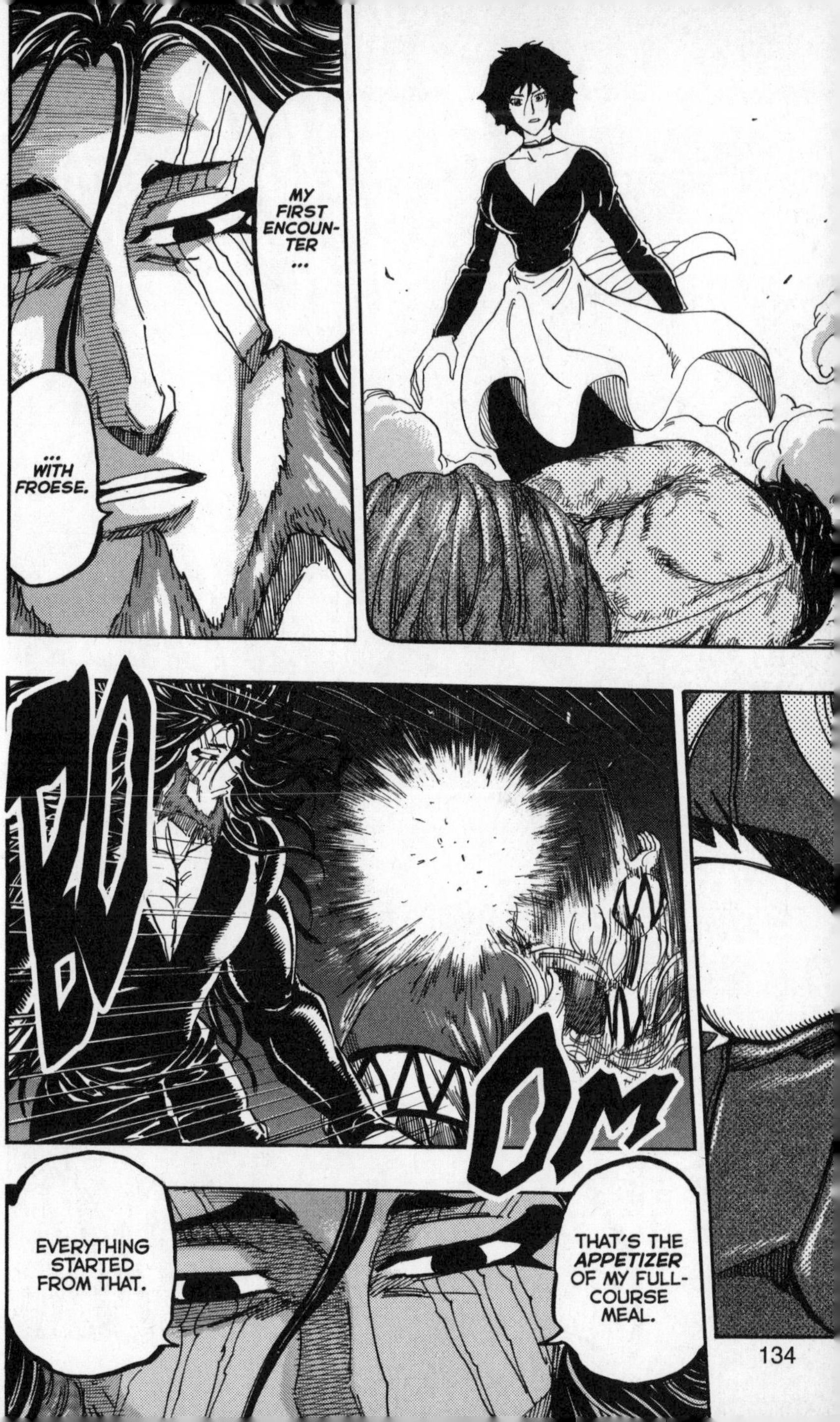
MY FIRST ENCOUN-TER ...
... WITH FROESE.
THAT'S THE *APPETIZER* OF MY FULL-COURSE MEAL.
EVERYTHING STARTED FROM THAT.

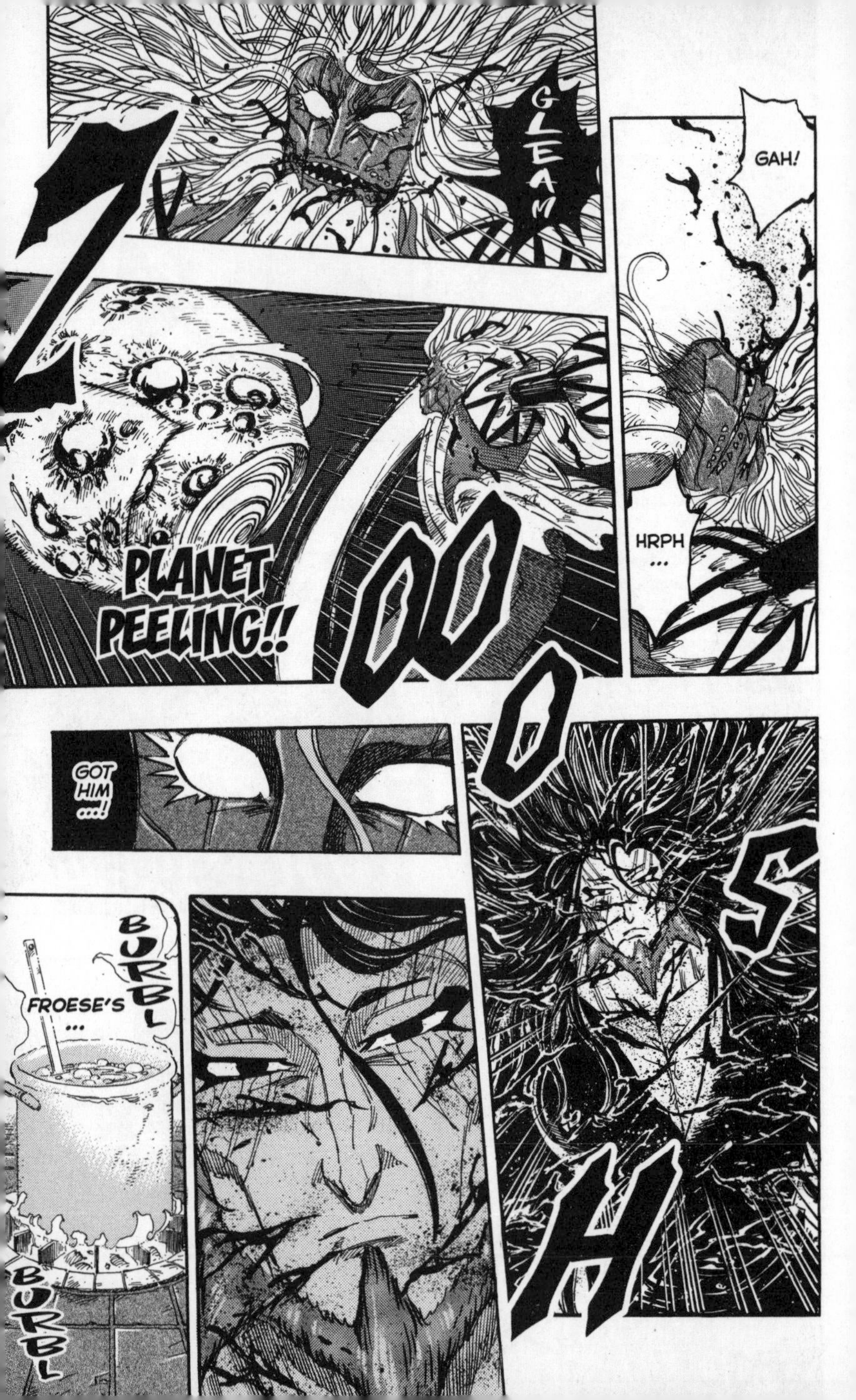
GAH!
HRPH ...
GLEAM
PLANET PEELING!!
OOO
GOT HIM ...!!
BURBL
FROESE'S ...
BURBL

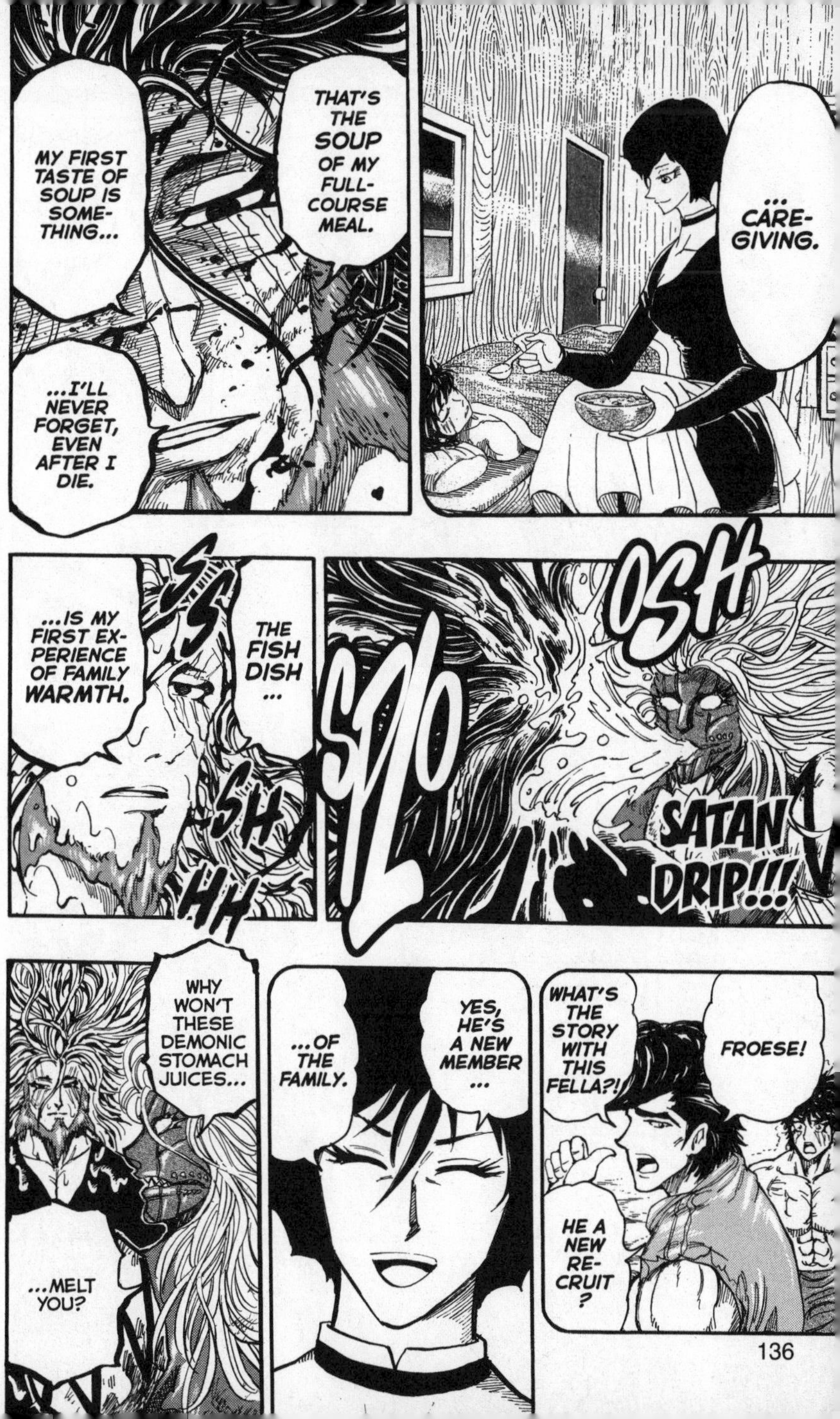
...CAREGIVING.
THAT'S THE SOUP OF MY FULL-COURSE MEAL.
MY FIRST TASTE OF SOUP IS SOMETHING...
...I'LL NEVER FORGET, EVEN AFTER I DIE.
OSH
SZLO
SATAN DRIP!!!
THE FISH DISH...
...IS MY FIRST EXPERIENCE OF FAMILY WARMTH.
SSS
SHHH
FROESE!
WHAT'S THE STORY WITH THIS FELLA?!
HE A NEW RECRUIT?
YES, HE'S A NEW MEMBER...
...OF THE FAMILY.
WHY WON'T THESE DEMONIC STOMACH JUICES...
...MELT YOU?

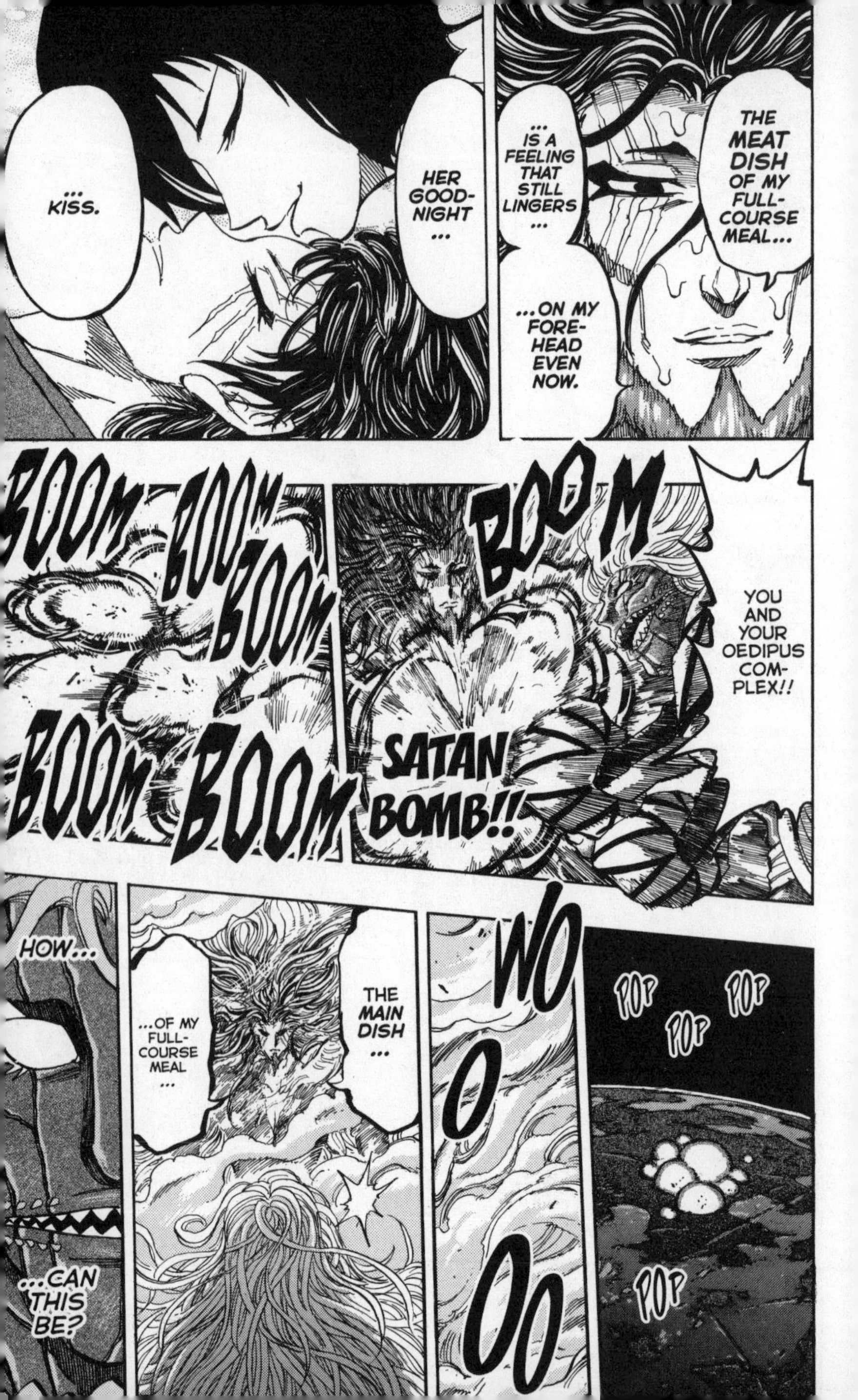
THE MEAT DISH OF MY FULL-COURSE MEAL...
... IS A FEELING THAT STILL LINGERS ...
...ON MY FORE-HEAD EVEN NOW.
HER GOOD-NIGHT ...
... KISS.
YOU AND YOUR OEDIPUS COM-PLEX!!
BOOM
SATAN BOMB!!
BOOM
BOOM
BOOM
BOOM
BOOM
POP
POP
POP
POP
WOOOO
THE MAIN DISH ...
...OF MY FULL-COURSE MEAL ...
HOW...
...CAN THIS BE?

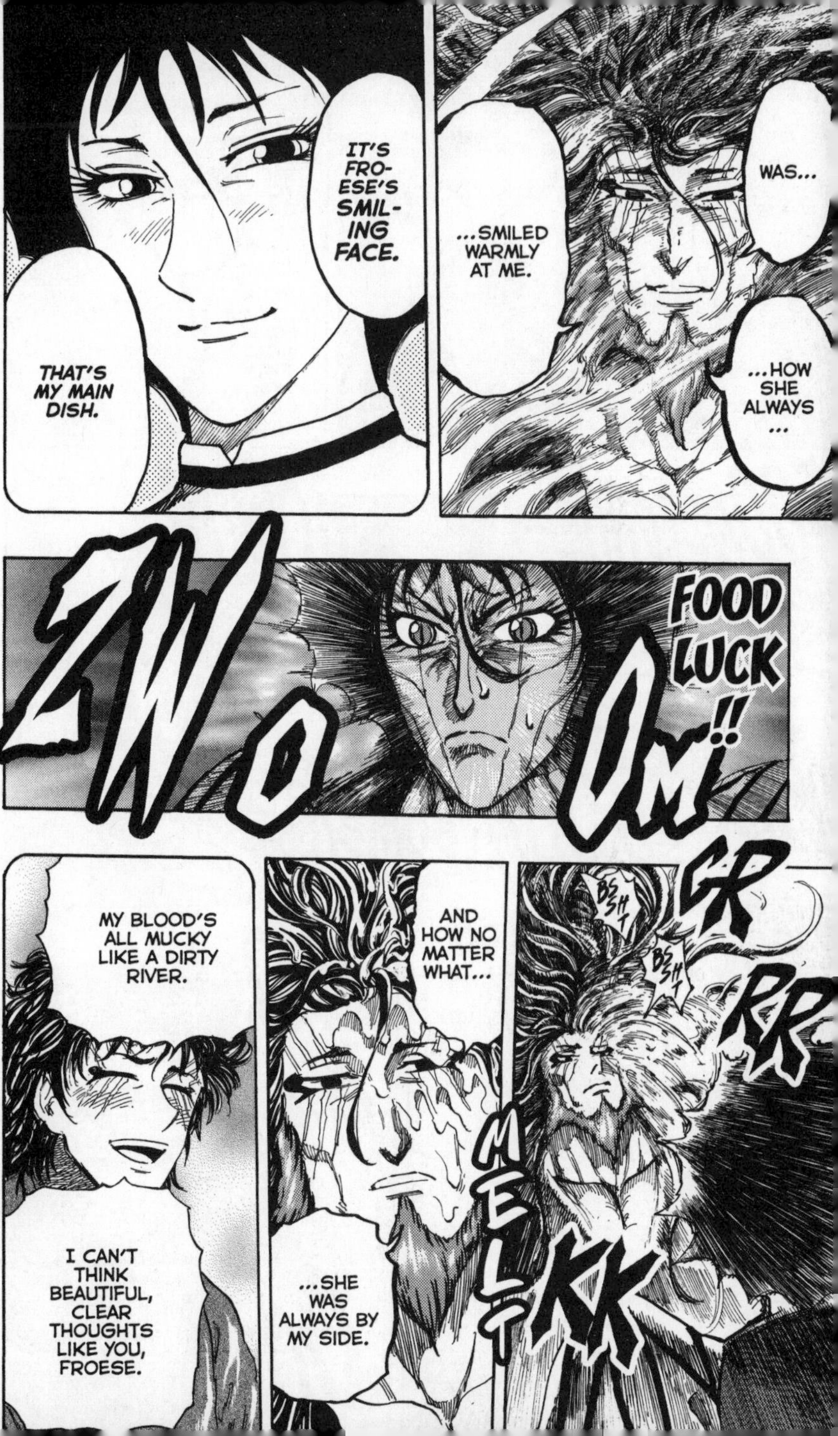
WAS...
...HOW SHE ALWAYS...
...SMILED WARMLY AT ME.
IT'S FROESE'S SMILING FACE.
THAT'S MY MAIN DISH.
ZWOOM!!
FOOD LUCK
GRRR
BSHT
BSHT
MELT
KK
AND HOW NO MATTER WHAT...
...SHE WAS ALWAYS BY MY SIDE.
MY BLOOD'S ALL MUCKY LIKE A DIRTY RIVER.
I CAN'T THINK BEAUTIFUL, CLEAR THOUGHTS LIKE YOU, FROESE.

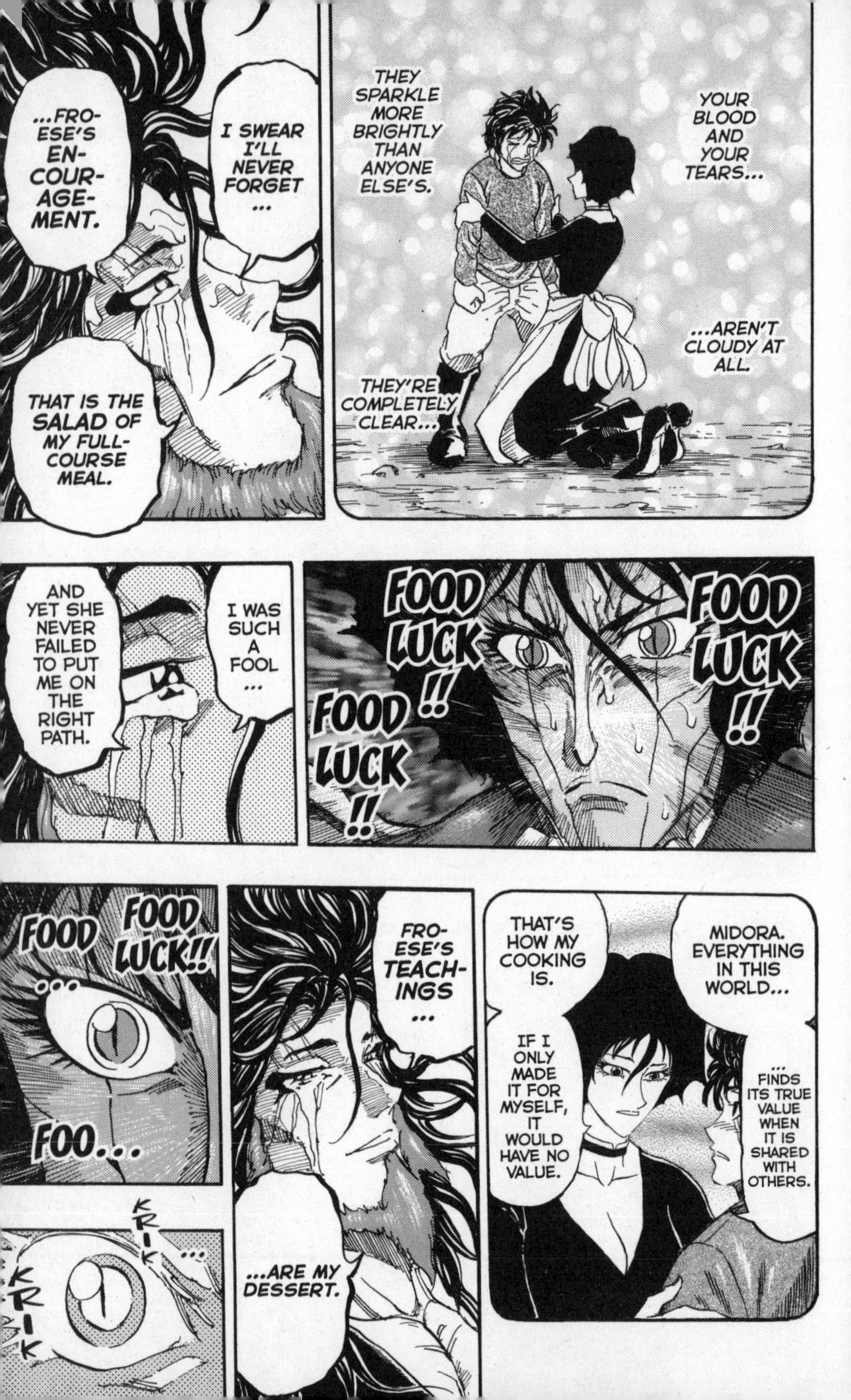
YOUR BLOOD AND YOUR TEARS...
THEY SPARKLE MORE BRIGHTLY THAN ANYONE ELSE'S.
...AREN'T CLOUDY AT ALL.
THEY'RE COMPLETELY CLEAR...
I SWEAR I'LL NEVER FORGET...
...FRO-ESE'S EN-COUR-AGE-MENT.
THAT IS THE SALAD OF MY FULL-COURSE MEAL.
FOOD LUCK!!
FOOD LUCK!!
FOOD LUCK!!
I WAS SUCH A FOOL...
AND YET SHE NEVER FAILED TO PUT ME ON THE RIGHT PATH.
MIDORA. EVERYTHING IN THIS WORLD...
...FINDS ITS TRUE VALUE WHEN IT IS SHARED WITH OTHERS.
THAT'S HOW MY COOKING IS.
IF I ONLY MADE IT FOR MYSELF, IT WOULD HAVE NO VALUE.
FRO-ESE'S TEACH-INGS...
...ARE MY DESSERT.
FOOD LUCK!!
FOOD...
FOO...
KRIK KRIK...

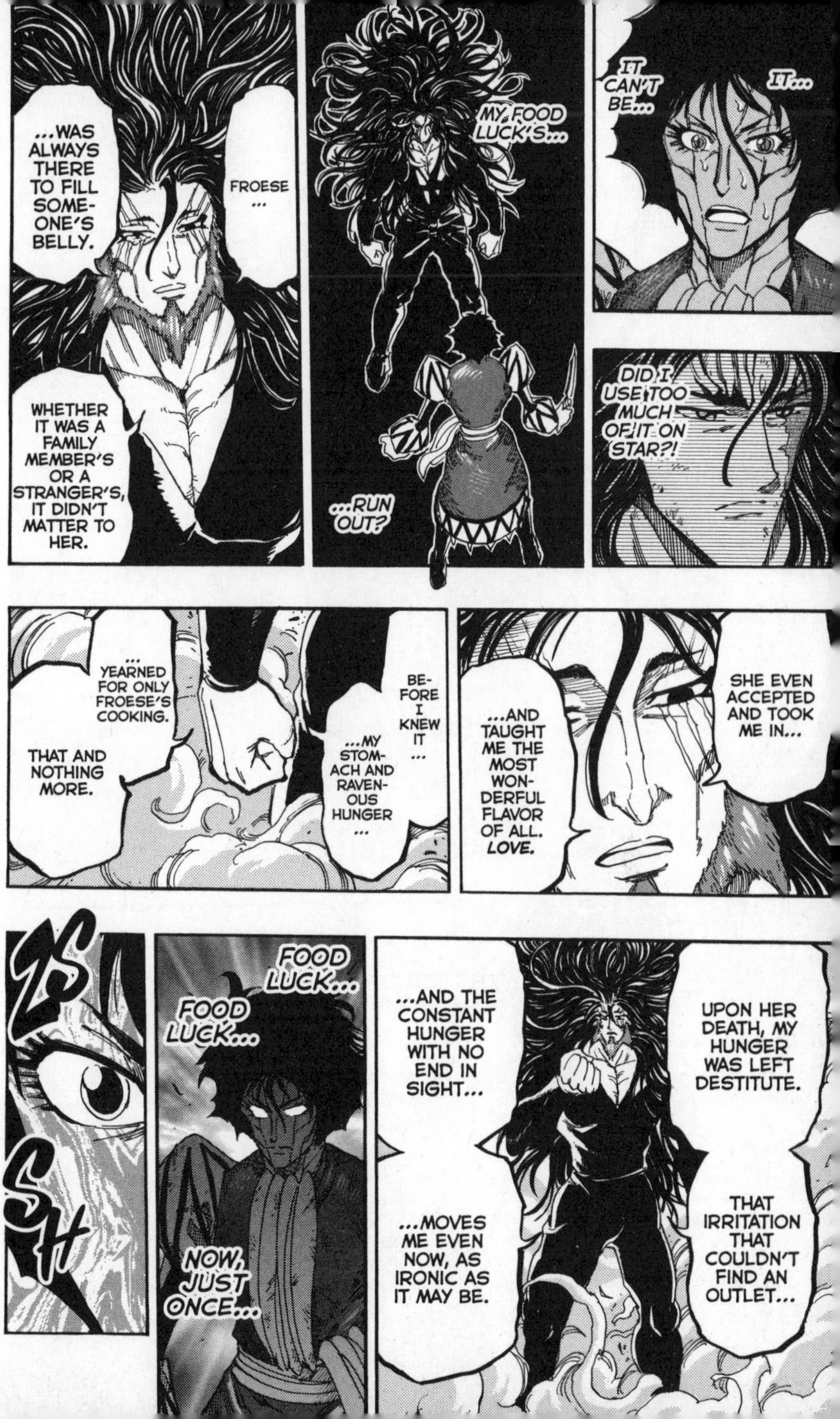
IT...
IT CAN'T BE...
DID I USE TOO MUCH OF IT ON STAR?!
MY FOOD LUCK'S...
...RUN OUT?
FROESE...
...WAS ALWAYS THERE TO FILL SOME-ONE'S BELLY.
WHETHER IT WAS A FAMILY MEMBER'S OR A STRANGER'S, IT DIDN'T MATTER TO HER.
SHE EVEN ACCEPTED AND TOOK ME IN...
...AND TAUGHT ME THE MOST WON-DERFUL FLAVOR OF ALL. *LOVE.*
BE-FORE I KNEW IT...
...MY STOM-ACH AND RAVEN-OUS HUNGER...
...YEARNED FOR ONLY FROESE'S COOKING.
THAT AND NOTHING MORE.
UPON HER DEATH, MY HUNGER WAS LEFT DESTITUTE.
THAT IRRITATION THAT COULDN'T FIND AN OUTLET...
...AND THE CONSTANT HUNGER WITH NO END IN SIGHT...
...MOVES ME EVEN NOW, AS IRONIC AS IT MAY BE.
FOOD LUCK...
FOOD LUCK...
NOW, JUST ONCE...
ZS
SH

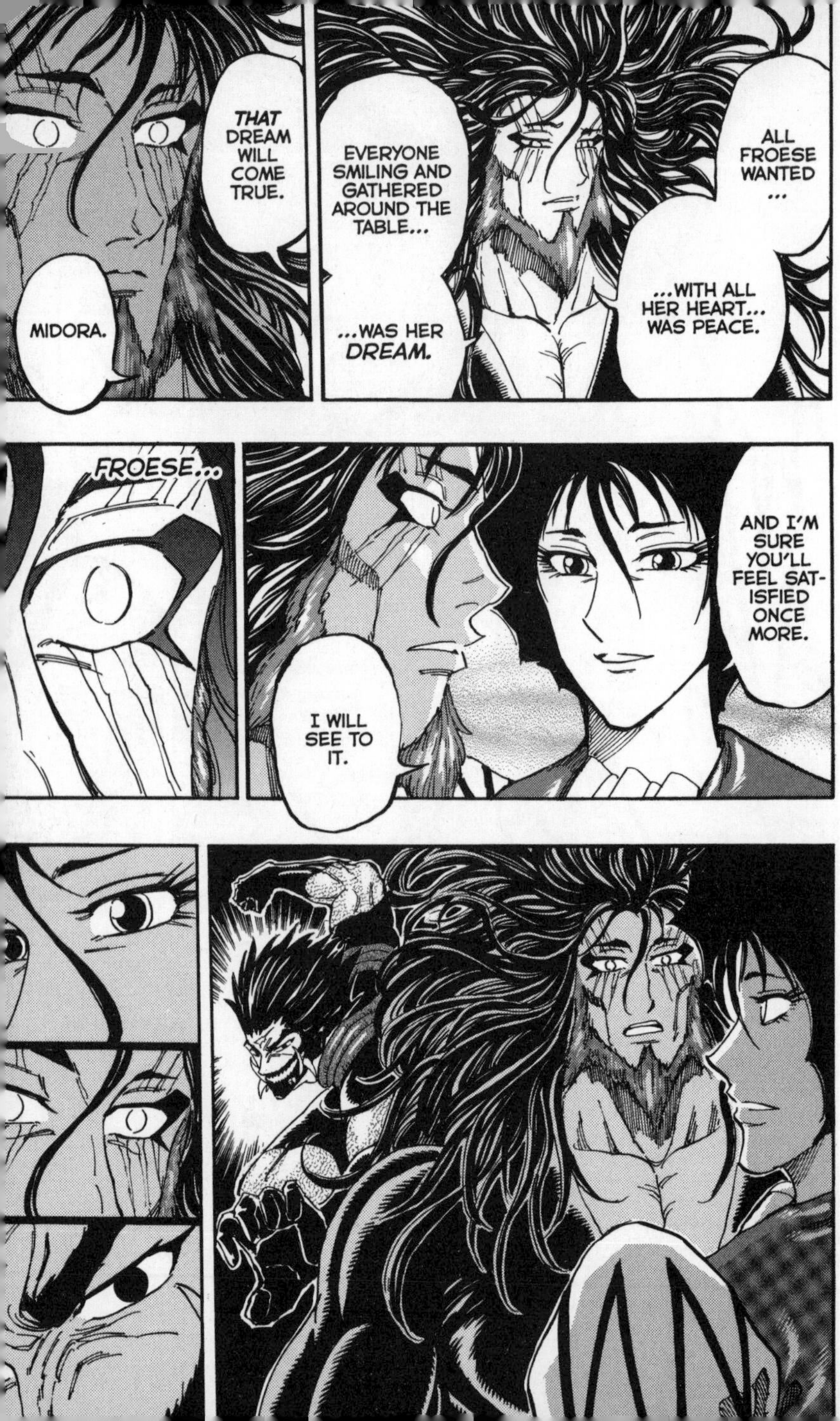
ALL FROESE WANTED...
...WITH ALL HER HEART... WAS PEACE.
EVERYONE SMILING AND GATHERED AROUND THE TABLE...
...WAS HER *DREAM.*
THAT DREAM WILL COME TRUE.
MIDORA.
AND I'M SURE YOU'LL FEEL SATISFIED ONCE MORE.
I WILL SEE TO IT.
FROESE...

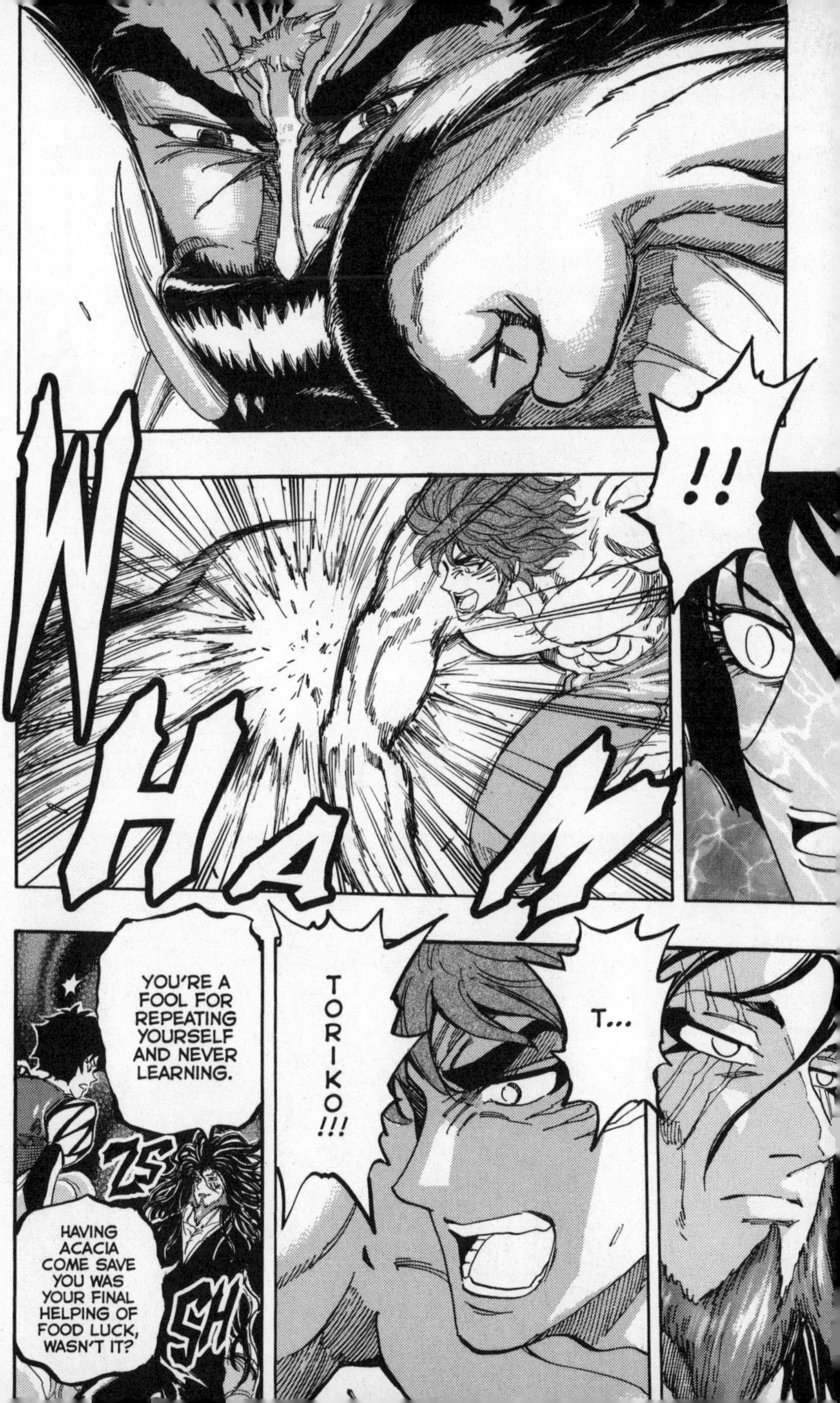

!!
WHAM
T...
TORIKO!!!
YOU'RE A FOOL FOR REPEATING YOURSELF AND NEVER LEARNING.
HAVING ACACIA COME SAVE YOU WAS YOUR FINAL HELPING OF FOOD LUCK, WASN'T IT?
ZSSH

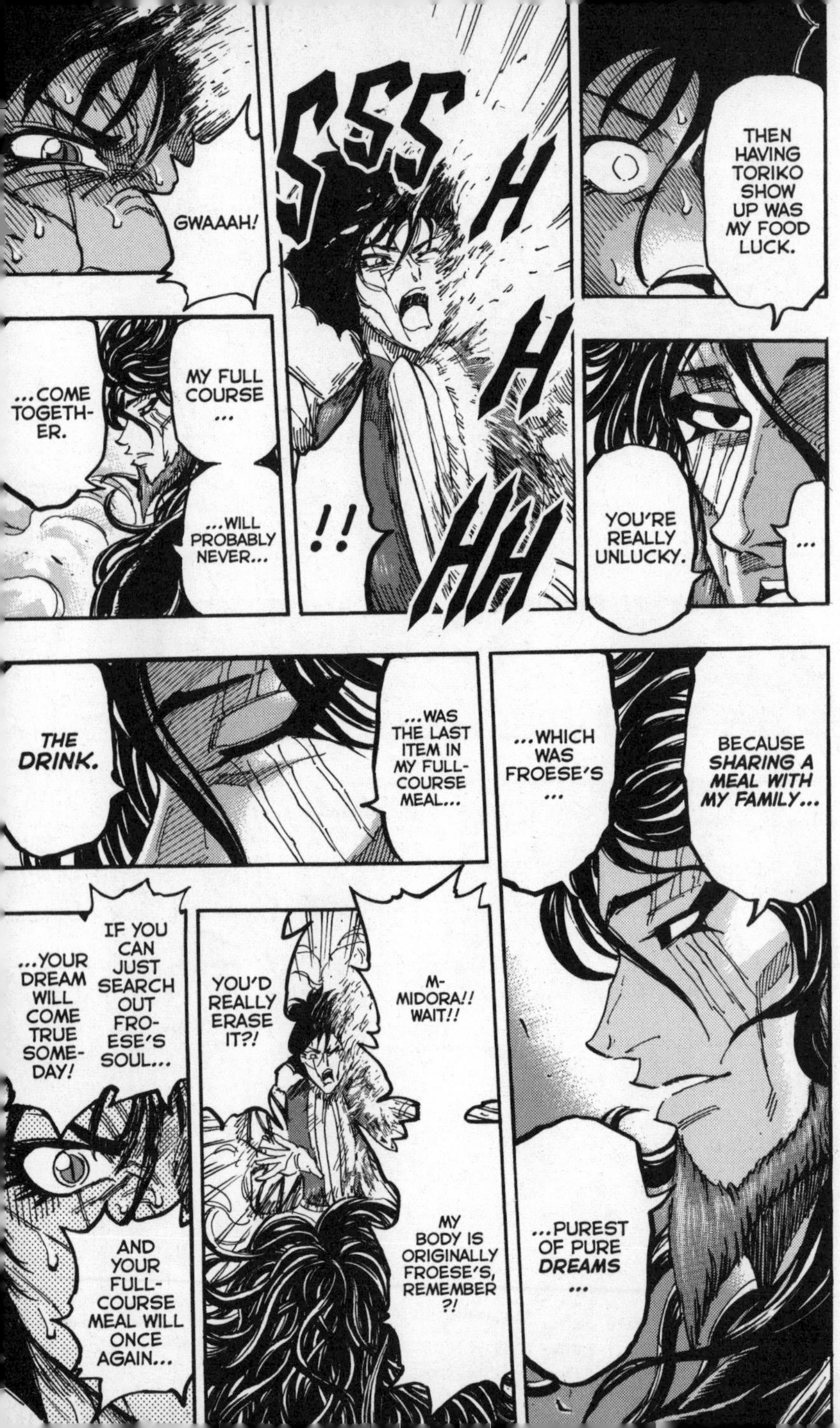
THEN HAVING TORIKO SHOW UP WAS MY FOOD LUCK.
YOU'RE REALLY UNLUCKY.
...
SSSHHHHH
!!
GWAAAH!
MY FULL COURSE ...
...WILL PROBABLY NEVER...
...COME TOGETHER.
BECAUSE SHARING A MEAL WITH MY FAMILY...
...WHICH WAS FROESE'S ...
...PUREST OF PURE DREAMS ...
...WAS THE LAST ITEM IN MY FULL-COURSE MEAL...
THE DRINK.
M-MIDORA!! WAIT!!
YOU'D REALLY ERASE IT?!
MY BODY IS ORIGINALLY FROESE'S, REMEMBER ?!
IF YOU CAN JUST SEARCH OUT FROESE'S SOUL...
...YOUR DREAM WILL COME TRUE SOMEDAY!
AND YOUR FULL-COURSE MEAL WILL ONCE AGAIN...

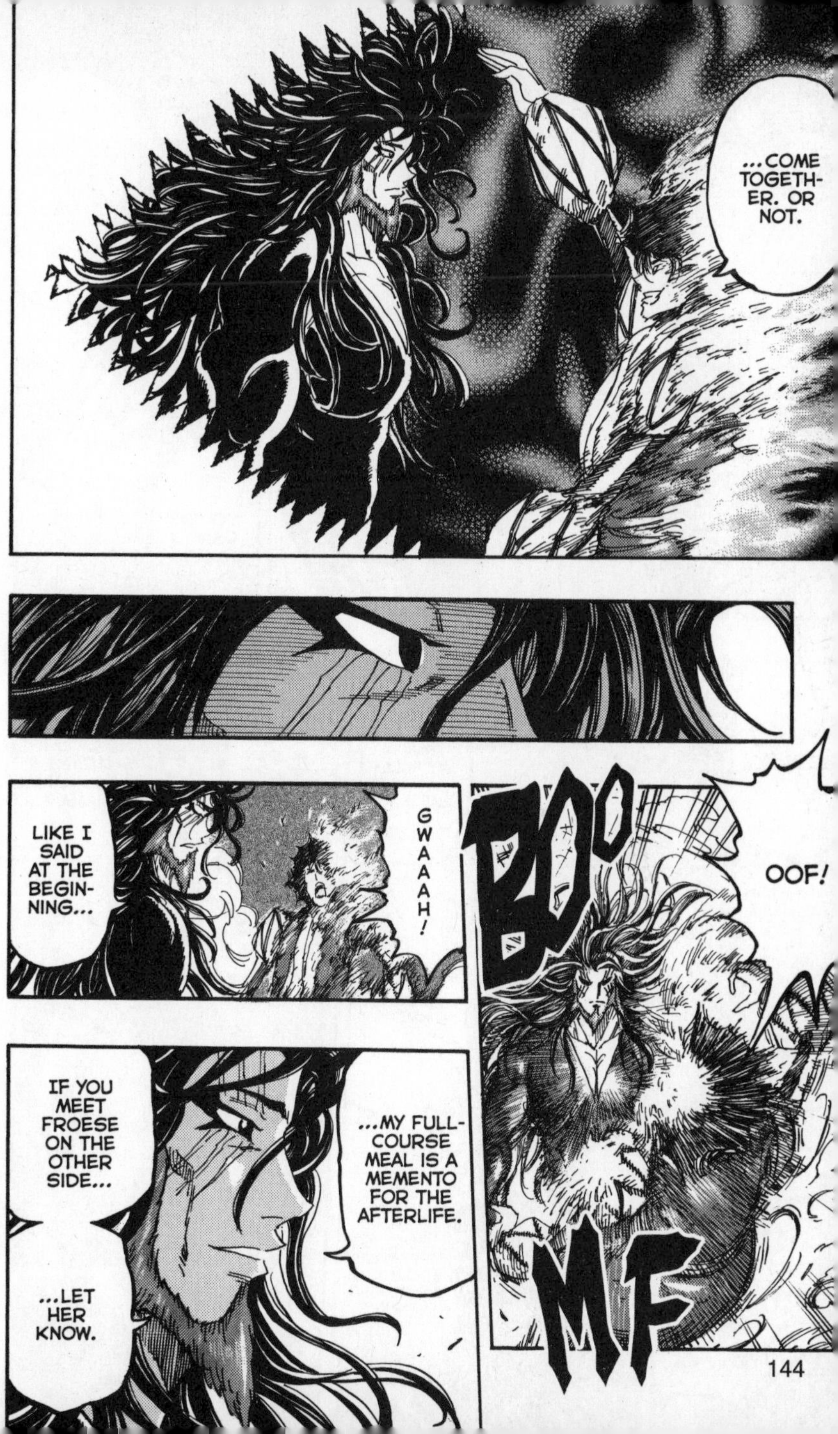
...COME TOGETHER. OR NOT.
BOOMF
OOF!
GWAAAAH!
LIKE I SAID AT THE BEGINNING...
...MY FULL-COURSE MEAL IS A MEMENTO FOR THE AFTERLIFE.
IF YOU MEET FROESE ON THE OTHER SIDE...
...LET HER KNOW.

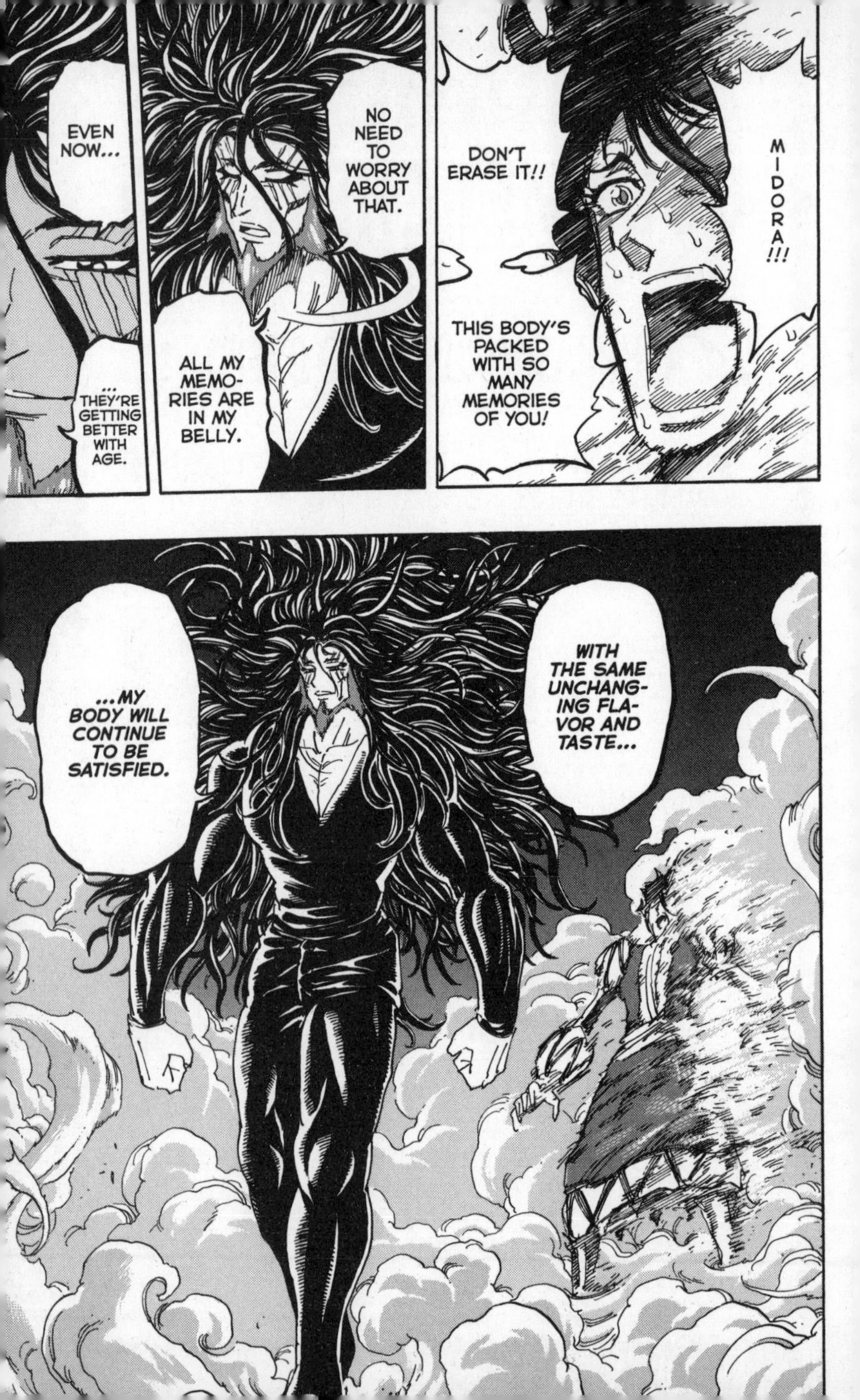
MIDORA!!!
DON'T ERASE IT!!
THIS BODY'S PACKED WITH SO MANY MEMORIES OF YOU!
NO NEED TO WORRY ABOUT THAT.
ALL MY MEMORIES ARE IN MY BELLY.
EVEN NOW...
...THEY'RE GETTING BETTER WITH AGE.
WITH THE SAME UNCHANGING FLAVOR AND TASTE...
...MY BODY WILL CONTINUE TO BE SATISFIED.

GOURMET CHECKLIST

Vol. 420

ASHURASAURUS (WILD BREED)
(DRAGON)

CAPTURE LEVEL: 4,990
HABITAT: THE FOREST ON SKY DEER'S HORNS
SIZE: 350 M
HEIGHT: ---
WEIGHT: 30,000 TONS
PRICE: 3,500,000 YEN PER 100 G

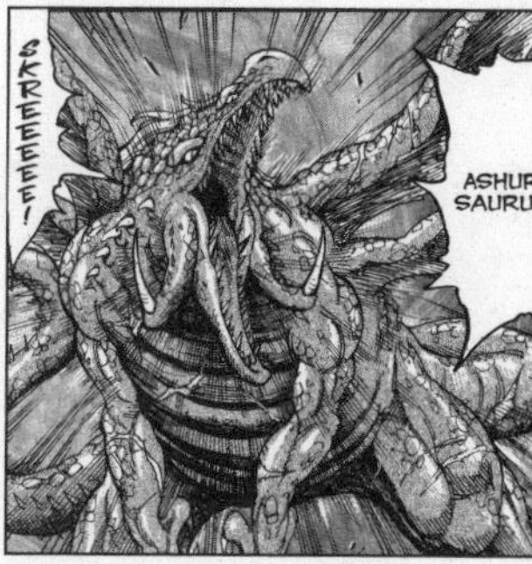
ASHURA-SAURUS?!
SKREEEEE!

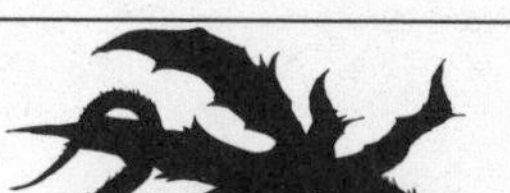

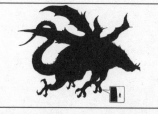

SCALE

A WILD BREED THAT LIVES IN THE FOREST IN THE DEER KING'S HORNS IN AREA 5. THIS FOREST IS ALSO KNOWN AS THE "DEN OF MONSTERS" WITH HORDES OF MONSTERS WHOSE CAPTURE LEVELS AVERAGE AROUND 4,000. PARTS OF ITS BODY ARE ON KNOCKING MASTER JIRO'S AND SETSUNO'S FULL-COURSE MEALS AS THEIR MEAT DISHES. IT'S SCARY BUT IT TASTES DELICIOUS! IN THE HUMAN WORLD, THIS INGREDIENT IS CONSIDERED A RARE DELICACY.

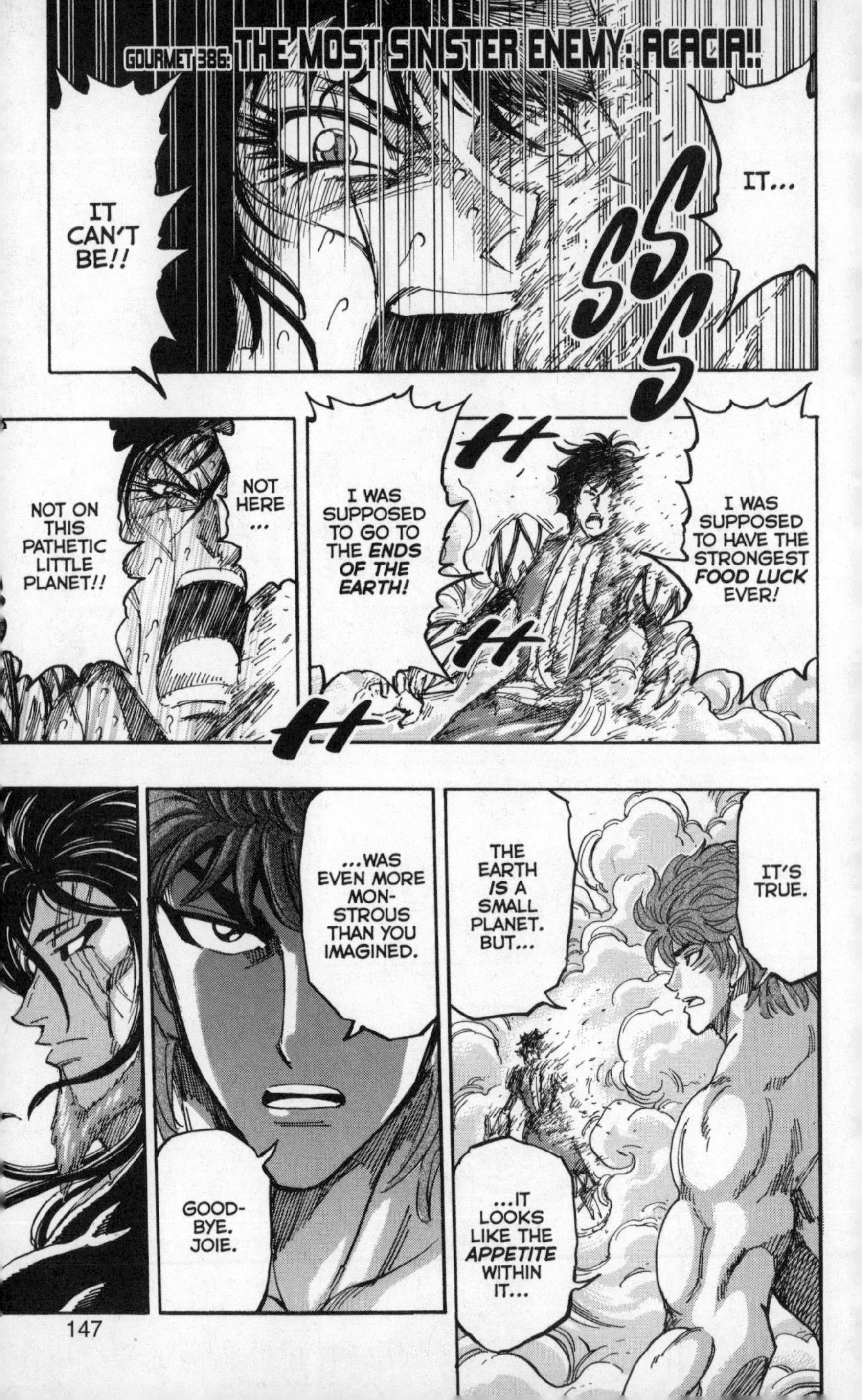
GOURMET 386: THE MOST SINISTER ENEMY: ACACIA!!
IT...
IT CAN'T BE!!
I WAS SUPPOSED TO HAVE THE STRONGEST *FOOD LUCK* EVER!
I WAS SUPPOSED TO GO TO THE *ENDS OF THE EARTH!*
NOT HERE...
NOT ON THIS PATHETIC LITTLE PLANET!!
IT'S TRUE.
THE EARTH *IS* A SMALL PLANET. BUT...
...IT LOOKS LIKE THE *APPETITE* WITHIN IT...
...WAS EVEN MORE MONSTROUS THAN YOU IMAGINED.
GOOD-BYE. JOIE.

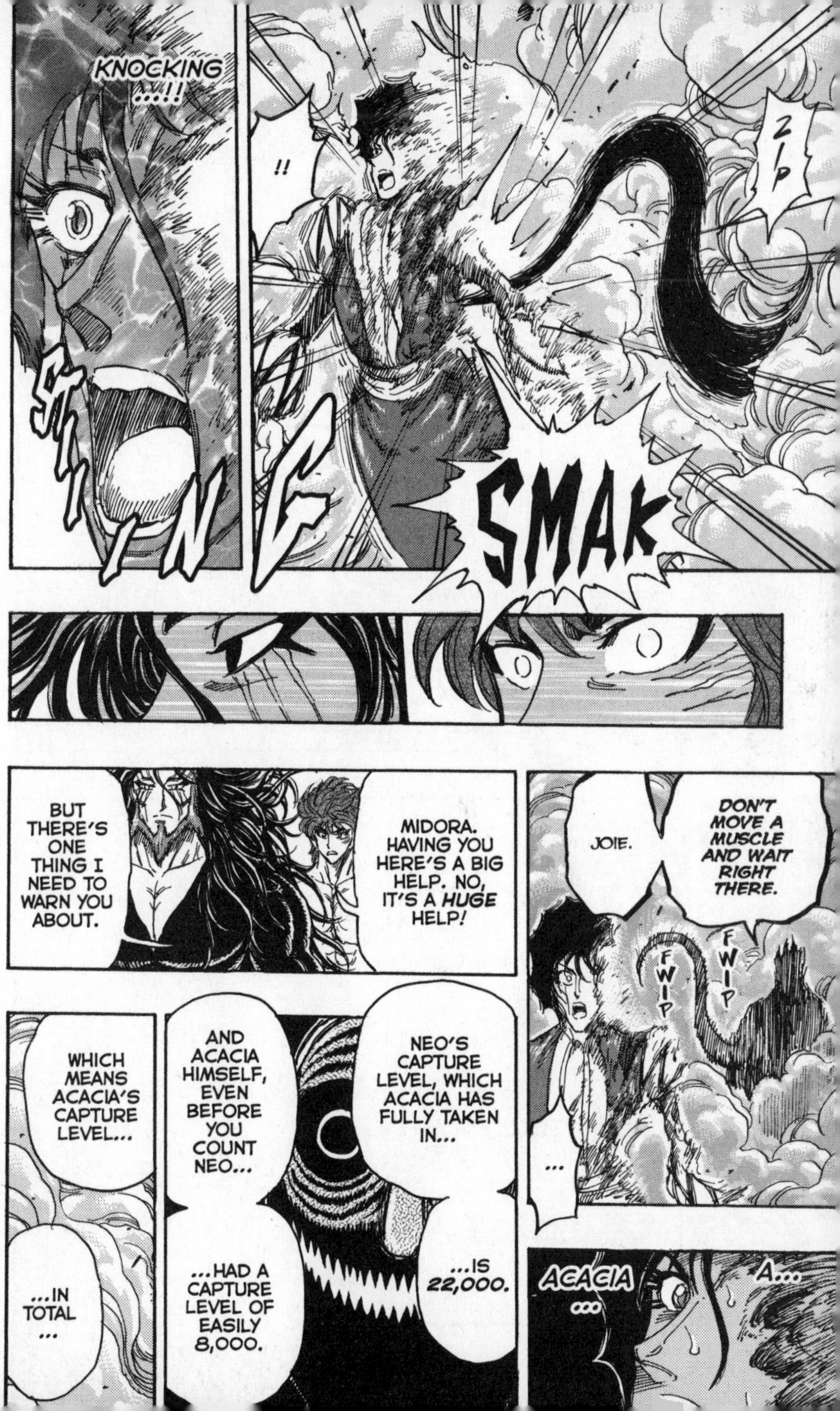
Zip
!!
SMAK
KNOCKING ...!!
SHIIING
JOIE.
DON'T MOVE A MUSCLE AND WAIT RIGHT THERE.
FWIP
FWIP
...
MIDORA. HAVING YOU HERE'S A BIG HELP. NO, IT'S A *HUGE* HELP!
BUT THERE'S ONE THING I NEED TO WARN YOU ABOUT.
NEO'S CAPTURE LEVEL, WHICH ACACIA HAS FULLY TAKEN IN...
...IS 22,000.
AND ACACIA HIMSELF, EVEN BEFORE YOU COUNT NEO...
...HAD A CAPTURE LEVEL OF EASILY 8,000.
WHICH MEANS ACACIA'S CAPTURE LEVEL...
...IN TOTAL ...
A...
ACACIA ...

GOURMET 386: THE MOST SINISTER ENEMY: ACACIA!!

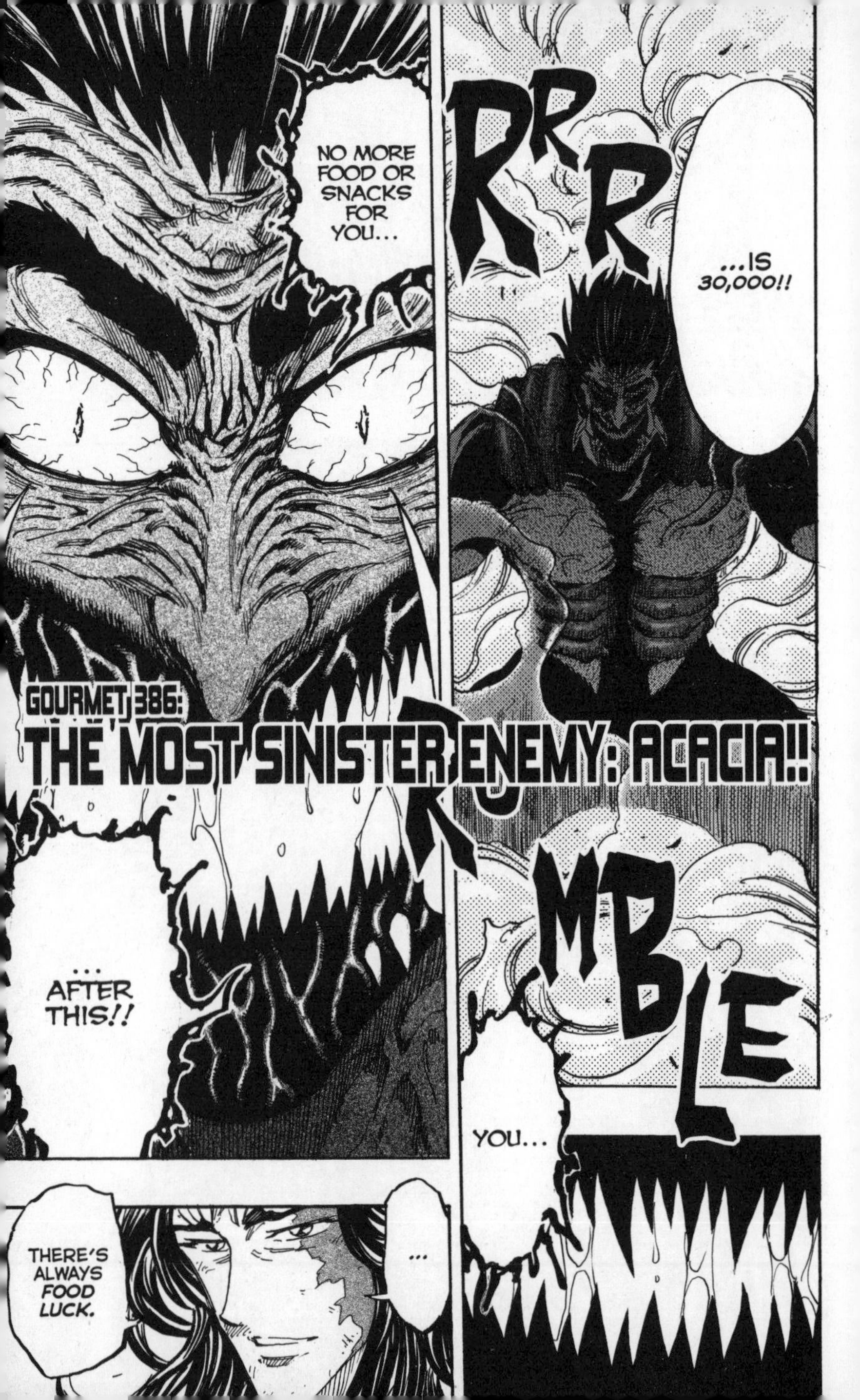

...IS 30,000!!
RRRRUMBLE
YOU...
NO MORE FOOD OR SNACKS FOR YOU...
...AFTER THIS!!
...
THERE'S ALWAYS FOOD LUCK.

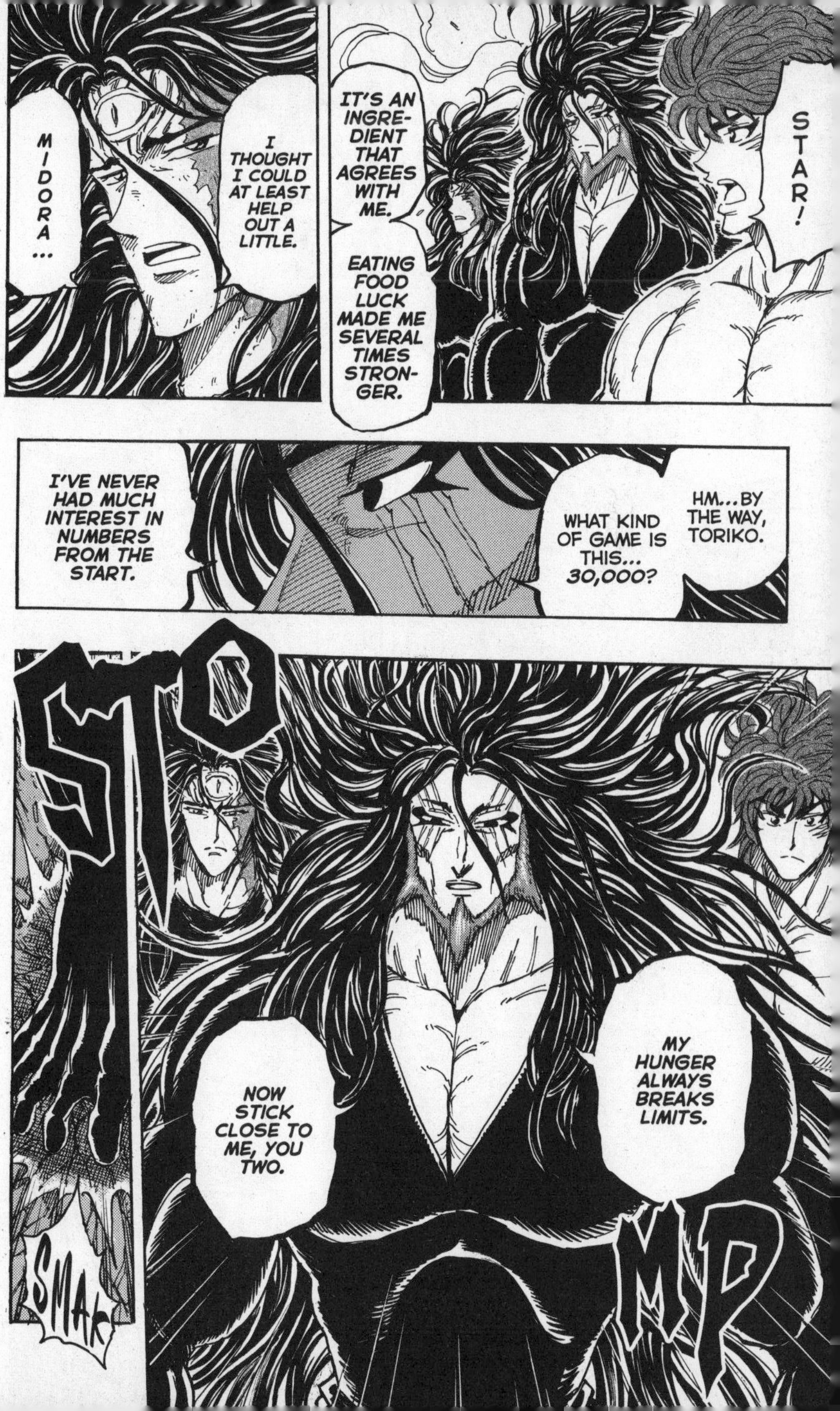
STAR!
IT'S AN INGREDIENT THAT AGREES WITH ME.
EATING FOOD LUCK MADE ME SEVERAL TIMES STRONGER.
I THOUGHT I COULD AT LEAST HELP OUT A LITTLE.
MIDORA...
HM...BY THE WAY, TORIKO.
WHAT KIND OF GAME IS THIS... 30,000?
I'VE NEVER HAD MUCH INTEREST IN NUMBERS FROM THE START.
MY HUNGER ALWAYS BREAKS LIMITS.
NOW STICK CLOSE TO ME, YOU TWO.
STO
MP
SMAK

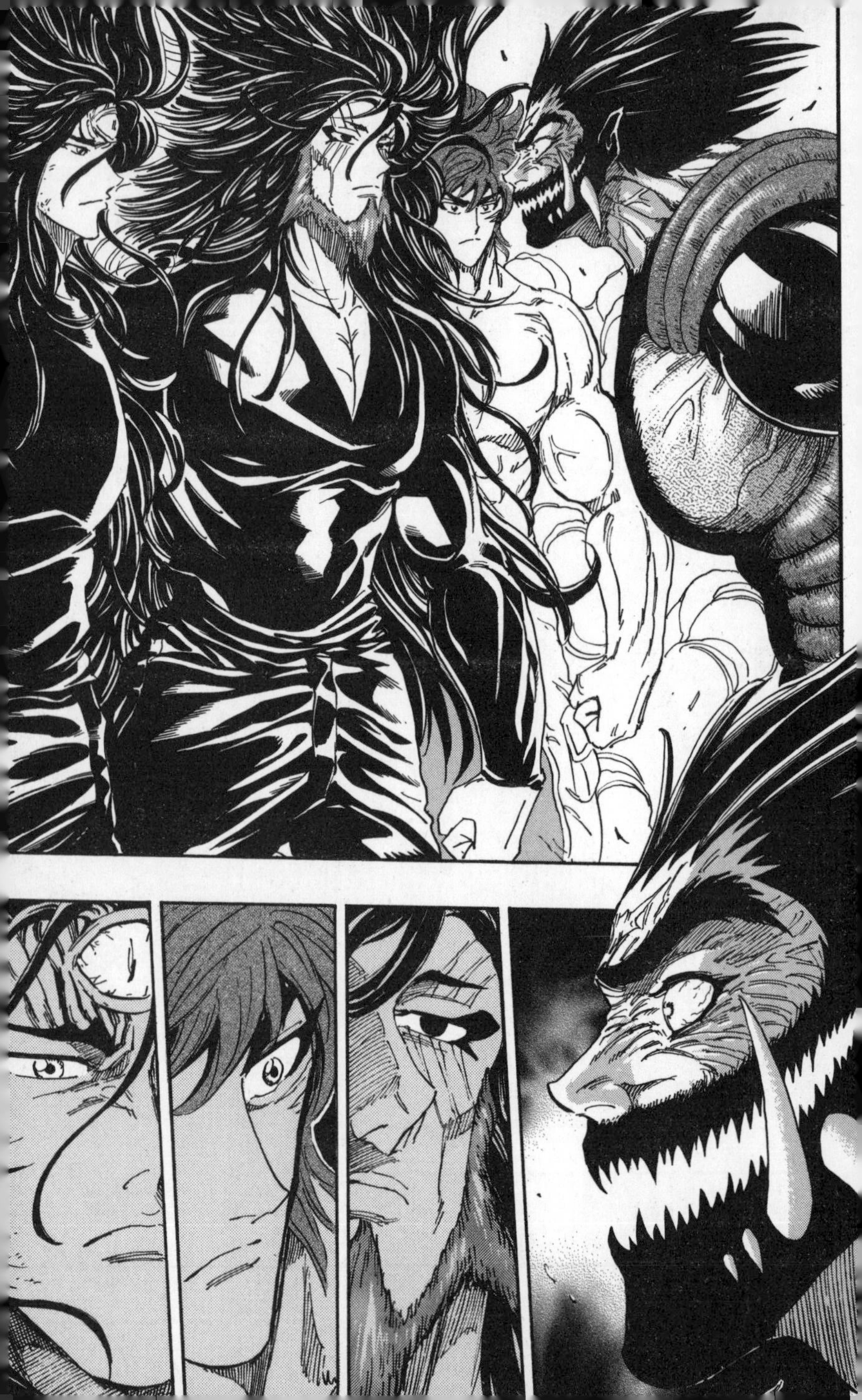

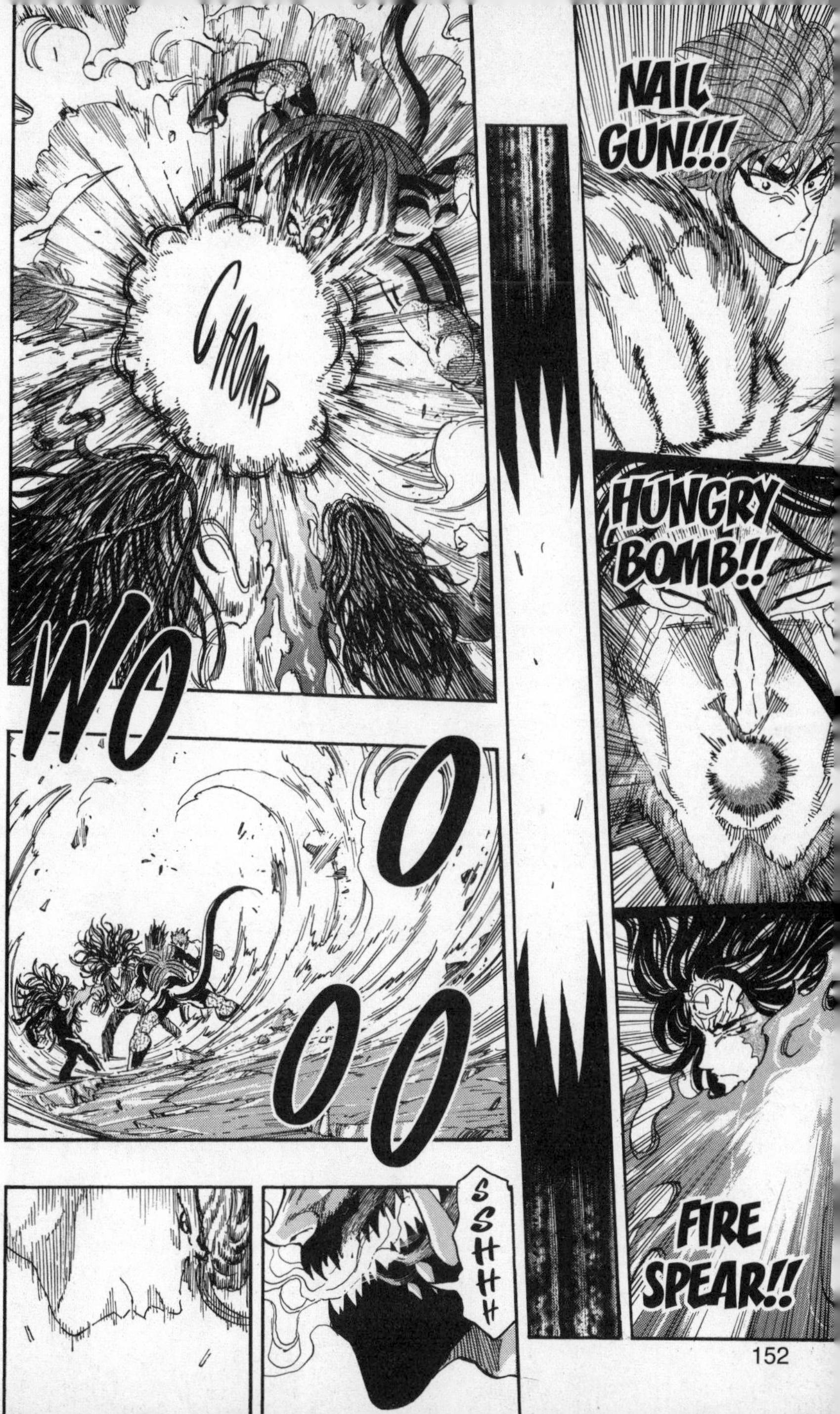
NAIL GUN!!!
HUNGRY BOMB!!
FIRE SPEAR!!
CHOMP
WOOOO
SSHHH

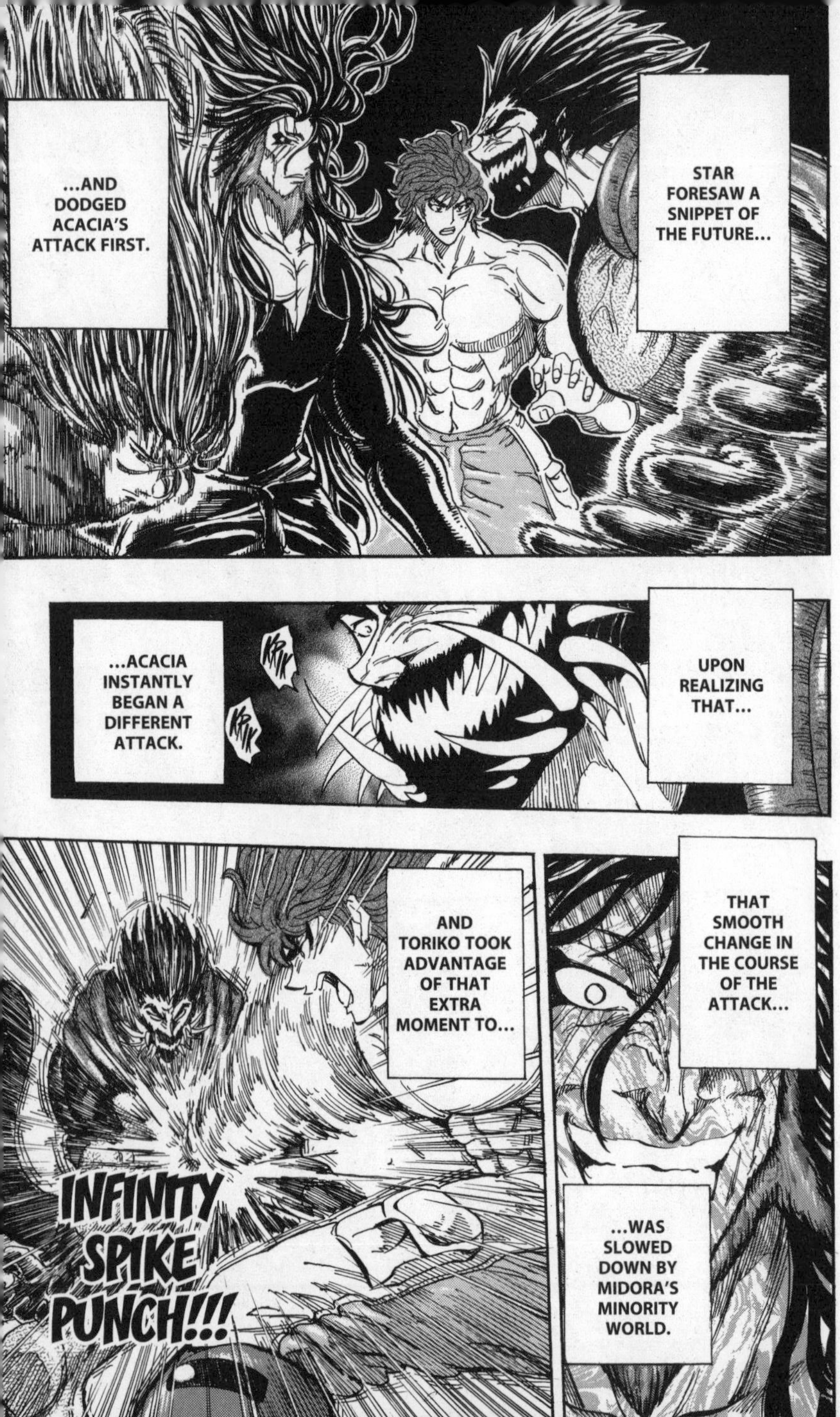
STAR FORESAW A SNIPPET OF THE FUTURE...
...AND DODGED ACACIA'S ATTACK FIRST.
UPON REALIZING THAT...
KRIK
KRIK
...ACACIA INSTANTLY BEGAN A DIFFERENT ATTACK.
THAT SMOOTH CHANGE IN THE COURSE OF THE ATTACK...
...WAS SLOWED DOWN BY MIDORA'S MINORITY WORLD.
AND TORIKO TOOK ADVANTAGE OF THAT EXTRA MOMENT TO...
INFINITY SPIKE PUNCH!!!

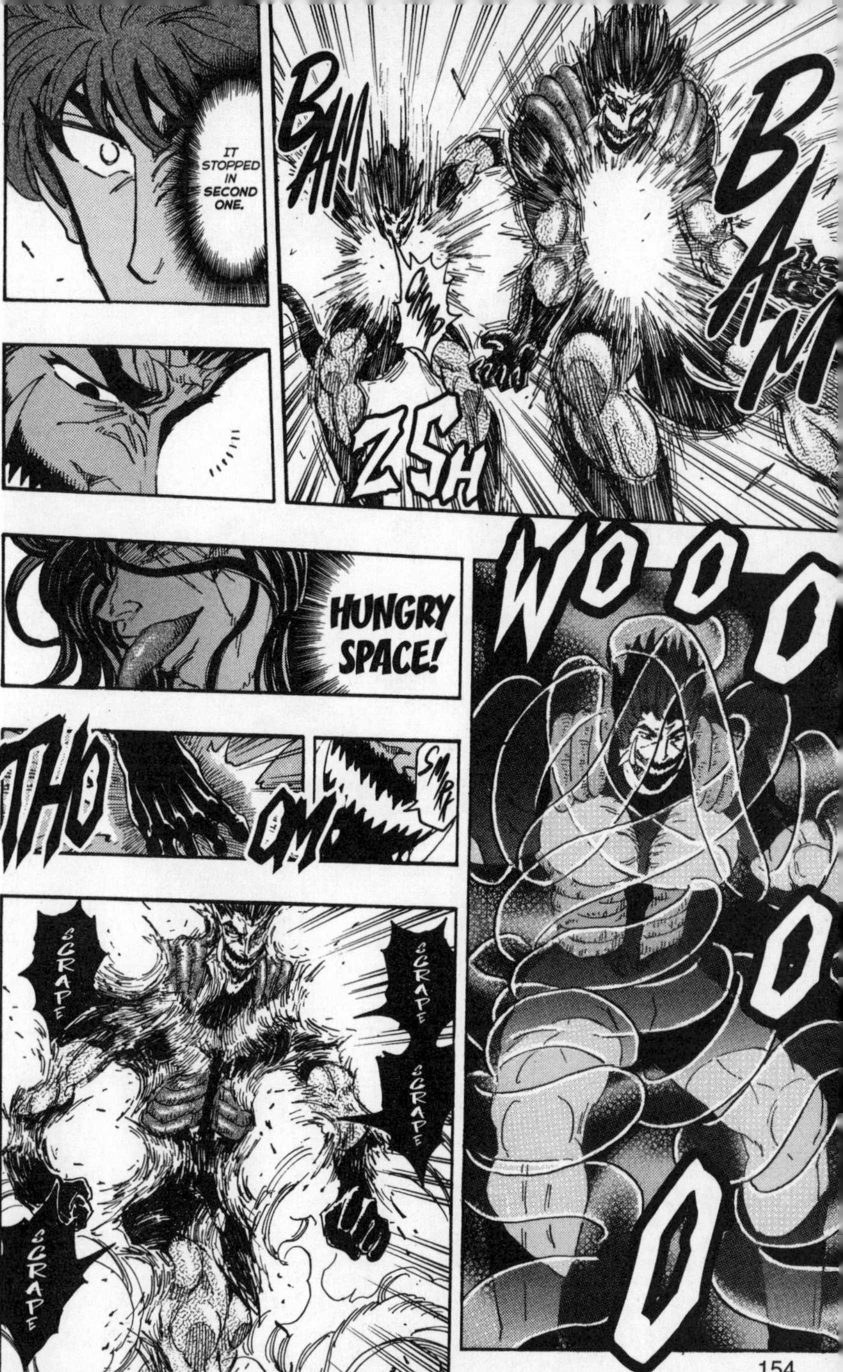
BAM
BAM
CHOMP
ZSH
IT STOPPED IN SECOND ONE.
WOOOOOO
HUNGRY SPACE!
THOOM
SMIRK
SCRAPE
SCRAPE
SCRAPE
SCRAPE

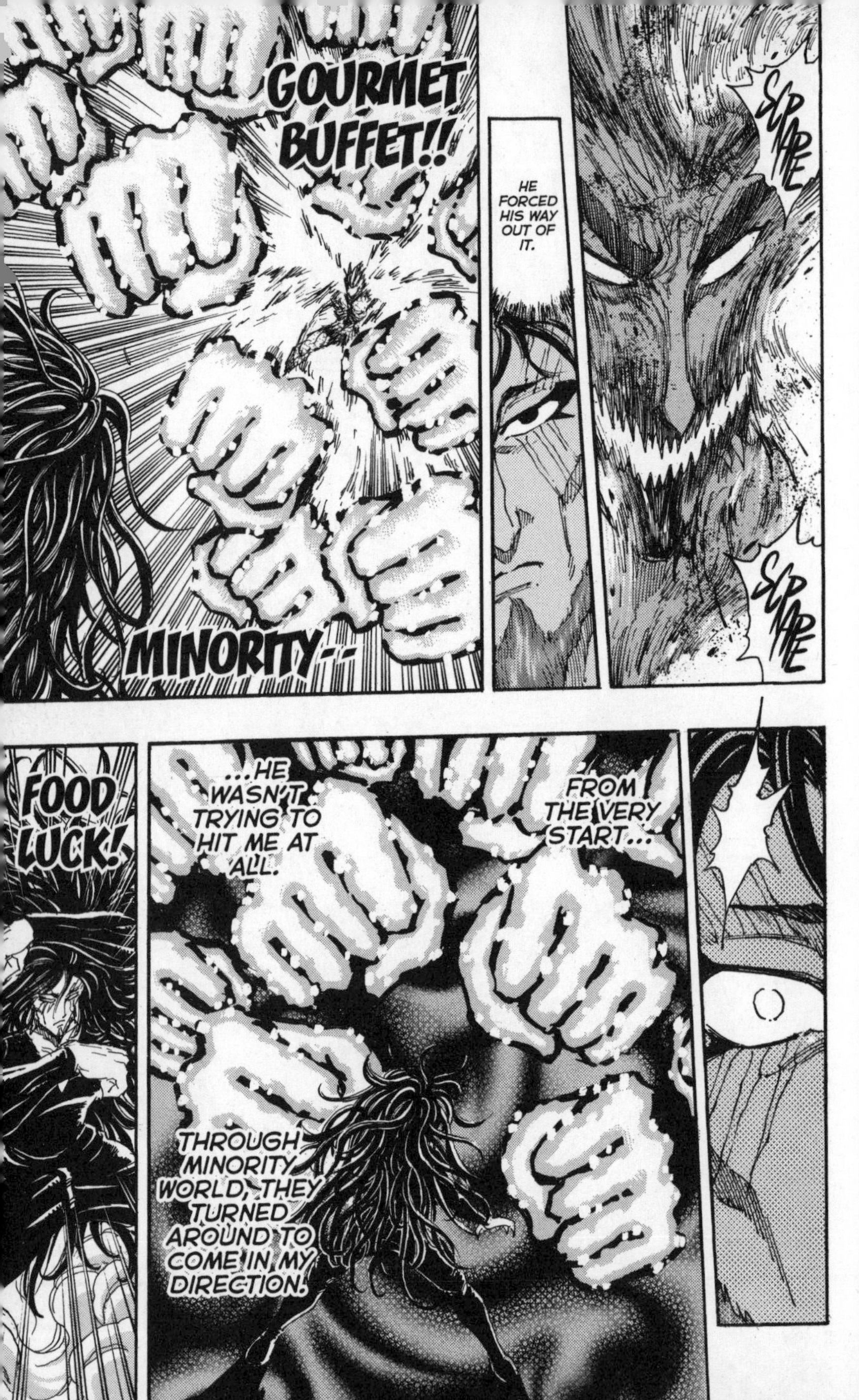
SCRAPE
SCRAPE
HE FORCED HIS WAY OUT OF IT.
GOURMET BUFFET!!
MINORITY--
FROM THE VERY START...
...HE WASN'T TRYING TO HIT ME AT ALL.
THROUGH MINORITY WORLD, THEY TURNED AROUND TO COME IN MY DIRECTION.
FOOD LUCK!

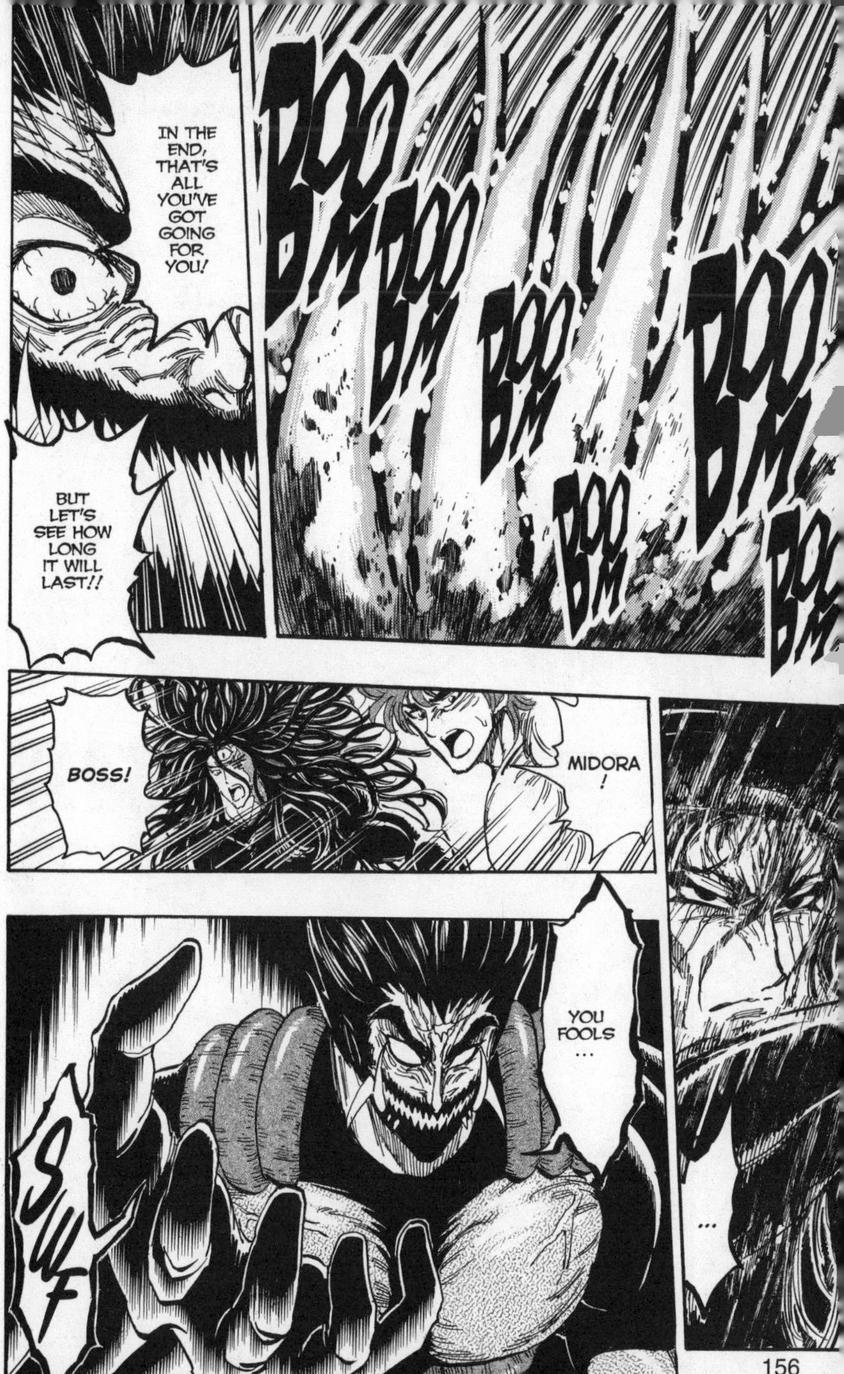
DOOM
DOOM
BOOM
BOOM
DOOM
BOOM
IN THE END, THAT'S ALL YOU'VE GOT GOING FOR YOU!
BUT LET'S SEE HOW LONG IT WILL LAST!!
...
MIDORA!
BOSS!
YOU FOOLS...
SHUF

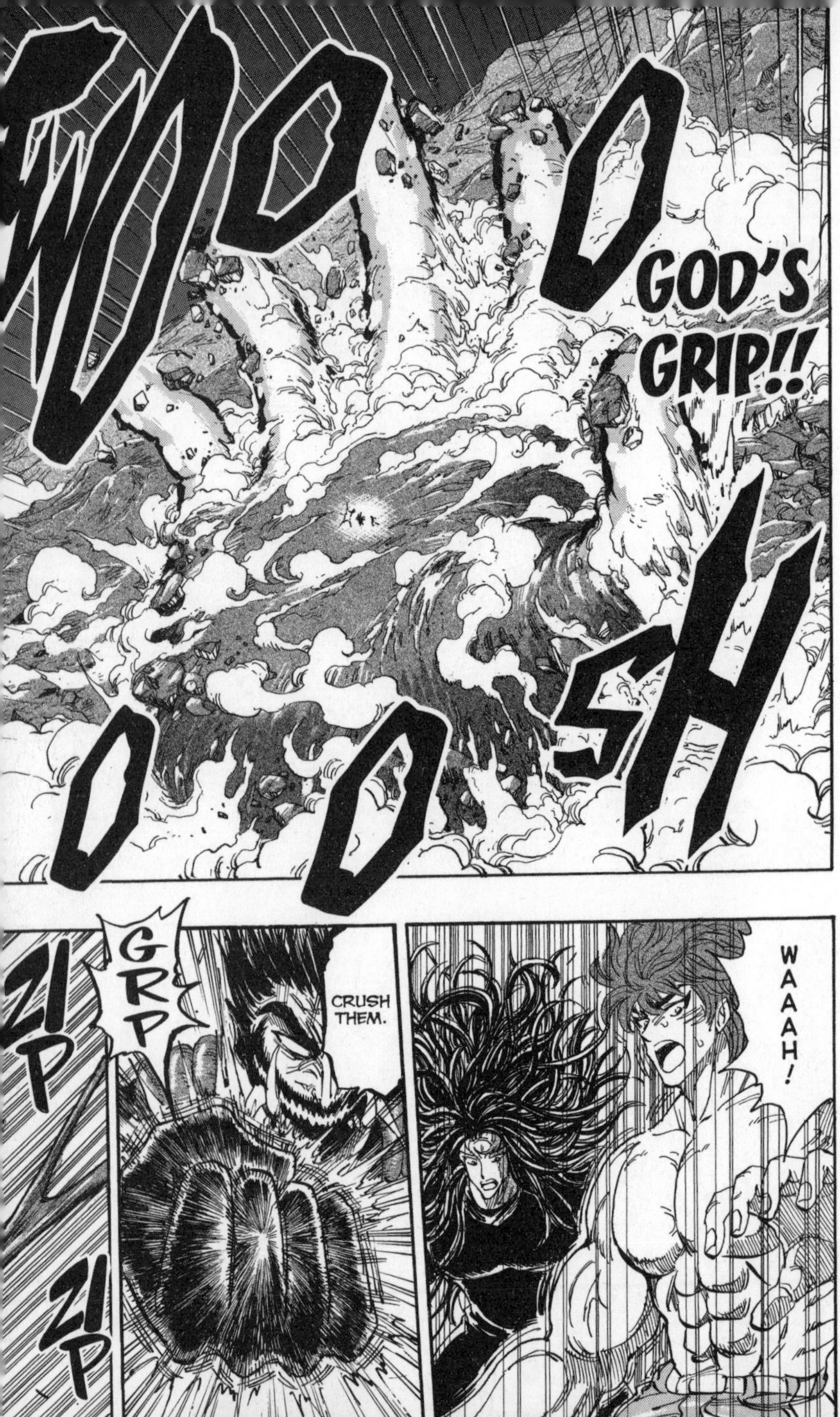
WOOOOOSH
GOD'S GRIP!!
WAAAH!
GRP
CRUSH THEM.
ZIP
ZIP

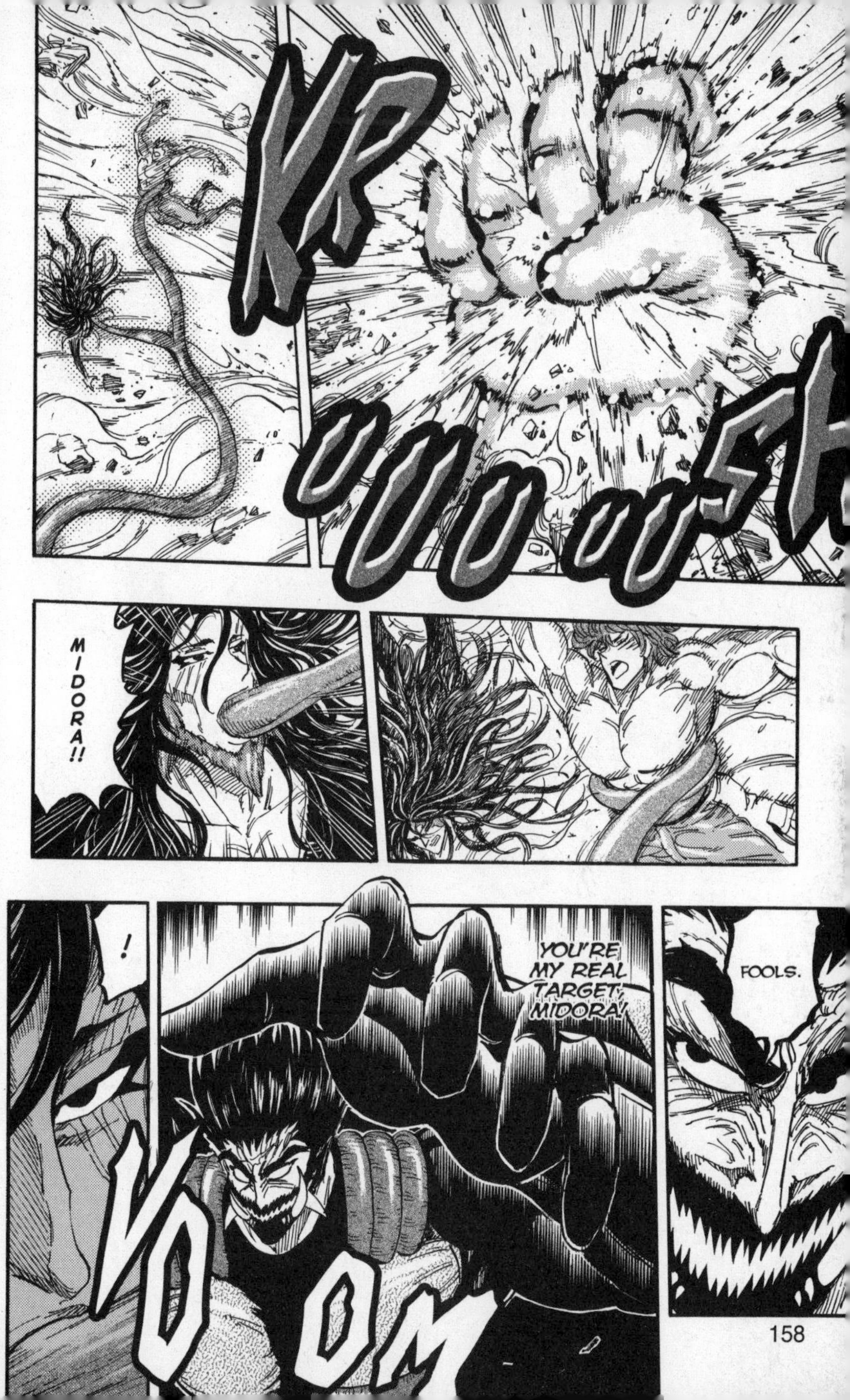
KR
MIDORA!!
FOOLS.
YOU'RE MY REAL TARGET, MIDORA!
!
VOOM

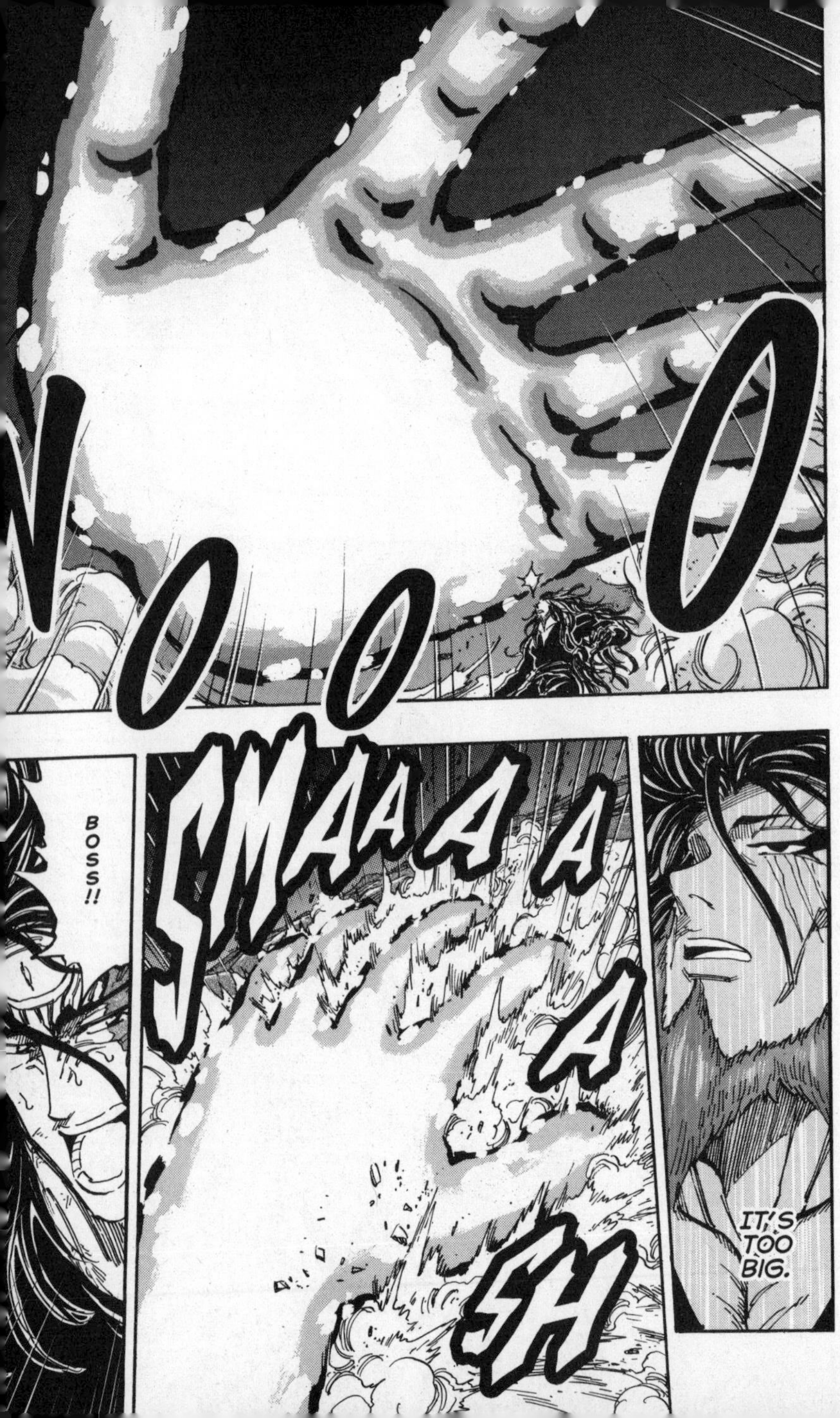
NOOO
IT'S TOO BIG.
SMAAAAASH
BOSS!!

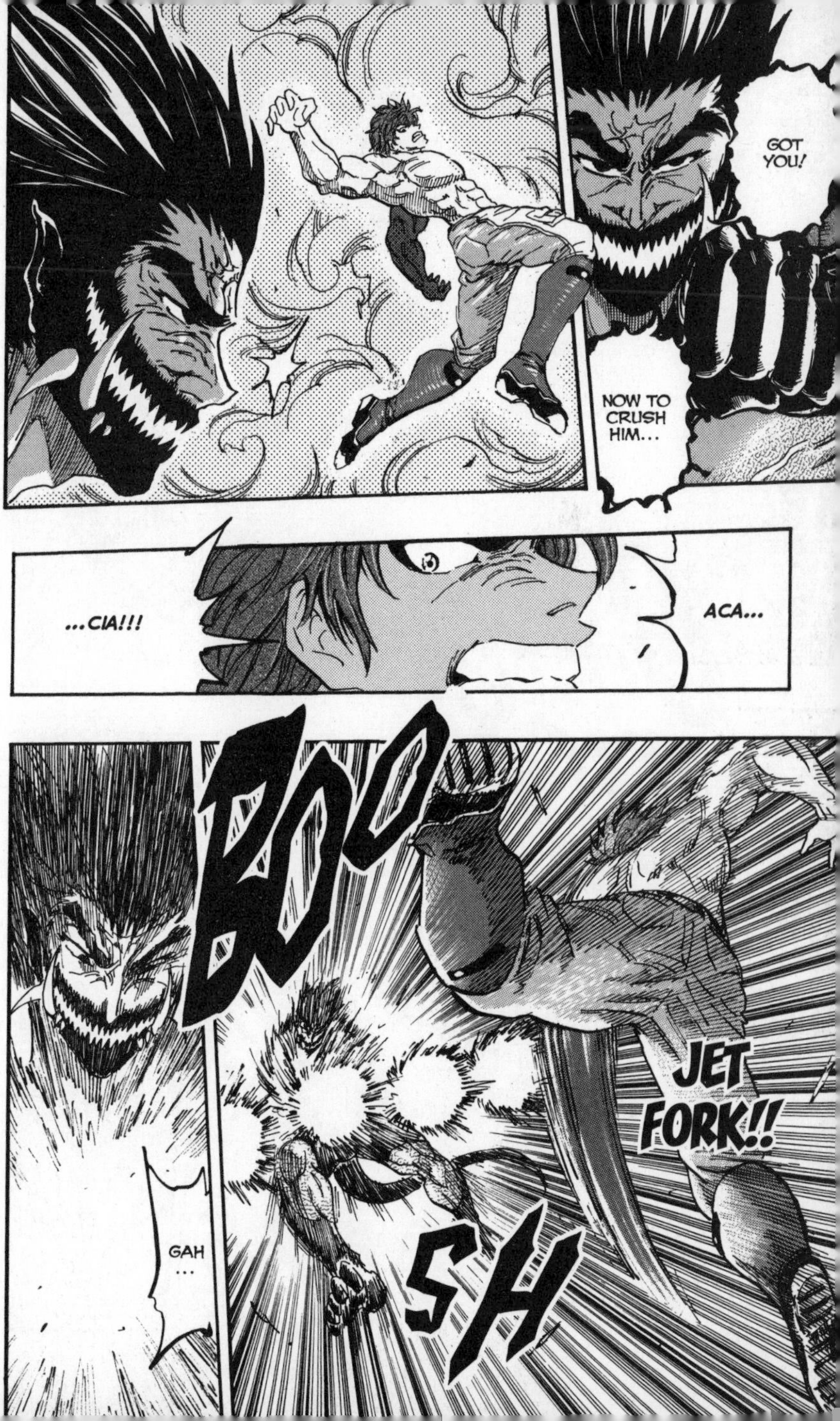
GOT YOU!
NOW TO CRUSH HIM...
ACA...
...CIA!!!
BOO
JET FORK!!
SH
GAH ...

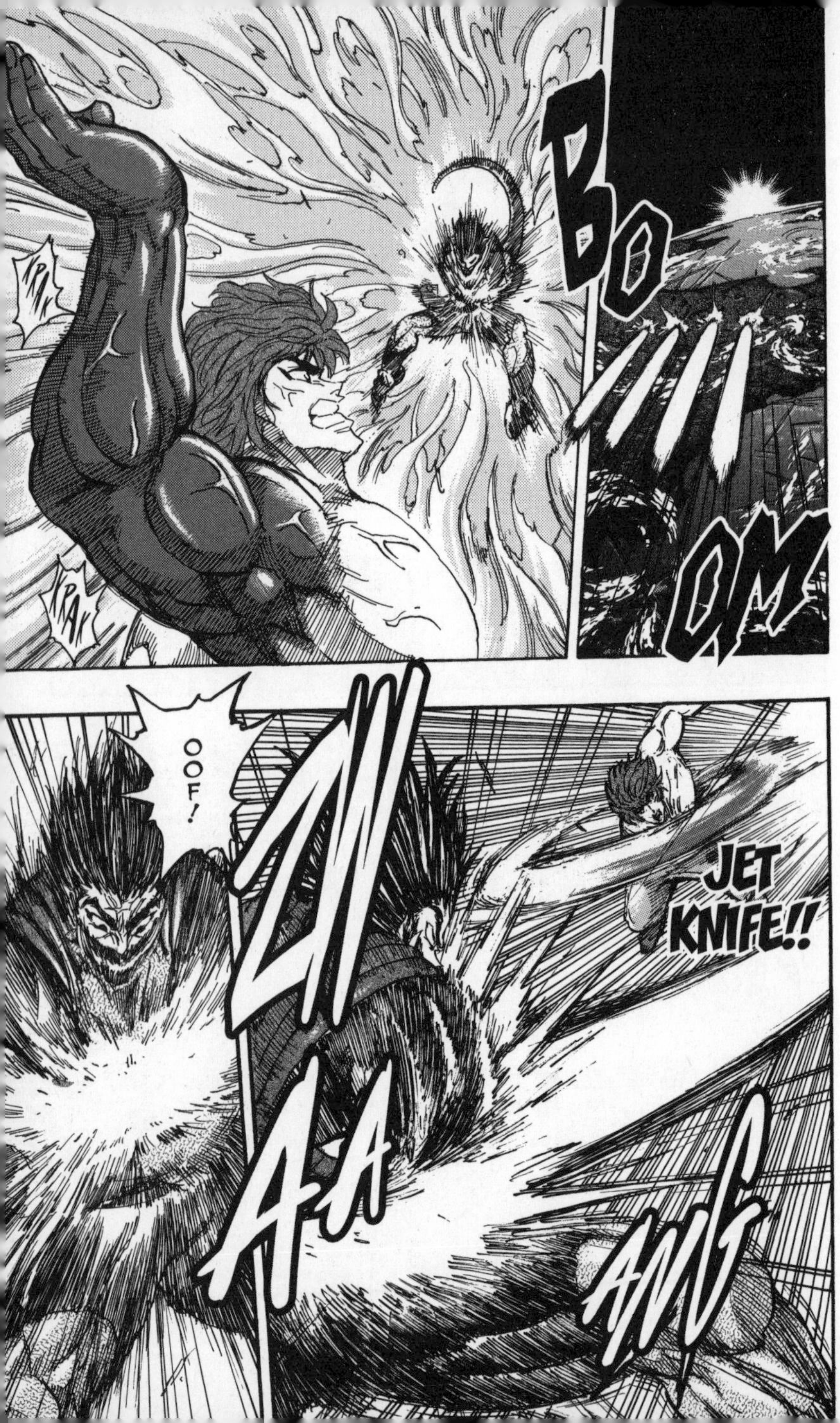
BOOM
KRAK
KRAK
JET KNIFE!!
OOF!
ZAAANG

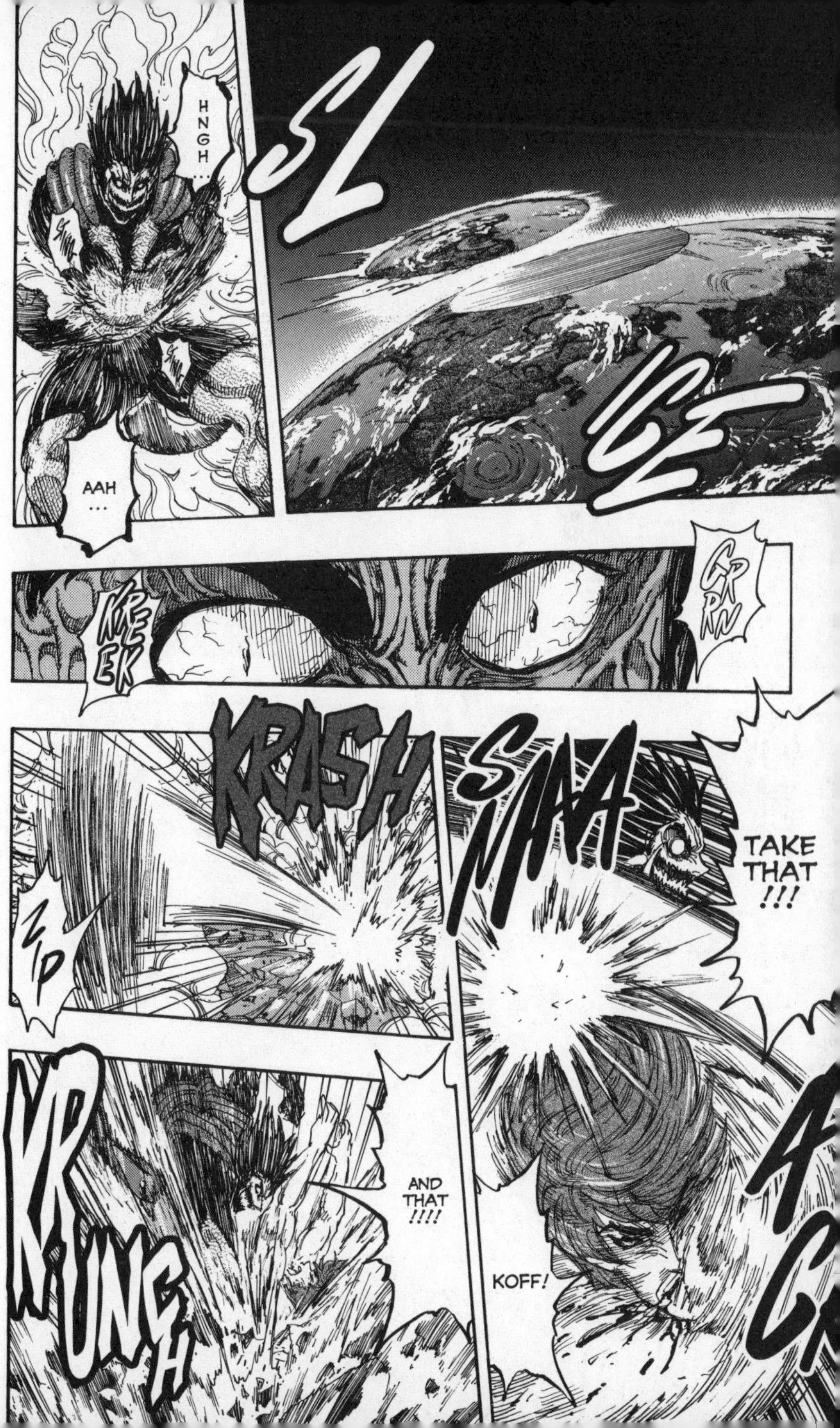
SLICE
HNGH...
AAH...
GRRN
KREEK
SMAA
TAKE THAT!!!
KOFF!
KRASH
ZIP
AND THAT!!!!
KRUNCH

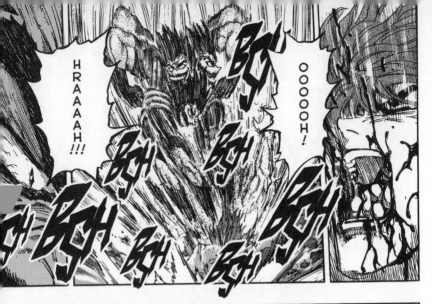

HRAAAAH!!!

OOOOOH!

BGH BGH BGH BGH BGH BGH BGH BGH BGH

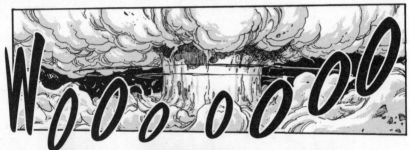

WOOOoOOOO

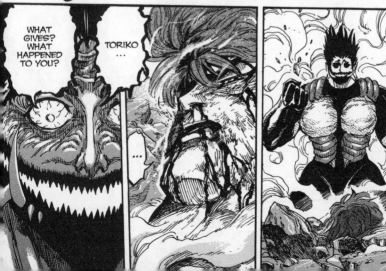

WHAT GIVES? WHAT HAPPENED TO YOU?

TORIKO...

....

KRMBL

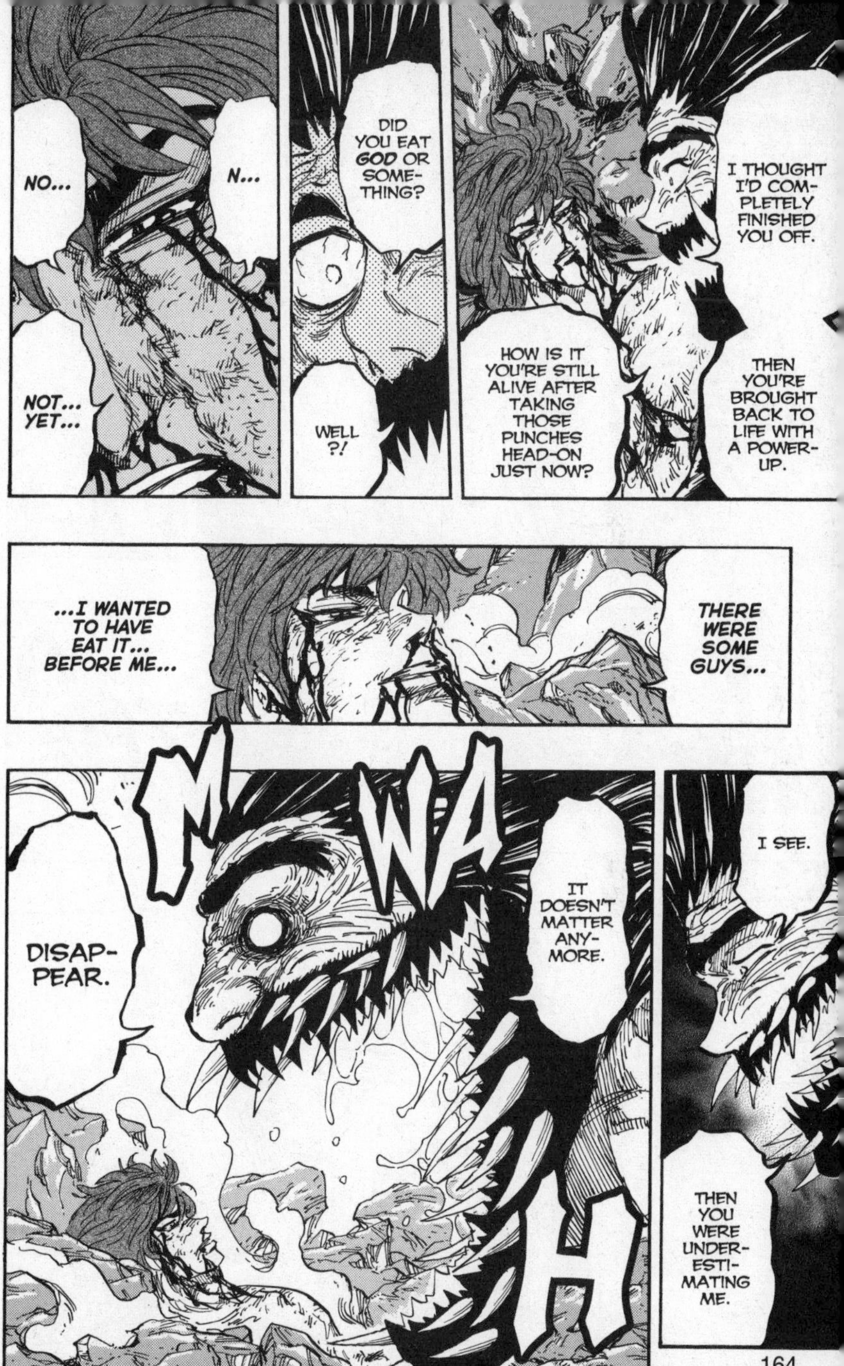
I THOUGHT I'D COMPLETELY FINISHED YOU OFF.
THEN YOU'RE BROUGHT BACK TO LIFE WITH A POWER-UP.
HOW IS IT YOU'RE STILL ALIVE AFTER TAKING THOSE PUNCHES HEAD-ON JUST NOW?
DID YOU EAT *GOD* OR SOMETHING?
WELL ?!
N...
NO...
NOT... YET...
THERE WERE SOME GUYS...
...I WANTED TO HAVE EAT IT... BEFORE ME...
I SEE.
THEN YOU WERE UNDERESTIMATING ME.
IT DOESN'T MATTER ANYMORE.
MWAH
DISAPPEAR.

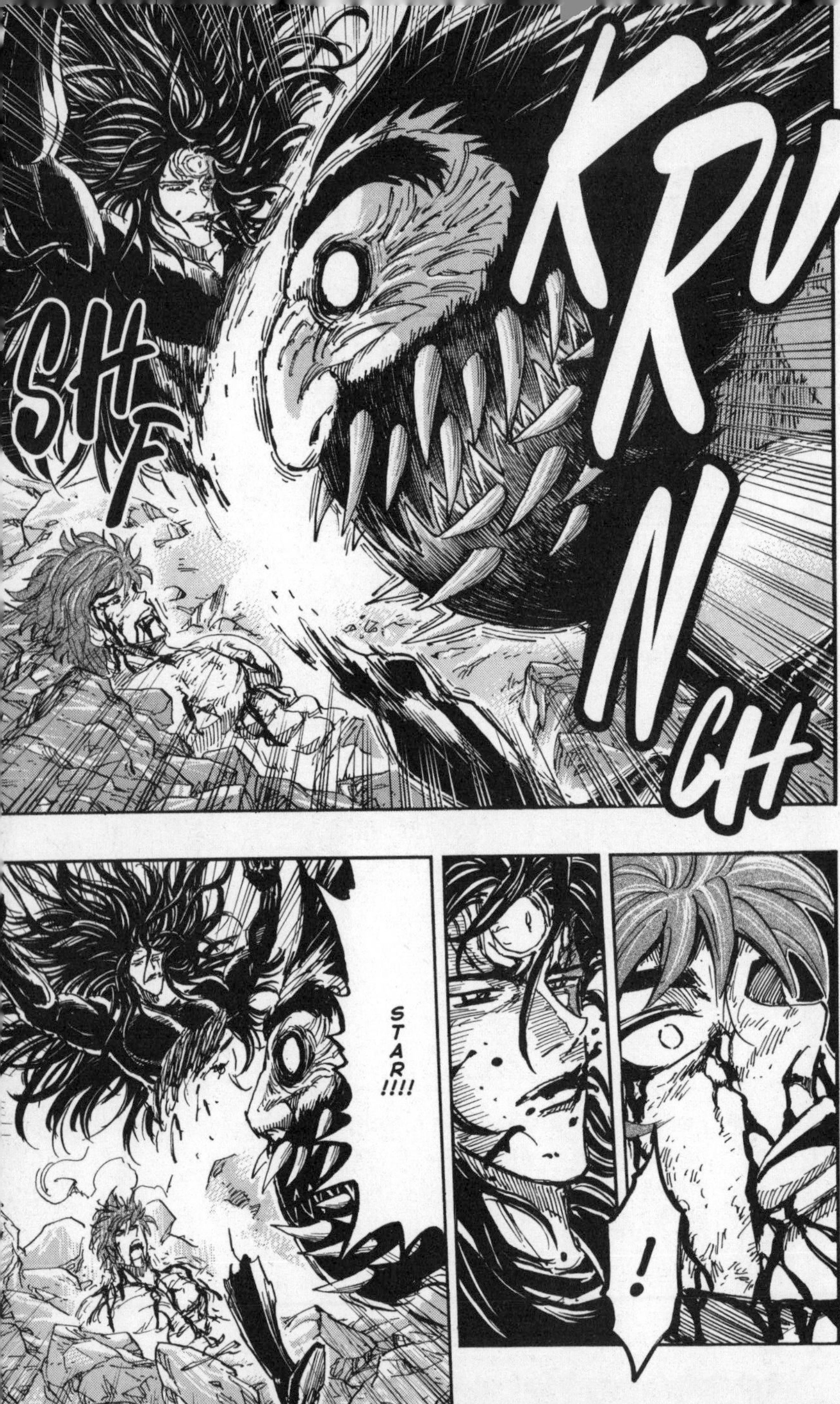
KRUNCH
SHF
!
STAR!!!!

TORIKO

GOURMET CHECKLIST

Vol. 421

SPACE TULIP
(SPACE PLANT)

CAPTURE LEVEL: UNKNOWN
HABITAT: SPACE
SIZE: ---
HEIGHT: 40,000 KM
WEIGHT: ---
PRICE: UNKNOWN

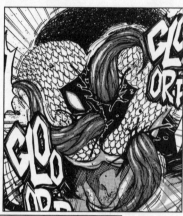

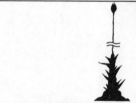

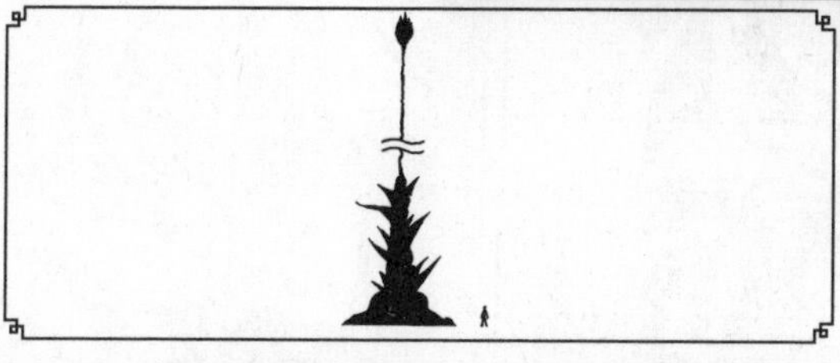

SCALE

A GOURMET FLOWER THAT GROWS IN SPACE. IT ABSORBS NUTRIENTS FROM
PLANETS AND GROWS UP AND OUT INTO SPACE BEFORE FLOWERING. THIS PLANT IS
INCREDIBLY DURABLE AND WILL SUCK NUTRIENTS FROM JUST ABOUT ANYTHING,
MAKING IT INCREDIBLY DESTRUCTIVE.

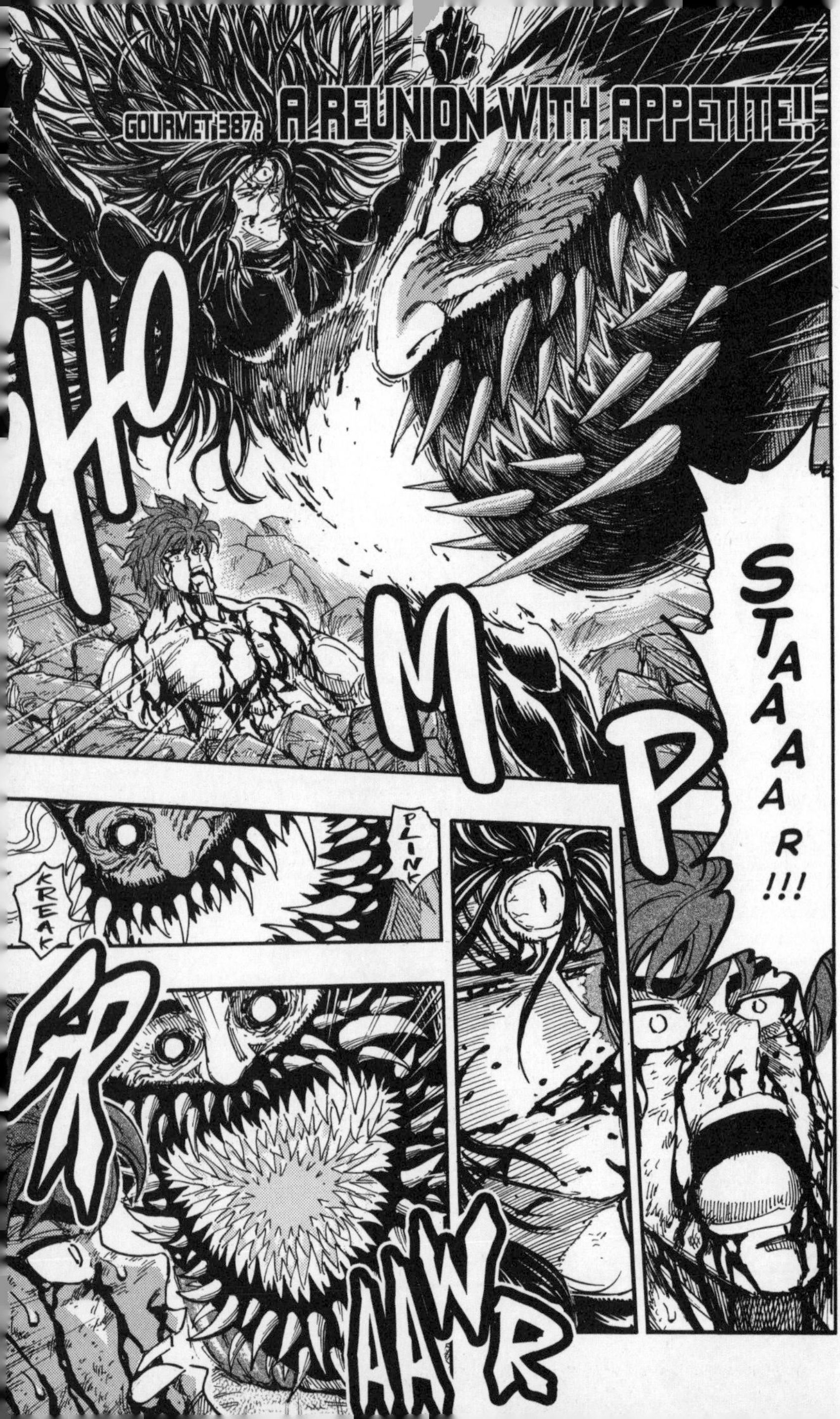
GOURMET 387: A REUNION WITH APPETITE!!
STAAAAR!!!
CHOMP
PLINK
KREAK
GRAAWR

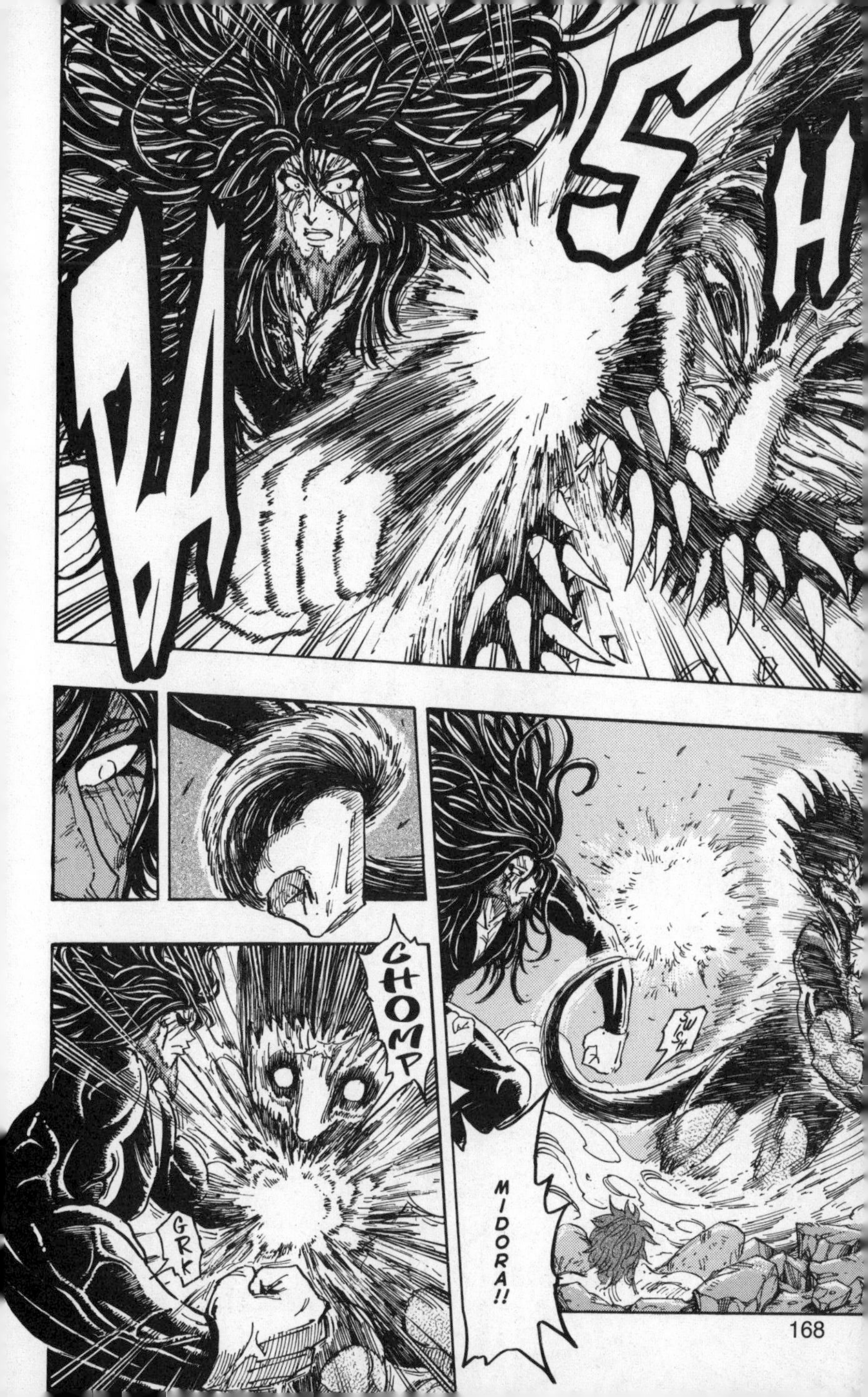
SH
SWISH
MIDORA!!
CHOMP
GRK

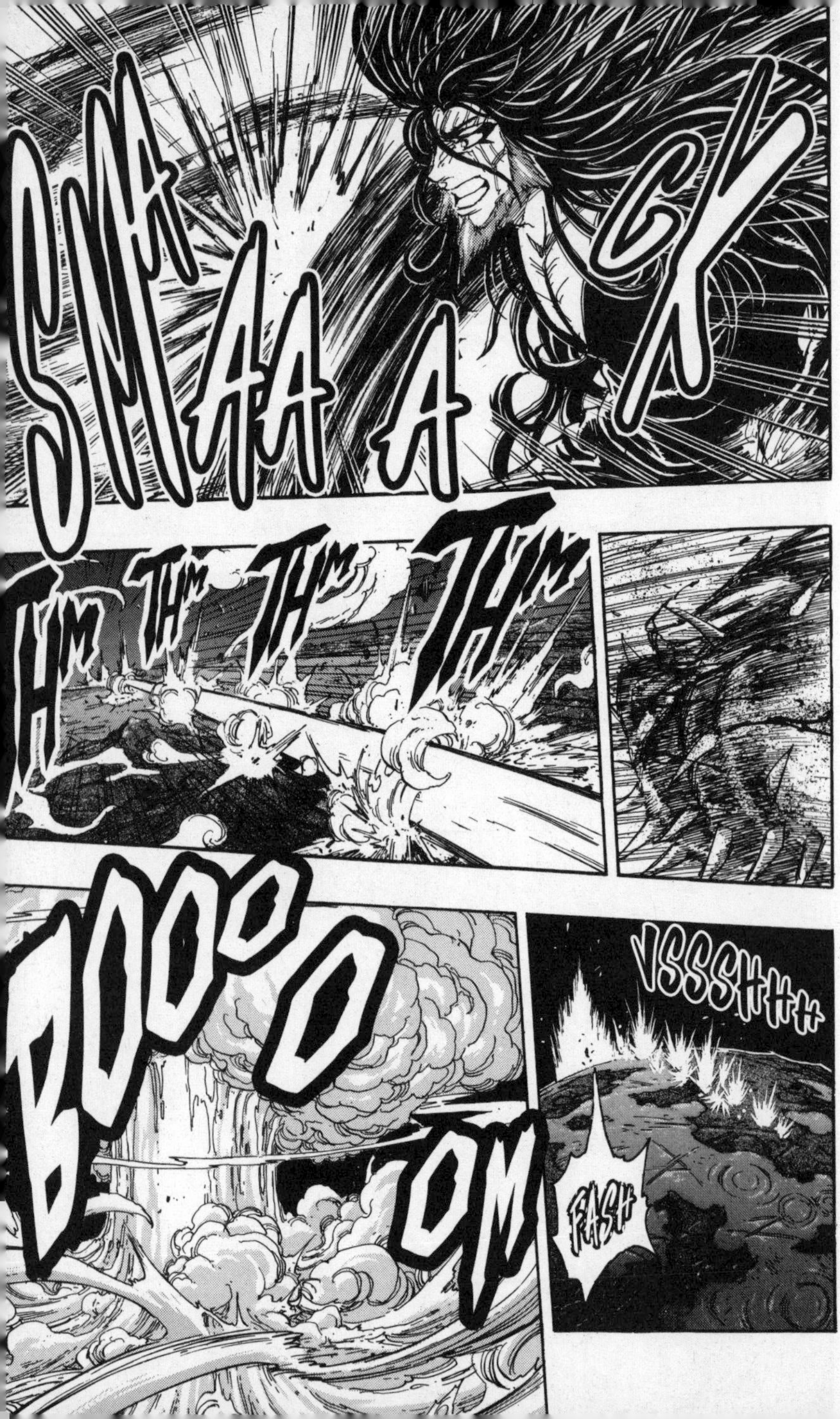
SMAAAACK
THM THM THM THM
VSSSHHHH
FRASH
BOOOOOM

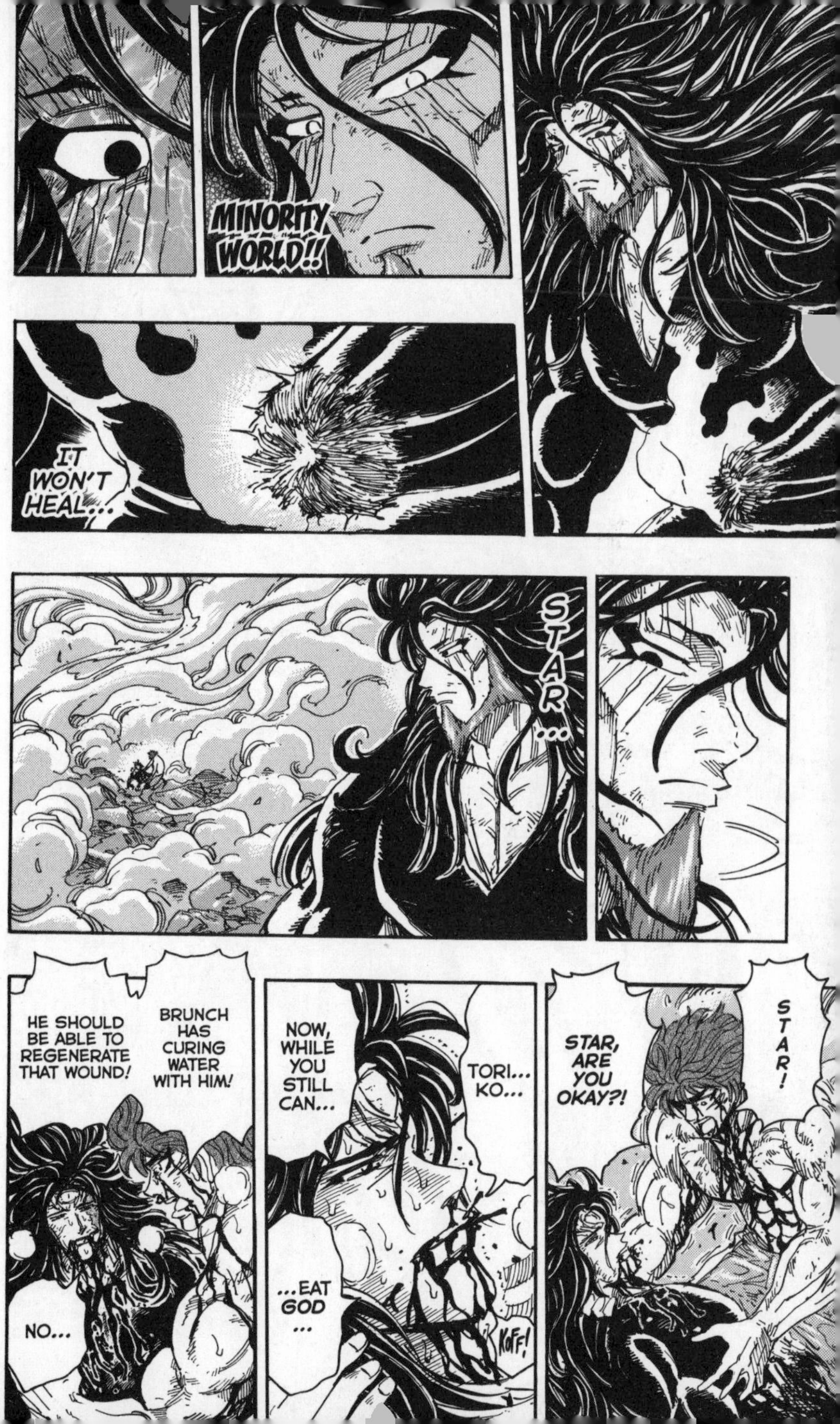
MINORITY WORLD!!
IT WON'T HEAL...
STAR...
STAR!
STAR, ARE YOU OKAY?!
TORI... KO...
NOW, WHILE YOU STILL CAN...
...EAT GOD...
KOFF!
BRUNCH HAS CURING WATER WITH HIM!
HE SHOULD BE ABLE TO REGENERATE THAT WOUND!
NO...

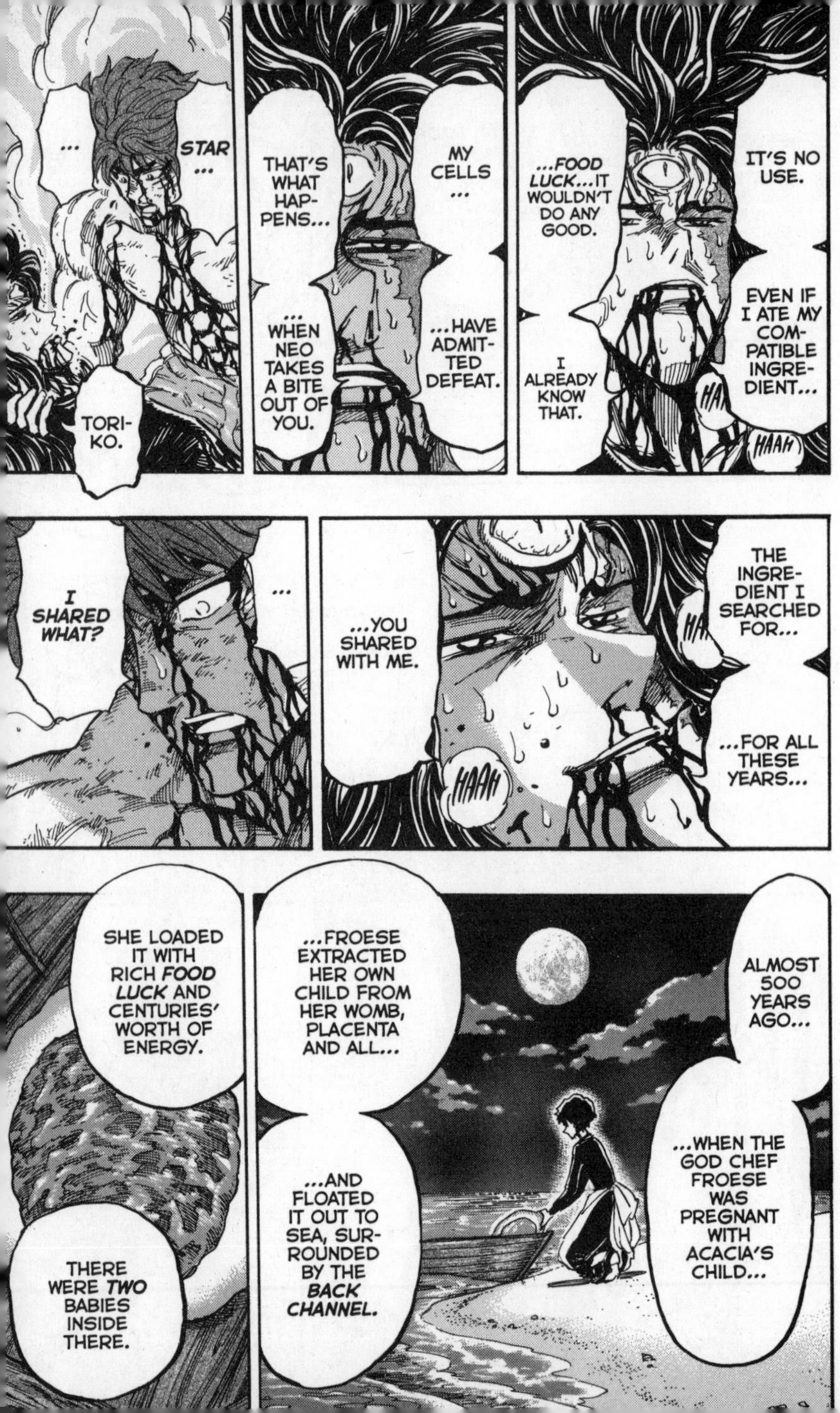
IT'S NO USE.
EVEN IF I ATE MY COMPATIBLE INGREDIENT...
...FOOD LUCK...IT WOULDN'T DO ANY GOOD.
HA
I ALREADY KNOW THAT.
HAAH
MY CELLS...
...HAVE ADMITTED DEFEAT.
THAT'S WHAT HAPPENS...
...WHEN NEO TAKES A BITE OUT OF YOU.
STAR...
...
TORIKO.
THE INGREDIENT I SEARCHED FOR...
HA
...FOR ALL THESE YEARS...
...YOU SHARED WITH ME.
HAAH
...
I SHARED WHAT?
ALMOST 500 YEARS AGO...
...WHEN THE GOD CHEF FROESE WAS PREGNANT WITH ACACIA'S CHILD...
...FROESE EXTRACTED HER OWN CHILD FROM HER WOMB, PLACENTA AND ALL...
...AND FLOATED IT OUT TO SEA, SURROUNDED BY THE BACK CHANNEL.
SHE LOADED IT WITH RICH FOOD LUCK AND CENTURIES' WORTH OF ENERGY.
THERE WERE TWO BABIES INSIDE THERE.

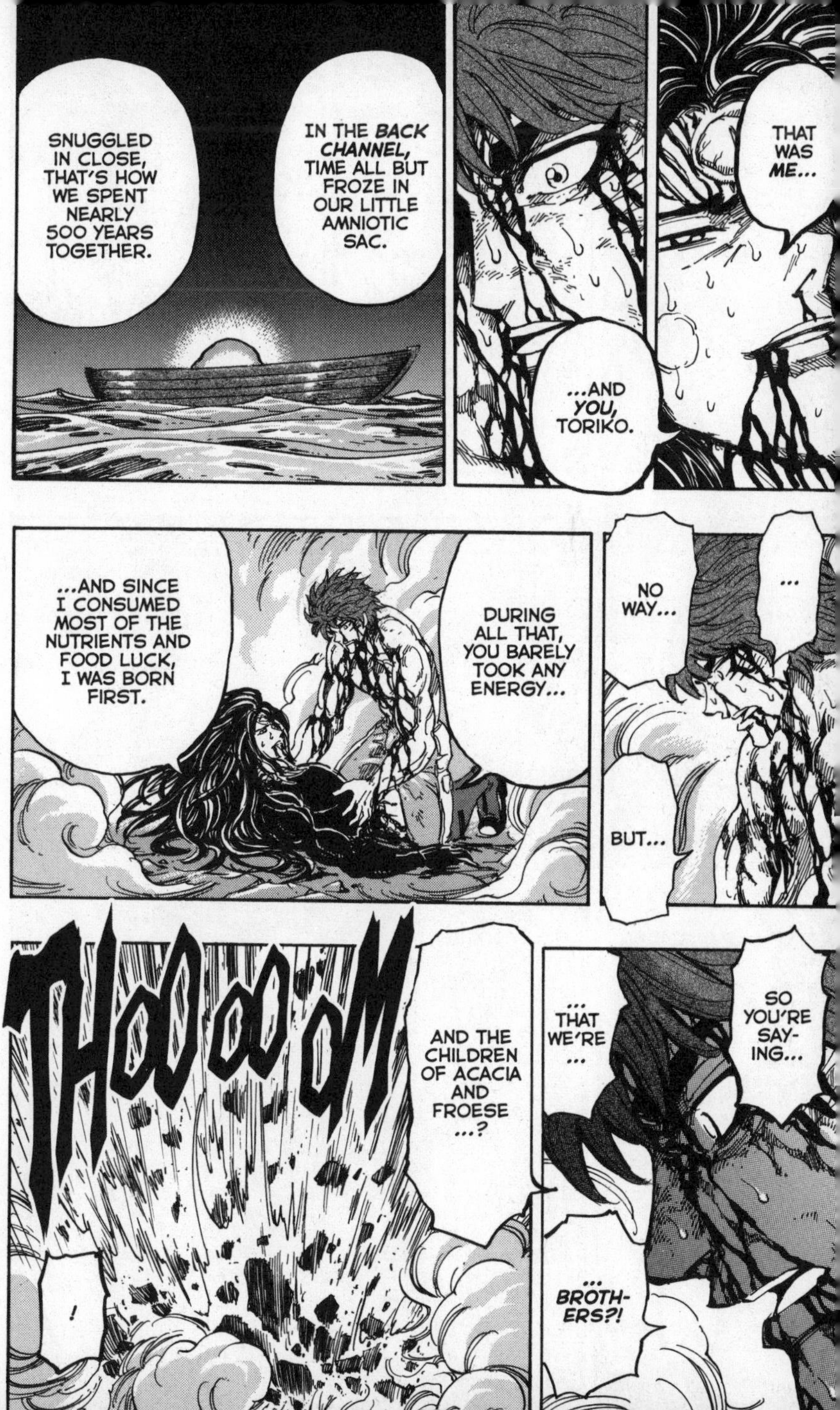
THAT WAS ME...
...AND YOU, TORIKO.
IN THE BACK CHANNEL, TIME ALL BUT FROZE IN OUR LITTLE AMNIOTIC SAC.
SNUGGLED IN CLOSE, THAT'S HOW WE SPENT NEARLY 500 YEARS TOGETHER.
...
NO WAY...
BUT...
DURING ALL THAT, YOU BARELY TOOK ANY ENERGY...
...AND SINCE I CONSUMED MOST OF THE NUTRIENTS AND FOOD LUCK, I WAS BORN FIRST.
SO YOU'RE SAYING...
...THAT WE'RE...
...BROTHERS?!
AND THE CHILDREN OF ACACIA AND FROESE...?
THOOOOM
!

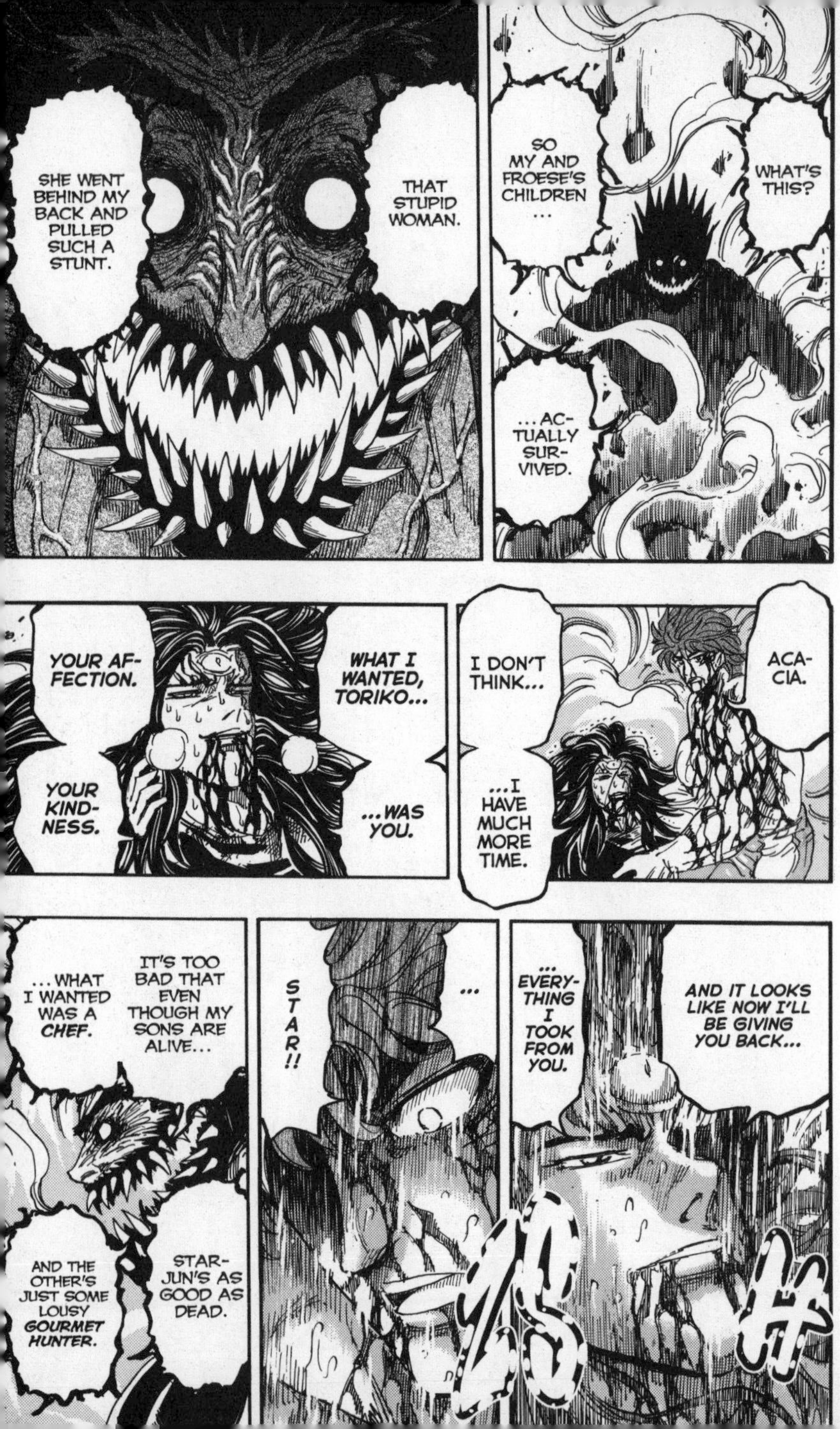
WHAT'S THIS?
SO MY AND FROESE'S CHILDREN ...
...ACTUALLY SURVIVED.
THAT STUPID WOMAN.
SHE WENT BEHIND MY BACK AND PULLED SUCH A STUNT.
ACACIA.
I DON'T THINK...
...I HAVE MUCH MORE TIME.
WHAT I WANTED, TORIKO...
YOUR AFFECTION.
YOUR KINDNESS.
...WAS YOU.
AND IT LOOKS LIKE NOW I'LL BE GIVING YOU BACK...
...EVERYTHING I TOOK FROM YOU.
...
STAR!!
IT'S TOO BAD THAT EVEN THOUGH MY SONS ARE ALIVE...
...WHAT I WANTED WAS A CHEF.
STARJUN'S AS GOOD AS DEAD.
AND THE OTHER'S JUST SOME LOUSY GOURMET HUNTER.

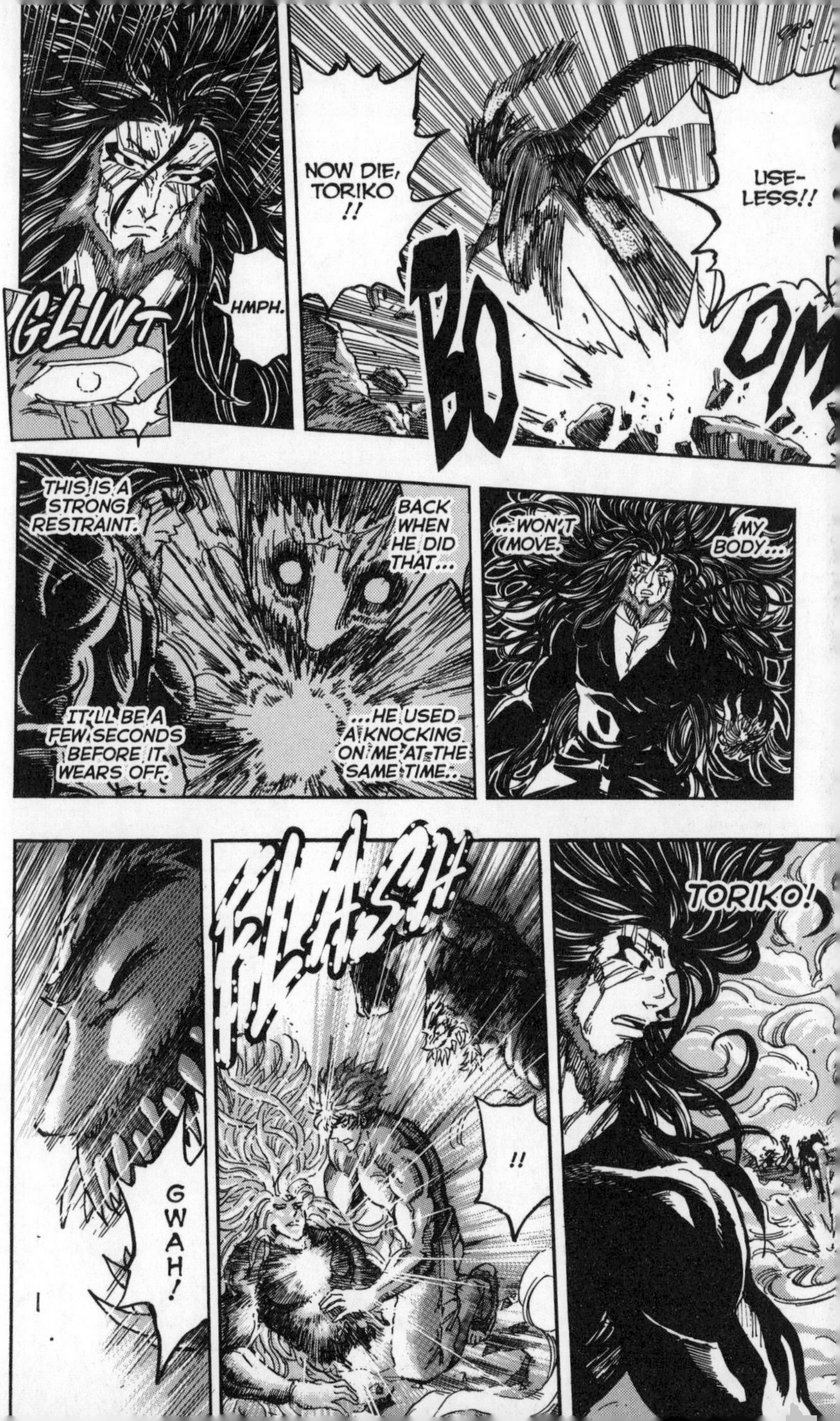
USE-LESS!!
NOW DIE, TORIKO!!
BOOM
HMPH.
GLINT
MY BODY...
...WON'T MOVE.
BACK WHEN HE DID THAT...
THIS IS A STRONG RESTRAINT.
...HE USED A KNOCKING ON ME AT THE SAME TIME..
IT'LL BE A FEW SECONDS BEFORE IT WEARS OFF.
TORIKO!
FLASH
!!
GWAH!

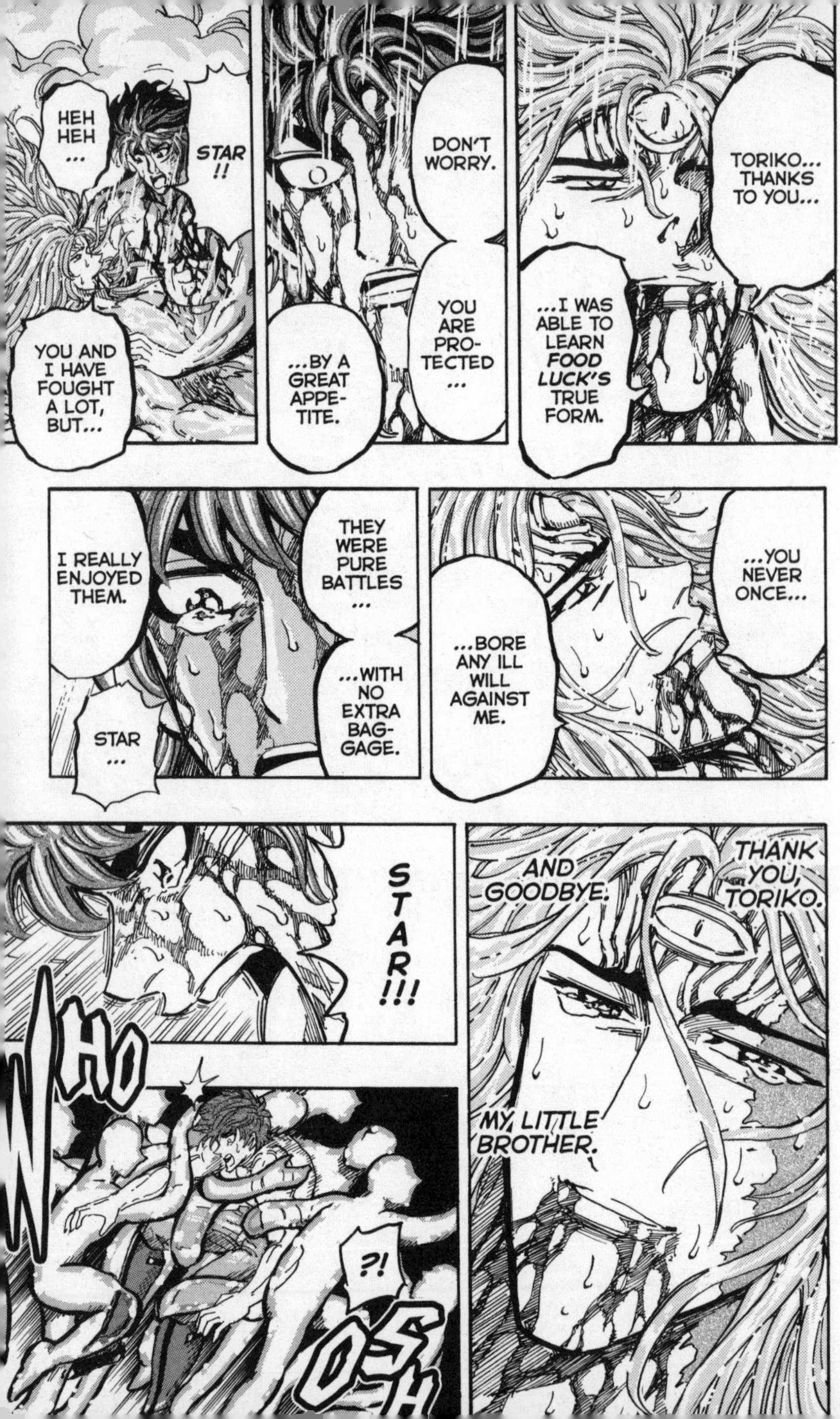
TORIKO... THANKS TO YOU...
...I WAS ABLE TO LEARN *FOOD LUCK'S* TRUE FORM.
DON'T WORRY.
YOU ARE PRO-TECTED...
...BY A GREAT APPE-TITE.
HEH HEH...
STAR!!
YOU AND I HAVE FOUGHT A LOT, BUT...
...YOU NEVER ONCE...
...BORE ANY ILL WILL AGAINST ME.
THEY WERE PURE BATTLES...
...WITH NO EXTRA BAG-GAGE.
I REALLY ENJOYED THEM.
STAR...
THANK YOU, TORIKO.
AND GOODBYE.
MY LITTLE BROTHER.
STAR!!!
WHO
?!
OSH

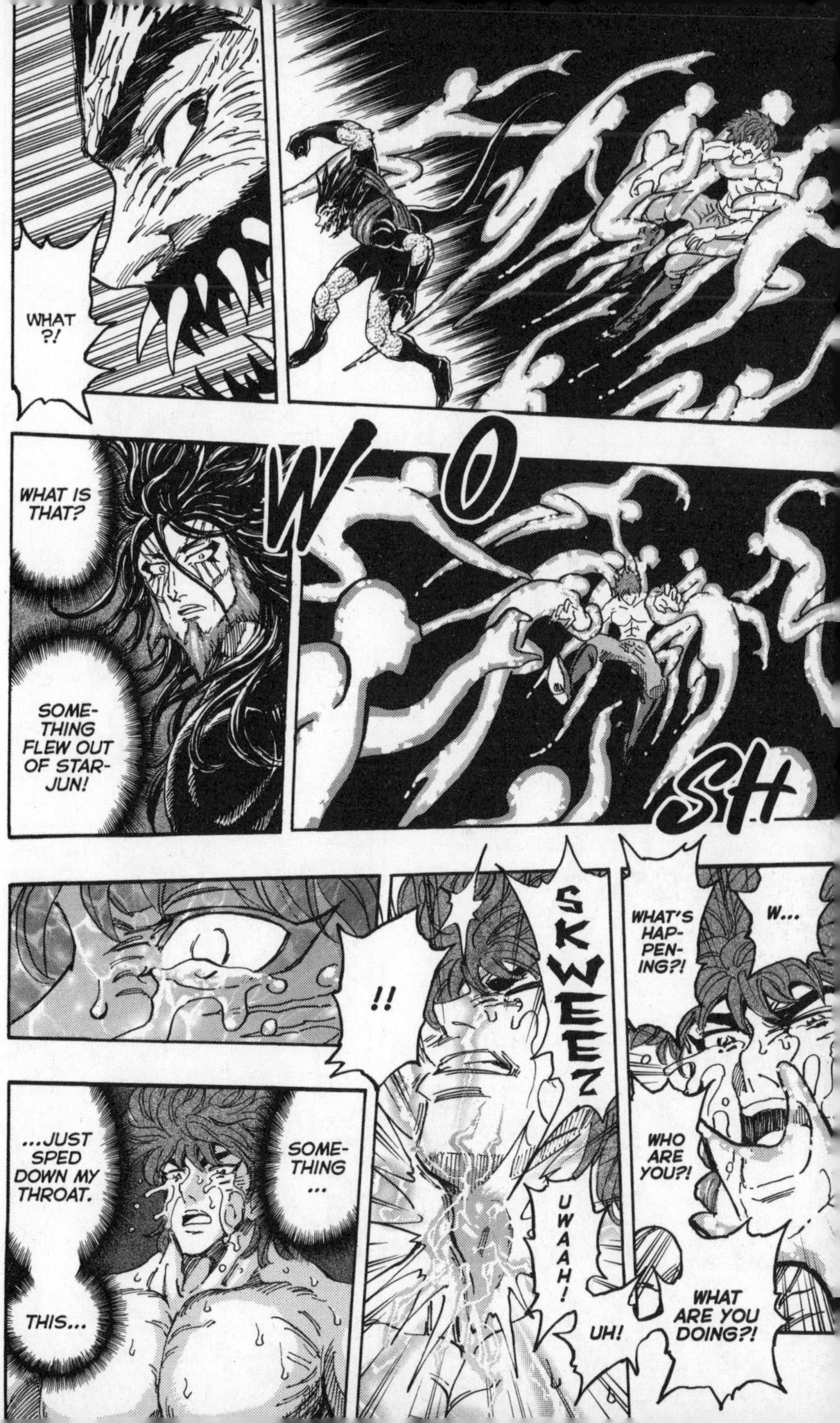
WHAT ?!
WO
SH
WHAT IS THAT?
SOMETHING FLEW OUT OF STARJUN!
W...
WHAT'S HAPPENING?!
WHO ARE YOU?!
WHAT ARE YOU DOING?!
SKWEEZ
!!
UWAAH!
UH!
SOMETHING...
...JUST SPED DOWN MY THROAT.
THIS...

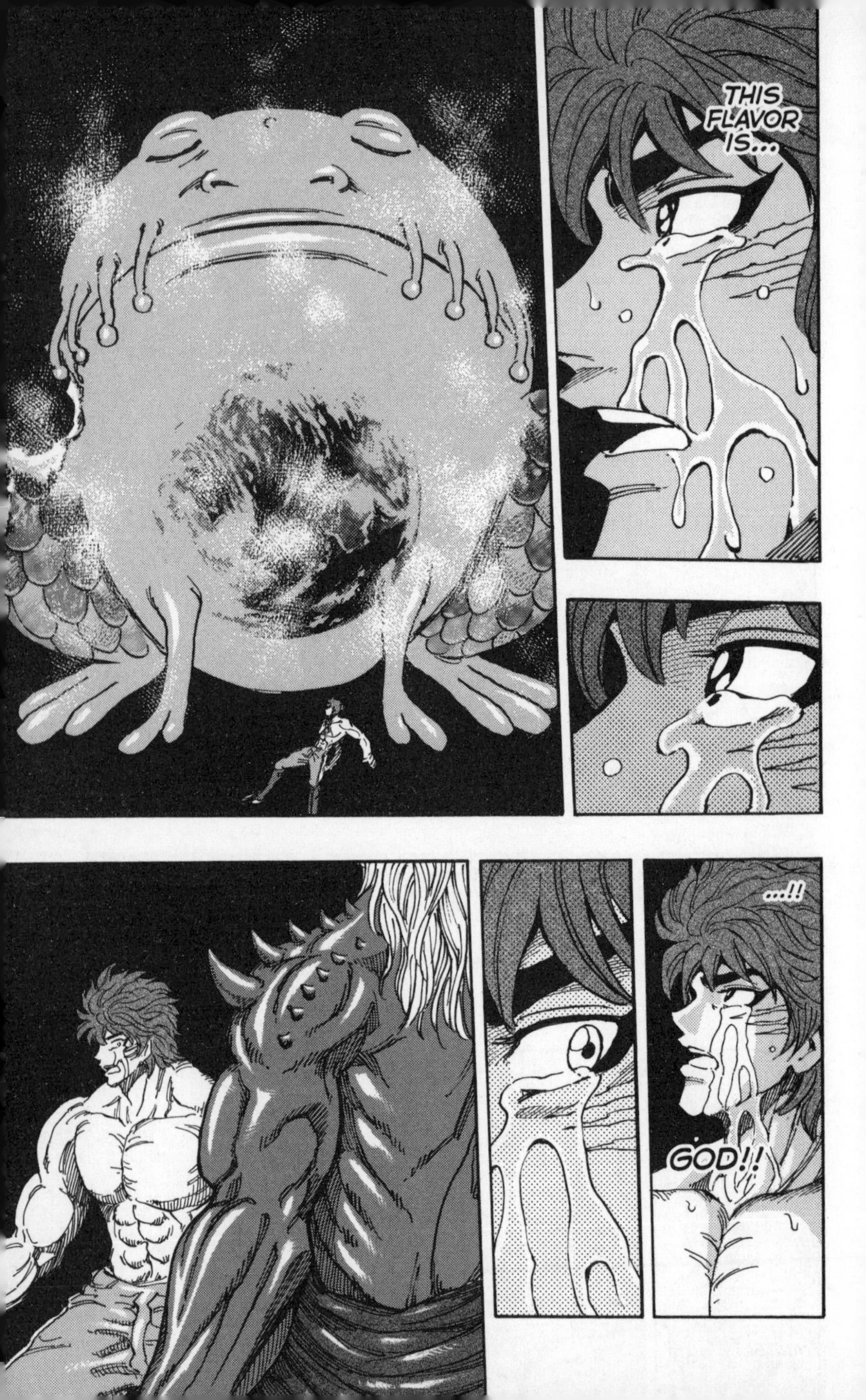
THIS FLAVOR IS...
...!!
GOD!!

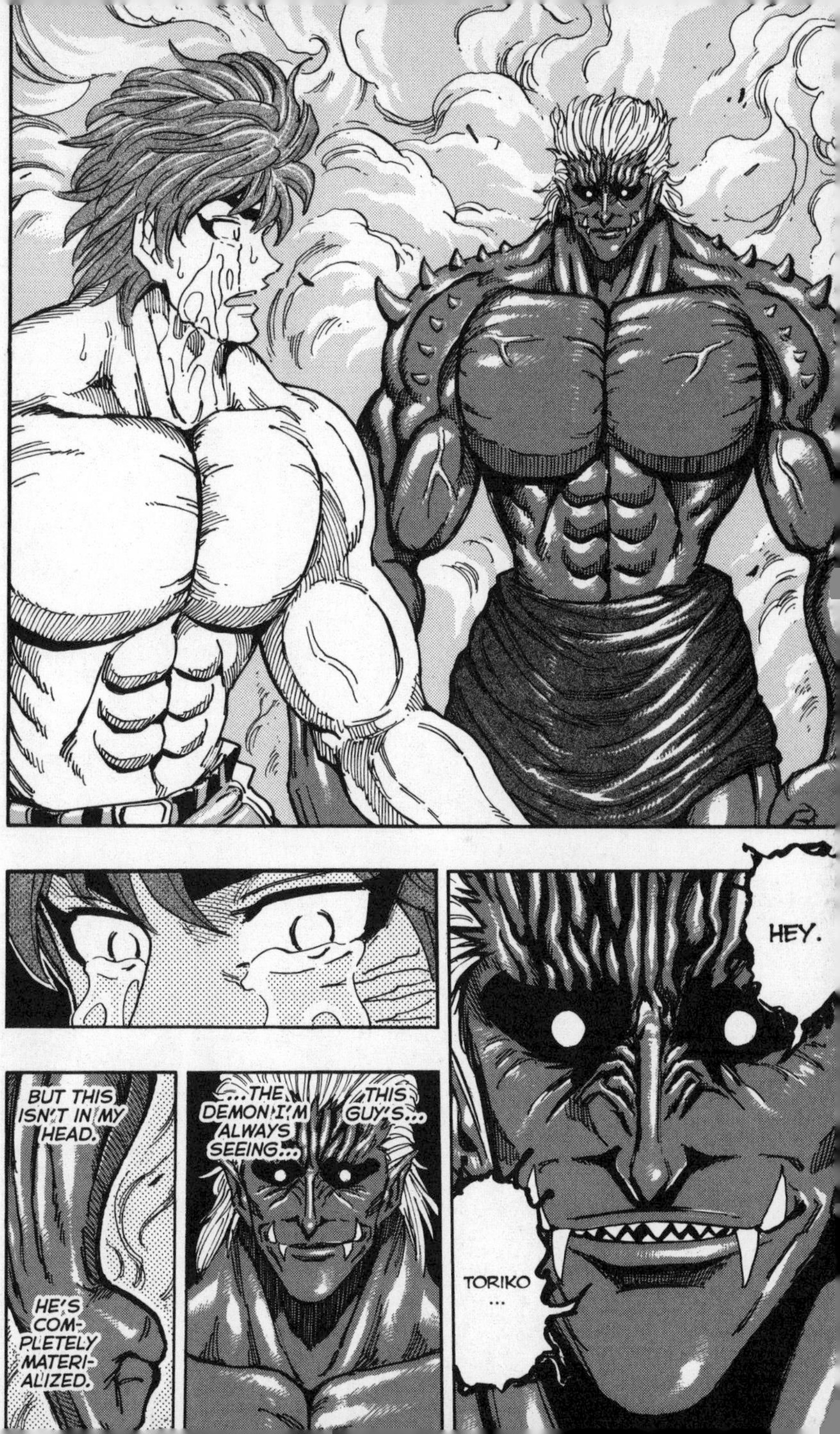
HEY.
TORIKO ...
THIS GUY'S...
...THE DEMON I'M ALWAYS SEEING...
BUT THIS ISN'T IN MY HEAD.
HE'S COM-PLETELY MATERI-ALIZED.

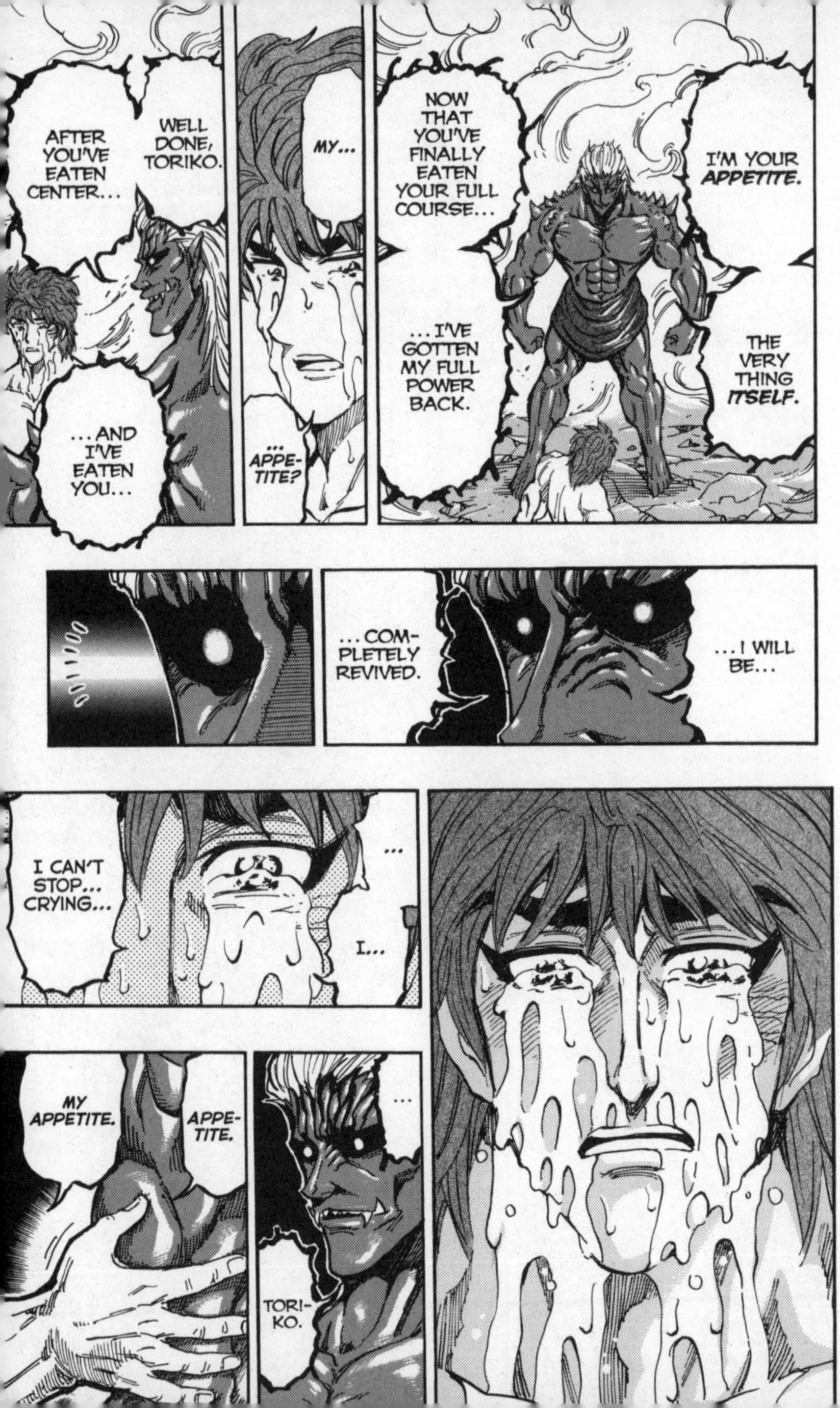
I'M YOUR *APPETITE.*
THE VERY THING *ITSELF.*
NOW THAT YOU'VE FINALLY EATEN YOUR FULL COURSE...
...I'VE GOTTEN MY FULL POWER BACK.
MY...
...APPE-TITE?
WELL DONE, TORIKO.
AFTER YOU'VE EATEN CENTER...
...AND I'VE EATEN YOU...
...I WILL BE...
...COM-PLETELY REVIVED.
...
I...
I CAN'T STOP... CRYING...
...
TORI-KO.
APPE-TITE.
MY APPETITE.

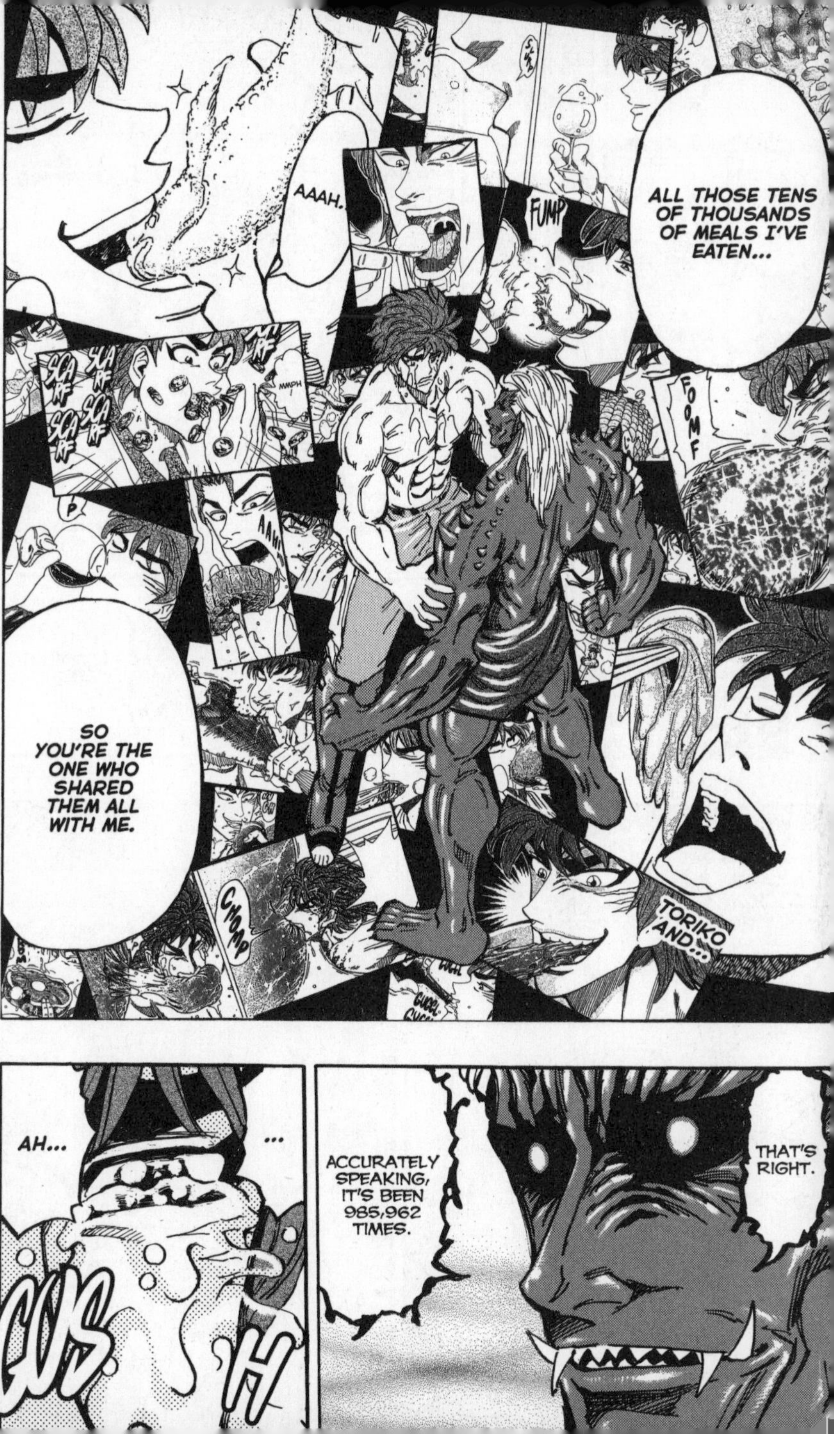
ALL THOSE TENS OF THOUSANDS OF MEALS I'VE EATEN...
FUMP
AAAH.
FOOMF
SCARF SCARF SCARF
MMPH
AAH!
TORIKO AND...
CHOMP
SO YOU'RE THE ONE WHO SHARED THEM ALL WITH ME.
THAT'S RIGHT.
ACCURATELY SPEAKING, IT'S BEEN 985,962 TIMES.
...
AH...
GUSH

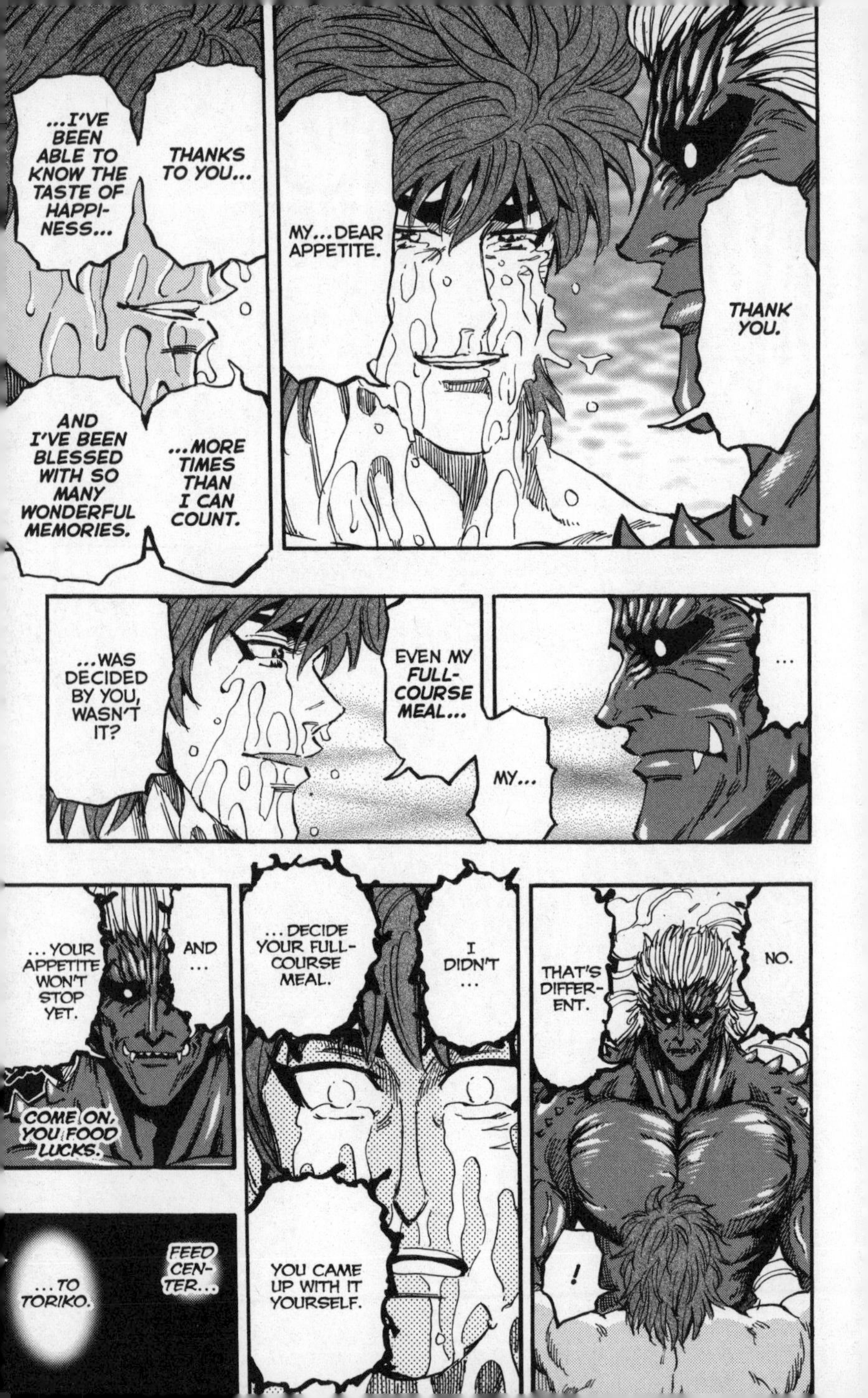
THANK YOU.
MY...DEAR APPETITE.
THANKS TO YOU...
...I'VE BEEN ABLE TO KNOW THE TASTE OF HAPPI-NESS...
...MORE TIMES THAN I CAN COUNT.
AND I'VE BEEN BLESSED WITH SO MANY WONDERFUL MEMORIES.
...
MY...
EVEN MY FULL-COURSE MEAL...
...WAS DECIDED BY YOU, WASN'T IT?
NO.
THAT'S DIFFER-ENT.
!
I DIDN'T ...
...DECIDE YOUR FULL-COURSE MEAL.
YOU CAME UP WITH IT YOURSELF.
AND ...
...YOUR APPETITE WON'T STOP YET.
COME ON, YOU FOOD LUCKS.
FEED CEN-TER...
...TO TORIKO.

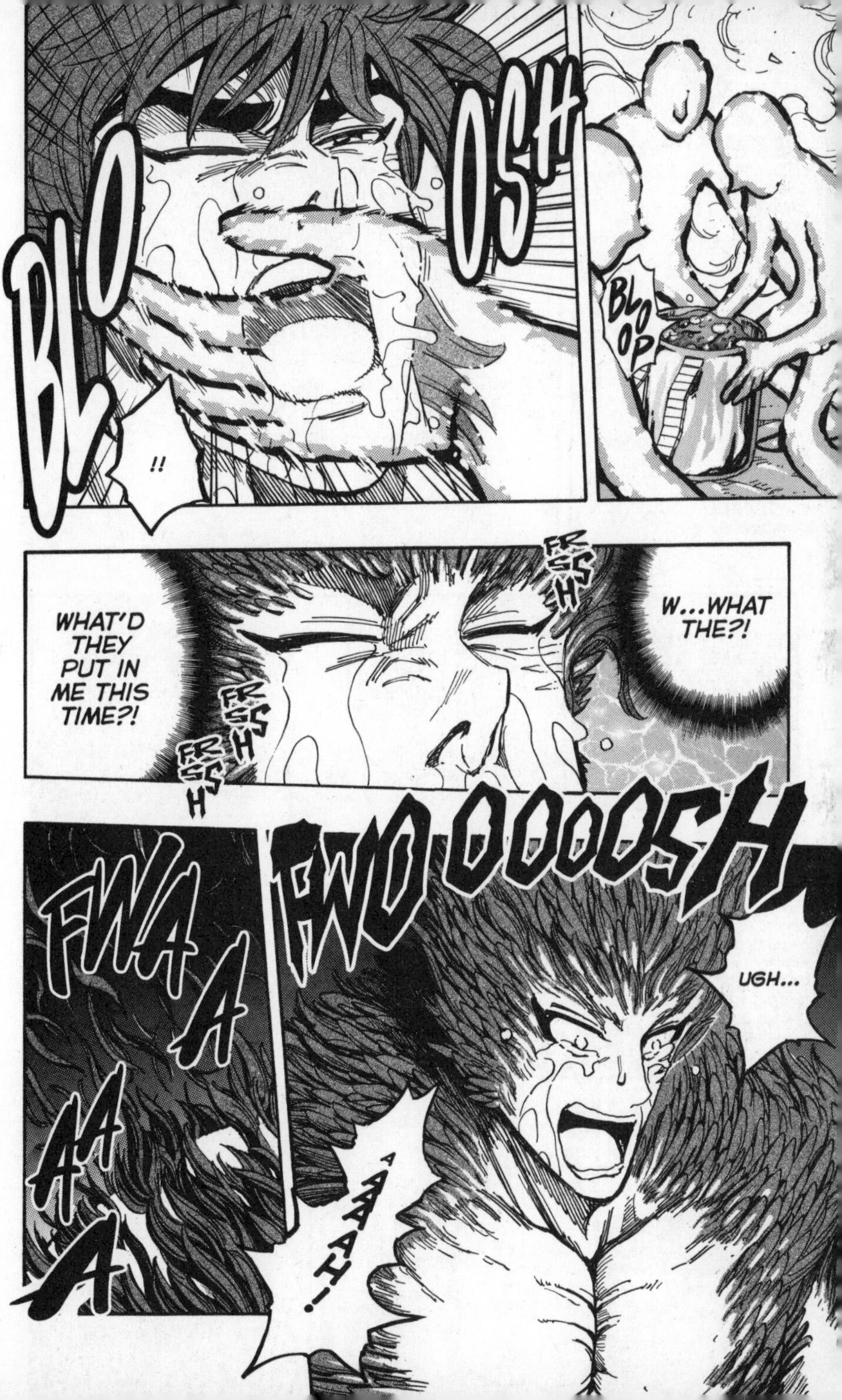
BLOOP
BLOOOSH
!!
W...WHAT THE?!
FRSSH
WHAT'D THEY PUT IN ME THIS TIME?!
FRSSH
FRSSH
FWOOOOOSH
UGH...
AAAAAH!
FWAAAAA

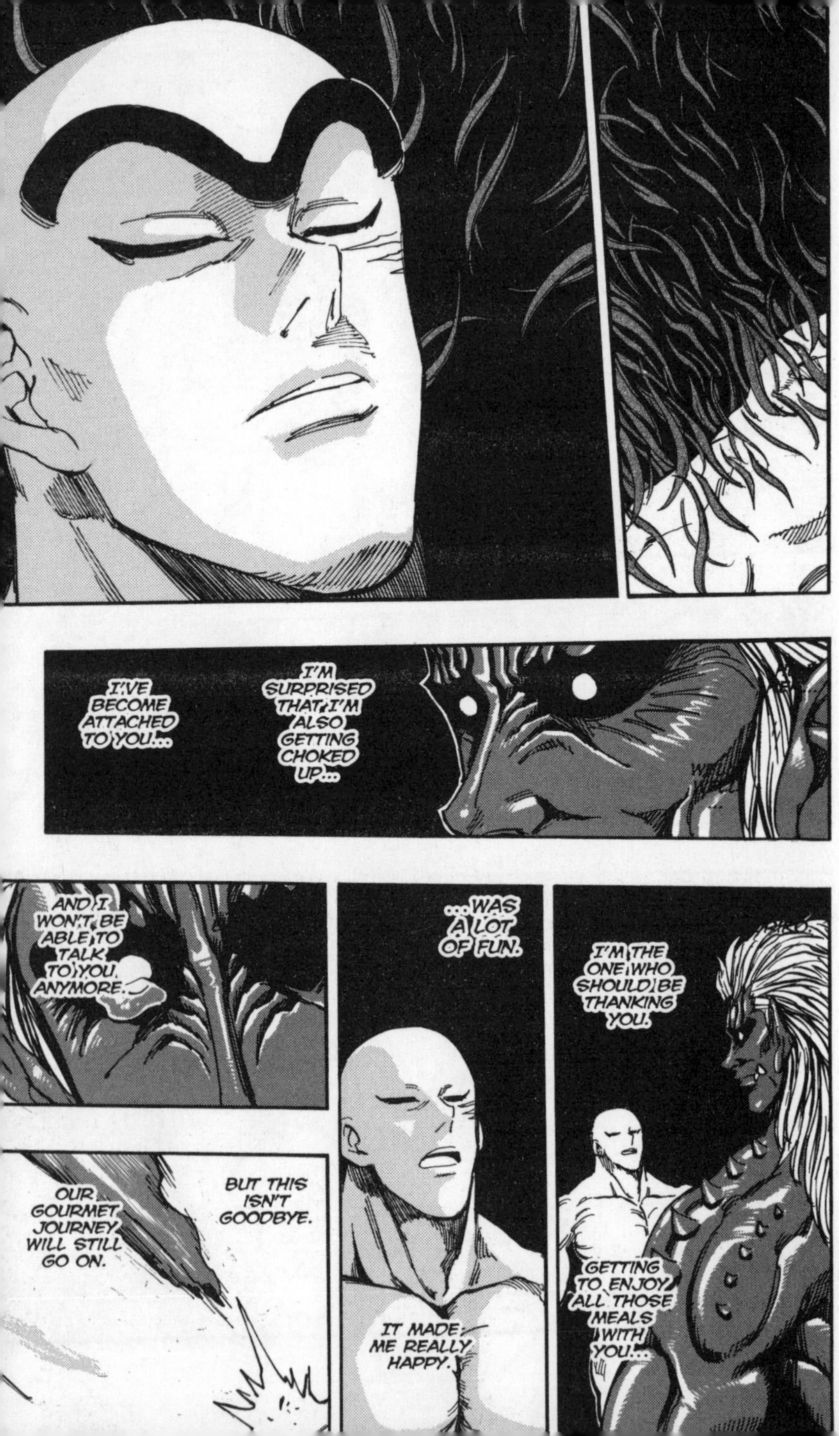
I'M SURPRISED THAT I'M ALSO GETTING CHOKED UP...
I'VE BECOME ATTACHED TO YOU...
I'M THE ONE WHO SHOULD BE THANKING YOU.
GETTING TO ENJOY ALL THOSE MEALS WITH YOU...
...WAS A LOT OF FUN.
IT MADE ME REALLY HAPPY.
AND I WON'T BE ABLE TO TALK TO YOU ANYMORE.
BUT THIS ISN'T GOODBYE.
OUR GOURMET JOURNEY WILL STILL GO ON.

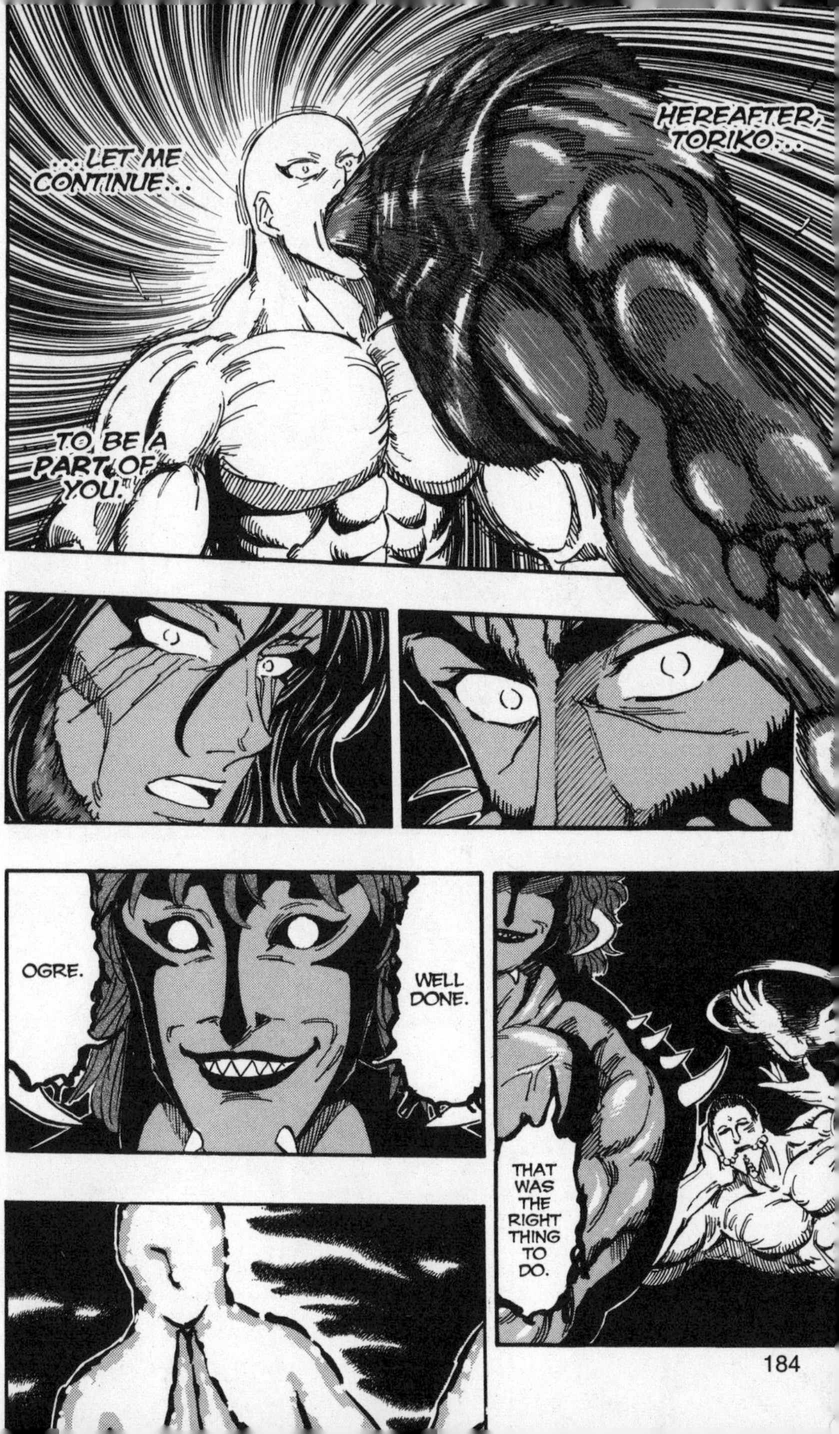
HEREAFTER, TORIKO...
...LET ME CONTINUE...
...TO BE A PART OF YOU.
THAT WAS THE RIGHT THING TO DO.
OGRE.
WELL DONE.

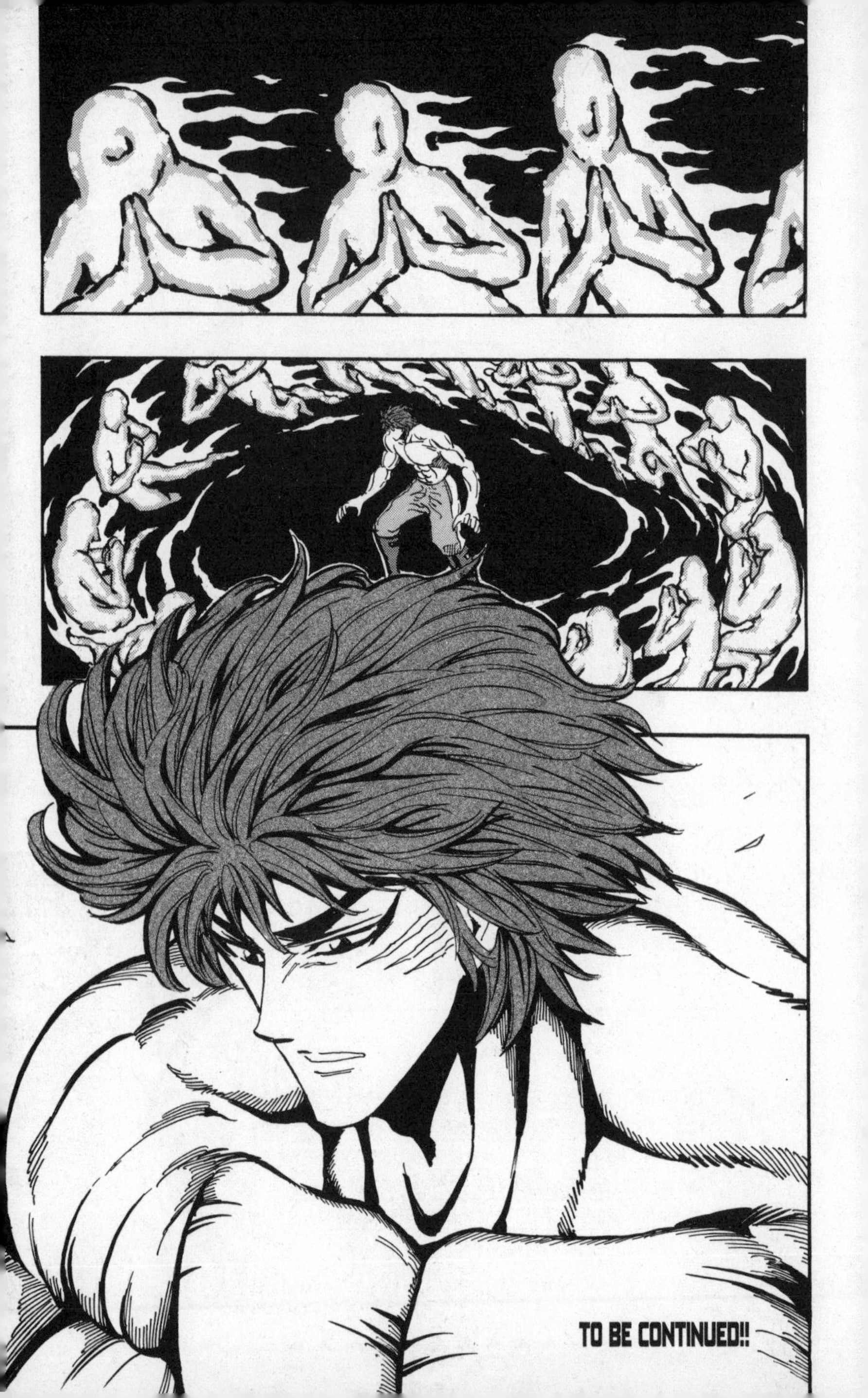
TO BE CONTINUED!!

GOURMET CHECKLIST

Vol. 422

CENTER
(GOURMET CELL NUCLEUS)

CAPTURE LEVEL: 10,000
HABITAT: AREA 0
SIZE:---
HEIGHT: ---
WEIGHT: ---
PRICE: ---

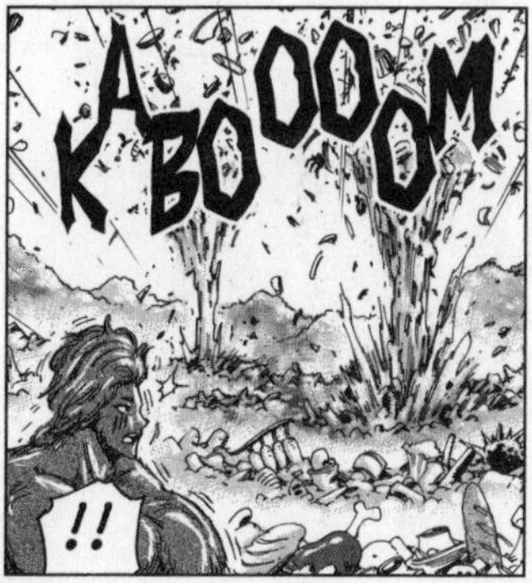
KABOOOOM
!!

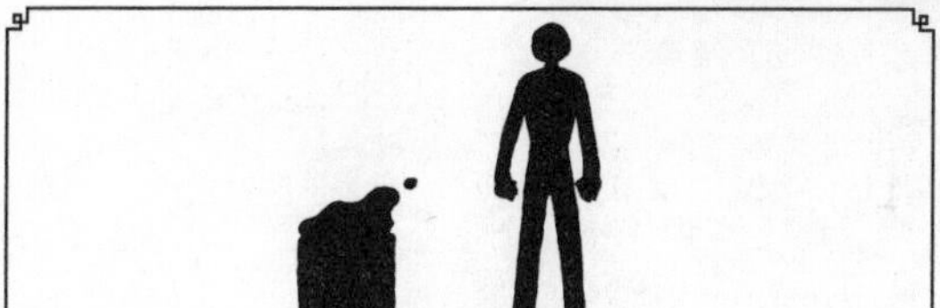

SCALE

THE ULTIMATE REVIVAL INGREDIENT AND THE HIDDEN APPETIZER IN ACACIA'S FULL-COURSE MEAL. CENTER IS 100 PERCENT PURE GOURMET CELLS AND OVERFLOWS WITH GOURMET CELL NUCLEI THAT ALLOW IT TO GIVE BIRTH TO ANY AND ALL INGREDIENTS AND NEW LIFE. IT'S THE FINAL INGREDIENT HOSTS MUST CONSUME IN ORDER TO REVIVE THEIR GOURMET CELL DEMONS.

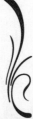

Character Profile

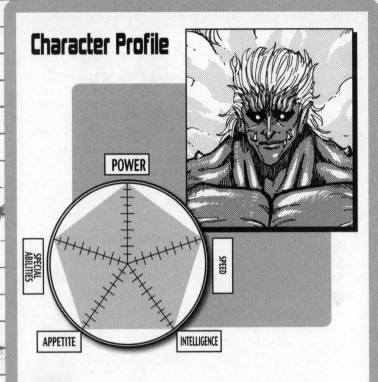

POWER
SPEED
INTELLIGENCE
APPETITE
SPECIAL ABILITIES

OGRE

AGE	UNKNOWN	BIRTHDAY	UNKNOWN
BLOOD TYPE	UNKNOWN	SIGN	UNKNOWN
HEIGHT	3 M	WEIGHT	2 TONS
EYESIGHT	20/1.5	SHOE SIGHT	UNKNOWN

SPECIAL MOVES ● JET FORK, JET KNIFE, DEVIL SENSE, JET PUNCH

THE GOURMET CELL DEMON THAT LURKS WITHIN TORIKO'S GOURMET CELLS. IT'S THIS VERY APPETITE THAT ORIGINALLY HAD ITS EYE ON ACACIA'S FULL-COURSE MEAL IN ORDER TO REVIVE ITSELF, BUT ULTIMATELY HAD TORIKO CONSUME HIM AFTER HE WAS REVIVED.

COMING NEXT VOLUME

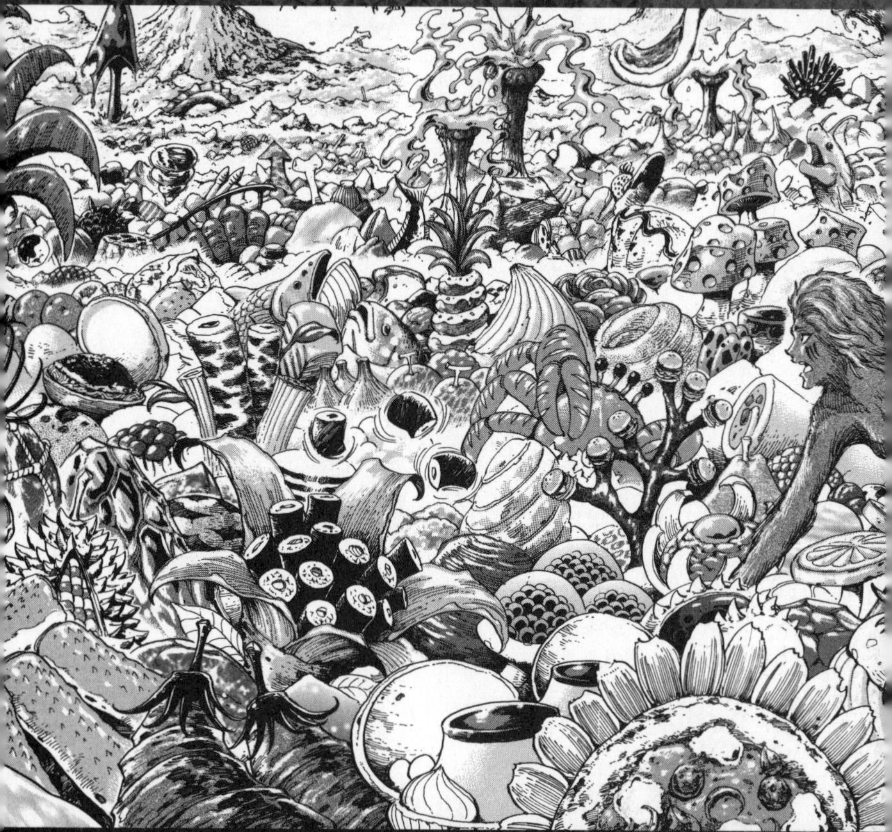

FINAL VOLUME: UNDISCOVERED INGREDIENTS

The battle for the fate of the world quickly approaches its climax. The Earth struggles to keep itself from falling apart with Center violently erupting under its crust. Toriko has already consumed Center and has the power he needs to defeat Acacia and Neo! But even with Starjun and Midora helping him, will it be enough to put an end to this earth-shattering battle? Find out in the final volume!

DON'T MISS THE EXCITING CONCLUSION!

AVAILABLE AUGUST 2018!

DRAGON BALL SUPER

STORY BY **Akira Toriyama** ART BY **Toyotarou**

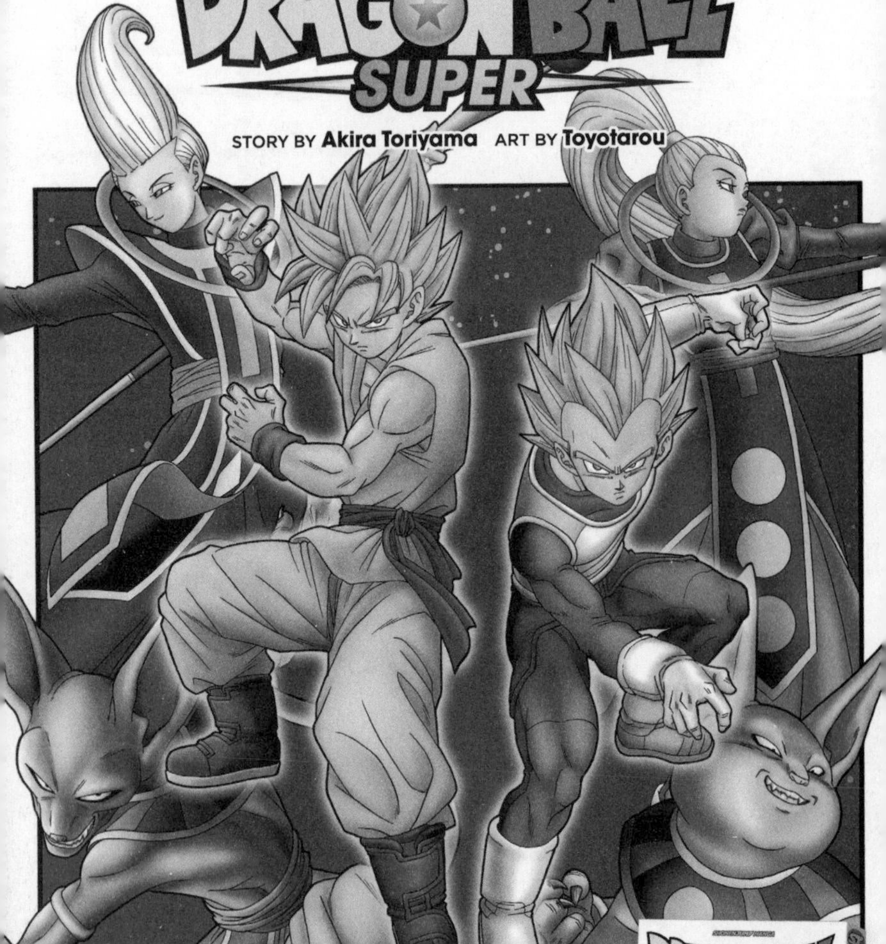

Goku's adventure from the best-selling classic manga *Dragon Ball* continues in this new series written by Akira Toriyama himself!

Ever since Goku became Earth's greatest hero and gathered the seven Dragon Balls to defeat the evil Boo, his life on Earth has grown a little dull. But new threats loom overhead, and Goku and his friends will have to defend the planet once again!

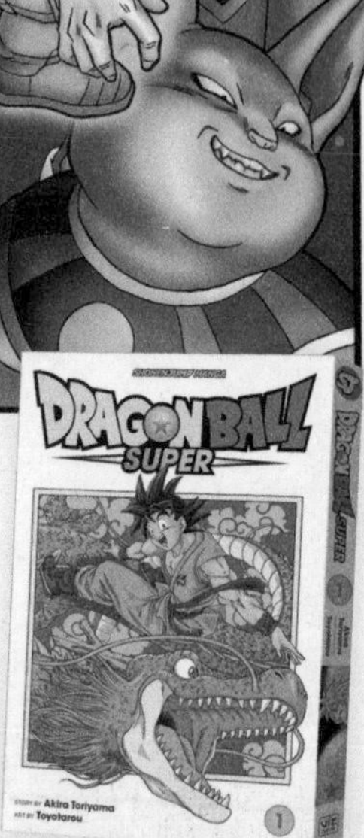

DRAGON BALL SUPER
STORY BY Akira Toriyama
ART BY Toyotarou
1

RATED T FOR TEEN

VIZ media

SHONEN JUMP

viz.com

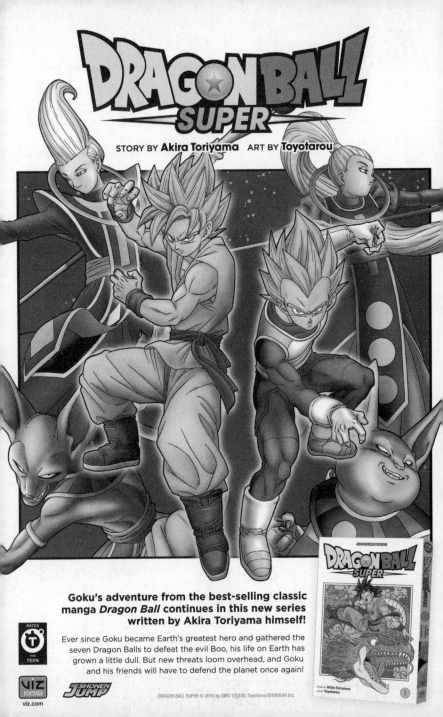

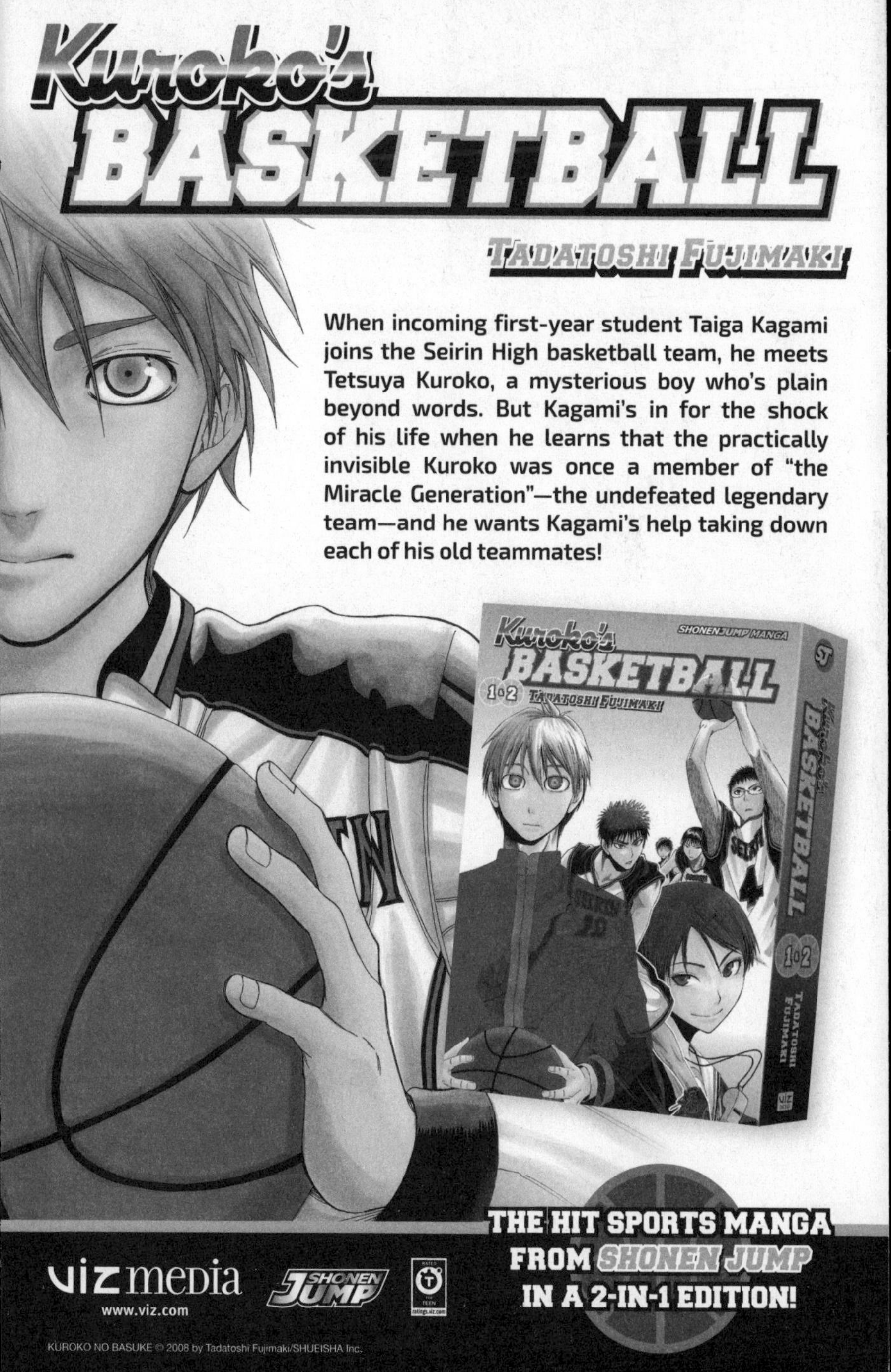
Kuroko's BASKETBALL
TADATOSHI FUJIMAKI
When incoming first-year student Taiga Kagami joins the Seirin High basketball team, he meets Tetsuya Kuroko, a mysterious boy who's plain beyond words. But Kagami's in for the shock of his life when he learns that the practically invisible Kuroko was once a member of "the Miracle Generation"—the undefeated legendary team—and he wants Kagami's help taking down each of his old teammates!
SHONEN JUMP MANGA
Kuroko's BASKETBALL
1•2
TADATOSHI FUJIMAKI
THE HIT SPORTS MANGA FROM SHONEN JUMP IN A 2-IN-1 EDITION!
viz media
www.viz.com
SHONEN JUMP
T TEEN
ratings.viz.com
KUROKO NO BASUKE © 2008 by Tadatoshi Fujimaki/SHUEISHA Inc.

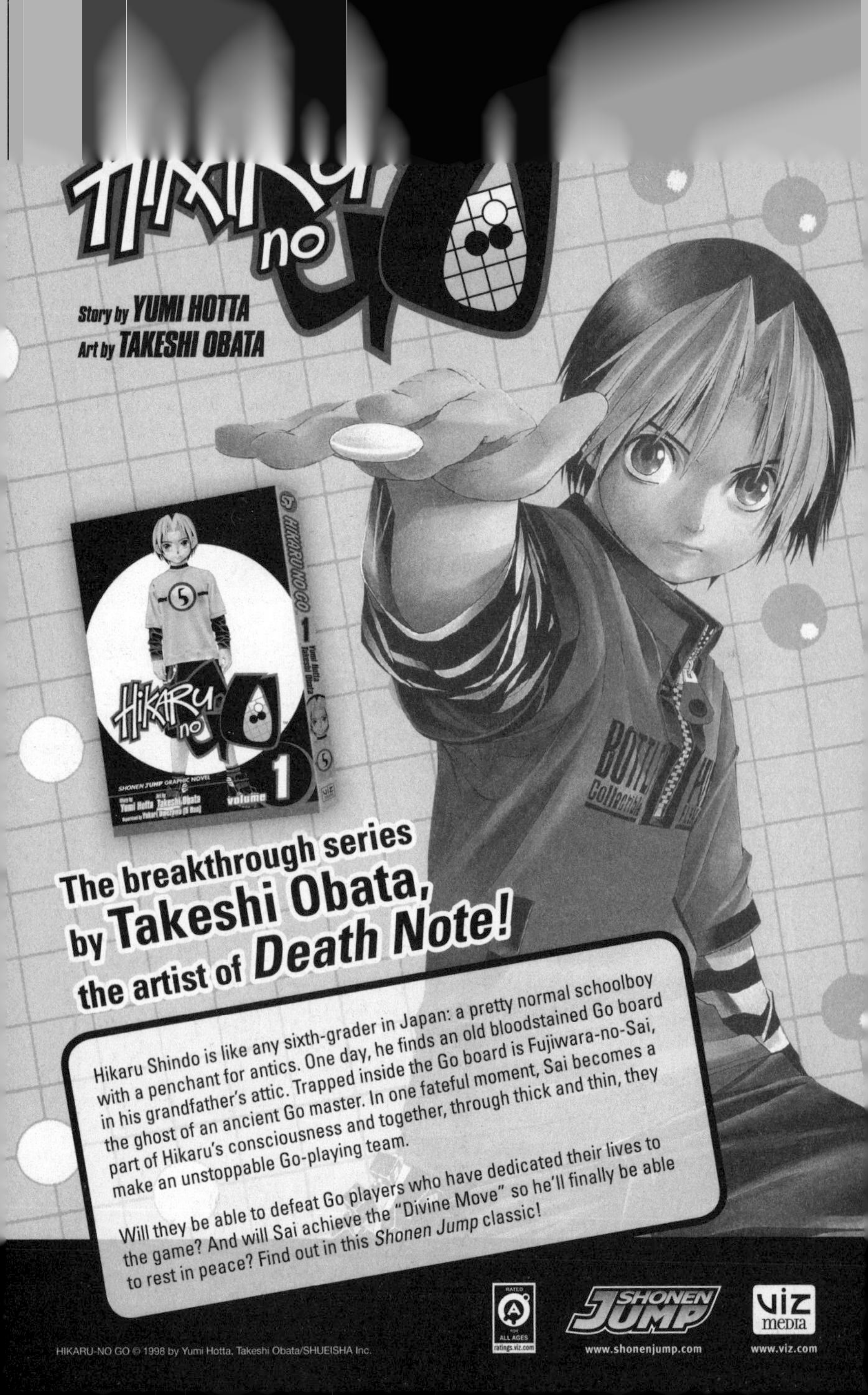
no
Story by YUMI HOTTA
Art by TAKESHI OBATA
HIKARU NO GO
1
HIKARU no
SHONEN JUMP GRAPHIC NOVEL
volume 1
The breakthrough series by Takeshi Obata, the artist of Death Note!
Hikaru Shindo is like any sixth-grader in Japan: a pretty normal schoolboy with a penchant for antics. One day, he finds an old bloodstained Go board in his grandfather's attic. Trapped inside the Go board is Fujiwara-no-Sai, the ghost of an ancient Go master. In one fateful moment, Sai becomes a part of Hikaru's consciousness and together, through thick and thin, they make an unstoppable Go-playing team.
Will they be able to defeat Go players who have dedicated their lives to the game? And will Sai achieve the "Divine Move" so he'll finally be able to rest in peace? Find out in this Shonen Jump classic!
RATED A FOR ALL AGES
ratings.viz.com
SHONEN JUMP
www.shonenjump.com
VIZ MEDIA
www.viz.com
HIKARU-NO GO © 1998 by Yumi Hotta, Takeshi Obata/SHUEISHA Inc.

You're Reading in the Wrong Direction!!

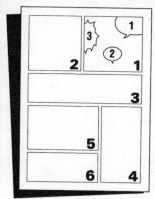

Whoops! Guess what? You're starting at the wrong end of the comic!

...It's true! In keeping with the original Japanese format, **Toriko** is meant to be read from right to left, starting in the upper-right corner.

Unlike English, which is read from left to right, Japanese is read from right to left, meaning that action, sound effects and word-balloon order are completely reversed... something which can make readers unfamiliar with Japanese feel pretty backwards themselves. For this reason, manga or Japanese comics published in the U.S. in English have sometimes been published "flopped"—that is, printed in exact reverse order, as though seen from the other side of a mirror.

By flopping pages, U.S. publishers can avoid confusing readers, but the compromise is not without its downside. For one thing, a character in a flopped manga series who once wore in the original Japanese version a T-shirt emblazoned with "M A Y" (as in "the merry month of") now wears one which reads "Y A M"! Additionally, many manga creators in Japan are themselves unhappy with the process, as some feel the mirror-imaging of their art skews their original intentions.

We are proud to bring you Mitsutoshi Shimabukuro's **Toriko** in the original unflopped format. For now, though, turn to the other side of the book and let the adventure begin...!

—Editor

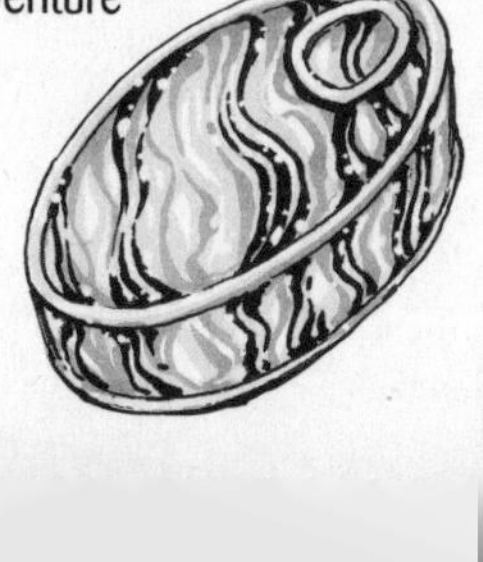

TORIKO

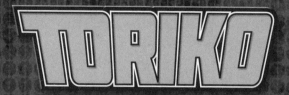

TORIKO VOL. 42
SHONEN JUMP Manga Edition

STORY AND ART BY **MITSUTOSHI SHIMABUKURO**

Translation/Christine Dashiell
Weekly Shonen Jump Lettering/ Erika Terriquez
Graphic Novel Touch-Up Art & Lettering/ Paolo Gattone and Chiara Antonelli
Design/Veronica Casson
Editor/Marlene First

Printed in the U.S.A.

Published by VIZ Media, LLC
P.O. Box 77010
San Francisco, CA 94107

10 9 8 7 6 5 4 3 2 1
First printing, May 2018

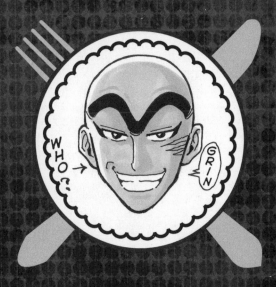

In the final chapter of this volume, there's a scene were Toriko suddenly grows a unibrow. That scene was drawn in honor of the 40th anniversary and final chapter of *Kochikame* in *Shonen Jump* in Japan. I know it has no direct relation to *Toriko*, so thank you for putting up with it. (My current weight is…70 kg!! Dang!! I'm going to try really hard until the very end!)

—Mitsutoshi Shimabukuro, 2016

Mitsutoshi Shimabukuro made his debut in **Weekly Shonen Jump** in 1996. He is best known for **Seikimatsu Leader Den Takeshi!**, for which he won the 46th Shogakukan Manga Award for children's manga in 2001. His current series, **Toriko**, began serialization in Japan in 2008.